RELIGIOUS IMAGINARIES

RELIGIOUS IMAGINARIES

The Liturgical and Poetic Practices of
Elizabeth Barrett Browning,
Christina Rossetti, and
Adelaide Procter

KAREN DIELEMAN

OHIO UNIVERSITY PRESS
ATHENS

Ohio University Press, Athens, Ohio 45701
ohioswallow.com
© 2012 by Ohio University Press
All rights reserved

To obtain permission to quote, reprint, or otherwise reproduce or distribute material from Ohio University Press publications, please contact our rights and permissions department at (740) 593-1154 or (740) 593-4536 (fax).

Printed in the United States of America
Ohio University Press books are printed on acid-free paper ∞ ™

20 19 18 17 16 15 14 13 12   5 4 3 2 1

Library of Congress Cataloging-in-Publication Data
Dieleman, Karen.
 Religious imaginaries : the liturgical and poetic practices of Elizabeth Barrett Browning, Christina Rossetti, and Adelaide Procter / Karen Dieleman.
   p. cm.
 Includes bibliographical references and index.
 ISBN 978-0-8214-2017-1 (hc : alk. paper) — ISBN 978-0-8214-4434-4 (electronic)
 1. Religious poetry, English—History and criticism. 2. Christian poetry, English—History and criticism. 3. Browning, Elizabeth Barrett, 1806–1861—Religion. 4. Rossetti, Christina Georgina, 1830–1894—Religion. 5. Procter, Adelaide Anne, 1825–1864—Religion. 6. Christian poetry, English—Authorship. 7. English poetry—Women authors—History and criticism. 8. English poetry—19th century—History and criticism. I. Title. II. Title: Liturgical and poetic practices of Elizabeth Barrett Browning, Christina Rossetti, and Adelaide Procter.
 PR508.R4D54 2012
 808.81'9382—dc23
                        2012016751

CONTENTS

	Acknowledgments	vii
	Abbreviations	ix
	Introduction *Liturgy and the Religious Imaginary*	1
1	Truth and Love Anchored in the Word *Elizabeth Barrett Browning's Religious Imaginary*	23
2	"Truth in Relation, Perceived in Emotion" *Elizabeth Barrett Browning's Religious Poetics*	61
3	"The Beloved Anglican Church of My Baptism" *Christina Rossetti's Religious Imaginary*	100
4	Manifestation, Aesthetics, and Community in Christina Rossetti's *Verses*	137
5	"The One Divine Influence at Work in the World" *Adelaide Procter's Religious Imaginary*	177
6	Religious-Poetic Strategies in Adelaide Procter's Lyrics, Legends, and Chaplets	211
	Conclusion *The Intricacy of the Subject*	254
	Notes	265
	Bibliography	293
	Index	307

ACKNOWLEDGMENTS

My first thanks in the writing of this book go to Grace Kehler, who nurtured it through its early form as a dissertation and modeled for me both the probing inquiry and the generous spirit that goes into worthy scholarship.

In the process of reshaping the early work into its present form, I owe much to the insights offered by colleagues at Trinity Christian College, particularly Craig Mattson and Keith Starkenburg. I am also grateful to my colleagues in the English Department for their support. Thanks also to Jamie Smith at Calvin College for encouraging words and for sending me the proofs of *Desiring the Kingdom* (2009) so that I could start reading ahead of its publication. I am also indebted to the readers for Ohio University Press for critical insights that spurred me to a final round of revision. Cynthia Scheinberg generously reviewed some chapters twice.

Librarians, archivists, and others have greatly aided me in retrieving source material and answering questions, both at Trinity and elsewhere. I acknowledge particularly Kate Perry, former archivist at Girton College Archives; Father Rupert McHardy, librarian and archivist at the Brompton Oratory; and Father Nicholas Schofield, diocesan archivist at St. James's Church, Spanish Place.

Much of my work on this book was enabled by Trinity Christian College summer research grants and interim and semester fellowships. I am grateful to the college for financial and other forms of support.

Working with the editors and staff at Ohio University Press has been a pleasure. I thank Joseph McLaughlin and Kevin Haworth for their support of the project, Nancy Basmajian for editorial advice, and Sally Bennett for meticulous copyediting. No doubt other people at the press played equally important roles in bringing this book into its present form. I thank them all.

Acknowledgments

Some remarks on liturgy and poetic practice in the introduction to this book were earlier published in the journal *Christianity and Literature* (2009) following a seminar on Christian scholarship and the turn to religion in literary studies; thanks to the editors for permission to reuse. A portion of chapter 1 first appeared in "Elizabeth Barrett Browning, Congregationalism and Spirit Manifestation," *Victorians Institute Journal* 36 (2008): 105–22, © *Victorians Institute Journal*, and is included here by permission. Other Barrett Browning material, now substantially revised, first appeared in *Victorian Poetry* 45, no. 2 (Summer 2007): 135–57, and enters the present book by permission of Hilary Attfield, journals manager at West Virginia University Press. Chapters 3 and 4 grew out of material published in *The Journal of Pre-Raphaelite Studies* 15 (Spring 2006): 27–49. Permission to quote from the Girton College Personal Papers of Bessie Rayner Parkes has been granted by the Mistress and Fellows, Girton College, Cambridge.

I also express my sincere appreciation to family and friends for regularly inquiring after the progress of this book. I know they will rejoice with me over its completion, as does my dear husband, Adrian. To him, I owe more than I can express. He rescued me regularly from a too-deep absorption in my work, so that I would not miss out on other delights of living.

ABBREVIATIONS

BC	Elizabeth Barrett Browning and Robert Browning. *The Brownings' Correspondence*. 18 vols. to date. Edited by Phillip Kelley, Ronald Hudson, and Scott Lewis. Winfield, KS: Wedgestone, 1984– .
CP	Christina Rossetti. *The Complete Poems*. Edited by R. W. Crump, with notes and introduction by Betty S. Flowers. Harmondsworth, UK: Penguin, 2001.
Diary	Elizabeth Barrett Barrett. *Diary by E.B.B.: The Unpublished Diary of Elizabeth Barrett Barrett, 1831–1832*. Edited by Philip Kelley and Ronald Hudson. Athens: Ohio University Press, 1969.
FD	Christina Rossetti. *The Face of the Deep: A Devotional Commentary on the Apocalypse*. London: SPCK, 1892.
FF	Elizabeth Barrett Browning and Robert Browning. *Florentine Friends: The Letters of Elizabeth Barrett Browning and Robert Browning to Isa Blagden, 1850–1861*. Edited by Philip Kelley and Sandra Donaldson. Winfield, KS: Wedgestone; Waco, TX: Armstrong Browning Library, 2009.
GCPP Parkes	Girton College Personal Papers of Bessie Rayner Parkes. Girton College Archive, Cambridge.
LA	Elizabeth Barrett Browning. *The Letters of Elizabeth Barrett Browning to Her Sister Arabella*. 2 vols. Edited by Scott Lewis. Waco, TX: Wedgestone, 2002.
LCR	Christina Rossetti. *The Letters of Christina Rossetti*. 4 vols. Edited by Antony H. Harrison. Charlottesville: University Press of Virginia, 1997–2004.

Abbreviations

LEBB	Elizabeth Barrett Browning. *The Letters of Elizabeth Barrett Browning.* 2 vols. Edited by Frederic G. Kenyon. New York: Macmillan, 1898.
LGB	Elizabeth Barrett Browning and Robert Browning. *Letters of the Brownings to George Barrett.* Edited by Paul Landis with the assistance of Ronald E. Freeman. Urbana: University of Illinois Press, 1958.
LO	Elizabeth Barrett Browning. *Elizabeth Barrett Browning's Letters to Mrs. David Ogilvy, 1849–1861.* Edited by Peter N. Heydon and Philip Kelley. London: John Murray, 1973.
PAAP	Adelaide Procter. *The Poems of Adelaide A. Procter.* Introduction by Charles Dickens. New York: Thomas Y. Crowell [1858]; reprint, Whitefish, MT: Kessinger Publishing [2004].
SPCK	Society for Promoting Christian Knowledge
WEBB	Elizabeth Barrett Browning. *Works of Elizabeth Barrett Browning.* 5 vols. General editor, Sandra Donaldson. London: Pickering and Chatto, 2010.

INTRODUCTION

LITURGY AND THE RELIGIOUS IMAGINARY

> All who believe in the being of a God, and consequently acknowledge the propriety of paying him their united homage in acts of worship, must allow it to be a matter of no small importance in what manner that worship is conducted; and all serious thoughtful persons must agree, that the public service of the Almighty ought to be performed in a way most conformable to his nature and will, most honourable to religion, and most conducive to genuine edification.
>
> But what that external mode of worship is, to which these characters are most justly applicable, wise and good men are by no means agreed.
>
> Samuel Palmer, 1812

As Samuel Palmer recognized already in 1812, nineteenth-century Christianity in England was both united and divided.[1] Though Christian churches held most of the central teachings of Christianity in common, they diverged significantly in polity, theology, and liturgy. For the ordinary churchgoing Christian, denominational divergence emerged most obviously not in theological discussions, seminary debates, or circulated writings but in the public worship service, where communal worship practices shaped and bespoke religious principle. True, the basic elements of Christian liturgy—Scripture reading, singing, prayer, sermon, sacrament—appeared in almost all worship services, of whatever denomination; but as Palmer points out, how these elements ought to be interpreted, or even conducted, remained a subject of disagreement. To affiliate oneself with a particular form of Christianity, therefore, meant most visibly to choose a distinctive set of liturgical practices. These practices and their import for the religious imaginary and for poetry are the subject of this book. My thesis—that distinctive religious-poetic voices can arise from religious imaginaries formed by and in response to liturgical practice—applies equally to devout men and women who engaged their forms of faith seriously. However, this book focuses on women's religious poetry, partly because the idea that women's religious writing shows mostly a conflicted relationship with church needs, at this time, more pressing emendation than an integrated study of men's and women's liturgical engagements could give; and partly because I believe the emerging conversation about women's religious poetry might be most enriched by my approach. That approach seeks not to align but to differentiate women's religious poetry. That is, recognizing that Victorian Christianity took many forms, this book is attuned to difference rather than resemblance in women's writing. Though they struggled with some of the same gender issues, Victorian religious women writers crafted individual voices, producing religious work that can more often be associated with male writers or speakers in their own denominations than with other Christian women writers. Religious identity features as importantly as—sometimes more importantly than—gender in the creation of distinctive religious imaginaries and religious-poetic voices. Though unified as Christians, religious women writers in Victorian England considered denominational difference to have enormous import for their understanding of the role of poet, the religious community, the act of scriptural interpretation, and the cultural weight of religious poetry.

In a cultural climate that advocates personal autonomy, it has perhaps been easy to believe that church affiliations largely hinder intellectual inquiry—if not now, then certainly in the past. We can then fail to appreciate the religious and literary value that Victorian men and women often assigned to their church experiences, believing instead that especially women sought to escape from or subvert the forms of Christianity that we (and sometimes they) have associated with patriarchy. But to do justice to women who showed themselves in various ways to be critically astute yet chose to affiliate themselves with traditional forms of faith, we need to ask whether we have too quickly ruled out the affirmative and generative possibilities of (Victorian) religious institutions for women's (and men's) writing. This study demonstrates the import of church practices for formal and conceptual experiments in religious poetry by Elizabeth Barrett Browning, Christina Rossetti, and Adelaide Procter.

At its broadest level, this book responds to Dennis Taylor's suggestion that the appropriate critical response to the ongoing "dilemma of skepticism" about religion may simply be to develop "a sense of the intricacy of the subject." Since (and even before) Taylor's call in 1998 for "religious interpretations that are substantial enough to enter into a productive and competitive relation with the reigning critical discourses,"[2] numerous studies of the intersections of literature and religion have appeared. Contributors to the 2006 inaugural volume of the new *ELN*—an issue devoted to literary history and the religious turn—offered potential reasons for the increased interest in religion by literary critics: a reaction to the mid-twentieth-century rejection of religion in favor of the secularized human sciences; a postmodern skepticism about secularism's exclusivist claims to truth; and twenty-first-century global events that reveal the ongoing strength of religious commitment. It seems necessary, one contributor wrote, to acknowledge religion as a form of thinking as well as spirituality. As had Taylor, another considered current historicized approaches to literary criticism to make such study more tenable than earlier value-laden approaches.[3] The challenge, all imply, is to find ways of maintaining intellectual seriousness in both critic and text while discussing subjects of faith. These remarks and Taylor's form the guiding principles for this book: I aim to combine intellectual seriousness with respect for faith commitments to increase our sense of the intricacy of the subject of religion in Victorian women's poetry.

In one sense, my work participates in what Jude V. Nixon, in the title to his 2004 edited collection, calls *Victorian Religious Discourse: New Directions*. In his introduction to this volume, Nixon also reflects on Dennis Taylor's advice as he writes that the goal of his collection "is not to re-present Victorian religious discourse as singular but as varied, informing and informed by culture."[4] The subsequent essays verify that Victorian Christianity was far from monologic, and the historicized approach of many of them reveals as untenable the earlier skepticism about religion's importance. Indeed, recent monographs on the subject of Victorian writers and religion—such as Mary Wilson Carpenter's *Imperial Bibles, Domestic Bodies: Women, Sexuality, and Religion in the Victorian Market* (2003), Jill Muller's *Gerard Manley Hopkins and Victorian Catholicism: A Heart in Hiding* (2003), and Jarlath Killeen's *The Faiths of Oscar Wilde: Catholicism, Folklore and Ireland* (2005)—frequently use historicized or material culture approaches to the subject. To some extent, I place the present book within this practice.

Still, I depart from the tendency in many of these studies to view Victorian religion mainly as a cultural construct, overlooked for a time but now properly recognized alongside class, gender, and race as a historical category worth attention. Nixon, for example, frames Victorian religious discourse primarily in terms of its importance to "British national identity" (1), particularly as tied to "masculinity, race and imperialism" (3). Here, at least by implication, the study of religion serves primarily to further our understanding of other (more important?) Victorian identities. Of course, study of Victorian religion does do that, and we benefit from examining how and why. But this approach might actually be limiting, disposed as it is to see religion only as discourse or ideology: as a set of verbal structures for analysis or as a scheme of ideas not supported by rational argument. Both terms, by assuming or implying religion's coerciveness, intolerance, or lack of sensitivity for the other, can reduce religion to a set of beliefs or ideas, most of them taken to be unexamined or oppressive. Thus, the critical project is predetermined by its terms to read religious-literary works either for their failures of self-examination—their complicity—or for signs of protest and rebellion. Again, Nixon supplies the example when he writes that Victorian literature is a site where religion, especially institutional religion, is "contested" or "problematically staged" (8). Many contemporary critics seem to have difficulty imagining Victorian religion, especially the church, as more than a contested cultural category or other than a set of unprobed ideas or language, much less as a generative place for literary work.

The seeking for signs of protest and revision has become, in the past decade or two, the primary critical approach taken toward, especially, women's religious writing. Cynthia Scheinberg observes that most narratives of feminist literary history (to 2002) assume that "women writers who actively supported religious institutions and affiliations were necessarily didactic, submissive, unenlightened, and uncreative reproducers of male religious hierarchy."[5] Because these terms run counter to the feminist project, critics often ignored religious writing by women or discounted it as a critical lapse in an otherwise worthy body of work. With the rise of interest in religion broadly, this critical position is being reassessed, with more and more work appearing that argues for the subtlety and creativity of women's religious writing. Scheinberg's declared goal in *Women's Poetry and Religion in Victorian England* "is to suggest that women's religious poetry is a site in which we find evidence of women's creative and original engagement with religious text and theology" (3). Similarly, F. Elizabeth Gray's recent *Christian and Lyric Tradition in Victorian Women's Poetry* argues for the creative contributions of Victorian women's religious poetry "to Christian discourse, to lyric tradition, and to contemporary views of womanhood."[6] This is welcome work. As with Nixon's, however, Scheinberg's terms imply that women's religious writing arises apart from women's affiliations with a church: she states that women used their poetry "to do the theological work from which they were excluded in most Victorian religious institutions" (3). In other words, exclusion, not participation, drives the poetry. And Gray, who rightly acknowledges that "Victorian women adhered to no one Christian faith," nevertheless aims to discuss their religious poetry "as a distinct, discrete body of work" (5). Women's denominational affiliations do not play significantly into Gray's analysis. While women's religious writing, therefore, has been recuperated into current critical endeavors in valuable ways, women's church lives have not (except, perhaps, for Christina Rossetti's). We seem unable yet to believe that Victorian Christian churches themselves could be generative for women's religious poetry, and that devout and astute women knew it. Scheinberg, for example, states in her study of two Christian and two Jewish women poets that "to explore the significance of the specific locations of these women in Christian and Jewish religious institutions . . . might serve to limit the ways these women can be read as original religious thinkers" (6). Church, in other words, probably restricts originality.

By contrast, I take the position that to understand religious writing by Victorian women of faith, we must pay *more* attention to their church affiliations. Whereas Scheinberg believes "these established labels often best refer to issues of practice and worship, but may not be useful when seeking to identify specific contours of the particular woman poet's religious thought" (6), I argue that the specific contours of each poet's religious imaginary can best be identified and understood within the context of her chosen denomination's worship practices. However, I see my work not as a rebuttal to or criticism of Scheinberg's or Gray's admirable work but as a response to the hope both critics have expressed for later scholars to link their work to studies of denominational difference.[7] The intricacy of the subject, I believe, requires this attention, not least because the Victorians themselves held denominational affiliation to be important.

My starting point, however, is not in theological differences, though such differences will inevitably play into my discussion. Nor will I attempt what some might call a worldview analysis: a detailing of each poet's perspective on the ultimate meaning of existence. Along with Roger Lundin—who labels sight (perspective, view) the "most imperial of the senses"—I am interested (in this project) less in *"getting the picture"* than in *"hearing voices."*[8] Therefore, I approach the question of denominational difference and its effect on religious poetry in terms of liturgy more than (though not apart from) theology. That is, I pay attention to the embodied practices of worship, not only the intellectual elements of belief. I do so mainly because I am persuaded that sustained practices—of any kind—have a powerful formative effect on how we imagine the world and our place in it and consequently on how we talk or write about it. In other words, I acknowledge what Charles Taylor calls a social imaginary that interpenetrates discourse and, forming that social imaginary, what James K. A. Smith calls liturgies, or rituals of ultimate concern.[9] The religious writing of Victorian women of faith, I suggest, takes particular shape and voice because it emerges from Christian religious imaginaries formed—deliberately but also in deeper, unconscious ways—by continual engagement in particular worship practices and environments. Thus, while most recent critics writing on Victorian religious texts focus on what a writer's religious discourse does to counter or revise institutional dogma or practice, I argue that the writers examined here *had* a particular religious imaginary because they willingly and regularly engaged in church worship in the first place. Their liturgical participation did not merely influence their religious poetics; it enabled, even generated, their respective religious-poetic voices.

My premises arise primarily from work by Smith, who draws on Taylor and Pierre Bourdieu. In *Modern Social Imaginaries*, Taylor describes the social imaginary as an understanding of "how we stand to each other, how we got to where we are, how we relate to other groups, and so on" (25). But Taylor does not actually mean anything as limited as a set of answers to questions. To make this clear, in *A Secular Age* he replaces his earlier definition of social imaginary with one that uses such terms as *imagine, notions, images,* and *underlie*: the social imaginary is "the ways in which [people] imagine their social existence, how they fit together with others, how things go on between them and their fellows, the expectations which are normally met, and the deeper normative notions and images which underlie these expectations." Taylor rejects the idea that our fundamental response to the world is determined by a set of articulated beliefs or propositions. He writes, "Humans operated with a social imaginary well before they ever got into the business of theorizing about themselves." He continues, "We are in fact all acting, thinking and feeling out of backgrounds and frameworks which we do not fully understand," backgrounds formed by all kinds of historical and social circumstances and unarticulated expectations. To some extent, we choose the frameworks that shape us, but often we do not. Either way, how we live in the world is at least as much a matter of what images or stories we carry as what propositions we hold.[10] Rephrased in terms of my project, how Victorian women writers of faith crafted their poetic voices is at least as much—and maybe more—determined by a religious imaginary shaped within their chosen worship experiences as by any set of articulated doctrines. This does not negate doctrine, any more than the social imaginary negates social theory. But it avers, with Smith, that a Christian religious imaginary existed before the early Christian church formulated its historic creeds and confessions: "Before Christians had systematic theologies and worldviews, they were singing hymns and psalms, saying prayers, celebrating the Eucharist, sharing their property, and becoming a people marked by a desire for God's coming kingdom—a desire that constituted them as a peculiar people in the present."[11] People worship before (or at least as) they formulate. A social imaginary directs us back before intellectualizing to a felt or imagined "standing in the world"—from worldview to what we might call worldsense.

Taylor's idea of a social imaginary can be juxtaposed with sociologist Pierre Bourdieu's concept of habitus to unpack further the notion of an imagined structure or set of dispositions in the individual (or the group) that are neither entirely subjectively nor objectively produced but arise as a "dialectic of expressive dispositions and instituted means of expression." Habitus, writes Bourdieu in a lengthy definition in *The Logic of Practice*, are "systems of durable, transposable dispositions, structured structures predisposed to function as structuring structures, that is, as principles which generate and organize practices and representations that can be objectively adapted to their outcomes without presupposing a conscious aiming at ends or an express mastery of the operations necessary in order to attain them." Such a habitus is produced by the "conditions associated with a particular class of conditions of existence." For Bourdieu, being immersed in what he calls a cultural field (institutions, rituals, categories) produces certain values and dispositions that then become naturalized and stay with people across contexts. These values and dispositions allow agency in that the individual can improvise and respond to shifting demands, but these responses are limited—even determined—by the habitus.[12] The concept of habitus, therefore, though more encompassing than Taylor's social imaginary in its inclusion of all dispositions, not only those related to social existence, corresponds to Taylor's concept in its argument that people interact with the world not strictly on the basis of principles or beliefs, nor strictly as products of their material or ideological environments, but in a constant, reciprocal process of negotiation, conscious and unconscious, between cultural fields and individual agency, according to

Introduction

a set of "structured structures predisposed to act as structuring structures." Further, like Taylor, Bourdieu emphasizes the place of practice in this dialectic. Practices are not simply the unthinking outcomes of a person's habitus, he notes, but instead result from "the relationship between, on the one hand, his *habitus* . . . and on the other hand a certain state of the chances objectively offered to him by the social world."[13] Practices, in other words, can be shaped, generated, creatively produced out of the dialectic of habitus and circumstance. It is this dialectic that the present book also explores, focusing on the "cultural field" called liturgical practice and on the women writers who generated their religious poetics out of the values and dispositions they acquired, consciously and unconsciously, by participating in certain "conditions of existence." However, throughout the book, I have chosen to refer to these women's basic orientation to the world, their structuring structures, not with Bourdieu's term *habitus* but with Taylor's and Smith's term, *the imaginary*, as the term more readily consonant with literary endeavor. Bourdieu's inclusion of values as part of the habitus will be useful to remember, though, particularly in the chapters on Elizabeth Barrett Browning, where the features of the Congregationalist imaginary might sometimes sound more like a set of moral values than a fundamental disposition toward the world.

In drawing on Taylor's idea of a social imaginary and Bourdieu's concept of habitus, Smith, in *Desiring the Kingdom*, also considers the relationship of practices to the imaginary, but he does so somewhat differently than Taylor and Bourdieu do. Where Taylor remarks on the reciprocity of practices and ideas ("If the understanding makes the practice possible, it is also true that it is the practice that largely carries the understanding")[14] and Bourdieu on the emergence of practices in the dialectic between habitus and circumstances, Smith insists on "the central role of formative practices" (24), or what he calls liturgies. Liturgies, he writes, "shape and constitute our identities by forming our most fundamental desires and our most basic attunement to the world" (25); they are "primarily formative rather than merely informative" (27). Developing what he calls an Augustinian anthropology that holds that our "primordial orientation to the world is not knowledge, or even belief, but *love*" (46), Smith claims a central role for the affective, which he defines as "a prereflective, imaginative 'attunement' to the world that precedes the articulation of ideas and even beliefs" (28n11). For Smith, a prioritizing of the affective over the cognitive, of embodiment over abstraction, of liturgy over doctrine rests on a proper understanding of humans as "fundamentally desiring creatures," not "primarily believing animals." He criticizes the "person-as-believer" and "person-as-thinker" models of the human for their disembodying and isolating effects: "Both the materiality of the body (along with attendant bodily practices) and the specificity of the church drop out of this picture" (45). Attention to the practices of worship—whether directed to secular or religious ends—helps us grasp something of the practitioner's religious imaginary because such bodily or material practices inscribe habits of being into the heart, to the extent that, though such habits are learned, they become "so intricately woven into the fiber of our beings that they function as if they were natural" (56). Moreover, bodily practices "don't float in society; they find expression and articulation in concrete sites and institutions" (62). Smith examines the liturgies of the mall, the stadium, and the university, as well as the church. About the latter he concludes that we need "to consider what Christians do—or more specifically, what the church as a people does together in the 'work of the people' (*leitourgos*); [we need] to read the practices of Christian worship in order to make out the shape of a distinctly Christian social imaginary" (134). Smith is not making here an argument about influence, about the unseen work or "flowing" of one person or thing upon another so as to affect the mind or action of that other. Rather, Smith proposes that the practices of worship actually form the religious imaginary. A distinctly Christian imaginary emerges through worship.

Smith's Augustinian anthropology and examination of secular as well as religious liturgies offers new ground and qualitative depth to studies of worship by such seminarians as E. Byron Anderson and Fred P. Edie. Anderson, like Smith, points to the embodied and affective dimensions of worship in *Worship and Christian Identity: Practicing Ourselves*. In an earlier article laying the groundwork for this book, Anderson first sums up James Fowler's position that an understanding of liturgy as dealing with the kinesthetics or sensory experience of faith allows one "to focus on the imaginal character of the liturgy and its power to suggest, form, and evoke the images that represent our convictional knowing"; he then declares, "The practice of the liturgy is a way of knowing self and other, person and community in the world that is other than and more than a cognitive knowing. Liturgical knowing is affective and physical, imaginal and embodied." Recognizing the power of embodiment, Anderson even adds that liturgy "may be a dangerous thing. Discussions about [language, gender, race, and disability] all serve to remind us that, as a way of knowing written in mind and body, the liturgy continues, in some cases, to reproduce patterns of patriarchy, hierarchical power structures, and disempowerment," though it can also "subvert" those very things.[15]

Introduction

If Anderson and Smith offer qualitative evidence for liturgy's kinesthetic as well as cognitive impact, Fred P. Edie and other liturgical theologians turn to recent studies in neurobiology to affirm the multiple dimensions of embodied knowing. Edie refers to a well-known 1994 study, *Descartes' Error*, by Antonio Damasio, in which Damasio, after extensive research, hypothesizes that (in Edie's words) "brain systems for emotion and cognition are often convergent, overlapping and integrally related. [Damasio] suggests that emotion focuses the attention of the organism and thereby sets the parameters for cognitive activity." Exploring such "relationally engaged" knowing, Edie finds communal worship to have the capacity "for firing on all epistemological cylinders (heart and body, as well as mind)."[16] In "Sensing the Other in Worship: Mirror Neurons and the Empathizing Brain," David A. Hogue agrees: "Carefully reading recent studies of the brain, it becomes increasingly difficult for us to consider ourselves as spiritual souls that temporarily inhabit material bodies."[17] Rather, our bodily experiences have significant import for our spiritual, emotional, and cognitive forms of knowing. Increasingly, in fact, neuroscience is offering evidence of an emotion-cognition convergence that counters a Cartesian body-mind duality.

Outside liturgical studies, neuroscience is also fuelling new feminist theories on the connection between bodily experience, emotion, cognition, and creativity. Perhaps most notable is the theory proposed by Elizabeth A. Wilson in *Psychosomatic: Feminism and the Neurological Body*. Wilson recounts first the twentieth-century disregard in the sciences for the study of emotion, then the "remarkable turnaround in neuroscientific interest in emotion" since the 1990s. After also citing Damasio's argument in *Descartes' Error* for the central role of emotion in rationality, she focuses on work by Joseph LeDoux, who uses neurological and evolutionary theories to build a "schema for the various affiliations between emotional and cognitive systems."[18] Wilson's purpose is to propose that feminists rethink their rejection of biology in theories of the body; but indirectly, this groundbreaking feminist book sustains Smith's assertions about the import of bodily practices for the formation of an imaginary. Wilson's summary that "emotional systems are more intimately connected to bodily sensations than are cognitive systems" (93) correlates with Smith's suggestion that liturgical practices and environments contribute to the way one imagines the world and one's place in it.

A few literary scholars are also turning to the neurosciences to reconsider creativity and the arts. Suzanne Nalbantian, in an article coauthored with neuroscientist Jean-Pierre Changeux, even speaks of "neuroaesthetics" as she explains data that suggest "art is concerned with the intentional cognitive processing of emotional and sensory material which mobilize defined limbic and sensory cortical territories." Creativity, in other words, though it has a cognitive dimension, also involves a physical process engaging brain regions that store and neurons that transmit images collected through emotional and sensory processes. "Fragmentary images or *prerepresentations*" marshal "combinations of pre-existing neurons," calling up "actual sensory precepts and stored memories from diverse brain territories." Further, this "reactivated memory processing is not simply a matter of retrieval but rather the result of internal testing and selection among alternative accounts, unconsciously biased by preexisting knowledge or by the emotional resonance of actual memories of past experience." Creativity is not a simple biological process but rather a complex interplay of cognitive, affective, and sensory components of the brain. As Nalbantian puts it, "In the course of *creation*, the work of imagination sooner or later engages a selection-by-evaluation mechanism that brings into play the limbic system and its outposts that are active in the context of emotion."[19]

Nalbantian's careful explanation of the selection-by-evaluation mechanism engaged in the work of imagination goes some way to dispel possible anxieties about reducing creativity—not to mention religious experience—to merely a biological process, with no room for such prized ideals as the free spirit or such theological concepts as free will. As Wilson points out in *Psychosomatic*, for feminists especially, biology has been seen as "reductive materiality stripped of the animating effects of culture and sociality" (3); feminists have typically, therefore, "foreclosed" on neurological data and relied heavily on theories of social construction (8, 13). In a challenging move, Wilson argues that tolerating and exploring biological reductionism might actually provide new accounts of the body, and she returns to overlooked elements in work by Freud, Darwin, and others to present her case. Others, such as seminarian Cliff Guthrie, turn again to Antonio Damasio to counter the fear of reductionism: "To discover that a particular feeling ... depends on activity in a number of specific brain systems interacting with a number of body organs does not diminish the status of that feeling as a human phenomenon. Neither anguish nor the elation that love or art can bring about [is] devalued by understanding some of the myriad biological processes that make them what they are."[20] But Nalbantian's account is perhaps most persuasive, or at least most attractive, in its presentation of creativity as biologically complex.

In recent years, though, some literary scholars, including Victorianists, have seemed not to need Guthrie-like reassurances or new feminist suppositions or even neurological data to justify their critical interest in relationships between the sensory and the affective, or the body, mind, and emotions. Indeed, Victorianists point out that the Victorians themselves often connected the body to the mind. Gregory Tate observes that Tennyson's poem "St. Simeon Stylites" repeatedly "draws attention to the way in which Simeon's body influences his mind," while the line "I am part of all that I have met" in "Ulysses" suggests that the speaker's "psychology is inseparable from the experiences and circumstances that have influenced it."[21] Similarly, Marie Banfield observes in her study of period terminology related to the sentiments that "the nineteenth century increasingly saw body and mind, thought, feeling and sensation as inextricably linked."[22] In *Embodied: Victorian Literature and the Senses*, William A. Cohen argues that, in fact, many nineteenth-century writers saw the body as a "sensory interface between the interior and the world." He notes, "Evolutionary biology and affiliated nineteenth-century sciences promoted the notion that consciousness developed out of the body rather than being implanted in it" and that such ideas clashed with long-held "philosophical and religious ideas of a self or a soul that could act independently of its corporeal habitation."[23] But, as Smith elsewhere points out, affirmation of the body and of the import of bodily practice has a long history within the Christian heritage as well, though it may have been forgotten at times. Augustine, Smith writes, affirmed embodiment by emphasizing three biblical concepts: the goodness of creation, wherein finitude is not lack but gift; the incarnation of Christ, "wherein the transcendent inhabits the immanent without loss"; and the resurrection of the body, wherein embodiment is affirmed as an eternal state, not a temporary, postlapsarian one.[24] To read Christian poetry through the lens of liturgical practices, therefore, is not to adopt nineteenth-century scientific frameworks that would probably have sat uneasily with the women who produced that poetry; rather, it is to focus on the formations of a religious imaginary through a mode that the writers themselves affirmed by their commitment to worship. At the same time, it grounds us in historical and material practices. As Cohen observes, "Attention to the experiential dimension of the body ... need not come at the cost of a historical or political account of power differentials" (24). Indeed, in this book, I give an account of such power differentials as they appear in questions of gender.

Putting together philosophical, sociological, liturgical, feminist, neurobiological, and literary studies, I contend that an approach to religious poetry that takes into account the practices of the church as experienced by the poets is not merely justified but perhaps necessary for a thorough appreciation of that poetry. In this study, I undertake a reading of worship as experienced by Elizabeth Barrett Browning, Christina Rossetti, and Adelaide Procter, in order to understand the distinctive shapes of their religious imaginaries and so read their poetry with care and distinction. That poetry I sometimes designate as religious and sometimes as devotional. G. B. Tennyson, in *Victorian Devotional Poetry*, helpfully distinguishes between these terms. Religious poetry, Tennyson writes, includes "all poetry of faith, poetry about the practices and beliefs of religion, poetry designed to advance a particular religious position, poetry animated by the legends and figures of religious history, and poetry that grows out of worship." Tennyson describes devotional poetry as that subset of religious poetry that "exhibits an orientation toward worship and a linkage with established liturgical forms."[25] In this study, I also use *religious poetry* as the more expansive term, to refer to, for example, poetry that examines faith or exegetes sacred text or recasts religious interpretation; but, as the foregoing pages indicate, I link this wider religious poetry as well as the subset of devotional poetry to "established liturgical forms." Like Tennyson, I use *devotional poetry* to refer to that which exhibits a worshipful posture toward the divine; but that posture, I assert, also often includes intellectual perception. In other words, the interrelatedness of cognition, emotion, and embodiment precludes too sharp a distinction between religious and devotional poetry, though the latter frequently carries a stronger worship ethos. Consequently, I sometimes speak of a religious poem as exhibiting a devotional impulse, even if as a whole it would not be characterized as a devotional poem, or of a devotional poem as exhibiting an interpretive impulse, even if as a whole it would not be characterized as exegetical.

    I also frequently use the term *voice* in this study to denote the rendering of the religious imaginary into language. It is, admittedly, a term with multiple meanings and a vexed reception, often linked to debates about the self or identity. I use it, however, neither skeptically (voice as always fabricated because the self does not actually exist) nor idealistically (voice as bespeaking a single, knowable, authorial identity). I use it instead in Peter Elbow's sense, as a resonant presence of the author, as words that somehow seem to "*have behind them* the unconscious as well as the conscious" of the writer.[26] In terms of my project, Elbow's description of resonant voice might be modified to read "words that have behind them the imaginary of the writer." Further, in intimating a physical body, *voice* fits better with my focus on embodied liturgical experience than would *discourse*, for example. Finally, because voice also intimates individuality, it implicitly allows for differences between persons (Elbow, *Everyone*, 187), in this case, differences between Barrett Browning, Rossetti, and Procter. In this study, therefore, *voice* means the expression of the imaginary, the resonance of the imaginary in the poetry, in all its complexity. But in using this term, I do not lose sight of that which is consciously explored, crafted, adapted, or dismissed by the poets. I maintain that these women poets *generated* poetry out of their liturgical experiences, that they also creatively experimented with voice, form, and issues associated with their worship lives. In this regard, I am less insistent than Smith that practices always precede beliefs, and I am more inclined to view practices as formative but also as critically examined by the women poets of this study.

Before I turn to exploring religious imaginary and voice in these three women poets, I offer a short interlude on Christian liturgy: what are, generally speaking, the practices of Christian worship? As later chapters in this book demonstrate, the exact shape of the liturgy differs by denomination (that is, named churches within Christianity, such as Anglican, Roman Catholic, Presbyterian, Baptist, and so on) or even by local church, but, as Smith points out in *Desiring the Kingdom*, "All Christian worship ... is liturgical in the sense that it is governed by norms, draws on a tradition, includes bodily rituals or routines, and involves formative practices" (152). It involves common elements that, taken individually and together, constitute opportunities to be in service to God, to acknowledge his worthiness. Before I break up the singularity of Smith's term "a distinctly Christian social imaginary," then, I draw on his exegesis of the Christian social imaginary embedded in Christian worship to describe the worldsense *shared* by the Victorian Christian women poets studied here.

As Smith explains, the historic Christian liturgy begins with a call to worship, often taken from one of the Psalms (for example, "Come, let us bow down in worship") (160). This call implies that the church is not a voluntary society but a people aware of being called by God to a certain kind of existence in the world. In recognition of their need for help in living before God appropriately, the people respond to the call by requesting mercy or naming their dependence (for example, "Our help is in the Name of the Lord, Maker of heaven and earth"). Usually using the language of Scripture, the minister then extends God's greeting and blessing to the people (for example, "Grace and peace to you from God our Father and the Lord Jesus Christ"). These opening elements of the liturgy take but a moment but become absorbed into the imagination. They reinforce the dialogic nature of Christian worship and its implicit founding on a relationship between God and people.

This dialogic nature of worship continues when God's blessing is followed by a reminder of God's law or requirements for Christian living: "The law," writes Smith, "though it comes as a scandalous challenge to the modern desire for autonomy, is actually an invitation to be freed from a-teleological wandering" so that adherents find the conditions that are "conducive to flourishing" (176). The law is followed by an honest confession of failure (in the form of a prayer or recitation) to live rightly and love fully, on personal, communal, social, political, and other levels. To this confession God responds with an assurance of pardon (for example, "The Almighty and merciful Lord grant you absolution and remission of all your sins, true repentance, amendment of life, and the grace and consolation of his Holy Spirit"). The people who admit failure find forgiveness, hope, and encouragement to action. The religious imaginary carried in the liturgy so far emphasizes a personal relationship founded on ongoing dialogue.

The church service also often includes several instances of song and prayer, as well as a creedal recitation. Smith notes that singing is a bodily action, drawing on stomach muscles, vocal cords, lungs, and tongues, and that song seems to become a mode of bodily memory. The church's songs can be "an affective, embodied means of training our speech, which is so centrally constitutive of who we are and how we imagine ourselves" (172). In addition, the people's singing reinforces the idea of community, reminding the people that worship is not strictly about personal spiritual flourishing but about communal human flourishing: "it is training for temporal, embodied human community" (174). This sense of belonging within community is also reinforced by the recitation of a creed, often the historic Apostles' Creed. Reciting this creed, or summary of the teachings of Christ's disciples, also contributes to the formation of a Christian imaginary. Smith describes it as a weekly declaration of citizenship in God's kingdom; as a situating of oneself within a long tradition of faith; and as a rehearsal of "the skeletal structure of the story" in which Christians find their identity (192). Prayer, too, shapes the imaginary, inasmuch as it is a conversation with someone not visibly present but nevertheless believed to be present and attentive, and inasmuch as it assumes that the God to whom the prayer is offered exceeds the worship space. Smith writes, "Prayer enacts an entire cosmology because implicit in the very act of prayer is an entire ontology and construal of the

Introduction

God-world relationship" (193). Prayer also implies "an epistemic humility ... [a readiness] to be dependent on a teacher outside of ourselves" (194). Song, creed, and prayer carry a worldsense of community, tradition, and story anchored in a God-human relationship.

A Christian worship service also includes reading from the Bible and some form of commentary or sermon on that reading. What does public reading from this book do for the formation of a Christian imaginary? It initiates a new way of reading the world, says Smith (197). Over time, the people who read and hear the exposition of the Christian Scriptures regularly in public worship "begin to absorb the plot of the story, begin to see [themselves] as characters within it" (196). The creation-fall-redemption-consummation narrative becomes the narrative in which they place themselves. They situate themselves on its continuum; its images become their images, until the entire Bible serves as "the fuel of the Christian imagination" (195). Its public reading and commentary validate its public scope, showing the worshippers how they fit together with others, how and why things go on between them (and God) as they do, what expectations are held for them, and the like.

Another important ritual in the Christian liturgy is that of sacrament. Whatever value or interpretation is placed on the sacraments by a particular denomination, all Christian churches practice at least two sacraments: baptism and the Eucharist. These rituals, in general, are seen as intensified moments of God's grace. The first, Smith writes, contributes to the formation of the religious imaginary by picturing and narrating three things: a religio-politico-social reality in which all believers are equal before God (all are baptized into the Father, Son, and Spirit); a reconfiguration of family beyond the sphere of the home (that is, the church family); and an affirmation of a fundamental antithesis in the world, between what pleases God and what does not (182). Baptism promises and makes "a new person and a new people" (183). The second sacrament, variously termed, is also an action, a ritual that shapes the religious imaginary. Smith calls it "an episode that compresses the gospel into an action" (198). Its meaning is understood in various ways, some of which are explored in later chapters; but generally, the bread and wine of this sacrament are taken to represent the body and blood of Jesus as he died on the cross, broken and poured out in an act of redemption for sinners. In taking bread and wine as symbols of himself, Jesus, Smith writes, hallowed the everyday, the material, the culturally produced. This sacrament therefore suggests that the kingdom of God does not cancel the world or human activity but transfigures it (199–200). Further, the sacrament reinforces Christian time by remembering the past and looking ahead to the future of restoration. It contributes to an eschatological imaginary, as also the observance of the liturgical calendar does in orienting the *telos* around a God-man who entered time, departed from it, and will return to it again. This orientation impresses on the Christian a deep sense of the future that also informs the present and stretches to the past (200–201). Finally, as an act of communal eating and drinking, the sacrament functions as a microcosm of the fellowship, justice, love, and hope necessary for the whole world (201–3). Participating in this sacrament shapes a worldsense in which these ends are obtainable through Christ.

The Christian worship service also includes an opportunity for financial giving, for what Smith calls a kingdom economics of gratitude. Worship, he notes, embodies an alternative economy, a reconfiguration of distribution and consumption that counters the capitalist imagination (204). Once again, a liturgical moment helps form a particular worldsense. After all this, the Christian liturgy ends with a sending out and another blessing. Having been for a while in a "practice arena," worshippers continue being human—as imaged within the liturgy—outside the church. "Thus," Smith concludes, "the church is a cultural center, not just a spiritual filling station" (206–7). Liturgy forms the prototype for living in the wider human community. It is a "dense and charged" time, "packed with formative power" (208). Kevin Irwin offers a similar recognition of the movement of liturgy from church to world: "Every Christian is influenced, in however minimal or maximal a way, by the liturgy" such that its effects carry over to "how one prays, reflects and acts outside the experience of liturgy."[27] Indeed, *liturgy* means "public service."[28] Its formative power or public service might be challenged by competing secular liturgies, but intentional Christian worship nevertheless powerfully shapes the religious imaginary of those who regularly engage in it, to the extent that their activities outside the liturgy—writing poetry, for example—can yet come forward out of that experience.

Finally, although Smith does not include church environment in his consideration of liturgy's effect on the Christian social imaginary, in the present study I include architecture and environment as formative for the religious imaginary. Indeed, the neurological studies surveyed earlier would indicate that physical surroundings—whether richly decorated or visually spare—form an important part of the sensory impact of worship on the mind and cognition. Jan M. van der Lans and Henri Geerts, in their study of the impact of setting on worshippers, conclude that the intended effects of liturgy depend on "physical components (building, visual and auditory stimuli) as well as social interaction."[29] Building materials, structures, colors, fabrics, spaces, décor, and the like all signify religious values and contribute images, even stories, to the imaginary, perhaps especially to an imaginary attentive to matters of structure and form in poetry.

Building on Smith's contention that liturgy plays a formative role in the religious imaginary, I nevertheless speak in my own work not of a single Christian imaginary or voice but of imaginaries and voices, since Christianity, for all its shared beliefs, is not a unified entity. As just one example, different Christian traditions term the sacrament involving bread and wine differently, as the Lord's Supper, Communion, Mass, or the Eucharist. Tyron Inbody explains how each term carries its own images and stories: the Lord's Supper—the term used by many Protestant churches, including all Dissenting groups in England—intends a fellowship meal rooted in the Hebrew Passover meal and refigured in Jesus's last meal with his disciples; consequently, it evokes a narrative of creation to consummation. Communion—the primary term among Anglicans—emphasizes the communal nature of the sacrament, the relationship between Christ and church rather than Christ and individual. Mass—the Roman Catholic term—emphasizes Christ's sacrifice on the cross and envisions a repeated redoing of that sacrifice as a continual renewing of God's favor to the individual. The Eucharist—the primary term among Orthodox groups—stresses thanksgiving for salvation; its mood is celebratory and joyful.[30] Though the three Victorian women poets I study all participated in the sacrament involving bread and wine, their very terms for it imply different assumptions, stories, and images within the broader Christian imaginary that Smith sketches. Indeed, I have chosen Elizabeth Barrett Browning, Christina Rossetti, and Adelaide Procter for this study partly because they each identified themselves as Christian poets in an age when many were giving up the Christian faith, and so their commitments seem deliberate rather than part of a conforming expectation; but also because they represent among them the three major strands of Victorian Christianity: Dissent, Anglicanism, and Roman Catholicism, respectively. In fact, each of these women made moves within Victorian Christianity that reinforce observations about their religious particularities: Barrett Browning repeatedly associating herself with one or another of the "Independents"; Rossetti becoming increasingly High Anglican; and Procter converting from Anglicanism to Roman Catholicism. Though these associations are increasingly recognized among critics today, they remain underexplored from the angle I propose.

I consider each poet in paired chapters. The first chapter of the pair explores the religious imaginary fostered by the liturgy of that poet's particular religious affiliation. Concomitantly, it outlines the issues that a particular liturgy presented to the woman poet who participated in it. Period conceptions of women's nature and roles figure into these chapter discussions. The second chapter of each pair reads each woman's religious poetry in light of the imaginary and the issues highlighted in the preceding chapter. Here the distinctive traits of the poetry emerge, the intricacies of the subject that Dennis Taylor suggested we seek. A pattern emerges in these chapters: traditional practices, forms, and beliefs to some extent restricted the woman poet's religious imaginary as it turned to poetic endeavor; but at the same time, participation in worship enabled the woman poet to imagine and experiment with form, message, and voice in innovative ways. That is to say, though these women were committed to their religious affiliations, they were not blindly or uncritically committed. They did not pretend satisfaction with all dimensions of their community's practices, but neither did they become religious rebels or even heterodox affiliates. Instead, they turned tension to creative account, conversing with the issues of the community and formulating their religious poetics in ways that both carry and criticize the community's worldsense.

Congregationalism, among other forms of Dissent, actually refused to use the word *liturgy* in reference to worship services, since it evoked the possibility of a prescribed form. As the next chapter demonstrates in more detail, Congregationalists, also called Independents, rejected anything that suggested an authority apart from Scripture, including form prayers, creedal statements, and a fixed pattern of liturgy. When Congregationalists wrote about liturgy, therefore, they did so carefully, offering advice rather than rules. *The Congregational Service Book* (1847), for example, noted of itself that it prescribed "neither Creed nor Prayers," while Samuel Clarkson's 1856 *Form or Freedom* stated that a fixed liturgy would be "as strange and eccentric in the 'Congregationalist,' as comets in the 'solar,' system."[31] Still, outlines for worship did appear from time to time for these churches. *The Congregational Service Book* lists as appropriate the following elements: a call to worship from one of the Psalms, prayer, psalm and hymn singing, Scripture reading, sermon, and parting blessing. Samuel Palmer's 1812 *A New Directory for Nonconformist Churches* lists Scripture reading, prayer, psalm and hymn singing, and sermon. Neither list mentions sacraments. Although Congregationalists observed baptism and the Lord's Supper, they seem not to have valued these as highly as the sermon, generally speaking of them only as a "perpetual obligation," with little further commentary.[32] Palmer rather complained, in fact, that Congregationalists "seldom speak of going to *worship*, but usually to *hear* this or the other preacher" (56). This liturgy, I suggest, cultivates a religious imaginary that privileges language over symbol. It attends to the narrative shape of Christianity, its expository inclinations, and its call to action in the world.

A Congregationalist—or, slightly more broadly, an Independent—religious imaginary permeates Barrett Browning's religious writing both in ways she consciously determined and in less intentional ways. Her religious imaginary privileges the verbal and dialogic over other modes of knowing or communicating. Although she held a broadly Christian view of the material world as testimony to the spiritual, Barrett Browning's religious imaginary is primarily formed not by symbols conveying grace but by language conveying truth. That is, her sense of the relationship between physical and spiritual worlds was not as theologically sacramental as Rossetti's. Her approach to religious subjects tended toward the expository rather than the meditative. Consequently, she began writing religious poetry by emulating the hymn, then drew increasingly on the sermon as an effective model for her poetry. Destabilizing elitist and gendered notions, she increasingly imagined the poet as busy with investigation and interpretation rather than awaiting divine revelation. Her poetry gravitates more and more toward expansive forms that feature multiple voices; these voices increasingly unite intellectual work and emotive language rather than consign them to separate types of poetry. It also increasingly sees right faith as leading to right work in the world. I discuss the early hymns, the midcareer dramatic lyrics, the verse-novel *Aurora Leigh*, and the later poem "A Curse for a Nation."

Anglo-Catholicism, as with all forms of Anglicanism, used *The Book of Common Prayer* as its liturgical guide. *The Book of Common Prayer* outlines what became the most important worship service for Anglo-Catholics, the Communion service. Historically, this service emphasized worship as an encounter with God. In the nineteenth century, the sense that God mainly manifests himself in sacrament and through heightened ecclesiology overcame in many Anglican churches the earlier, more balanced sense that God reveals himself through manifestation *and* proclamation. At the same time, a heightened liturgical ritual in many churches tied (so it was imagined) the present church to its ancient heritage and underscored the communion of saints. This Anglo-Catholic double focus on communion—with Christ and with fellow believers across the ages—nevertheless arose from a historic Anglican liturgy to which Rossetti criticism has been less attentive than to its nineteenth-century offshoots. But Anglican worship was a devotional style that even non-Anglicans noticed. However much Dissenters rejected the Anglican Church, at least some of them were conceding at midcentury that while "the preaching of the Established Church is, on the whole, inferior to that of educated Nonconformists, the impression is prevalent that the former excels the latter in the devotional spirit which seems to characterise its public services."[33] These public services, I suggest, cultivate a religious imaginary that privileges encounter and symbol over narrative and exposition, that attends to community and communion, and that calls for discipleship.

Rossetti's twice-weekly participation in Anglican and, increasingly, Anglo-Catholic church services was perhaps her most frequently repeated, lifelong intellectual, bodily, emotional, and spiritual act. With its emphasis on encounter and discipleship, the historic Anglican liturgy opens the way for a religious poetry with an ontological focus: how ought one to be vis-à-vis Christ and others? Because, for Rossetti, religious poetry examines the spiritual condition more than anything else, it relies primarily on short but intense poetic forms that encourage introspection or contemplation. Further—and especially under the formative effects of the ecclesiological and ritualist movements—religious poetry derives its power mainly from its attunement to a sacramental aesthetic, where sacrament means both enactment of the gospel and conveyance of grace through symbol. With its appeal to the sense as well as the mind and spirit, Anglo-Catholicism encouraged a religious poetry that also gave attention to structure, arrangement, and material appearance to underscore the importance of religious formation. But such poetry does not withdraw from communal issues; it quietly offers whatever vision might be required to restore fractured communities to wholeness. It does this primarily by examining modes of being and relationship rather than by persuasive exposition or narration.

Turning to my third poet, I theorize liturgy again as the ground from which Adelaide Procter developed her religious poetics, this time two quite different liturgies within nineteenth-century English Roman Catholicism. Procter attended St. James's Church in Spanish Place, where the Tridentine Mass reflected the sober patterns of historic Catholicism as laid out in the traditional *Roman Missal*; this liturgy privileged the canon of the Latin Mass, with its solemnity, mystery, and cultivation of private, parallel devotions alongside the church's liturgical activity. Procter also attended the London Oratory, where additional worship services followed a revivalist mode expressed in newly written prayer and song books, and sermons drew more attention than celebrations of Mass; revivalist Catholicism preferred expressive, even flamboyant services that drew public notice, encouraged religious-social activity, and encouraged submission to the pope. These two liturgies, I suggest, allow for a versatile religious imaginary from which Procter generated diverse kinds of religious poetry.

Though well received in its own time, Procter's poetry, especially the religious verse, has not generally been highly valued since. Actually, even critical Victorian readers such as Barrett Browning saw it as having "little force & originality," as being high in "moral tone" but lacking in "vigour & artistic development."[34] I include Procter in the present work not to dispute this assessment but to examine how the most popular Roman Catholic poet of the period also created her verse out of a particular church experience, much as her (potentially more gifted) peers did. Religious poetry for Procter attended not primarily to exegetical work or aesthetic intricacy but, on the one hand, to a tradition of reserve about religious mystery, a tradition that nevertheless encouraged (experimental) private devotion, and, on the other hand, to devotional expressiveness and affect. Some of Procter's poems build on particular moments and phrases drawn from the Mass, offering themselves as alternatives to vernacular texts provided by clergy for use during Latin Mass. Others adopt effusive language to convey a religious ardor that properly avoids undue scrutiny of form, expression, or text. In many poems, a moral-didactic voice takes precedence over genuine dialogue, social and emotional fervor over theological precision. Yet these strategies, though sometimes problematic, are also sometimes deliberate, arising from a revivalist conviction that affect can do powerful work. Surveying Procter's poetry widely enables the reader to see how different modes of worship within one faith commitment can lead to an equally versatile religious poetics.

Some Victorian writers, men and women, gave up their commitments to traditional Christianity under the pressures of the age. Others maintained their ties to the Christian faith but expressed their anxieties or rebellions against it in their writings. Still others—such as the women poets examined here—cultivated their religious imaginaries through their church lives and so created distinctive religious-poetic voices for themselves. In the process, they engaged liturgical, poetic, and broader cultural questions in both creative and critical ways, and so perhaps prompt a rethinking of our own cultural assumptions about the value of religious practice.

CHAPTER ONE

TRUTH AND LOVE ANCHORED IN THE WORD

Elizabeth Barrett Browning's Religious Imaginary

Because Barrett Browning's connection to Congregationalism in her adult life has been under-recognized to date, this chapter necessarily begins with remapping the poet's postmarriage religious commitments. Though somewhat preliminary to the main argument of the chapter, the opening pages resituate Barrett Browning within—or at least close to—a church group that has mistakenly been judged in its midcentury character by the theology and practice of an earlier time. The mistake matters for literary studies because it has marred our perception of the importance of religion to arguably the most important woman poet of the period. Certain of Barrett Browning's remarks have led to suppositions that the poet distanced herself from her earlier commitment to Congregationalism; consequently, while critics have rightly ascribed innovation and independence to her, some have also underplayed or denied an ongoing religious context that actually reveals her innovation and independence more forcefully. In aligning the mature poet and her remarks more closely with Congregationalism and its affiliates than others have done, I do not mean to limit Barrett Browning as a religious thinker and writer; in fact, I see the clarifications I offer on Barrett Browning's theology vis-à-vis Congregationalist teaching as somewhat ancillary to my main focus, which is on religious practice. Nevertheless, religious practice, to be rightly understood, must be situated within its denominational context. I hope in doing so to advance our knowledge of Barrett Browning's creativity, originality, and skill as a writer of religious poetry, by exploring in detail the religious imaginary that stands behind her creative work, an imaginary developed within and by the poet's chosen church affiliations.

Once the grounds for seeing Barrett Browning as linked with Congregationalist and like-minded churches throughout her life have been established, the chapter proceeds with its main purpose, which is to explicate the enabling as well as the challenging dimensions of the Congregationalist ethos broadly, and its liturgy specifically, for the formation of a woman adherent's religious imaginary and poetic voice. In Congregationalism, the verbal dimensions of worship took precedence over visual, meditative, or ceremonial possibilities, because they best illustrated—and, in reciprocal motion, formed—the deepest postures of Congregationalism: its valuation of Scripture as the highest authority and of intellectual and spiritual independence as necessary for every believer and congregation. Sermons and hymns thus figure importantly in Congregationalist worship, because they create and reinforce Word/word centrality and dialogic-democratic temperament. From these modes, I believe, Barrett Browning shaped her religious-poetic experiments. She first pursued the emotive and generic opportunities offered by the relatively new religious-literary field of hymn writing. Later she turned to expansive poetic forms such as the dramatic lyric, lyrical drama, and epic-narrative hybrid. These forms, while emulating the sermon in scope and interpretive work, also permit more substantial dialogue among speakers than does the lyrical voice of the hymn. Moreover, the Congregationalist grassroots concept of the preacher played an important role in Barrett Browning's thinking about the (woman) poet. With it, she modified the prevailing Romantic paradigm of the poet as an authoritative, prophetic figure. Yet even while she employed these liturgical models and figures, Barrett Browning also experimented with them, remaining alert to a larger cultural context that challenged some of the denomination's practices. The most significant dimensions of Barrett Browning's poetic development arise, I argue, when the hymn and sermon become spaces where religious thought and language confront both a Victorian ideology of gender that distinguished between men's and women's modes of being and of expressing themselves, and a Victorian homiletic theory that called (male) preachers to infuse their sermonic expositions with a more feeling (that is, "feminine") language. Congregationalism did not escape these issues. Attentive as it was to hymn and sermon—that is, to word-oriented practices—it had to consider what kind of speaker and what kind of language best served the goals of religion. As a woman participating in such language-laden practices, Barrett Browning, too, considered the point: If an intellectually sophisticated language expresses religious truth best, then how might a woman poet write in an age when gender theory assigns the intellectual primarily to men? If an emotive or passionate language expresses religious truth best, how might a woman poet committed to serious, scriptural interpretation—as is the preacher—produce work that moves beyond the sentimentalism expected of her as a woman? Word-orientation, independence, dialogism, style: these matters frame my study of Barrett Browning, with the present chapter exploring her religious imaginary as generated within (and sometimes against) the Congregationalist liturgy, particularly hymn and sermon; and the next chapter reading mainly her religious poetry as creatively and critically arising from this imaginary.

Barrett Browning, Congregationalism, and the Free Church of Scotland

Barrett's early and well-known association with Congregationalism needs only a brief recounting here.[1] The poet's diary and early correspondence tell of Barrett's regular participation (excepting periods of illness) in Congregationalist gatherings such as the Hope End schoolhouse-chapel, Sidmouth Marsh Independent Chapel, and London Paddington Chapel.[2] By contrast, Barrett Browning's postmarriage correspondence does not name any Congregationalist chapels among her places of worship. This absence—especially when coupled with such remarks as "There is nobody in the world with a stronger will & aspiration to escape from *sectarianism* in any sort of sense" (*BC*, 8:76); "[I am] a believer in a Universal Christianity" (*BC*, 9:120); and "I could pray anywhere & with all sorts of worshippers, from the Sistine chapel to Mr. Fox's [Unitarian chapel]" (*BC*, 11:10)—has led critics to conclude that the poet moved toward heterodoxy or outright disavowal of organized religion. Simon Avery, for example, states that during her years in Italy, Barrett Browning increasingly "took up the firm dissenting stand of staying at home to read and interpret the gospels by herself."[3] However, although illness certainly kept Barrett Browning at home much of the time, she remained invested in communal worship throughout her life. In her thirties, she affirmed to William Merry that a "rational person" could, without being called a "controversialist," "class himself or herself with the particular class of Christians which appears to approach nearest his or her view of Scriptural truth" (*BC*, 8:47); continuing the conversation in her next letter, of early 1844, she identified the "class of Christians" she chose as her own: "I am not a Baptist—but a Congregational Christian,—in the holding of my private opinions" (BC, 8:150). When she and Robert discovered during their courtship that their religious ideas resonated well together, she wrote to him, "You go quickest there, where your sympathies are least ruffled & disturbed—& I like, beyond comparison best, the simplicity of the dissenters." She then qualified her remark about being able to pray anywhere, even in Fox's Unitarian chapel, with the statement, "I would prefer as a matter of custom, to pray in one of these chapels, where the minister is simple-minded & not controversial,—certainly wd. prefer it. Not exactly in the Socinian chapels, nor yet in Mr. Fox's—not by preference" (BC, 13:154). These statements in themselves caution against any quick conclusion as to Barrett's rejection of Congregationalism or, more broadly, of organized religion. More substantially, though, other evidence points to a sustained—though not uncritical—relationship with the denomination.

To uncover that evidence requires a brief foray into church history. W. B. Selbie's study of Congregationalism reveals that the denomination, rooted in sixteenth-century England, formed also in Scotland, Ireland, Wales, America, Canada, Australia, and other outreaches of the British Empire, but not in Europe.[4] That is to say, Barrett Browning never had the opportunity in Europe to affiliate herself in public worship with Congregationalists so-named. But her sense of fellowship with Congregationalism continued, though it necessarily appeared in a different guise, primarily as an affiliation with the Free Church of Scotland. The Free Church of Scotland began in 1843 when it broke from the (Scottish) Established Church over the question of legislative authority.[5] In resisting the increasingly heavy-handed practice of patronage appointment of ministers and the civil courts' enforcement of that practice, the Free Church declared its own principles to be those of "non-intrusion and spiritual independence"; further, whereas members of the Established Scottish Church could declare, "What makes the church of Scotland, but the law [of the land]?" the Free Church emphatically stated, "God is her Author, Christ is her King, and the Bible is her law."[6] In these declarations, the Free Church of Scotland endeared itself to Congregationalists, who appreciated the convictions that led to independent establishment. Though their views on the sacrament of the Lord's Supper differed somewhat—a point to which I will return—Congregationalists and adherents of the Free Church concurred on most theological and liturgical points. In fact, in Scotland many Congregationalists were absorbed into this newly established Free Church,[7] while in London they quickly became acquainted with these like-minded believers when the majority of churches in the London "Scots Kirk" Presbytery decided, also in 1843, "to sever connection with the Church of Scotland" and become "Free."[8] These Free Churches existed in good harmony with Congregationalist churches, often in near proximity.[9] Barrett seems early to have recognized the affiliations between the two groups. When she desired to attend church a few weeks before her marriage, but not amid the crowds of worshippers at her Congregationalist Paddington Chapel, she went with Arabella to what she called the "Scotch church" in her neighborhood (BC, 13:284); as the guest preacher of the day later noted, this church was "the chapel of Mr. Chalmers (Free Church)," not the Established Scottish Church (BC, 13:286n7).

A London Congregationalist relocating to Europe would mostly likely, then, have sought the Free Church of Scotland as an alternative place of worship. Because of the work of its Continental Committee, the Free Church of Scotland had a presence in several important European cities in the nineteenth century.[10] Barrett Browning repeatedly referred to it in her letters to Arabella. As before, she called it the "Scotch church" and frequently expressed either a longing for or a satisfaction at finding this church in her neighborhood. At Pisa, she wished "the Scotch church at Leghorn were here."[11] In Paris, where no Scotch church had been established, she attended the Reformed churches, which she referred to, not insignificantly, as "the French independents" (LA, 1:407, 436, 485; 2:182, 239). True, she also expressed appreciation for the pastor of the Paris church associated with the Newman Street churches of London (later named the Catholic Apostolic Church and led by Edward Irving), but she based her regard on private encounters with him and made a point of saying she had never been to Mr. Carré's church (LA, 1:483–85). Upon arriving in Florence, she and Robert first chose rooms that had the "advantage" of having "the French protestant church close by" (LA, 1:178), but when, two years later, a Scotch church was established there, they began attending its services instead (LA, 1:323, 347, 524). The minister in this church, Robert Maxwell Hanna, had been ordained at Girthon and Anwoth, Scotland, in 1844, in a congregation that had "gone out" of the Establishment the year before; he arrived in Florence in 1850 to serve the Free Church of Scotland there,[12] and he was highly regarded by both Brownings (LA, 1:323). In Rome, the Brownings attended St. Peter's on Christmas Day, a visit often taken as evidence of their ecumenicalism; but Barrett Browning's account of the experience reads more like a tourist's report than a worship participant's: "It was warm enough to admit of my going out to St Peters to hear the grand mass. It was very fine, the spectacle (two Kings present besides pope & cardinals) & the music most affecting" (*LA*, 2:199). Moreover, she wrote to Arabella that their usual practice was to "attend the Presbyterian worship in a private room of the American embassy" (*LA*, 2:52). Once again, this small gathering was the Scotch church. During the last years of her life, when no longer able to attend church herself, Barrett Browning, having allowed her son, Pen, to visit numerous Roman Catholic churches with his nurse in his early years, decided that, now that he was older, he should go with Robert to the Scotch church (*LA*, 2:269). Finally, whenever Barrett Browning returned to London to visit, she continued to attend the Congregationalist services at Paddington Chapel (*LA*, 2:172). Her worship pattern in Europe suggests it was not sisterly affection alone that caused her to join Arabella at these services.

Given this information, Barrett Browning scholarship needs to reexamine the assumption that the poet rejected her early religious affiliation later in life. To be sure, this reading derives from many of Barrett Browning's own remarks. The poet declared Scripture to be indefinite about "any doctrine of particular election" (*Diary*, 122–23), the sacraments to be merely memorial signs and not instruments of grace (*BC*, 7:211), Isaac Watts's hymns used in Congregationalist chapels to be not all in good taste (*LA*, 2:104), the impulse to sectarianism to be detestable (*LA*, 2:117), and the scriptural phrases about hell to be simply symbolic.[13] When these remarks are set within the wider context of nineteenth-century Congregationalism, though, they produce a different effect than when read in isolation. Histories of nineteenth-century Congregationalism reveal that the denomination's theology shifted over time, its parameters gradually widening. Gerald Parsons states of midcentury Congregationalists, "In practice the majority had quietly replaced the old 'high Calvinist' doctrine that only the elect would be saved by a more moderate, effectively Arminian, belief in the possibility of salvation for all." Significantly, Parsons emphasizes the exploratory aspects of the Congregationalist approach to doctrine: "Nonconformists (and especially Congregationalists and Unitarians) explored various liberal and critical versions of theology." He then specifies what three well-known Congregationalist ministers were teaching from their pulpits: "As early as the 1840s Thomas Binney was rejecting belief in eternal torment, and in 1846 Edward White expounded the view that immortality was found only in Christ and that the ungodly would not suffer eternal punishment but would be destroyed.

... Others, among them Baldwin Brown, pressed further and advocated universalism and the eventual salvation of all."[14] These doctrinal shifts and contests with regard to salvation and the nature of hell were accompanied by changing attitudes to the sacraments and hymn singing. The midcentury Congregationalist minister R. W. Dale observed that, with regard to the sacraments, "the overwhelming majority" of Congregationalist ministers had given over the view that the benefit to the participant is brought to the sacrament by Christ in favor of the view that the efficacy of the sacrament is determined by the degree of faith the participant brings to it.[15] About the denomination's hymns, J. Briggs writes that a new tolerance crept into the hymns over the course of the century, a worry about claiming uniqueness.[16] Congregationalist historian Albert Peel points out with regard to sectarianism that many Congregationalists resisted being formed into even a loose association among themselves lest they appear as an independent *church* rather than independent *congregations*.[17] Now to reread Barrett Browning's midlife declarations is to see just how well these expressions fall in line with the theological positions then being taken up by major Congregationalist figures in England. The poet's divergence from some points of historic Protestant theology, in other words, is mid-nineteenth-century Congregationalism's divergence. Although the Free Church of Scotland did not manifest these shifted theological positions (though at least one critic has described Thomas Chalmers—the leading figure in the Scottish Disruption of 1843—as "soft on Calvinism"[18]), Barrett Browning clearly maintained her Congregationalist sensibility while worshipping in the Scotch church. Though she told a friend in 1854 she could not "help thinking that all these church-walls, English, Scottish, Roman, equally, must all be swept away, before Christ can be seen standing in the midst," she did not herself sweep away church distinctions.[19] She looked beyond any single church for what she called Truth and Love; but she mainly chose for her own place of worship Congregationalist and Free Church of Scotland churches. And the liturgy and ethos of these churches were what shaped her religious imaginary.

Forming the Congregationalist Imaginary: A Liturgy of the Word

I now focus on the liturgical experience—its practices and the key principles that interpenetrated them—that shaped the nineteenth-century Congregationalist imaginary. We can think of the Congregationalist liturgical experience as a set of concentric circles, in which the deeper one penetrates, the closer one comes to the core value. For Congregationalists, that core was Scripture: its divine inspiration and authority, its perspicuous nature, its summons to individual engagement. The entire Congregationalist worship experience embodied a confidence that God and his saving grace are not hidden in language but made explicable by it. Because of this high regard for the Word/word, the liturgy privileged the verbal over other forms of religious expression. At the heart of the worship service, Congregationalists placed the sermon, as the exposition of Scripture. But moving inward to and outward again from that core moment, the worshipper participated in a continuous enactment/formation of the significance of the Word/word. It began with the environmental configurations of the worship space and went on to prayer, the singing of hymns, and Bible reading together with the sermon. These practices both expressed and formed the distinctive features of the Congregationalist imaginary: its valuation of independence, dialogue, and verbal work as the way to religious meaning.

To participate in Congregationalist worship, then, meant first of all to enter a building that bespoke disregard for a rich visual or ritualist experience. Congregationalists constructed plain, unadorned chapels in which to worship so that the eye might not distract the ear. Whereas other denominations, notably Anglican and Roman Catholic, crafted the visual, symbolic, and ceremonial dimensions of their liturgies and buildings carefully, Congregationalists underplayed, if not downright ignored, these. A contemporary, John Blackburn, described Paddington Chapel, for example, as "bare and unsightly," and a period drawing of the exterior confirms the description.[20] Similarly emphasizing economy and function rather than aesthetics, the Free Church of Scotland—having given up all its churches, manses, and schools by departing from the Established Church—determined that its new edifices should be built in an "unpretending style of architecture." The builders were to pay attention to "acoustic properties and general convenience," under the conviction that "it needs no gorgeous cathedral, no fane rich in the glories of architecture, in order that God's message of forgiveness may be preached to sinful men."[21] In such plain churches and chapels, the pulpit held front and center position, indicating its importance as the place from which the Word was read and preached. Blackburn, editor of the 1847 *Congregational Year Book*, reiterated the point: "The pulpit, not the altar, the teacher, not the symbol, must be conspicuous" (160). Even when simplicity in Congregationalist architecture no longer elicited much support and—under the influence of the Gothic Revival—chapels began to acquire spires, chancels, and painted windows, the pulpit kept its central position.[22] Contemporary ecclesiological pressures—to be further detailed in the chapters on Rossetti—could not persuade Congregationalists that anything could outdo the word in effectively communicating religious truth.

As early as 1826, Barrett expressed a similar sentiment in a poem entitled "An Essay on Mind": "thoughts uncloth'd by language are, at best, / Obscure," she wrote. Therefore, "spurn not words," for "no freedom, Learning's search affords, / Of soul from body, or of thought from words."[23] Further, though Barrett declared there was "unspeakable poetry in Christ's religion" (BC, 3:179), she insisted that a religion reliant on language was more powerful than a religion reliant on the visual or symbolic. She criticized the Roman Catholic worship experience as merely "picturesque—*not poetical*" (BC, 3:208)—too dependent on predetermined visual effect. A "religion of the sense," she writes, is weaker than a "religion of the imagination" (BC, 5:182), by which sleight of hand she claims the Congregationalist language-oriented mode of worship as more imaginative than the Roman Catholic—or, for that matter, the Anglo-Catholic. True, she mentions favorably the crucifix and incense in the cathedral service at Pisa, but she hastens to add that the glitter and ritual were soon "all weariness of the flesh and no edification of the spirit" (LA, 1:9–40)—meaning they brought her no physical or spiritual benefit. Elsewhere she explains that her reference to such sensual elements as altar candles and priests in her poem "The Dead Pan" is "altogether spiritual" and not to be taken as "compromising any truth" (BC, 8:261). Presumably the same is true for the altar and incense of "A Vision of Poets." "God will give of His beauty & fragrance," she writes in reference to the preaching, "to the least word" (BC, 8:148–49). That is, language already bears God's presence, even lowly language; so nothing additional—visual or olfactory—is required. The Congregationalist worship environment seems likely to have contributed to, if not actually formed, this confidence in the verbal over a multisensory religious mode.

Interlude: Sacrament

This faith in the verbal rather than the metaphorical or connotative possibilities of the visual, tactile, or olfactory also marked the Congregationalist celebration of the Lord's Supper. Some readers may have wondered why sacraments were not included in the earlier list of key liturgical episodes in the Congregationalist service, and though it forms a long interlude here between my remarks on Congregationalist architecture and prayer, I must explain the absence. Put briefly, the sacrament of the Lord's Supper as practiced by Congregationalists virtually ignored the metaphorical meanings so important to other denominations, and again put the accent on narrative and exposition. When Congregationalists participated in the celebration of the Lord's Supper, they—like members of the Scotch church and other Presbyterians[24]— usually sat around a table set up for the purpose but afterwards put away again; that is, the table served only a functional purpose, not a symbolic one. The minister read relevant verses of 1 Corinthians 11, but because Congregationalists emphasized the instruction of Christ "Do this in remembrance of me" rather than the description "This is my body" (or blood), the celebration did not include an invocation or blessing on the elements of bread and wine.[25] Instead, it leaned on Paul's words, "For whenever you eat this bread and drink this cup, you proclaim the Lord's death until he comes." Remember and proclaim: these were the key words, and they reflected a Zwinglian sensibility of sacrament, as a contemporary Congregationalist statement makes clear: "[We] believe in the perpetual obligation of Baptism, and the Lord's Supper: . . . the latter to be celebrated by Christian churches as a token of faith in the Saviour, and of brotherly love."[26] The Zwinglian term here is "perpetual obligation." Distinguishing his ideas from interpretations put forward by Calvin or Luther, Zwingli—their contemporary in Switzerland—described the Lord's Supper as a memorial meal only, to be celebrated because Christ so instructed, or ordained it. As an ordinance rather than a sacrament, the meal was not understood to evoke Christ's presence or God's grace; its elements were not understood as symbolic. Instead, the meal was simply a recollection, in solemnity and faith, of a past event. As one Congregationalist of the time remarked, "It is simply a memorial—a memorial of an absent Friend and Lord."[27] As Tyron Inbody explains, whereas a sacramental view of the Lord's Supper takes the meal as "a way to experience anew the reality of Christ," the memorialist view interprets the supper "primarily as a narration of salvation history, a recital of what God did in Christ." He continues, "When seen strictly as an ordinance, the emphasis [in celebration] falls on our recollection, our public testimony of our commitment and loyalty to the life of Christ and to his preaching and teaching of the kingdom of God."[28] There is no holy presence, only a renewed proclamation.

Barrett Browning most decidedly aligned herself with this memorialist view of the Lord's Supper. She wrote in 1843, "I can never see anything in these sacramental ordinances except a prospective sign in one (Baptism), and a memorial sign in the other (the Lord's Supper), and could not recognize either under any modification as a peculiar instrument of grace, mystery, or the like. The tendencies we have toward making mysteries of God's simplicities are as marked and sure as our missing the actual mystery on occasion. God's love is the true mystery and the sacraments are only too simple for us to understand" (BC, 7:211–12; see also 8:47). Barrett uses a common church vocabulary of *sacrament* and *sacramental* here, but clearly her principal terms are *ordinances* and *memorial sign*; there can be no mistake about her rejection of symbolic interpretations of the supper at this point in her life.

Thereafter, Barrett mentioned the Lord's Supper infrequently. In all her travels, what concerned her was finding a church where the Word was preached, not where the Lord's Supper might be celebrated. Indeed, Congregationalists were not concerned with frequency of celebration, because to them Scripture far outranked ordinance as the narration of salvation history. Only twice in her letters to Arabella did Barrett mention the meal. In 1851, when she and Robert were in France attending services of the French Reformed Church, she wrote, "Robert was quite vexed that I wouldn't stay [for] the communion this morning at the church—He 'does dislike going out in that way.' Really I had not courage, for fear of being asked, our business there—Still perhaps they wd. have let us stay. We can try another time" (LA, 1:412). Barrett Browning did not explain her anxiety here, but it may be deduced by recognizing that the French Reformed churches followed more in the tradition of Calvin than of Zwingli. Calvinist practice of the Lord's Supper typically includes an admission to the table only after consultation with appointed members of the church council. If Barrett Browning knew of this practice, she would have been uneasy about staying for the supper without permission. Thus, her remark would be about procedure rather than any sense of unworthiness (a sense not in keeping with memorialist views anyway).

Two years after this moment, Barrett Browning mentioned the Lord's Supper to Arabella again, this time from Rome, where she and Robert were attending the Free Church of Scotland. She wrote,

> For our part, we attend the presbyterian worship in a private room of the American embassy, where Mr. Baird officiates— ... Robert & I received the Lord's supper from his hands the sunday before last, and though a portion of the service was read we both of us enjoyed it much—indeed those were the happiest moments I have had in Rome. I never saw the sacrament so administered, Arabel—there were great pieces of bread as large as two of

my fingers. For the rest, not more than five or six communicants besides ourselves, and those, women. We stayed without any permission, beyond the general invitation to christians of all denominations given in the sermon—we saw at once that we were free to stay. Mr. Baird is of the church of Scotland. (*LA*, 2:52)

Though compelled to note the fixed liturgy of part of the service (a portion "was read")—a practice totally at odds with Independent emphases—and astonished at the size of the bread pieces, Barrett Browning felt "free to stay." This is intriguing because the Free Church of Scotland interpretation of the Lord's Supper was not memorialist. Through John Knox, Calvinist interpretations prevailed in the Scottish churches; that is to say, the supper was viewed as a sign and seal of God's grace, and celebration included a blessing on the elements. But as in Congregationalism, the celebration was a simple affair. It privileged the word of blessing, and Free Church members concurred that "no mystic rite, no blaze of taper, and cloud of incense [need] accompany the celebration of the sacraments, in order that they may impart their efficacy to the worshippers."[29] The Lord's Supper celebration, therefore, would have felt very much the same in Congregationalist and Free Churches, though the interpretation differed. The theological variance seems not to have deterred Barrett Browning from celebrating in Free Churches. In fact, in both letters quoted here, she uses nonmemorialist terms such as *communion* and *sacrament*, even to her Congregationalist sister. It is possible that she held the memorialist position less firmly in her forties than earlier; but it is also possible that she retained her own views while feeling free to celebrate in a denomination whose beliefs and practices aligned closely with her own on other (to her, more important) points. The celebration as a *sacrament* simply did not signify largely in her religious imagination.

By this point, some readers may be protesting that Barrett Browning's poetry, or even her prose, does not bear out my assertion about the minimal role of the sacrament in her religious imagination. What about Aurora's declaration, "Earth's crammed with heaven / And every common bush afire with God"?[30] Or Barrett's assertion in the preface to "A Drama of Exile," "As if life were not a continual sacrament to man, since Christ brake the daily bread of it in His hands" (*WEBB*, 2:569)? Or the statement in "The Book of the Poets" that "Nature is God's art—the accomplishment of a spiritual significance hidden in a sensible symbol" (*WEBB*, 4:462)? Or the comment to Isa Blagden that reviewers ignored "the double action of the metaphysical intention" in *Aurora Leigh* (FF, 115)? Such phrases certainly seem in keeping with a sacramental poetics. But in truth, not only do such expressions rarely appear in Barrett Browning's writings, but when they do, they reflect the influence of romanticism and Swedenborgianism more than of sacramentalism per se. That is to say, Barrett Browning's occasional "sacramentalism" almost never takes the shape of seeing, touching, or tasting—so to speak—the crucified Christ in particular elements of nature or culture. Whereas for Rossetti the sacramental is almost synonymous with the redemptive and has rich theological meaning, for Barrett Browning the sacramental is imaginative; it has a Romantic spiritualized meaning detached from historic, doctrinal roots. As such, it is a relatively young concept. As Roger Lundin observes, "The aesthetic call to transfer incarnational and sacramental powers from the history of redemption to the workings of the imagination" arose out of "a strong degree of nostalgia for re-enchantment among many western Christians" in the modern industrial and skeptical age. The Romantic notion of sacramental art is a contingent term: "To speak of the sacraments in the mid-sixteenth century would have been to join a great debate over Christ's power, not poetry's, and over the meaning of divine grace rather than the measure of human creativity."[31] Rossetti's sacramentalism, I demonstrate later, followed from such sixteenth-century or earlier theological understandings. Barrett Browning's did not. Indeed, the phrases in *Aurora Leigh* that posit a correspondence between earth and heaven ("the double action of the metaphysical intention") derive mainly from Barrett Browning's reading of Swedenborg, as Nathan Camp and others have shown.[32] And when Romney says in the poem that his "daily bread tastes of" Aurora's poetry, the reference has less incarnational meaning than the texture of Swedenborg's statement that "[t]he Lord's 'blood' means his Divine Truth and the truth of the Word, because His 'flesh,' spiritually understood, means the Divine good of love."[33] That is, Romney refers to Aurora's poetry as drawing him up to heights of truth and love; but he does not attach these meanings to the incarnated Christ. The same is true much earlier in the poem, when Aurora recounts how her father's life was changed when he met her mother: "He too received his sacramental gift / With eucharistic meanings; for he loved" (1.90–91). The liturgical weight of the sacrament that so shapes Rossetti's poetry is not felt in these lines, which do not unpack their potential the way a Rossetti poem does. While, therefore, I am led to new recognitions of Catholic presences in *Aurora Leigh* through Maria LaMonaca's provocative reading of the poem as Aurora's effort to "acknowledge and embrace" her "inner Catholic,"[34] I am not ultimately persuaded by the suggestion that Aurora's eventual uniting of physical and spiritual desires carries the resonance of the Roman Catholic Mass, even covertly—not so much because Barrett Browning emphatically rejected Catholicism (which LaMonaca acknowledges) but because she was not persuaded that any sacramental act could embody truth as well as language could. Gestures toward sacrament generally remain thin in her poetry. It is the narrative and expository impulse that prevails instead: the urge to testify to the Word more than to contemplate the symbol.

For this reason, even in a poem ripe with potential for (Romantic) sacramentalism—"Earth and Her Praisers"—Barrett does not cast the natural world as veiling an immanent divinity. Indeed, in the poem the poet with the "ecstasy-dilated eye" is completely misguided as to why Earth should be praised, and his self-aggrandizement is corrected by "a Christian" who praises Earth because both its beauties and its harshness direct him to think of a future world in God's presence—a world which, significantly, he has read about in "God's dear book" (*WEBB*, 1:472.106, 162, 201). Similarly, when in "The Book of the Poets" Barrett declares nature to be God's art, her next sentence moves rapidly from sacramentally laden terms to intellectually laden ones: "Poetic art (man's) looks past the symbol with a divine guess and reach of soul into the mystery of the significance,—disclosing from the analysis of the visible things the synthesis or unity of the ideal,—and expounds like symbol and like significance out of the infinite of God's doing into the finite of man's comprehending. Art . . . does not imitate, she expounds" (*WEBB*, 4:462). Moreover, the two sentences together seem less about God's immanence in nature—and certainly not about Christ's incarnation or redemptive work—than about God's creative act of the past: nature is the *accomplishment* of a spiritual significance hidden in a sensible symbol; poetry discloses the infinite of God's *doing*. That is, Barrett believes nature testifies to God's existence and activity, but she does not suggest nature embodies God or testifies to the incarnation. Poetry looks "past the symbol," not at it. The "mystery of the significance" lies beyond nature, not in it. While, therefore, romanticism and Swedenborgianism sometimes propelled Barrett Browning toward a spiritualized view of nature that can seem like sacramentalism, ultimately she did not have a deep theological feeling for sacrament; she saw little sign of grace or redemption in it. Thus, this excursion into the sacramental returns us to the point that the most deeply formative elements of the liturgy for her were those first and foremost oriented to the Word: to language, disclosure, exposition, narrative.

Interpreting the Word: The Hymn as Potential and Problem

While the unornamented environments of Congregationalist and "Scotch" churches drew no attention to themselves but instead encouraged worshippers to focus on the pulpit and sermon, prayer in the Congregationalist liturgy drew considerable attention—but not much of it positive. Rather, church prayer shaped the Congregationalist imaginary more by its failings than by its vibrant presence. Surprisingly for such a linguistically attuned body, public prayers were so long and wearying that congregants sometimes avoided them by coming late to the service; Samuel Palmer observed that too many of them regarded prayer as "little more than an introduction to the sermon."[35] Later in the century the long prayer was divided across the service, but even then, records of the liturgy show the prayers being differentiated more by length (short, long) than purpose (pastoral prayer, supplicatory prayer, offertory prayer, and so forth).[36] Moreover, these prayers were the subject of extensive controversy as to whether they should be prepared beforehand or composed and delivered extempore. The debate arose from a centuries-old aversion to any kind of set form, which Congregationalists associated with the Established Church. In the main, their own sensibility was for free expression, though more often than not, this practice led to meandering or disjointed or even showy prayers that few people had patience for.[37] Despite its potential for being one of the most formative elements of a liturgy so attentive to the verbal, Congregationalist public prayer did not contribute meditative, supplicatory, or adorative postures to the Congregationalist imaginary. This is not to say that Congregationalists did not supplicate or adore during the worship service but that, generally speaking, the prayers did not serve as strong, consistent opportunities or models for such formations. Not surprisingly, though Barrett Browning sometimes in her correspondence mentions private or family prayers, of liturgical prayer she says not much more than "If the spirit crieth Abba in us, why sh.^{d} we not cry it with our lips,—without reading a form of speech from a prayerbook" (BC, 8:150). Her allusion to Romans 8:15 in defense of free prayer places her among the majority of Congregationalists on this point. But for a poet interested in religious work, the lack of rich liturgical prayer may have been an unnameable absence in the formation of her devotional poetry.

However, the failure of the Congregationalist public prayer to offer rich meditative, supplicatory, or adorative moments in the liturgy did not, as I have said, mean these postures were not at all found in the Congregationalist liturgy: worshippers experienced and performed these postures through the hymns they sang together, three or four per service. As an embodied practice, congregational singing has its own formative impact on the worshipper. First, to recall Smith's analysis, because singing draws on muscles, lungs, tongues, and vocal cords, it can be a mode of bodily memory, a means of forming the singer's speech and, consequently, sense of self. Nineteenth-century Congregationalists such as Palmer at least partly recognized the bodily impact of singing by recommending that the congregation stand to sing, since standing is "universally esteemed a necessary expression of respect."[38] Palmer's association of singing with respect indicates how hymns can function also as prayers, as respectful or devotional addresses to God. A glance through the *Congregational Hymn Book* of 1836 (as through any hymnbook) reveals just how many hymns are cast this way. The editor chose such hymns deliberately, observing in his preface that too many modern hymns had a "descriptive, sentimental, or didactic character, instructive and edifying in themselves, but not in the form or spirit of either prayer or praise."[39] In the *Congregational Hymn Book*, then, could be found the meditative and devotional postures apparently missing from the public prayers—now enacted by the people instead of the preacher and necessarily appearing in set forms.

Yet in Congregationalist circles, the potential of the hymn to invite singers into prayerful, devotional postures could sometimes be hindered by the drive to make every element of the service do instructive verbal work as well. In the preface to the *Congregational Hymn Book*, Josiah Conder writes, "In compliance with the wishes of the Committee . . . the Editor has prefixed to every hymn an appropriate passage of Scripture,—furnishing as it were a key-note to the general strain, and making the volume 'a sort of running metrical commentary on the Bible.'"[40] Conder appears to be quoting someone—perhaps the aforementioned committee—and so there is some sense of community or consensus here, but his words more readily indicate how the hymn, for Congregationalists, could not be overlooked as an opportunity for theological or biblical exposition. The affixed Scripture texts, in other words, did not turn the volume into a devotional handbook to the Bible. Rather, they turned it at least partly into an excursus on the Bible, as if the act of devotion were inadequate without an adjoining commentary.

Congregationalists themselves attempted to articulate this deep impulse toward the instructive and interpretive word. In 1833 the newly formed Congregational Union of England and Wales—probably feeling the need both to clarify for others why a group of churches whose alternative name was "Independents" would form a union at all and to assuage its own worries about potential loss of autonomy—issued a "Declaration of the Faith, Church Order and Discipline of the Congregational, or Independent Dissenters."[41] Although the declaration might appear prescriptive in its theological and liturgical principles, in fact it did no more than name for public reference what had always been its reciprocating principles and practices. Assuring readers that participation in the Union was voluntary and meetings were to be a forum for mutual support rather than decision-making opportunities, the declaration attempted to give discursive shape to a Congregationalist ethos already some centuries old. Two of the leading statements capture the Congregationalist Word-orientation. First, Congregationalists accept Scripture as "divinely inspired, and of supreme authority" in all matters, with all controversies over its meaning to be settled by resort to "the languages in which they were originally written." Here, a belief in Scripture's divine origin combines with a historical-grammatical exegetical method that holds that the true meaning of a biblical text can be found by studying its original linguistic and cultural contexts. Second, Congregationalists insist on congregational and individual independence in religious matters: "Human traditions, fathers and councils, canons and creeds, possess no authority over the faith and practice of Christians"; rather, all members have "the right to form an unbiased judgment of the word of God." That is to say, the designation "Independent" signified, in the Congregationalist ethos, both the denomination's relationship to the Established Church and each adherent's relationship to any model of authority other than Scripture itself.[42]

Barrett maintained these Congregationalist valuations of scriptural authority and independent interpretation throughout her life. Her wide scriptural knowledge informed many of her diary entries in her midtwenties; on one level it exceeded that of fellow churchgoers in that she learned Hebrew and Greek (*Diary*, 177, 238; *BC*, 4:144) and could thus apply the historical-grammatical method to scriptural interpretation in ways that the majority of worshippers could not. Given the declaration's statement that the original languages of Scripture were the final grounds for settling disputes, this was no small matter. Moreover, Barrett gave absolute primacy to Scripture as the source of divine truth. As late as 1854, she wrote, "No doctrine should be received from spirits, who are always fallible but only from the Word."[43] At the same time, she insisted that individuals were always limited in their perception; when she declared Truth and Love as her hope of a church, she parenthetically remarked of Truth, "as far as each thinker can apprehend it" (*BC*, 8:76).

This dual impulse toward confessing scriptural authority and insisting on individual interpretation creates both the power and the tension of the Congregationalist imaginary. To demonstrate my meaning, I turn again to the liturgical hymn before moving on to the sermon and preacher. Traditionally, Nonconformist churches, like the Established Church, had sung metrical versions of the Psalms—the words of Scripture placed in the mouths of believers as their response to Scripture. These psalms provided worshippers with many religious postures (meditative, celebratory, mournful, supplicatory, thanksgiving) and modes (narrative, lyric, dramatic). But in the eighteenth century, the hymn virtually erupted as an alternative to or expansion of psalm singing. Richard Arnold illustrates how the rise of hymns provoked controversy as to whether such human compositions were suitable for use in the church;[44] but Nonconformists, who emphasized "the importance of the individual in his relationship to God rather than the corporate identity of the church," were drawn to hymns as a means of expressing the layperson's participation in the church service.[45] Hymns, clearly, could incorporate contemporary language and individual experience in a way that versified psalms could not. Perhaps even more enticingly for those who liked to "explore various liberal and critical versions of theology" (to use Parsons's words again), hymns gave far more room than the metrical psalms (which were basically a rearrangement of biblical words into chant or song) for theological variance. Hymns allowed the different theological casts of the hymnists to show themselves. Wesley's hymns, for example, emphasize individual spiritual experience and the "bliss of conversion," while the more Calvinist-minded Isaac Watts's hymns emphasize "the relationship between human and divine" and are more "decorously ordered."[46] Such opportunity for theological and linguistic individuation sometimes resulted in controversy, as in the case of a Congregationalist minister who, on account of his hymns, was accused of being deist.[47] The duration and passion of the ensuing controversy in the denomination's newspapers show that Congregationalists recognized the potential power of the hymn as an exposition of Scripture; as one of their ministers said, "Let me write the hymns of a Church . . . and I care not who writes the theology."[48] Such influence, of course, could have positive ends as well, as in Conder's attempt to foster an ecumenical spirit in the users of the *Congregational Hymn Book*. In his preface, Conder pointed out the inclusion of hymns by "Episcopal clergymen, Moravians, Wesleyan Methodists, Independents, and Baptists—all harmoniously combining into one metrical service—prov[ing] that 'by one Spirit we are all baptized into one body,' and that there actually exists throughout that body 'a Communion of Saints.'"[49] Given the potential influence of hymns in the church, the construal of the hymn as both an opportunity for independent religious expression and a threat to scriptural authority or religious stability is no surprise.

Period concepts of gender complicated this picture, especially for women hymnists. The *Congregational Hymn Book*—which Barrett would likely have used in Paddington Chapel, whose minister supported the Union's endeavors[50]—speaks to a change that overcame women's hymn writing from the eighteenth to early nineteenth centuries. Most hymnbooks in use in the early nineteenth century built on the work of eighteenth-century predecessors, men and women. Prominent names included Isaac Watts, John and Charles Wesley, Philip Doddridge, John Newton, Anne Steele, and Anna Barbauld. To these were added hymns by contemporary writers, again both men and women. In terms of women writers, the *Congregational Hymn Book* included ten hymns by Steele and one by Barbauld but also four by Mrs. J. Conder, wife of the editor, and one each from the sisters Jane Taylor and Ann Taylor (later Gilbert), best known for their *Hymns for Infant Minds*. Strikingly, both the subject matter and the placement of the hymns within the collection differ between the eighteenth- and nineteenth-century women writers. Steele's hymns do work that the editor apparently comfortably acknowledges: he recognizes a liturgical intention in the hymn he heads as "For the Lord's Supper"; expository work in the two hymns he groups together under "Didactic and Expository: New Testament Subjects"; and public value in the hymn he names as "A Hymn of National Mercies." Clearly it was acceptable not only for Steele to write such hymns in the eighteenth century but also for Conder to feature them in a nineteenth-century hymnal. The contributions by the nineteenth-century women, by contrast, almost uniformly address private experience in terms that foreground (women's) weakness, resignation, or fear. Though Mrs. Conder ventures toward what Conder calls a "New Testament subject," it is only to call on the image of Mary weeping over Jesus's feet as a proper model of (women's) penitence and humility. Perhaps these women also produced hymns of a stronger theological cast, but if so, such hymns were not given public recognition. In fact, to reinforce the nonliturgical (that is, nonpublic) position of these contemporary women's hymns, Conder groups them all under the heading "Private and Family Worship" and places them last in the book.

What happened to occasion this shift in attitude, even by women, with regard to women's hymns, I suggest, was the growing influence of an ideology that distinguished between women's and men's abilities and spheres of action. Numerous critical works have by now familiarized us with the Victorian period's configuration of men as intellectual and rational by nature, women as emotional. In his 1864 lecture to the working-class men of Manchester, for example, John Ruskin formulated the ideology in these now well-known terms: "Now their separate characters are briefly these. The man's ... intellect is for speculation and invention; [b]ut the woman's ... intellect is not for invention or creation, but for sweet ordering, arrangement, and decision. ... [For a woman, it is not] an object to know; but only to feel, and to judge." Scientists, lawmakers, church figures, and others concurred with Ruskin that the binary oppositions in this ideology were natural ones.[51] Though actually the Victorians both constructed and contested these binary oppositions, the concept of separate spheres and, indeed, separate modes of being for men and women permeated the Victorian period, shaping the cultural roles, expectations, and productions of both groups. The assignment of intellection to men and emotion to women also had implications for the type of language each was expected to use, whether written or spoken. In their (at least, theoretical) acceptance of women's interpretive abilities, therefore, Congregationalists somehow had to negotiate the contemporary denial of them—no easy task, as Angela Leighton has shown in *Victorian Women Poets: Writing Against the Heart*. Already by the first third of the nineteenth century, much women's religious verse had all but replaced an earlier participation in theological work with an outpouring of emotive language. Devotion replaced interpretation; this had the added effect of at least partly easing the tension between Scripture's authoritative word and the hymnist's interpretive moves.

Despite the potential opportunities that the hymn provided for women's engagement with theology and liturgy, therefore, a woman poet writing in the 1830s and beyond could feel restrained by the expectation that she privilege sentiment over intellect in her work. A model of the (woman) poet as a witness to or exemplar of religious feeling but not as a religious interpreter simply could not, in the long term, prove satisfactory for a writer with a strong inclination toward independence of thought (or Independent thought). Even apart from gender issues, hymn writing presents other constraints, if designed for congregational use. The hymn cannot be too individualized, too reflective of a particular personal moment, or too radical in its theology. The hymn writer who hopes to contribute to the church's liturgy without provoking a storm of theological controversy is conscious that what she voices must, to a certain extent, be what others wish to voice as well.

To totally disregard the community's beliefs in the pursuit of an individual theology would destroy any prospect of influence within that community. In addition, hymns tend to become communal property, with the name of the hymn writer rapidly forgotten or pushed to an index of first lines (as in the *Congregational Hymn Book*) and the hymn itself frequently changed by editors and compilers to suit their own or their congregation's preferences. As Susan Drain notes, many early hymn editors "counted their responsibility to liturgical, theological and hymnological standards more important than merely literary responsibility to an author."[52] As a kind of public property, then, the hymn included in church hymnals seldom contributes to personal distinction or fame. Further, because hymns usually conform to preexisting melodies, the hymn writer has a limited choice of metrical patterns and rhyme schemes, the most usual being common measure. While hymn writing challenges one to be creative within the given frames, the poet seeking innovative ways of producing religious poetry might feel constrained by these frames.

As the next chapter details, in pursuing her own religious poetics Barrett began with the hymn. She titled or subtitled several of her early religious poems as hymns and also used the metrical structure and devotional voice of the hymn in poems not titled as such. It was the most obvious model offered by Congregationalism for religious poetry, and Barrett saw its intellectual and spiritual possibilities. She expressed fondness for many of Watts's hymns (*LA*, 2:104) and knew from her own experience that such hymns could be an effective way of evoking religious response in readers/singers. She also understood that hymns performed some measure of theological work, and she became increasingly skilled in using her own hymns for scriptural interpretive work. For example, in the early "Hymn" (*WEBB*, 4:271), Barrett cites two Psalm texts as epigraphs, but these texts do not function in the poem other than as thematic reinforcement: "The Lord is nigh unto them that call" (Ps. 145:18) is simply the biblical parallel to Barrett's "Abide with us in weal and woe" (3). In contrast, in "The Measure: Hymn IV" Barrett actually scrutinizes her biblical epigraphs, poses a question that arises from them, and proceeds to answer that question as well as pray for patient learning.

In other hymns, too, Barrett successfully joins intellectual and devotional ends. For example, "The Mediator: Hymn II" (*WEBB*, 4:313) combines praise and prayer with a careful pondering on the gospel. Each stanza opens with an exclamation acknowledging a characteristic of God and contrasting it with human failure; the stanza then pivots in its third line to bring in Christ as the one who makes it possible for the Father to be in relation with people. High, pure, strong, and kind, God sees the low, impure, weak, and unkind only through Christ—and the speaker prays in the closing line that this may always be so:

> How high Thou art! our songs can own
>   No music Thou couldst stoop to hear;
> But still the Son's expiring groan
>   Is vocal in the Father's ear.
>
> How pure Thou art! our hands are dyed
>   With curses, red with murder's hue—
> But HE hath stretched HIS hands to hide
>   The sins that pierced them from Thy view.
> ....
> High God, and pure, and strong, and kind!
>   The low, the foul, the feeble, spare!
> Thy brightness in HIS face we find—
>   Behold our darkness only *there!*
>
>   (1–8, 17–20)

In five short stanzas, the poem explicates the biblical themes of sin and redemption in Christological fashion yet maintains the note of worship and prayer usually associated with the genre of the hymn—an intellectual-devotional accomplishment explored further in the next chapter.

But despite this success, Barrett seems also to have chafed against the limitations of the hymn. The avenues of publication she sought suggest that her goals differed from those of hymn writers who wished to have their hymns used in chapels or churches. Barrett sent her hymns not to denominational magazines or newspapers but to literary journals, a choice that suggests she never intended her hymns to function exclusively as religious expressions of a community, however much the model proved useful in developing her individual voice. Moreover, the intellectual complexity of her hymns, especially the later ones, makes them unsuitable for singing, since continuous singing does not allow for sustained analysis of any one image or line. The hymn, Barrett soon saw, served as a springboard for her further religious work, not its endpoint. After 1838, she wrote no new hymns; perhaps tellingly, when in 1842 she translated three Greek hymns of Gregory of Nazianzus she chose verse paragraphs rather than stanzas as her form. Though in future work she sometimes cast the female poet as prophet to contest standard gender ideologies, she also engaged another model for the poet, that of the preacher, whose primary rhetorical means was not hymn but sermon.

Mutual Talk: Poet-Preachers and Truth

To this point I have focused on word-orientation and independence as crucial to and for the Congregationalist imaginary. I have also several times gestured toward Barrett's formulation of Truth and Love as the essential markers of Christian religion. In turning now to the formative influence of preacher and sermon on Barrett Browning's religious imaginary, I draw in the third element outlined in the chapter introduction as significant to the Congregationalist imaginary, namely, the valuation of dialogue, and I give more sustained attention to those words *Truth* and *Love*, which Barrett used in 1843 to express her vision of a church. Bemoaning the schisms and controversies of the present age, she declared, "Truth (as far as each thinker can apprehend it) apprehending,—& Love, comprehending—make my idea . . . my hope of a church" (BC, 8:76). For her, Truth and Love were coterminous, but for the purpose of analysis, I treat them somewhat separately below, examining her hopes for Truth in relation to Congregationalist conceptions of sermon and preacher, and her hopes for Love in relation to denominational and wider debates about homiletic style.

First, then, how did Congregationalists expect to find Truth? As Briggs writes, "It is no exaggeration to say that the sermon was the focus of nonconformist life in the nineteenth century, at once the central experience of the church, the imperative to morality, to philanthropy and evangelism."[53] It occupied the greatest amount of time in the Congregationalist church service and elicited the most commentary afterwards. Its significance was understood to lie in its superior ability to explicate the Scriptures, words making known the Word. As stated earlier, it was typically based on a historical-grammatical exegetical method that closely examined the original linguistic and cultural contexts of a passage to grasp its meaning and then apply it to the life of the present congregation. As such, it was the result of intensive intellectual labor, though it aimed to promote reverence and thankfulness as well as knowledge in its listeners. But it was not regarded as an authoritative discourse; rather, it was construed as social and dialogic. This may seem surprising, given that the sermon is typically delivered by a preacher to a silent congregation, but both the Greek word *homilia* and the Latin word *sermo* signify conversation or mutual talk.[54] Although this root meaning is not audible in the worship service, the sermon remains implicitly dialogic and social, and the preacher a participant in a wider communal imperative to interpret Scripture. That Congregationalists understood sermons and preachers this way appears in two more of their regular practices: their Bible behavior in church and their process of selecting a minister.

Scripture's centrality in the service and the individual's responsibility to interpret meshed in the Congregationalist habit of taking a Bible to church and holding it open for study throughout the sermon. Historian Owen Chadwick refers to a contemporary description of a Congregationalist congregation as "one great Bible class; there was a Bible open in almost every hand."[55] Given that the denomination as a whole repeatedly reset its theological parameters to accommodate ideas that Scripture did not explicitly deny, the open Bible in each hand was not a meaningless gesture. Because independent thinking was expected, divergent interpretations were likely to arise and be accommodated, as listeners judged the sermon against their own knowledge of Scripture. Because Congregationalists tended to be members of the well-educated middle classes—much like their counterparts in the Free Church of Scotland, considered the "most intellectually-active and academically-inclined denomination in Scotland" in the nineteenth century—their habits of independent religious inquiry often led them to substantial knowledge of the Scriptures, as was the case with Barrett.[56] The preacher, then, knew that even as he delivered the sermon, his listeners were speaking back to him in their minds, and he had to anticipate and respond to their thoughts. Sometimes this led him to actually verbalize what he thought their questions or objections might be. The ancient rhetorical term for such inserted imaginary dialogue is, significantly for my argument, *sermocinatio*, and this dialogic sensibility—even sensitivity—remained alive in the Congregationalist ethos of the sermon. A sermon could never be authoritative to a Congregationalist. One could always talk back, Scripture in hand.

Such a potential proliferation of independent interpretations could conceivably end in outright conflict, of course, but Congregationalists did not believe that independent interpretation of the Bible in itself would lead to the breakdown of a coherent, religious community or of religious truth. On the one hand, they trusted—some might say naively—to a certain level of responsible intellectual and religious behavior in each other and a certain measure of conformity. The declaration, for example, expressed the orthodox Christian beliefs Congregationalists expected each other to hold, such as belief in the Trinity and the two natures of Christ. As one of their ministers observed, Congregationalists did not mean "licentiousness of opinion" or "*unaided* judgment" when they referred to their "right of private judgment."[57] The reading of biblical commentaries or writings by the church fathers was encouraged, even expected as part of the ongoing conversation. Responsible interpretation included thoughtful consideration of what respected theologians had already offered. Barrett showed herself at an early age to have participated in this responsible activity: when she studied particular Bible passages, she often considered interpretations given by such early church writers as Gregory of Nazianzus and Chrysostom, and by later theologians such as Richard Hooker and David Clarke (*Diary*, 121; *BC*, 6:193, 8:147). Her copies of works by Gregory and Chrysostom are filled with her marginal and end notes, dated as late as 1839. Barrett never felt bound to agree with these theologians (indeed, in "Some Account of the Greek Christian Poets" she wrote, "Devoted and disinterested as many among them were, they, themselves, were at most times evidently and consciously surer of their *love*, in a theologic sense, than of their knowledge in any" [*WEBB*, 4:370]), but neither did she assert that her conclusions outweighed theirs. Like other Congregationalists, she was confident enough in the clarity of Scripture on essential points to live comfortably with disagreement on lesser points. Basically, Congregationalists were convinced that "when each believing man comes independently for his religious faith and practice to the unpolluted source of truth [that is, Scripture], it is morally impossible that such should be the ambiguity of the oracle, as that the Christian life of the church should become generally or radically wrong."[58] Barrett formulated her own understanding of this concept in stronger (and ungendered) terms: "The more thought & enquiry, the better for Truth. Error is the result of half-thinking" (*BC*, 5:236). Notably, for Barrett, to be Christian does not negate critical reflection; rather, she insisted, Truth emerges more clearly with widespread thought and enquiry. She characterized error as the result of insufficient critical probing. Only an irresponsible Christian, she implied, could be satisfied with half thinking or could leave the thinking up to others. To accept "the church [rather than the responsible individual] as an *interpreter* of scripture" absolutely dismayed her (*Diary*, 170). While thought and enquiry might lead to disagreement in the short term, in the end they could only produce a better understanding of the Truth. When Congregationalists, therefore, sat in church with open Bibles, figuratively they held in their hands entire conversations that involved the preacher, themselves, and other commentators. The sermon not only produced but also, in its very nature, demanded this kind of conversational interchange.

On the other hand, Congregationalists did not rest on good faith and common commitment alone to prevent the privileging of any single person's reading (or preaching) of Scripture over another's. They extended their refusal to submit to councils and creeds in religious matters also to matters of local church polity, and this refusal likewise had its liturgical appearance in the person of the minister. Unlike the Established Church and the Roman Catholic Church, which view the clergy as inheritors of apostolic authority, Congregationalists expressed in the declaration what again had been long practice among them, namely, "that church officers, whether bishops or deacons, should be chosen by the free voice of the church," and ministers "call[ed] forth" from the membership to be pastors.[59] The Free Church of Scotland likewise insisted on the congregation's calling of a minister rather than his appointment by a patron. Because what was freely given or called forth could also be taken away, ministerial status in such a community depended on the regard in which the people held the preacher and could fluctuate depending on his performance. Not always appropriately, each service could be an opportunity to measure the minister. A glance at the process by which a minister became associated with a congregation reveals the vigor with which Congregationalists clung to their democratic ideals.

Candidates for the ministry invariably attended seminary for several years before being ordained (a practice not yet standard in all denominations);[60] yet they still had to earn the respect of a particular congregation before being appointed. In fact, in both Congregationalist and Free Church of Scotland circles, they were chosen and appointed only after a probationary period and only by the "suffrage of the people," as one Dissenting minister put it.[61] At a meeting of the congregation, a motion to call a particular candidate would be either supported or defeated by a vote. If supported, the candidate received a letter of invitation, signed by women as well as men of the congregation.[62] He would respond with his own letter of acceptance. Though the preacher would, therefore, gain a prominent position from which to voice his interpretations of Scripture to the congregation, it was absolutely clear to all parties who gave—and who could remove—this platform. And removals did happen: Congregationalist minister George Macdonald (later an author of fantasy stories) was forced by his congregation to resign in 1853 because of his doubtful doctrines and interest in higher biblical criticism. Similarly, Samuel Davidson, professor at the Congregationalist Lancashire

Independent College, was required to resign his post in 1857 for his denial of Scripture as divinely inspired. Service after service, when the minister ascended the pulpit, the full weight of this practice of appointment and dismissal lay behind his appearance, the sense that while his words merited attention, they did so because the people had agreed to it. In the main, Congregationalist ministers did not object to this democratic process, for they claimed an honor in their task but not a divine or even historical authority. One of them, for example, reminded himself and his congregation of their "deep-seated belief that the ministry is not a divine order of men having exclusive possession of a superior kind of grace, but only men whom God has called to the high honour of preaching his truth and ministering to the spiritual wants of the world."[63] This Congregationalist practice (also maintained in the Free Church of Scotland) again set limits on the authority or power that any one interpretive voice could gain in the religious community, even as it encouraged a high level of scriptural inquiry by each individual. In short, the entire dynamic involving Bible study, sermon, and preacher underscored the belief that collective investigation in a dialogic community would be, to use Barrett's words again, "better for Truth."

Importantly for Barrett's later thinking about the poet figure, Congregationalists did not explicitly exclude women from the position of church officer or preacher. The declaration refers to "members" who are qualified "by the Holy Spirit" and called to certain "church offices" by the congregation.[64] In the United States, at least, a woman named Antoinette Brown was ordained as a Congregationalist minister in 1853, though she later resigned her position.[65] Even if such ordination did not occur in England, the dismissal of any claim to a male, apostolic succession for ordained clergy shows that nineteenth-century Congregationalism was more open to the possibility of female preachers than contemporary Anglican or Roman Catholic churches could be. However, Barrett Browning never commented on the point, either to concur with or to contradict it; but she may have been compliant with an unwritten proscription against women preachers for at least two reasons. First, she steadfastly refused to challenge the meaning of Scripture where it seemed plain enough. As she wrote to Arabella in 1853, "[T]o accept doctrine or direction in contradiction to the written Scripture, or to obvious duty must be in the highest degree blamable [sic]" (LA, 2:17). If the injunction against women speaking in the church could not be defended as a doctrine, it might be called a scriptural direction, and if so, Barrett was not likely to contest it. If this lack of inquiry into Scripture's words about women's silence seems out of line with Barrett's usual practice of interpreting scriptural texts in innovative ways (a practice discussed in the next chapter), the second possible reason for her silence may be more credible. For most of her adult life, Barrett experienced intense discomfort, even inarticulateness, in public situations. She was far more expressive and vibrant in her correspondence than in face-to-face encounters, especially encounters outside her own rooms.[66] The idea of actual, public speech of any sort may have been so discomfiting to her that she easily accepted a general restriction that she had no personal wish to cross. Moreover, although Congregationalist practice did not include women preachers, it did involve them in choosing a minister and in visiting candidates for membership and providing testimony to the church of the candidate's faith commitment, after which the church collectively would extend the membership.[67] In other words, Congregationalist churches took the words of women seriously. When Barrett began to envision the (woman) poet as a preacher, therefore, she engaged a concept that for her carried more weight as a democratic than a gendered model, though the latter inflection did not disappear.

I believe that primarily because of its dialogic and democratic connotations, Barrett found in the poet-preacher image a viable alternative to the widely held contemporary paradigm of the (male) poet as seer, prophet, or sage—that is, as one who has wisdom or insight that others lack—even though at times the prophet model appealed to her as well. Sage discourse—defined by John Holloway as the expression of "notions about the world, man's place in it, and how he should live"—seemingly appealed to Victorian writers as a mode of expression because the rapidly shifting dynamics of their age seemed to call either for new understandings of human significance or for the recovery of values that were being lost.[68] Thomas Carlyle set the terms of sage discourse early in the period: whoever else "may forget this divine mystery [of the Universe]," he declared, "the *vates*, whether Prophet or Poet, has penetrated into it; is a man sent hither to make it more impressively known to us."[69] Carlyle's language rubs against democratic ideals at several points: the sage apparently has exceptional powers to penetrate into mysteries; by implication, others have less access. The sage is sent, apparently by a higher authority; by implication, he stands at least somewhat apart from the rest of the community (the "us"). And he does not converse with the community, he impresses his vision upon it. Further, as the gendered wording of Carlyle's (and Holloway's) definition reveals, Victorian sage discourse identified the *vates*, or poet-prophet, as a man. According to this configuration, only male poets and prose writers could claim the visionary authority of an Old Testament prophet to critique Victorian culture and offer alternative worldviews. As discussed in the previous section on hymns, the ideological configurations of respectable femininity also discouraged women writers from participating in such public and authoritative discourse. Yet as Thaïs Morgan argues, women writers frequently critiqued and subverted the patriarchal model of sage discourse by boldly entering "the 'masculine' world of socio-economic conflict, theological polemic, and sexual politics," despite the risks associated with "adopting a 'masculine' tone of authority," such as defamation in the press or influential social circles.[70] As Marjorie Stone and others cited in the next chapter have shown, Barrett Browning does sometimes adopt the mantle of prophet as she enters the "masculine" world of theological polemic in her poetry.

However, I believe that the poet-prophet paradigm, with its Romantic overtones of the poet as authoritative visionary, had an unsettled position in Barrett Browning's democratic, religious imaginary. Even Barrett's 1844 "A Vision of Poets," though often read as endorsing the poet-prophet model, is actually quite ambivalent about the *vates* figure. In this poem, the speaker witnesses a poet receive a vision of "God's prophets of the Beautiful" (*WEBB*, 1:194.292) gathered around an angel and an altar. The poet-prophets acknowledge that they have all responded to a higher call, one that is now extended to the new poet, who falls in obedience at the angel's feet. As Stephanie Johnson observes, most critics of "A Vision of Poets" have focused on the portion of the poem involving these "king-poets." But the poet-prophet configuration so important to the interior narrative of the poem is not actually endorsed by the poem's speaker, who seems somewhat detached from all that happens—even looking away when the male poet enters the visionary company. When, in the poem's conclusion, the speaker meets the son of the now-dead poet and hears the son echo his father's words, "KNOWLEDGE BY SUFFERING ENTERETH, / AND LIFE IS PERFECTED BY DEATH" (*WEBB*, 1:214.1004–5), the speaker does not reply. Johnson observes that Barrett uses the frame of the poem to distance the speaker from "the self-abnegation of the apocalyptic vision of the framed narrative." Instead, Johnson finds, the narrator's listening and questioning suggest an "ethical model ... defined by human relationship and feeling" rather than the prophetic model of the king-poets. The speaker, whom Johnson identifies as female, describes an apocalyptic vision but also contains it, operating herself in a much more communitarian mode. Her tone throughout the narration is that of a curious bystander—somewhat moved, perhaps, but ultimately unconvinced, even skeptical about the visionary tradition.[71] The appearance of a prophetic figure in Barrett's poetry, then, does not in itself mean that Barrett consistently imagined or approved such a model for a poet. In her prose descriptions of the poet's task, Barrett never refers to the poet this way. In her religious poetry especially—much of it contemporaneous with "A Vision of Poets"—the model does not figure strongly. Indeed, Barrett Browning's liturgical experiences perhaps supplied the alternative paradigm of poet-preacher rather too readily; otherwise, in searching for a model that stressed the educative element of the poet's task, she might have considered the poet-priest. Though *priest* perhaps most immediately conjures a sacrificial or sacramental mode not in keeping with a Congregationalist imaginary, Barrett Browning would have known that the priests of ancient Israel had important teaching functions among the people as well, and that at least one significant prophet, Moses, needed his well-spoken brother (the soon-to-be-priest Aaron) to help him carry out his task. She might then have extrapolated, along with the apostle Peter, from the ordained priesthood of ancient Israel to the "priesthood of all believers" in the Christian era—a firmly Protestant move with generative possibilities for a democratic poet figure.[72]

But Barrett Browning did not imagine a poet-priest in her writings. Certainly her primary liturgical experiences supplied no such figure to her religious imaginary. Instead, her alternative image for the poet is that of the preacher, a model she named more than once. Already in an early poem, "An Essay on Mind," she gives as an example of a rapt poet the flamboyant preacher Edward Irving (*WEBB*, 4:105.910–15). Then, during the years of her affiliation with Paddington Chapel, she directly articulated her poet-as-preacher paradigm. Spurred by what she considered Tennyson's failure to clasp and speak Christian truth broadly in poetry, she asserted, "The poet is a preacher & should look to his doctrine" (*BC*, 8:6). That is, poetry, like preaching, is not self-preoccupation; like preaching, it publicly declares religious truth, and its declarer bears a responsibility to speak only after careful examination of Scripture. This association between preaching and poetry was still alive for Barrett in 1838, when she sent a sonnet to Mary Russell Mitford, wherein she comments of Mitford and her poetry, "Thou art unperplext— / . . . / To preach a sermon on so known a text!" (*WEBB*, 2:71.10, 14). Her ostensible praise of Mitford implies that she herself *is* perplexed about how to preach a sermon in poetry, especially on well-known texts. Antony Harrison notes, "In her letters of the 1830s Elizabeth Barrett does in fact mount the pulpit, only sometimes apologizing for 'seeming, or seeming to try, to be a sermon writer.'"[73] But converting this stance into good poetry proved challenging because for Barrett Browning, good poetry—like her ideal church—involves not only Truth but also Love. Of course, the subject matter of sermons, as of poetry, could or should show the interconnectedness of the two: Barrett declared her system of divinity to arise from Christ's loving prayer for his disciples (BC, 6:129); and as the next chapter shows, her religious poetry often foregrounds divine love. However, the final section of this chapter focuses less on sermonic subjects than on sermonic style as signifier of the role of Love in religious formation.

Homiletic Style: Poet-Preachers and Love

According to theorists of style, style reflects or even models human behavior, perspective, or attitude. Prose theorist Richard Lanham writes, "Every statement about style makes . . . a statement about behavior. Style does not provide a peripheral cosmetic accompaniment to the exposition of self-standing ideas but choreographs the whole dance of human consciousness."[74] Debora Shuger likewise associates style with consciousness, particularly with religious perceptions. In her study of ancient and Renaissance sacred rhetoric, she writes that style speaks "to the role of emotion and imagination in the mind's journey toward God, to the relation between thought and feeling, to the Christian concept of selfhood." According to Shuger, the Christian grand style of the Renaissance—"at once ardently expressive, deeply spiritual, and highly rhetorical"—borrowed from Augustinian anthropology to connect emotion "to man's noetic and spiritual activities." The Christian grand style "follow[ed] from [the] conviction that man comes to God through love and desire" rather than knowledge. Rejecting both "the ostentatious and playful self-display of the sophists" and "the whole intellectualist tradition," it "appeals to the imagination and is therefore able to move and transform the desires of the heart."[75] Barrett's poetics of (Truth and) Love is, I believe, related to a homiletic style of the nineteenth century similarly grounded in affective theory, one that reminds us that "ardently expressive" language is not inherently gender grounded, however much the Victorian period gave it that overlay.

This affective homiletic style of the nineteenth century had two sources, both of which played especially into Barrett's midcareer religious poetics. The first source has been most recently detailed by O. C. Edwards in *A History of*

Preaching.[76] Edwards first accounts for the partial collapse of the Renaissance grand style in preaching by observing that the rise of modern science, on the one hand, and a Protestant commitment to individual reading of Scripture, on the other, led to the favoring of a plain style, supposedly more in keeping with "natural" sources of truth. He notes that by the eighteenth century, the chief characteristics of this strand of preaching were "serene good taste" and "abhorrence of enthusiasm" (404). Shaped by Enlightenment rationalism, such sermons reflected the assumption that the individual journeyed toward God through knowledge or reason, which "was not so distorted by the fall as to be unable to recognize the advantages of good over evil." Preachers tended, therefore, to call their congregants to "the practical goodness [already] apparent to natural reason but made abundantly clear in biblical revelation" (404). However, Edwards continues, the sixteenth and seventeenth centuries also saw "an insistence that in order to be real, religion had to be experienced affectively" (426). He traces these religions of the heart from the early Puritans and Pietists to various evangelical awakenings of the eighteenth century (Whitefield and Wesley) and nineteenth century (Spurgeon). He then examines Romantic preaching as a blend of rationalistic and emotive preaching: "It saw feeling as a path that ultimately gave greater access to knowledge than reason"; yet those who held this view were not "anti-intellectual or opposed to critical thought" (591). Edwards names the rediscovery of Longinus, an ancient Greek rhetorician, as an important influence on this homiletic development, for Longinus's treatise *De Sublimitate*—which Barrett read (BC, 2:218, 10:168)—"contained the first statement of the view that persuasion was not the only purpose of oratory. It also had the aim of enabling an audience to experience sublimity" (595). Influential Romantic heirs of Longinus described the preacher as a creative writer, sermons as works of art, and narratives of individual biblical lives as better than abstract reasoning for experiencing truth deeply (596, 597). Edwards concludes that this influence continued, even deepened, through the nineteenth century, as Victorian preachers "made frequent appeals to the emotions, especially pity and fear [and] delighted in scenic grandeur" (601). As an 1881 guide to sacred rhetoric put it, "A Sermon aims at its effect chiefly by acting on the sensitive part of our nature. Consequently, the Preacher should be thoroughly conversant with the feelings, sentiments, and passions of the human heart."[77] To sum up, Romantic and Victorian homiletics reflected, as did the Renaissance grand style, the supposition that imagination and emotion also played important roles in the spiritual journey toward God.

In addition to what Edwards recounts, I propose a second source for the increased attention in nineteenth-century homiletics to the role of affect in religious discourse, one that also has bearing on Barrett's religious poetics. After all, many Protestants of the nineteenth century resisted affect's association with evangelicalism, distrusting Methodism, for example, for its belief that "intuition and emotion" on their own could be "reliable sources of spiritual enlightenment."[78] Congregationalists especially, with their emphasis on theological training, study of Scripture in its original languages, and careful textual exegesis, were unlikely to take lessons from Methodist preachers, who often had little theological training—and little belief that it was necessary. Likely, Congregationalists, at least early in the century, would have found gratifying rather than discomfiting religious historian Owen Chadwick's observation that their "best sermons were less warm and direct, but more profound than those of Methodists."[79] This would have been true for many Protestant groups of the period, including the Anglican Church from which the Methodists eventually seceded. Consequently, a seventeenth- to eighteenth-century heritage of affective religion does not, I think, fully account for the return of the passionate style in Victorian homiletics. Instead, Victorian homiletic theory and practice also resulted I suggest, from a widespread interest among churches broadly in the writings of the so-called church fathers. That is, Victorian homiletics was at least partly shaped by the same ancient Christian rhetoric that created the Renaissance grand style of Shuger's analysis.

This assertion finds grounding in Michael Wheeler's *The Old Enemies: Catholic and Protestant in Nineteenth-Century English Culture.*[80] In a detailed chapter entitled "On the Origin of Churches," Wheeler demonstrates that both Catholics and Protestants of the 1830s and 1840s "were feverishly researching the first centuries of the Christian era, in order to prove that their own traditions either originated in the early Church ... or were most closely modelled upon the primitive Church described in the New Testament and in the writings of the Fathers, which needed to be translated from the *original* Greek and Latin, and then edited" (51–52; original italics). Among the other evidence of this activity that Wheeler lists are the Catholics Berington and Kirk's 1813 compilation of passages from Christian antiquity, retranslated by Kirk in a second edition in 1830 and then again by James Waterworth in 1846; the Anglican William Keary's 1828 *Common-Place Book to the Fathers*, intended as a Protestant foothold against any misleading emphases in the first Berington and Kirk compilation; reprints of Joseph Bingham's eighteenth-century compilation of the writings of ancient church fathers in

1838 and again in 1840; the Tractarian "Library of the Fathers" project, begun in 1838; and the 1844 work of David Welsh, professor of church history in the newly formed Free Church of Scotland (61–63, 53). Wheeler concludes that between 1821 and 1855, "debate between Catholics and Protestants over the origin of Churches was at its height," with all parties intensely at work with the "historical source material" (52).

All this "feverish" activity of rereading the church fathers in the second quarter of the century may have been motivated by the debate over church origins, but at least one result of such rereading—the one most pertinent to the present study—was a reawakened sense of the power of the Christian grand style. In these early church writings could be found a rhetoric of passion with far more venerable roots and a more persuasive claim than any modern religion of the heart. Barrett's translation of Gregory of Nazianzus's "Oration on the Nativity" demonstrates the ardent and imaginative rhetoric characteristic of the church fathers:

> But now receive for me his birth,—& leap if not in the womb as John, yet as David at the resting of the ark. And reverence the enrolment by which thou wast enrolled in Heaven, & venerate [o/w onto honor][81] the birth by which thou are freed from the chains of thy [o/w onto thine] birth,—& honor the little Bethlam which hath restored thee to paradise [. . .]. Whether thou art of those who are pure & under the law, & of contemplative natures, & fitted for sacrifice—whether thou art yet of the pure, & of those unlawful to be eaten or [o/w onto &] of those unlawful to be sacrificed, & of the Gentiles— run with the star, & with the magi offer gifts, gold & frankincense & myrhh [sic], as unto to [sic] thy King, as unto thy God, as unto Him who was a corpse for thee,—with the shepherds owe glory, with the angels dance, with the archangels hymn His praise. (WEBB, 5:466–67)

The scriptural density of this passage (more than ten allusions) does not weigh down its rhetorical vigor and its appeal for joy. Not for nothing does Barrett write in her 1842 essay on the Greek Christian poets that the ancient theologians knew how to preach so as to "warm hearts"; asking (in *sermocinatio* fashion) whether the "Fathers" are obsolete in the present age, she responds, "Surely not. . . . [W]e may learn devotedness of them and warm our hearts by theirs; and this . . . in the capacity of theological oracles" (WEBB, 4:370). In other words, sermons or theological orations—what Barrett here calls oracles—can lead to Love.

Gregory (A.D. 326–89), renowned as the Theologian for his great intellect, was, in fact, highly praised in the nineteenth century for his rhetoric and passion. The 1881 *Sacred Rhetoric; or, The Art of Rhetoric as Applied to the Preaching of the Word of God*, names Gregory along with Augustine, Basil, and Chrysostom as "the most accomplished orators that human ears perhaps have ever listened to."[82] Henry Clay Fish, in his 1856 *History and Repository of Pulpit Eloquence (Deceased Divines)*, also names Gregory as one of the four most eloquent Greek preachers of the early church.[83] Although Barrett read the other three famous Greek preachers as well—Chrysostom, Basil, and Gregory of Nyssa—Gregory of Nazianzus perhaps received her greatest attention. As mentioned, she translated—at age eighteen—his "Oration on the Nativity of Christ" onto some twenty closely written pages of a notebook now held in the Huntington Library. She clearly spent significant time on this task, for her manuscript often offers two, or even three, translation possibilities for many phrases in the sermon. She also read and made notes in her copy of Gregory's *Theologia Opera*, memorized over a thousand lines of his poetry, and studied his letters in the early 1830s. In 1841, she read his "Hymns and Prayers" and observed that she preferred them to his "grand work De Virginitate" (*BC*, 5:138). In 1842, in her essay on the Greek Christian poets, she declared that Gregory was "noble and tender" and a greater orator than the "golden mouth" (that is, Chrysostom), though his eloquence consisted "less of music than of power." He was, the essay continues, "full and rapid in allusion, briefly graphic in metaphor, equally sufficient for indignation or pathos, and gifted peradventure with a keener dagger of sarcasm than should hang in a saint's girdle" (*WEBB*, 4:378, 379). Though his poetry often had "monotony of construction without unity of intention" (*WEBB*, 4:379), his sermons impressed her—lingering in her memory enough that in her 1860 *Poems before Congress*, she returned to his "Oration on the Nativity" for an epigraph for "Christmas Gifts." Over a span of at least thirty-six years, then—a span of time in which she was clearly not a religious anomaly but a participant in a wide religious and cultural activity of reading the church fathers—Barrett Browning found Gregory a preacher worth her consideration, worth her attention even for poetry, in part for his theology but even more for his noble, allusive, and emotive oratory. In fact, when the preachers whom she heard prior to her moves to Sidney and London (that is, prior to her attendance at Congregationalist chapels) seemed hesitant to incorporate a sympathetic element into their intellectually grounded sermons, Barrett unsparingly criticized them. On more than one occasion, she expresses in her diary "disappointment about [the preacher's] eloquence" despite "satisfaction about his scriptural knowledge" (*Diary*, 4). Indeed, her desire for a sermon that would make her really "*glow*" even prompted her on one occasion to talk "*boldly* about the Wesleyans" (*Diary*, 10; original italics)—boldly, perhaps, because the Barrett family was at that time attending services where Wesleyan emotional intensity was not much favored.

It appears, though, that Barrett found a living, satisfactory model for the effective combination of intellect and emotion in James Stratten of Paddington Chapel, where she worshipped (when not ill) from 1836 to 1846. Stratten's homiletic style during these years shows him at the forefront of those preachers shifting toward a more affective mode than past practice favored in denominations noted for their intellectual vigor. Barrett maintained a great regard all her life for Stratten, whom she viewed as a preacher of intellect and power and from whom she learned the effectiveness of emotive language used with restraint. When temporarily forced to Torquay for her health in 1838, Barrett wrote home to her sister Arabella to inquire after "Mr. Stratten," adding, "It is a pleasant placed hope to me that I shall get out beside you in the chapel at Paddington & hear with you what we used to hear so delightedly" (BC, 4:93). She confided to Robert Browning during their courtship that she had "the greatest respect" for Stratten because he had "a heart of miraculous breadth & depth,—loving further than he can see, pitying beyond what he can approve, having in him a divine Christian spirit, the 'love of love' in the most expansive form." She added, "How that man is beloved by his congregation, the members of his church, by his children, his friends, is wonderful to see—.... His children have been encouraged & instructed to speak aloud before him on religion & other subjects in all freedom of conscience—.... I believe for my part that there never was a holier man" (BC, 13:315–16). Barrett seems to have appreciated Stratten for his able scriptural exposition, which permitted others to interpret differently; for his largeness of heart and sincerity, which imbued his sermons with conviction; and for his personal life of humility. From Stratten's extant sermons, one can see how his listeners found his sermons compelling, for his rhetoric is passionate without being flamboyant, stylistically effective without appearing artificially contrived; it puts forth doctrine in personal terms and expounds Scripture as revelatory of grace and wonder; it calls for a response of faith as well as knowledge. In his sermon "The Titles and Offices of Christ," for example, Stratten scrutinizes Christ's diverse prophetic, priestly, and regal offices and concludes with this expression of his aim as preacher: "O, I have desired to occupy your minds, and to fill my own with ideas and conceptions of the greatness and grandeur, the unsullied holiness, the transcendent beauties of our Lord Jesus Christ. . . . [L]et him be pre-eminent in your hearts and minds, enthroned upon your affections; he is worthy of all your love."[84] The opening exclamation, the first-person voice, the amassing of phrases (so redolent of Gregory's sermon), and the address to heart and mind all contribute to the emotive effect of the sermon's conclusion, an effect impressed on Barrett every time she sat in Paddington Chapel.

For Barrett, who wrote of the "unspeakable poetry there is in Christ's religion" (*BC*, 3:179), such integration of Truth and Love in religious speech became formative for her midcareer religious poems "The Seraphim," "The Virgin Mary to the Child Jesus," and "A Drama of Exile." True, these poems are sometimes criticized as being somewhat highly colored and excessively emotive. As Rebecca Stott notes, Barrett sometimes struggled with finding the right degree of emotional or persuasive language;[85] perhaps she initially overresponded to unimpassioned sermonic language. If so, however, her later, more moderate language may likewise have acquired its overtones from her exemplars in the pulpit. By the 1850s, much Victorian homiletic theory was rejecting an "ornamented oral rhetoric [in favor of] a plainer, more natural, more literary approach to sacred speaking," "a simple, conversational rhetorical style";[86] Stratten seems likewise to have manifested quiet composure under emotional stress. On a visit to London in 1855, Barrett heard him preach with dignity, tenderness, and conviction shortly after the death of his four-year-old daughter. She reflected afterwards, "For a man to speak so, in his position, . . . with his heart breaking in his bosom, as he must have felt it . . . was to me the very triumph of Christian experience, & made me cry as no eloquence of lamentation could have done" (*LA*, 2:172). In Florence, she witnessed the same composure in the Scotch minister Robert Hanna, who preached with a "bright & serene" face the day after his mother's death. She concluded, "Such things preach better than a hundred sermons and a hundred thousand added to those—They are always very impressive to me" (*LA*, 2:308). From these preachers as well as homiletics, Barrett Browning learned the powerful effect of restrained emotion.

Though Barrett Browning formulated her poet-as-preacher paradigm before her marriage, her conviction as to its relevancy for poetry did not change in her European years, though she seems not to have repeated the metaphor. The implicit dialogic form of the sermon, the grassroots figure of the preacher, and affective homiletics remained for her powerful models for a religious poetics aimed at Truth and Love, though these models often failed to meet her expectations. A few months after her marriage, when she and Robert were in Pisa, she wrote extensively to Arabella about their experience in the cathedral service. After describing the apparent irreverence of the people, she wrote, "We have tried again & again to hear a sermon preached—but it seems the most difficult thing possible, to hear a sermon. The giving of religious instruction in that form, seems shrunk from," and the result was an Italy "melancholy beyond all my expectations. [It has] the sun, & no light" (*LA*, 1:40). A few months later, she wrote that during the period of Lent, the Pisa cathedral sermons still did not fully satisfy her but they at least outdid the "imbecillity [*sic*] & inconsequence" of the Rev. Henry Greene at the "English church" (*LA*, 1:52, 53). The greatest impression the cathedral sermons made on her resulted not from their contents, which showed not "the least trace of original thinking," but from their delivery—"the voice, the articulation, the vibrative earnestness of the tones of the preacher"—and from the response in the listeners, "thronging, standing, leaning against the columns with uplifted dark Italian faces." She concluded, "Just see how this people give their attention & reverence when they *understand*—It makes all the difference, the understanding. The chanted, muttered Latin mass leaves them as I told you, a congregation of promenaders—but the words of their own language, appealing to their sympathies & experience, draw them, fasten them, impress them. . . . [T]he silence in the great crowd seemed to take away your breath" (*LA*, 1:53).

For Barrett Browning, the way to Truth and Love was through language that combines intellect ("the understanding") with feeling ("appealing to their sympathies"). Such words impress the body, take away the breath, compel attention and reverence—make all the difference. To such words she aspired in her poetry also. To that poetry I now turn, with the aim of tracing in it the constellations of independence, dialogue, intellect, and feeling mapped here as the shape of Barrett Browning's religious imaginary.

CHAPTER TWO

"TRUTH IN RELATION, PERCEIVED IN EMOTION"

Elizabeth Barrett Browning's Religious Poetics

In 1845, Barrett gave her definition of poetry to another prominent woman poet of the day, Sara Coleridge, as follows: "Would you agree to such a definition of poetry as this? *Truth in relation, perceived in emotion?* I think that if I had to try at a definition, or at my idea of a definition, I might put it so. I have often thought it" (BC, 10:168; original italics). Truth in relation, perceived in emotion: the phrases evoke Barrett's earlier words that Truth apprehending and Love comprehending constituted her hope of a church; and the evocation underscores the deep bearing Barrett Browning's religious imaginary had on her poetry. Turning now to read the poetry in detail, this chapter examines the variety of ways in which Barrett Browning's religious imaginary compels her creative and critical poetry. It argues that Barrett Browning's valuations of a democratically constituted community of interpreters together conversing their way to knowledge, of the erudite yet passionate speaker, and of language as above all able to convey religious truth and love all inform the poet's theory and practice in complex ways. The chapter proceeds chronologically through selected poetry, with the named valuations structuring the analysis. I sketch these further below, linking them to the poet's choices about genre, poetic speakers, and poetic language.

The question of a poetic voice at once instructive and democratic, knowledgeable and emotive, involves Barrett Browning in experiments with a range of generic forms. From (adaptations of) the hymn to dramatic lyric and epic, Barrett Browning used poetic form to explore the issues central to her imaginary. I suggest that in the hymn she found a genre that has the potential to embody what Martha Nussbaum, in *Upheavals of Thought*, calls a cognitive-evaluative view of emotions, however often that potential may fail in other hands.[1] Her seven named hymns explore the relationship between intellection and passion. However, possibly because the hymn ultimately failed to permit the kind of dialogic work that she associated with vibrant, religious investigation, Barrett Browning eventually abandoned that form, turning instead to dramatic and epic genres. In them she found what E. Warwick Slinn calls discursive practices that reject subjective isolationism. These genres allowed her to place the individual in dialogue with a community. The two dramatic poems feature two or more speakers, neither serving as instructor to the other (or to the reader) but jointly interpreting an important event; *Aurora Leigh*'s hybrid nature likewise reinforces a democratic poetics, for the first-person limited subjectivity of the poem denies the omniscient voice that might otherwise be permitted by its epic qualities. Genre, then, served as one means by which Barrett Browning weighed out critical and emotive stances, and it ensured a communal grounding for the poet's voice. Further, genre enabled her increasingly to challenge gender norms. While the hymns initially minimize these concerns by relying on ungendered, plural pronouns, the move toward more expansive, discursive, and epic forms—first in "The Seraphim," "The Virgin Mary to the Child Jesus," and "A Drama of Exile," and later in *Aurora Leigh*—contests the usual Victorian designation of such forms as belonging to the "masculine" and prophetic sphere. Refusing to accept such restrictions on the woman poet's use of form, Barrett Browning crafted genres that insist on exchange and mutual recognition.

Barrett Browning's concerns with authority and independence, particularly as these relate to gender, also emerge in how speakers are cast in the poems. The communal, lyric voice of the hymns prevents the explicit figuring of a woman speaker within them, but the midcareer dramatic poems and *Aurora Leigh* feature women in key roles. At first tentatively, and then more confidently, Barrett Browning cast women as poet-preachers—that is, as informed speakers with sophisticated interpretive and linguistic skills. Elevating women speakers to instructive roles without invoking the poet-prophet paradigm did, however, present Barrett Browning with the challenge of mediating between independence and authority—a fraught issue especially for women speakers. "The Seraphim" least resolves this issue, while "The Virgin Mary to the Child Jesus," "A Drama of Exile," and *Aurora Leigh* increasingly depict women who interpret within dialogic communities.

The challenge of the poet-preacher configuration for women also resides in the issue of verbal style, and the challenge of finding effective language or style permeates the poetry from early to late. Appreciative of the homiletics that recovered the passionate oratory of the church fathers and willing to challenge the period's gendering of feeling as feminine (weak), Barrett Browning experimented with different rhetorical modes as she sought to align emotive with intellectual knowledge. In her early hymns she works toward the integration of devotion and exegesis, turning to more positive ends the usual stereotype of tears as weakness. In her midcareer poems, she introduces women whose perception of truth involves both intellectual and emotive knowledge: Truth and Love conjoined. In *Aurora Leigh*, however, she most succeeds in creating a sophisticated woman poet-preacher who is able to use language effectively, value the cognitive in the emotive and the emotive in the cognitive, and help others (men) value this interpenetration also. Experiments with language, therefore, figure centrally in Barrett Browning's effort to integrate scholarly and emotive work. In short, Barrett Browning turned the tensions between disparate impulses—whether between the authoritative and the independent word, or between emotion and intellect—to productive ends as she sought to live up to her own composite definition of poetry as truth in relation, perceived in emotion.

Early Experiments with Religious Poetry

To understand why Barrett began with the hymn as a model for religious poetry when her other early poetry follows more classical modes, we need to look at the first religious poems that she published, "The Dream" (1826) and "Who art thou of the veilèd countenance" (1827). In subtitling "The Dream" as "A Fragment," Barrett signals her recognition of the gaps and failures in this unfinished poem. In the first three stanzas, the speaker relates how, in a dream, her spirit is freed from Time and travels back to the age of Paradise. The poem then interposes a line of ellipses and resumes with an imaginative picture of the Flood destroying the earth. The fall into sin lies unmentioned, avoided, in the ellipsis. The closing stanzas then describe the pervasiveness of Sin in the human heart in the ages that follow the Flood. The poem ends with four lines that relate how Christ's death brings renewed life. This final moment arrives abruptly and ends quickly, leaving the reader surprised and dissatisfied. While Barrett obviously felt the fragment merited publication, the poem serves more as an indication of what she had not yet learned to do than what she could successfully do, in terms of handling religious or scriptural material. Moreover, the Spenserian stanza form evokes association with poems of allegory or myth (such as *The Faerie Queene*, "The Eve of St. Agnes," and part 1 of "The Lotus Eaters") and jars somewhat with Barrett's acceptance of the biblical narrative as an actual historical account. The gaps in narrative and the limits of the chosen form suggest that in 1826 Barrett had not found a way to write effectively about the central stories of Christianity. She abandoned this subject matter and mode for some other starting place for her religious-poetic work. Though she later returned to such ambitious religious projects as discussing the fall into sin or the redemption of humanity via a divine act, she temporarily withdrew from the ambitious scope and unsatisfactory form of her first biblical poem.

Barrett's second major religious poem, published in 1827 in *The Jewish Expositor, and Friend of Israel*, deals with its chosen subject without gaps but may have dissatisfied the poet on different grounds. The untitled poem, written in blank verse rather than Spenserian measure and beginning with the line "Who art thou of the veilëd countenance" (*WEBB*, 4:168–70) picks up the themes and language of Lamentations, as well as Revelation, Exodus, and the Psalms, to create a dialogue between the fallen city of Jerusalem, represented as a woman, and a male passerby. Although the woman refuses to answer the man's initial question, "Who art thou," until the man describes to her the most wonderful and the most desolate sights he has seen (Jerusalem in its glory and its desolation), ultimately the woman's despair turns to hope only when he shares his greater knowledge: the dialogue concludes with the (Jewish) city/woman appealing to the Christian man to give her the Book that tells about the Crucified One who redeems Israel. After its initial appearance in *The Jewish Expositor*, Barrett neither republished the poem, as she did with many other works first appearing in periodicals, nor produced another so reminiscent of biblical prophecy. Perhaps she recognized its tensions, for even though the poem frames prophecy as dialogue—suggesting just how early in her career Barrett associated religious understanding with exchange, and Scriptural exposition as necessary to full knowledge—it also ascribes largely ineffectual emotion to a woman and understanding to a man. Although Barrett may have felt compelled to gender Jerusalem as female because Scripture does so, no clear reason exists why she did not also cast the passerby with the Book as a woman. The Book-holder need not be a man for the poem to do its work. In fact, publishing the poem in a journal aimed at converting Jews to Christianity positions Barrett herself as a woman with the Book, a woman able to share knowledge of Christ; but the poem does not depict women this way. Perhaps because she did not yet see a way to resolve the various tensions engendered in her first two religious poems, Barrett abandoned both the dialogic mode and the large narrative scale of these early poems and turned instead to the liturgical model of the hymn for her religious work of the 1830s. In doing so, she did not capitulate to the prescribed limits of women's devotional writing but explored how emotion and cognition might function in more integrative ways.

Early Religious Poetry: The Hymns

As the 1826 "An Essay on Mind" testifies, Barrett did not lack intellectual ability in her early career. From childhood on, she was intellectually gifted and avid to learn, which she was able to do through extensive reading, sharing her brother's tutor, and maintaining correspondence and friendship with the scholars Sir Uvedale Price and Hugh Boyd. Given her rather astounding erudition in "An Essay on Mind," not to mention the (attempted) complexity of "The Dream" and "Who art thou of the veilèd countenance," the poems titled or subtitled as hymns seem disappointingly superficial. Perhaps as a result, when twentieth-century criticism paid any attention at all to these hymns, it did so disparagingly. Glennis Stephenson criticized their "somewhat adolescent morbidity" and Dorothy Mermin their sinking "into renunciation and gloom" and their lack of "struggle."[2] If, however, we measure the hymns against eighteenth- or nineteenth-century standards for the genre, we see success, not failure. For example, the (easy) resignation to death in Barrett's hymn "Remonstrance" successfully emulates that of her successful (male) Congregationalist predecessor, Isaac Watts, as the following excerpts from each demonstrate:

> Fix not thy sight, so long and fast,
>   Upon the shroud's despair;
> Look upward unto Zion's hill,
>   For death was also *there!*

(WEBB, 4:260.33–36)

> Why do we mourn departing Friends?
> Or shake at Death's Alarms?
> 'Tis but the Voice that *Jesus* sends
> To call them to his Arms.
>
> (Watts, *Hymns and Spiritual Songs*, Hymn 2.3)

Again, the uncomplicated theology, expression of utter dependence, and desire for divine proximity in Barrett's "Hymn"

> Since without Thee we do no good,
>   And with Thee do no ill,
> Abide with us in weal and woe,—
>   In action and in will.
> . . . .
> Abide with *us*, abide with *us*,
>   While flesh and soul agree;
> And when our flesh is only dust,
>   Abide our souls with *Thee*.
>
> (WEBB, 4:270.1–4, 25–28)

resonate well with Watts's stanza

> I cannot bear thine Absence, Lord,
> My Life expires if thou depart:
> Be Thou, my Heart, still near my God
> And thou, my God, be near my Heart.
>
> (Hymn 2.117)[3]

We could extend these comparisons beyond Watts to show Barrett successfully participating in this vein of hymn writing, but rather than "defend" Barrett's hymns along these lines, I propose to examine them as conducive to Barrett's exploration of religious devotion and intellection because they make room for what Nussbaum calls a cognitive-evaluative view of emotions. Primarily a public intellectual, Nussbaum does not call on neuroscientific data to recover emotion's value, but her account of the emotions is as persuasive as the neuroscientific arguments outlined in the introductory chapter.

Nussbaum argues that emotions are not what many have long taken them to be, "'unreasoning movements,' unthinking energies that simply push the person around" (24). On the contrary, she builds a case for emotions as their own kind of cognition. Emotions, she writes, "always involve the thought of an object combined with thought of the object's salience or importance; in that sense they always involve appraisal or evaluation" (23). Emotions are always about something, and their "aboutness" embodies a way of seeing, and includes a set of beliefs about, that something, a perception of its value for (or against) the person's own flourishing (27–31). For Nussbaum, emotions are judgments of value. This view of emotions has tremendous value for thinking about the hymn. As a genre that presupposes the worthiness of God, that embodies a way of seeing God and includes a set of beliefs about Him, that perceives God's value for the hymn singer/writer's own flourishing, the hymn has the potential to be an emotive genre on Nussbaum's terms: which is to say, a cognitive-evaluative genre. Though in certain hands it may collapse into mere sentimentality, in other hands it may render, even embody, judgments of value.

Barrett, I suggest, came to recognize the inherent potential of the hymn to make such judgments of value. Over the course of a decade, she strove to create an exegetical-evaluative balance in her hymns that many contemporary religious hymns, succumbing to gender theory, had thrown off. Her early hymns lean more heavily toward the emotive than the cognitive, but they do not thereby relinquish judgment. Conversely, her later hymns become more intellectually laden, but they do not give up their emotive quality. Rather, all the hymns strive to manifest in the treatment of their subjects what the form itself encourages (though it may be burdened also with other concerns), namely, what Nussbaum calls the intelligence of emotions. Helpfully, because the hymn was an approved form for women's religious writing, it actually allowed Barrett to concentrate on this matter of cognition and emotion without the distraction of gendered criticism. In fact, by relying on ungendered first-person, often plural, voices, Barrett's hymns ultimately figure emotion as intimately associated with religious knowledge for all believers. Further, the hymns also manifest the poet's early preoccupation with independence, though subtly. The early children's hymns depart in important ways from male and female precursors, and the final hymn nearly breaks the limits of what a hymn can sustain, in erudition and form. Yet after 1838 Barrett wrote no more hymns (later we will see why).

The earliest of Barrett's extant hymns are two unpublished children's hymns, written sometime before 1828, possibly though not necessarily before "The Dream: A Fragment" and "Who art thou of the veilèd countenance," and, according to their manuscript title, "sung on the occasion of the annual sermon for the benefit of the Sabbath School."[4] Although somewhat deprecated by the poet as her "experimental simplicity" (BC, 2:165), these earliest hymns already mark Barrett's recognition of the genre's formative power, both intellectually and emotively, also for children. One of Barrett's important precursors in children's hymn writing, the influential Anna Laetitia Barbauld, had composed her hymns for children in prose and defended this choice in her preface: "It may well be doubted, whether poetry *ought* to be lowered to the capacities of children, or whether they should not rather be kept from reading verse, till they are able to relish good verse."[5] Barrett, who at age thirty-nine could still quote the opening page of Barbauld's reading primer, *Lessons for Children* (1778–79), may have been familiar with Barbauld's *Hymns in Prose for Children* (1781), which was designed to follow *Lessons* and went through seventeen editions before 1824.[6] She clearly did not agree with the sentiments Barbauld expressed: that hymns cannot be good verse and should probably not be composed for children. By contrast, Barrett seems to have understood hymns as an embodied approach to children's faith. She objected to her Congregationalist predecessor Isaac Watts's children's hymns, which she took as attempts to theologize children, and that, poorly. Although she sang these hymns herself as a child, years later she criticized the "flames & eternal damnations" in them as scare tactics, an altogether "erroneous mode of appeal" in teaching children to turn to God (LA, 2:104). Watts's verses, Barrett seems to have felt, forget that the hymn as a genre is premised on the recognition of God's worth, not a person's sinfulness. While no doubt hymns may contain a didactic element, they functioned for Barrett first as expressions of value about God and his importance for the singer's own flourishing. They should be cast as prayer postures, in both truth and love. In composing her own children's hymns, Barrett aimed to create such postures of praise and supplication, while also recognizing the intelligence of emotion. Take, for example, this stanza from Hymn 2:

> Children we—oh! thine esteem us;
> Poor—thy bounty may we share.
> Sinful—pity and redeem us—
> Helpless—take us to thy care.
>   Israel's Shepherd
> In his arms the lambs will bear.
>
>   (WEBB, 5:444.7–12)

Though Barrett's broken phrases somewhat confuse sense, the stanza moves from the children's plea to be esteemed especially as *God's* children to the quiet confession that they will indeed be so esteemed simply because God is a Shepherd who carries lambs. The hymn does not deny that children are sinful, but neither does it warn children to obey God for fear of flames and damnation. Instead, it states a truth to evoke a trust.

The same effort to balance knowledge with feeling characterizes Hymn 1, where the singers first recall the words of Jesus to his disciples to let the children come unto him, and then translate such coming into the Lord's presence from an earthly moment to a heavenly one:

> A babe once lay in sweetest rest
> Within thine arms, on mercy's breast—
> Dear Saviour, thus to condescend,
> The Lord of heaven—the infant's friend.
>
> And now, tho' on a throne above
> Thou reignest—'tis a throne of love.
> For infant hosts around it stand,
> Redeemëd by thy victor hand.
>
> In heavenly beauty there they shine,
> And sing in harmony divine
> Hosannas to the Eternal word,
> To David's son & David's Lord.
>
> (*WEBB*, 5:443.9–20)

While these lines may strike the modern ear as exasperatingly sentimental, even heavy-handed, in fact, they are busy with biblical interpretation. The last stanza alone draws on at least three scripture passages to create a heavenly parallel to the scene evoked in the first stanza: John 1:1, which (historically understood) names Christ as the Word from the beginning; Luke 20:41–43, which defends the paradox of Christ's being both David's son and David's Lord; and Matthew 21:15, which recounts children's singing "Hosanna to the Son of David" to Jesus in the temple. Yet all this exegetical work does not overwhelm the essentially thankful posture of the hymn, which acknowledges that Christ deserves the child-singer's gratitude because, while earlier he could hold children in his arms, now, as a king, he can also redeem them by his "victor hand." The simple, familiar rhythmic pattern of this hymn further imprints on the singer this posture of childlike trust based on real knowledge. To sum up, if Barrett's two children's hymns demonstrate simplicity, they are also—to use Barrett's own adjective—experimental, in both our and her sense of the word. They are her cognitive-evaluative poetic *experiments*, and they recognize that children's religious *experience* should have intellectual and emotive dimensions. Many of those who first heard the hymns sung by children in a service where Watts's hymns usually predominated may have appreciated their judgments of value and their tenor of praise or prayer rather than didacticism or even threat.

Whether Barrett wrote these two hymns before or after "The Dream" and "Who art thou," she obviously thought they did not merit publication, despite their experimental nature. Confronted by the difficulties of the longer poems, she either turned or returned to hymn writing. Her five hymns of the 1830s show the same effort as did the children's hymns to make the genre bear out its emotive potential (that is, its potential for cognitive-evaluative work). Four of these hymns appear to have been written around the same time, despite the fact that only one of these—the simply titled "Hymn"—was published in 1833. The remaining hymns later formed a set in *The Seraphim, and Other Poems* (1838), but manuscript evidence suggests that Barrett had already written the first three by 1833. Hymn III of the 1838 set is transcribed in Barrett's hand on the flyleaf of a book given to a friend in 1833, and elsewhere Hymns I, II, and III are copied on a single leaf.[7] Perhaps *Poems* had already gone to press when Barrett wrote her three other poems of that year, so she joined them with a later one to form the set of four in 1838. The intellectual and structural sophistication of Hymn IV over the other hymns of the set supports this conjecture as to the gap in composition. At the same time, the grouping together of the four hymns in the 1838 volume effectively highlights their repeated valuation of emotion—often figured through tears—as a form of knowledge.

As expressive of suffering or sorrow, tears were considered appropriate in women's poetry of the nineteenth century; but whereas many of these tearful poems fail as the "hermeneutical acts" J. R. Watson thinks hymns can be, Barrett's do not.[8] In Barrett's hymns for adults, tears are a judgment of value in material form. The image features innovatively in her hymns, rather than as the stereotypical emblem of complaint, resignation, weakness, or grief so dominant in the women's hymns that round off the *Congregational Hymn Book*. In Barrett's "Hymn," the speaker pleads with God to abide with us even

> In woe,—that, while to drowning tears
>   Our hearts their joys resign,
> We may remember *who* can turn
>   Such water into wine.
>
> (WEBB, 4:270.9–12)

It is not merely that Christ can turn water into wine, as at the wedding feast in Cana (John 2:1–11), but that he can turn wine into spiritual celebration. Human tears, therefore, have potential to display Christ's power and grace. As one reviewer of the poem put it, "This is an exquisite use of the miracle!" (BC, 4:397). In "A Supplication for Love: Hymn I" and "The Weeping Saviour: Hymn III," Barrett again reworks the conventional usage of tears in poetry by or about women by representing tears as a sign of understanding rather than weakness or resignation. "A Supplication for Love" reflects on a preacher's assertion that the ascended Jesus, who once wept on earth over the city of Jerusalem (Luke 19:41–42), still gazes on his Church from heaven. The speaker of the poem implores the "loving Lord" to weep again on the fallen Church, that we also may "view each other's face, and weep" in a collective acknowledgment of the Church's failure to love sufficiently (WEBB, 4:310.5, 32). Jesus's tears figure again in "The Weeping Saviour"; the speaker, recalling that Jesus wept at Lazarus's grave (John 11:35), begs that the Saviour's tears be turned not upon dead bodies but upon sinning souls, that "as Thou weepedst, *we* may weep" and so break through hardheartedness to repentance (WEBB, 4:315.16; original italics). In both these hymns, Jesus's weeping acts cathartically to release the human weeping that signifies comprehension of sin, of offense against one who deserves infinitely better from his people; such weeping necessarily precedes forgiveness. That is to say, only weeping restores the believer's relationship with the Saviour, because it signifies cognitive-evaluative knowledge rather than mere cognition or false sentiment. Thus, as Barrett writes near the end of "The Weeping Saviour," "we may weep to *know*," not we may weep to *feel* (WEBB, 4:315.17; my italics).

In the final 1838 hymn, the image again features crucially in the poem, but this time it makes a greater intellectual demand on the reader, to the extent that the poem's devotional impulse struggles to be felt. The poem is a kind of threshold moment for Barrett: either she can continue to write hymns whose judgments of value emerge (perhaps only faintly) through their devotional texture or she can cross into genres whose cognitive-evaluative work occurs (perhaps more noticeably) through exegetical or expository means.

"The Measure" begins her tip toward the latter. Despite its identification as a hymn, it pursues a scriptural exegesis not found in Barrett's earlier devotional work. Barrett had signaled her participation in intellectual communities in Hymns I through III by taking epigraphs from the scholar Hugh Boyd and the poet John Donne, but she had not displayed the full scope of her mental powers in them. For example, with her knowledge of the original languages of Scripture, she might have, but did not, differentiate in Hymn III between the Greek words used to describe Jesus's weeping and the others' weeping at Lazarus's grave.[9] However, in "The Measure: Hymn IV," Barrett endeavored to make the hymn do more explicit intellectual work. She cited two biblical epigraphs and gave parenthetically the Hebrew word for "measure" that appears in each text. She then footnoted the hymn with the (incorrect) observation that this word "occurs in no other part of the Hebrew Scriptures" (*WEBB*, 2:320). As Cynthia Scheinberg notes, knowledge of Hebrew was "often considered the highest proof of serious exegetical ability," so Barrett's conscious display of Hebrew knowledge was a way of garnering "a particular kind of intellectual and theological authority" in Victorian England.[10] Having set this scholarly tone, Barrett brought two apparently disparate Old Testament texts into a speaking relationship with each other through a New Testament Christology and knowledge of their shared Hebrew word. She did so by uniting the dust of one text with the tears of the other. I quote the poem in full, beginning with the epigraphs:

"He comprehended the dust of the earth in a measure" (שליש).—*Isaiah xl.*
"Thou givest them tears to drink in a measure" (שליש).—*Psalm lxxx.*

I.

God the Creator, with a pulseless hand
Of unoriginated power, hath weighed
The dust of earth and tears of man in one
    Measure, and by one weight:
    So saith His holy book.

II.

Shall we, then, who have issued from the dust
And there return,—shall we, who toil for dust,

And wrap our winnings in this dusty life,
> Say "No more tears, Lord God!
> The measure runneth o'er"?

III.

Oh, Holder of the balance, laughest Thou?
Nay, Lord! be gentler to our foolishness,
For His sake who assumed our dust and turns
> On Thee pathetic eyes
> Still moistened with our tears.

IV.

And teach us, O our Father, while we weep,
To look in patience upon earth and learn—
Waiting, in that meek gesture, till at last
> These tearful eyes be filled
> With the dry dust of death.

(WEBB, 2:320)

The opening stanzas of the hymn unite the two texts by calling on the single appearance of the Hebrew word for measure as evidence that God gauges earthly dust and human tears equally; they then refigure the dust of the earth into our dusty existence (created from dust, toiling for dust, surrounded by dust) so that what God co-measures is not nonhuman and human, but two elements of the human. The speaker then pleads with God to be gentle in the face of a human foolishness that, without knowing the extent of the dustiness that needs to be counterbalanced in the measure, believes sufficient tears have been shed. The speaker grounds her plea on Christ's assumption of our dust (his taking on of human form) as well as our tears (sins and sorrows). The final stanza again associates weeping with learning; it depicts weeping as appropriate meekness, not undesirable weakness. The closing image, though somber in its evocations, suggests that tears and dust achieve equilibrium only at the moment of death—which is, in Christian theology, the moment of new life as well. This final hymn, retaining its devotional character most strongly in its fourth stanza, nevertheless shows how much Barrett has shifted within the space of the hymn from the strongly emotive voice of such early lines as

> Oh! then sleep comes on us like death,
> All soundless, deaf and deep.
> Lord! teach us so to watch and pray,
> That death may come like sleep.
>
> ("Hymn," *WEBB*, 4:271.21–24)

to more challenging cadences and concepts. In "The Measure," devotion and intellect both inform the poem and form the poem's subject matter. Further, in affixing scriptural texts as epigraphs and exegeting these texts by reference to their original linguistic contexts, Barrett exhibits an interpretive impulse that reminds us of the inability of the *Congregational Hymn Book* to let hymns stand alone as devotional, or even hermeneutical, acts. The urge toward scriptural exposition is very strong—it may not be insignificant that the *Hymn Book* preceded this last hymn of Barrett's by only two years. At the same time, this last hymn wavers from the sustained, prayerlike posture of the earlier hymns: its first stanza declares, its second interrogates fellow worshippers, and only its third and fourth address God. Perhaps the judgment of value that emotions supply was beginning to slip as Barrett became restless with the hymnic form.

For Hymn IV indicates in its very structure that Barrett was literally moving beyond the traditional hymnic form. The most common stanzaic and metric form for a hymn is the quatrain, either in tetrameter or with alternating tetrameter and trimeter lines, in an *abab* or *abcb* rhyme scheme. Barrett's second children's hymn, in having six-line stanzas with the fifth line in dimeter, does not follow this pattern (though it could be read as having *abab* quatrains with appended dimeter-tetrameter closing lines). But all the rest of Barrett's hymns except the last fit the common pattern. As if wondering whether intellectual expansion might be accompanied by a break from the typical structures of the hymn, however, each stanza of "The Measure" has three lines in pentameter and two more in trimeter, none of which rhyme. The *Congregational Hymn Book*, at least, contains no model for this structure. Thus, although Barrett had found the hymn helpful in her initial efforts to fuse intellectual and emotive religious commitments, she apparently came to feel constrained by its limits, both actual (prescribed form, communal voice and property) and implied (women's verse). Perhaps for these reasons, she did not write any new hymns after 1838. In her 1850 and 1856 poetry publications, both of which reprinted almost all the 1838 poems, the only hymn reprinted is the final one, "The Measure." Of the hymns not included, Barrett wrote to Arabella that they were "weak & inferior" (*LA*, 1:330). Thus, the poem least like a hymn most satisfied her when considered from the perspective of her later poetics. If Barrett indeed wrote this hymn some years after the others, it marks well her step from one genre for religious poetry to another. Her midcareer religious poems turn away from representing the poet as hymnist toward exploring the concept of the poet as preacher. This turn may have been already embedded in Barrett's decision to publish her hymns as literary poems instead of congregational songs. By giving up the formative bodily impact of the sung hymn, the five poems implicitly long for the power of expository speech rather than the power of lyric song. They do, however, explore the relative (and related) roles of emotion and intellect, love and truth, in poetry and faith.

Midcareer Poems: The Dramatic Lyrics and Lyrical Dramas

The religious poems of Barrett's midcareer emulate the rhetorical flexibility and structural capaciousness of the sermon rather than the concise form of the hymn, but certainly not through mere sermon versification, to which Barrett strongly objected (*BC*, 5:228, 271). Instead, they participate in a sermonic mode by becoming more explicitly social in dimension and by investigating and expounding from new perspectives the essential stories of the Christian faith rather than single devotional texts or moments. Instead of relying on the unified voice of the hymn, they are structured by *sermocinatio*: imaginary dialogue, commonly employed by the church fathers Barrett read, by contemporary preachers, and by the apostle Paul in, for example, the letter to the Romans, a book Barrett studied at great length with Hugh Boyd.[11] Longer by far than the earlier hymns, "The Seraphim" (1838) considers Christ's crucifixion through the imagined dialogue of two angels (1,051 lines); "The Virgin Mary to the Child Jesus" (1838) consists of Mary's address to the sleeping Jesus shortly after his birth (180 lines); and "A Drama of Exile" (1844) imagines the conversations of Gabriel, Lucifer, Adam, Eve, and Christ on the first evening after the expulsion from Eden (2,270 lines). These hybrid dramatic-lyric-narrative poems successfully replace Barrett's inadequate rendering of biblical narratives in "The Dream" with a religious poetry of new expository power and effect.[12] In shying away from visionary modes, they also participate in a larger reaction to what Victorians perceived as a limited Romantic subjectivity. As E. Warwick Slinn notes, "The move in Victorian poetry away from personalized and homogeneous lyrics toward dramatic-lyrical and epic-narrative-lyrical hybrids suggests a growing dissatisfaction with the essentialist assumptions of organic poetics. Such hybrids shift individual expressiveness away from isolated subjectivism toward social contexts and culturally produced discursive practices."[13] Philip Davis adds that dramatic monologues likewise create "a context for the 'I' that [is] implicitly social rather than solitary," and Slinn pointedly includes the monodrama among those forms that reinforce "a move toward social connections and ideological contextualizations."[14] Barrett's generic choices for these mid-career biblical poems, then, respond to a larger Victorian poetic context, but they also reflect a deep sense that "mutual talk" (*sermo*) can promote both devotion and learning in a democratically minded religious community.

This mutual talk signifies a resistance to authoritative pronouncement by any one figure, while the conversations themselves reveal Barrett's ongoing attention to emotion as a vital form of religious knowledge. Although the choice of angels as key figures in "The Seraphim" (*WEBB*, 1:81–115) may appear to grant poetic speakers heavenly authority, Barrett does not actually invest these celestial figures with particular insight or visionary power. The seraphim are rather hesitant and confused, hardly daring to follow the other angels to earth at God's command. For all their celestial nature, Zerah and Ador learn the meaning of Christ's sacrifice rather slowly. When they initially view the crucifixion, they are appalled, yet Zerah must still ask Ador, "Where shall I seek him [Christ]?" When Ador points to the three crosses, Zerah responds, "Nay—let me rather / Turn unto the wilderness!" Ador, no less shocked, bursts out with "And men weep only tears?" (425, 465–66, 499). Only through impassioned dialogue—underscored visually by multiple, broken lines on the page—do they eventually come to understand Christ's agony as an expression of divine Love:

> ADOR.   And ONE!—
> ZERAH.   And ONE!—
> ADOR.   Why dost thou pause?
> ZERAH.   God! God!
> Spirit of my spirit! who movest
> Through seraph veins in burning deity
> To light the quenchless pulses!—
> ADOR.   But has trod
> The depths of love in Thy peculiar nature,
> And not in any Thou hast made and lovest
> In narrow seraph hearts!—

> ZERAH.   Above, Creator!
> Within, Upholder!
> ADOR.   And below, below,
> The creature's and the upholden's sacrifice!
>
> (539–47)

Although Zerah and Ador do at last offer an interpretation of the event, they do so not because they possess celestial wisdom but because Barrett as poet has taken a "less usual" (*WEBB*, 4:290) imaginative stance and cast them together in the experience of bewilderment, from which position they seek mutual understanding. Barrett may even have drawn imaginatively on a sermon published in 1837 by Stratten, in which he "incline[s] to think that there is a distinction" between seraphim and angels, the first "more characterized by prayer" and the second by "vast intelligence" and "clear vision."[15] If so, it is striking that Barrett chose not angels—not creatures of vast intelligence and clear vision—but seraphim for her poem and that she characterized them at least initially as uncertain, however adoring.

The seraphim are not the only ones in the poem deeply moved by the crucifixion. Barrett also depicts a weeping woman at the foot of the cross in order to consider again the relationship between emotion and knowledge. Zerah draws Ador's attention to the woman "with her lips asunder, / And a motion upon each. / Too fast to show or suffer speech—" (478–80; 1838 text [revised in the 1856 edition to a weeping woman who "feels, / With a spasm, not a speech"]). Ador initially scorns such weeping, even as Barrett, in a later version of the poem, clarifies that emotive knowledge applies to men as well as women:

> Weep blood—weep blood—   Weep? Weep blood,
> All women! yea!   All women, all men!
> These water-tears are vain   He sweated it, He,
> They mock like laughter!   For your pale womanhood
>   And base manhood. Agree
>   (1838 text; *WEBB*, 1:98,   That these water-tears, then,
>   notes to lines 485–88)   Are vain, mocking like laughter!
>   Weep blood!
>
>   (485–92, 1856 text)

In both renditions, Ador understands that tears arise from powerful emotions, not necessarily weakness; he would have those emotions wrenched out in blood, as was the case for Christ in the Garden of Gethsemane. But Ador does not adequately distinguish between human sorrow and divine suffering. Zerah does. He replies, "Mine Ador! it is all that they can! Their being / And being's strength make issue but in those" (1838 text; *WEBB*, 1:98, notes to lines 499–500). He goes on to suggest that tears are gifts of love that seraph eyes should gaze upon with wonder (in a series of lines rendered more simply in 1856 as "Tears! the lovingest man / Has no better bestowed / Upon man" [503–5]). Zerah understands that to bestow (genuine) tears on a fellow being is to acknowledge a depth of relationship that the tearless cannot know. He thus addresses the woman, "Thou woman! weep thy woe! / I sinless, tearless—loving am, and weak!" (513–14 [clarified in 1856 to "Thou woman that weepest! weep unscorned of us! / I, the tearless and pure, am but loving and weak"]). Zerah's association here of tearlessness with weakness or with a lesser love recurs in the poem. Seeing the depth of love in Christ's eyes, Ador and Zerah lament that their unfallen nature prevents them from experiencing the deep gratitude for Christ's payment for sin that humans can feel; less a command than an acknowledgement of human privilege in this regard, their "Love him more, O man, / Than sinless seraphs can!" (696–97) bespeaks regret over their own limited emotive potential. To be able to weep at the cross, then, means to know in a way that seraphim cannot know. What Linda Lewis calls Ador and Zerah's "central revelation" thus recalls those instances in the hymns where weeping signals deep knowledge—to use Nussbaum's words again, a judgment of value.[16] Though the woman in "The Seraphim" lacks speech, she is not thereby lacking.

Nevertheless, if Barrett intended to assign a positive value to the woman's weeping here, the suggestion that a woman's inarticulateness may be the only appropriate response to the (temporary) silence of the "Master-word" contrasts notably with her own dexterous handling of the biblical and poetic word. In its linguistic and interpretive adroitness, "The Seraphim" marks its author as a skilled expositor of Scripture and literary heritage. "The Seraphim" takes as its theme what Barrett elsewhere identifies as her system of divinity, the depth of Christ's love for believers: "What can there be in language more divine than the seventeenth chapter of John's gospel [Christ's prayer for his disciples/believers]? We hear in it the last beating while on earth of the heart of the Redeemer,—holy, tender, pathetic,— . . . & *we*, learning so the full loving nature of that Heart, learn also the sufficiency of what we trust. That seventeenth chapter of John's gospel is my system of divinity" (*BC*, 6:129). Barrett foregrounds this theme of Christ's love by affixing two epigraphs to each of the two parts of her poem (*WEBB*, 1:78). For "Part the First," which takes place outside the shut heavenly gate where Ador and Zerah linger after the other angels have departed for earth, Barrett quotes Orpheus (in Greek) and Giles Fletcher, a contemporary of John Donne. The Orpheus lines translate as "Long-suffering angels stand by the fiery throne" (*WEBB*, 1:115n2), while the Fletcher excerpt, from *Christ's Triumph over Death* (1610), reads, "I look for angels' songs and hear Him cry." For "Part the Second," which takes place in the skies above the crucifixion scene, Barrett quotes the early church father Chrysostom (in Greek) and Edmund Spenser. The Greek epigraph here, drawn from book 2 of Chrysostom's "On the Priesthood," translates as "For otherwise I do not know how to love, except that I also surrender my life" (*WEBB*, 1:115n3), words which Chrysostom credits his friend Basil with saying when he aided a friend in danger, but which also echo Christ's definition of perfect love (John 15:13). The Spenser excerpt, taken from "A Hymn of Heavenly Love" from *Four Hymns* (1596), reads,

> O blessed Well of Love! O Floure of Grace,
> O glorious Morning Starre! O Lampe of Light!
> Most lively image of thy Father's face,
> Eternal King of Glorie, Lord of Might,
> Meeke Lambe of God!
>
> (*WEBB*, 1:78, 115n4)

In keeping with the movement of the poem from struggle to comprehension, the part 1 epigraphs emphasize angels' suffering and confusion, while the part 2 epigraphs emphasize divine love, sacrifice, and glory. But this skillful thematic and literary work actually reinforces Barrett's difference from the isolated woman in the poem who has no speech.

In fact, by pairing ancient and medieval texts as leads for her own work, Barrett adroitly places her text within a long tradition of male-authored reflections on this scriptural theme. Her linguistic ingenuity appears in the poem proper as well, as Barrett alludes to texts in Genesis, Samuel, Job, Isaiah, Revelation, all four Gospels, and the epistles of John and Peter to elucidate her theme or various elements of it. The dense biblical allusiveness of her poem seems akin to Stratten's yoking together of a multitude of biblical texts to solidify a theme. In a sermon entitled "Entrance to the Holiest by the Blood of Jesus," for instance, Stratten explicates his theme through a continuously triggering series of biblical images or allusions: the tabernacle, Moses at the burning bush, the Ten Commandments, Melchizedek, Solomon's temple, Isaiah, the candlesticks of John's vision, Abel's sacrifice, Aaron's sacrifices, the Passover initiated in Egypt, cleansing of lepers, Calvary, Adam, John the Baptist, the Lamb that is slain, the Pharisee and the publican, the two spies who entered Canaan, Jacob's dream at Bethel, the stoning of Stephen, and Paul.[17] For both Stratten and Barrett, Scripture formed a metaphorical and thematic unit richly inviting for linguistic choreography. Decades later, Barrett was still practicing such biblical dexterity as she revised this poem. In the 1838 text Barrett has Ador, in viewing the cross, say,

> Unto Him, whose forming word
> Gave to Nature flower and sward,
> She hath given back again,
> Instead of flowers, the thorn.

(WEBB, 1:96, note to line 439)

But in 1858, she replaced the last line with "For the myrtle, the thorn." With the revision, Barrett created a relationship between two seemingly unrelated biblical passages in much the same way as she did with the two texts in "The Measure." In Isaiah 55:13, the prophet visualizes Israel's return from exile as a positive movement represented in the growth of the myrtle tree in place of the thorn. In John 19:2, the gospel writer records, "The soldiers platted a crown of thorns, and put it on [Christ's] head." Although this latter text makes no mention of myrtle, Barrett has Ador, when viewing the crucifixion, reverse the movement of the text in Isaiah and say, "For the myrtle—the thorn." Technically classified as eisegesis rather than exegesis (leading in rather than leading out a meaning), the maneuver reinforces what the early version of the poem already shows, that the poet of "The Seraphim" has a sophisticated voice—though the woman in the poem does not.

At the same time, having experienced sermons well-grounded in scriptural truth but sadly lacking in emotional power, Barrett desired to produce a poetry wherein language elicits emotion as well as intellectual response. In her midcareer poems, she seems to have tried to elicit such emotion by emulating the passionate rhetoric of the preachers she admired, whether ancient or contemporary. "The Seraphim" sounds in places very much like her translation of Gregory's "Oration on the Nativity." It relies heavily on exclamations, repetitions, accumulations, alliterations, typographical signals, and sudden shifts in meter to create its fervor, as here:

> My heaven! my home of heaven! my infinite
> Heaven-choirs! what are ye to this dust and death,
> This cloud, this cold, these tears, this failing breath,
> Where God's immortal love now issueth
>   In this MAN's woe?
>
> (611–15)

Compare not the subject but the linguistic pattern of these lines to Gregory's "|O|f these things what do the revilers say? What, the bitter |scorners| against deity, the condemners of what is admirable, they who are in darkness around the light, uninstructed at the feet of wisdom, for whom Christ freely died, ungrateful creatures, formations of the devil?" (WEBB, 5:465). The two passages have the same manner of direct address followed by an elongated question loaded with parallel structures. Or compare Ador's speech below to the passage from Gregory that immediately follows it. They have the same pattern of negative reiteration building to a climax meant thereby to have greater emotional impact:

> There is a silentness
>   That answers thee enow,—
> . . . .
> Hear it. It is not from the visible skies
>   Though they are very still,
> . . . .
> It is not from the hills, though calm and bare
> . . . .
> It is not from the places that entomb
> Man's dead—though common Silence there dilates
> . . . .
>   Not there—not there!
> Nor yet within their chambers lieth He
> A dead one in His living world!
>
> (548–70; 1838 text)

And how shall this be? Let us not crown the porches, let us not constitute the choirs, let us not adorn the streets, let us not feast the eye, let us not bring music to the ear, let us not make delicate the smell–, nor luxurious the palate–, let [o/w *onto those*][18] us not gratify the taste, for |those| ways open

> unto wickedness, & the entrance doors of sin. Let us not be effeminate in vestures both soft & flowing, & of which the most beautiful [tiful o/w onto ty] is {?vanity}. Not with the lustre of gems [o/w onto precious], not with splendour of gold, not with the wiles of colours falsely imitative of natural beauty, & devised in order to sin against the divine image—not with feastings & drunkenness, unto [o/w onto with] which every kind of impurity we know, is yoked,— ... Let us not {?fire} lofty {?rushes},—building the *things* [o/w onto den] of luxury into tabernacles for the appetite. Let us not *honour / prize* the flower-scent of wines, the enchantments of the table, the preciousness of ointments. Let not the earth & sea offer unto us that expensive dust / dross—for thus I have learnt how to value luxury. Let us not emulate each other in intemperance. [...] But we by whom the word is worshipped, if we must needs luxuriate, let us luxuriate in the word, & in the divine law, & in other narrations[.] (WEBB, 5:460)

Barrett's emotive rhetoric feels almost controlled compared to Gregory's, though both writers seem to "luxuriate in the word"—so much so that, sustained over more than a thousand lines of poetry, this strategy tends to overreach its ends. This was not a problem Barrett faced in the hymns, where stanzaic regularity and brevity impose their own controls. The more open form of a dramatic lyric or lyrical drama, however, has no such inherent stop on affective accumulation. Barrett could luxuriate as she pleased, heaping phrase upon phrase, exclamation upon exclamation, descriptor upon descriptor. The very form of her midcareer poems seems to have enabled her to do to readers what she considered a good sermon should do to auditors: "draw them, fasten them, impress them"—appeal to their emotion as well as understanding.

In a long dramatic lyric, such affective language sometimes tested even a Victorian receptivity toward expressiveness. On publication of "The Seraphim," the *Athenaeum*'s reviewer lamented that Barrett "addresses herself to sacred song with a devotional ecstacy [*sic*] suiting rather the Sister Celestines and Angelicas of Port-Royal, than the religious poets of our sober protestant communities" (BC, 4:375). While the remark reveals its denominational preferences as well as the usual assignment of feeling to women (sisters), the reviewer's objections seem justified by such lines as

> O meek, insensate things,
> O congregated matters! who inherit,
>   Instead of motive powers,
>   Impulsions God-supplied;

> Instead of vital spirit,
> A clear informing beauty;
> Instead of creature-duty,
> A motion calm as rest.
> Lights, without feet or wings,
> In golden courses sliding!
> Broad glooms! 'neath masses, hiding,
> Whose lustrous heart away was prest
>   Into the argent stars!
> . . . .
>   O brave
> And subtle elements! the Holy
> Hath charged me by your voice with folly.
> Enough, the mystic arrow leaves its wound.
> Return ye to your silences inborn,
> Or to your inarticulated sound!
>
> (383–95, 401–6; 1838 text, as drawn from notes to these lines)

Zerah's accumulated and somewhat fanciful descriptions of the elements (continued in the ellipsis) sometimes obscure rather than express meaning. Apparently, Barrett had not yet learned in midcareer what she later learned from the sermon Stratten preached after his daughter died, that restraint can be more effective than eloquence of lamentation or devotional ecstasy. Nevertheless, as Heather Shippen Cianciola notes, the seraphim in this poem have had "a language-altering experience," one that is shared by the speaker of the epilogue—whom Cianciola reads as Barrett. As the soul reflects on its own process of spiritual formation "as an act of articulation," the epilogue reveals that "what is at stake for Barrett is language itself."[19] It is not the only thing at stake, of course—but what language to use and who can use it are certainly central issues in Barrett's religious poetics here.

    In the other two dramatic poems of her midcareer, Barrett develops her considerations of authority, dialogue, gender, emotion, and intellect by taking biblical history's two key women as her central speakers: Mary in "The Virgin Mary to the Child Jesus" (*WEBB*, 1:481–86) and Eve in "A Drama of Exile" (*WEBB*, 1:10–71). Both poems maintain a commitment to a democratic poetics by being dialogic rather than visionary or declarative. Genuine dialogue, of course, may be hindered by such things as unequal relations between speakers or self-aggrandizement, so that dialogic poetry does not guarantee a democratic poetics, although it furthers its possibility. Some critics, consequently, acknowledge the dramatic or conversational modes of "The Virgin Mary to the Child Jesus" and "A Drama of Exile" yet argue that Mary and Eve assert themselves as authoritative speakers. Cynthia Scheinberg and Marjorie Stone, for example, have each argued that the first poem presents Mary as having religious power.[20] Scheinberg pays particular attention to what she sees as Mary's linguistic as well as spiritual power in the poem: Mary asserts her right to name the child, aligns herself with Moses, commands Jesus's crowning, prophesies the baby's dread future, and "erases God 'the Father'" from the equation" when she claims Jesus as her son (83). I admire Scheinberg's larger argument regarding Barrett Browning's relationship to Hebrew and Hebraic figures, yet I believe the poem does not sustain these claims about Mary's linguistic power. Certainly, Barrett repositions the usually silent and passive Mary of the nativity scenes as a key speaker addressing the sleeping Jesus—and in a period anxious about the emancipation of Roman Catholics and hovering near the pope's declaration of the Immaculate Conception of Mary, Barrett must have been aware of the poetic and religious risks of featuring Mary this way. But the poem does not make Mary an authoritative speaker.

The poem indeed opens with Mary pondering what name to call the child: "My flesh, my Lord!—what name? I do not know / A name that seemeth not too high or low, / Too far from me or heaven" (2–4). But the question seems prompted by confusion more than assertiveness, with the memory of the name "given / By the majestic angel" coming back to Mary almost as a relief in her dilemma of how to reconcile the human ("my flesh") and divine ("my Lord") natures of the child in a suitable name: "My Jesus, *that* is best!" (5). Next, when upon kissing Jesus, Mary recalls the tradition by which Moses died with the kiss of God on his lips, she does not so much align herself with Moses's prophetic power as with Moses's sense that, having tasted such divine love, he has nothing more to ask of life: "I feel I could lie down / As Moses did, and die" (36–37). Further, when Mary commands the universe to "crown me Him a King" (123; not "crown me a King"), she immediately acknowledges that her command is ineffectual:

> What is my word?
> . . . .
> The child-like brow, crowned by none,...
> Keeps its unchildlike shade.
> Sleep, sleep, my crownless One!
>
> (127, 130–32)

Moreover, when she perceives that the Child before her will be "'despised,'" "'rejected,'" and smitten with a "sword" (146, 144), she is not prophesying but knowingly echoing the prophecies of Isaiah and Zechariah, as the internal quotation marks indicate (see Isaiah 53:3 and Zechariah 13:7; Barrett intensified the prophetic context in 1856 by adding quotation marks also to "smites the Shepherd" in line 145). Mary's sudden knowledge of the Child's future derives not from her own visionary powers but from familiarity with historic Jewish prophecies widely known in her community. Again, when Mary declares, "[F]or me alone / To hold in hands created, crying—Son!" (71–72), she might be erasing Joseph from the equation, but "hands created" does not erase God the Father. Finally, one does not typically interpret a mother's soft murmuring to a child to "sleep, sleep" as an imperative. While, therefore, I agree that "the poem resists constructing Mary as a speaker offering a conventional devotional address to Jesus,"[21] I cannot see Mary as particularly prophetic or powerful in it. While Ingrid Hotz-Davies may venture too far in asserting that the Mary of this poem is "a perfect example of Victorian womanhood," I concur with her that Mary is not particularly radical or powerful: "She is very definitely not a goddess, and Barrett Browning seems to go out of her way not to call up or, if called up, to defuse those aspects of the Virgin Mary which can be—and have been—used to exalt her."[22] Instead, Mary's importance in Barrett's poetic experimentations lies, I believe, in Mary's dialogic and communitarian habits, as well as integrated emotional and intellectual being.

Whereas "The Seraphim" employs two speakers to create its dialogic mode, "The Virgin Mary to the Child Jesus" experiments with a different genre to achieve the same effect. This time Barrett constructed the poem as thirteen verse paragraphs, which she pointedly numbered. Given that the poem has only one speaker, this structure helps accentuate its changing verbal drama as Mary addresses several different auditors. Chiefly, she addresses Jesus, as the title suggests. But she also speaks to herself, seraphim, the universe, and future generations; at times she adopts a narrative stance as well. Conscious of her social context, Mary draws her auditors into imagined conversation, in *sermocinatio* fashion. She addresses the invisible seraphim with "I am 'ware of you, heavenly Presences" (38; see also 57, 76, 149); and she questions the Child, "[A]rt Thou come for saving?" "Art Thou a King, then?" and "Wak'st thou, O loving One?" (13, 122, 180). The lack of verbal response does not erase her essentially dialogic mode, for she continually shapes the direction of her speech according to the nonverbal responses she receives (or imagines). For example, after telling the seraphim they are but fellow worshippers with her, she responds to their apparent response, "Yea, drop your lids more low" (56). At other moments, the addressee is less clear, but given the various presences named in the same section (kine, shepherds, wise men), Mary's questions do not seem entirely self-directed, even when they seem rhetorical, as in her query, "Can hands wherein such burden pure has been, / Not open with the cry, 'Unclean, unclean!' / More oft than any else beneath the skies?" (114–16). Further, at least once in the poem, Mary situates herself within a community, however limited it might be: "We sate among the stalls at Bethlehem" (59). Given that the seraphim are standing, and that the section goes on to describe the arrival of the shepherds and wise men, the "we" here must needs refer to herself and someone else, perhaps Joseph. In any case, the poem as a whole casts Mary as a woman in dramatic action, turning first to one auditor, then another, then speaking to herself, to the child, the seraphim, the stars, the seraphim again, the child again, and so on. She sits, she bends over the baby, she straightens up, she holds up her hands, she gestures. Deeply moved at the presence of the Child, she—unlike the woman in "The Seraphim"—neither weeps ineffectually nor "feels with a spasm, not a speech." She considers, she interprets, she verbalizes. Against her existent knowledge of Scripture, she poses questions that lead her (and the listening seraphim? and the reader?) to ever greater understanding. At the end of the poem, the Child wakes, not when Mary grasps that the prophetic word applies to him but when her silent tear falls. As in the hymns, this tear does not represent weakness, fear, or resignation, but relational knowledge. It binds her to the Savior because it signifies that the process of inquiry, begun in wonder and awe, has reached its proper end in devotion, not mere comprehension. Indeed, throughout the poem, Mary has demonstrated the strength of both her feeling and her thinking. Barrett's "system of divinity" emerges again as she represents love as grounded in understanding, and knowledge as requisite to devotion.

"A Drama of Exile" (WEBB, 1:10–71) returns to a more obvious dialogic mode by participating in the pursuit of truth through multiple speakers. Barrett chose a dramatic mode to represent "the new and strange experience of the fallen humanity" (WEBB, 2:567) in order that both Adam and Eve might speak without narratorial intervention—as Stone observes, they do so in relatively equal proportions.[23] They come to understand only through conversation with each other and Christ that exile from the Garden does not mean eternal condemnation. Notably, when Christ appears in a vision, he does so to Adam and Eve together. Neither receives a special revelation or lapses into silence in his presence. Also, when a scene involves Lucifer, both members of the yet-limited human community participate in the conversation. Earth spirits and other imagined voices further contribute to the conversational-dramatic mode, the mutual talk, of this poem.

Though less easy to see than the dialogic mode of the poem, an emotive-intellectual relationship also lies at the heart of "A Drama of Exile." With the notable exception of Alexandra Wörn's careful theological reading of the poem, critical debate on this poem so far has centered on whether Barrett depicts Eve "as an acquiescent woman" and the poem as "a silencing of Eve's expressive voice" or whether Eve, despite an apparent subscription to Victorian ideologies of gender, actually subverts them and becomes Adam's teacher.[24] But Barrett may be less preoccupied with this question in this poem than this debate suggests. If the poem wavers in its presentation of Eve as an independent thinker and slips into occasional acquiescence with Victorian ideology, it may be because Barrett's central interest here is, as she states in her preface, "lyrical emotion" (*WEBB*, 2:567). Eve's grief, she writes, "appeared to [her] imperfectly apprehended hitherto, and more expressible by a woman than a man" (567)—an allusion, of course, to Milton's treatment of Eve in *Paradise Lost*, as well as to Robert Montgomery's 1832 *The Messiah*, which mostly omits Eve from its Genesis scenes.[25] Notably, in Barrett's phrasing it is not Eve (or Eve's power) but Eve's grief that has been imperfectly apprehended. Perhaps because Barrett intended to consider Eve's grief or emotion, the poem does not represent Eve as, say, a figure whose persuasive powers Adam could not resist. Instead, Barrett shows that Eve's emotional response to the fall into sin and exclusion from the Garden expresses a deep understanding of justice, mercy, and consequence. Barrett does not bar Adam from such understandings. She gives it to him to say,

> Our spirits have climbed high
> By reason of the passion of our grief,
> And, from the top of sense, looked over sense
> To the significance and heart of things
> Rather than the things themselves.
>
> (991–95)

But perceiving "the significance and heart of things" leads Adam and Eve in different directions: he to hostility, she to empathetic relation. When the Spirits of Inorganic and Organic Nature bitterly confront Adam and Eve,

Adam reacts by stating, "There must be strife between us, large as sin," while Eve disagrees: "No strife, mine Adam! . . . [rather] pardoning grace" (1175, 1176, 1188). Fully acknowledging the disharmony between Nature and herself after the fall, she nevertheless asks for the Spirits' patience; by contrast, Adam continues to demand their reverence. When the Earth Spirits scorn Eve's request and Adam's demand, Adam asserts human superiority: "We are yet too high, O Spirits, for your disdain!" Eve contradicts him again:

> Nay, beloved! . . .
> We confront them from no height.
> We have stooped down to their level
> By infecting them with evil.
>
> (1511, 1512–15)

When the Earth Spirits become more threatening, Adam appeals to God's power for help, but Eve appeals to God's pity (1745, 1746). In every situation, Barrett formulates Eve's response as gently corrective to Adam's. Though Adam and Eve possess the same cognitive knowledge of events, the woman's emotive judgment differs from the man's. Eve rightly posits God as the wronged party; Adam posits humans. His cognitive-evaluative judgment is skewed; hers is not. Thus Barrett assigns more value to Eve's responses than to Adam's. Eve's continual tears, therefore—while no doubt reducing the intellectual fortitude some would like to see in a woman poet's representation of Eve—do not mean, for Barrett, Eve's inferiority to Adam, who does not weep. On the contrary, when Christ appears in a vision, he again validates the power of tears by declaring, "The tears of my clean soul shall follow [all sins], / And set a holy passion to work clear / Absolute consecration" (1976–78). Tears set consecration in motion. Once again, Barrett gives tears redemptive or restorative value.

As these exchanges between Eve and Adam intimate, "A Drama of Exile" differs significantly from "The Seraphim" in its representation of a woman who speaks rather than sobs in silence. Grief no longer silences but liberates female expression. But as with "The Seraphim," there remains a discord in "A Drama of Exile" between the woman of the poem and the woman poet who created her. Though Barrett writes elsewhere that religion ought to be "a subject of *feeling*, of real warm emotion & feeling" (*BC*, 4:182) and though she admits this feeling when she names reverence and adoration as the principles behind her inclusion of Christ as a speaker in the poem (*WEBB*, 2:569), in her preface she again underscores her own intellectual or critical faculty even while in the poem she leaves Eve somewhat lacking in this regard. In the preface, Barrett justifies the length of the twilight in her poem by referring to and explaining the Hebrew word for twilight used in Genesis: it "signifies a 'mingling' and approaches the meaning of our 'twilight' analytically" (*WEBB*, 2:569). As a reader of Scripture in its original languages, this move seems to say, she engages not in flights of fancy but in skilled interpretation—as indeed she states more explicitly elsewhere when she writes about poetry and Scripture this way: "Certainly we are not called to write fantasies, but interpretations—we are to read wisdom from an open book, & not to dream over it, idly" (*BC*, 10:186). "A Drama of Exile" is just such an interpretation of the "open book" of Scripture, the poet's "wisdom" everywhere evident as Barrett weaves together scriptural allusions that neither Adam nor Eve could actually know.

But Barrett perhaps reveals her inventiveness in "A Drama of Exile" most when she incorporates into a poem based on a biblical narrative an imagined celestial system most often associated with pagan or secular astrology: the zodiac. Fully half the poem takes place under the umbrella of the twelve zodiacal figures, which Adam and Eve first see as dubious and rather frightening shapes, then interpret as foreshadows of humanity's experience. Earth and other spirits, Lucifer, and Christ himself all appear within the circle of the zodiac before it finally fades away near the end of the poem. Barrett may have known that the zodiac had a place in ancient and medieval Christian iconography. Mary Charles Murray observes that in the fourth century, Christian writings assigned allegorical meaning to the zodiac in two contexts: baptism and the preaching of the twelve apostles. By the time of Bede, these Christian interpretations disappeared as the zodiac became a more secular symbol, applied to the labors of the months. But then in the medieval period the symbol was again appropriated into Christian contexts when it was inscribed on Romanesque church doorways all over Europe. Murray writes, "This time it is not a question of baptism or preaching, but the bringing of all the work of the year into the orbit of religion."[26] This puts Barrett's zodiac within a larger tradition of Christian imaginative work. Or perhaps Barrett's zodiac, like her Eve, serves more directly as part of her reworking of Milton, who alludes to zodiacal figures in books 10 and 11 of *Paradise Lost*. Yet again, the zodiac may signify Barrett's comprehensive vision of the entire 1844 volume of poems, for it appears in her last as well as first poem in the volume. In "The Dead Pan," Barrett writes,

"Truth in Relation, Perceived in Emotion"

> O twelve gods of Plato's vision,
> Crowned to starry wanderings,—
> With your chariots in procession,
> And your silver clash of wings!
> Very pale ye seem to rise,
> Ghosts of Grecian deities—
> Now Pan is dead.
>
> (WEBB, 2:377.57–63)

The next stanzas enumerate these gods, each reduced to a ghost of its former self because Christ's victory on the cross crushes the Greek system of belief ("Pan is dead"). What is interesting here is that in *Phaedrus*, Plato aligns the twelve Greek gods with the twelve signs of the zodiac. In "The Dead Pan," the zodiac retains this classical pagan association, wherein the twelve gods are antithetical to Christ. But in "A Drama of Exile," the twelve zodiacal signs serve the narrative of Christian history, so that Christ arises in their midst. Whether as Christian allegory, Miltonic reworking, or classical revision (for Barrett knew her Plato well), the zodiac testifies to Barrett's intellectual and creative skills, and she was quite pleased with it (*LGB*, 116–17). But problematically, Barrett does not yet ascribe such astuteness to Eve, who still needs Adam to name and interpret the zodiac for her. In other words, Eve is not yet the skilled exegete, the poet-preacher, however close Barrett might be drawing to that aspiration. Whatever failing this might be for Barrett's Eve, it at least highlights again the dialogic nature of Barrett's poem: for all her patient teaching of Adam as to appropriate responses to fallen creatures and spirits, Eve, too, needs instruction.

Taken together, "The Seraphim," "The Virgin Mary to the Child Jesus," and "A Drama of Exile" show an emerging individuality in Barrett's work. Barrett herself later desired "to acknowledge nothing *before* [her] volume of Seraphim poems," in which, she said, "I *broke my shell*, & came out, however unworthily & weakly, yet in my own nature & individuality" (*BC*, 9:52, 57). At least part of that nature and individuality derives from a religious imaginary formed within a Word-centric liturgy, drawn to the narratives of salvation history, and desirous of an integrated Truth and Love. As if her achievement in this volume increased her confidence, Barrett's post-*Seraphim* correspondence increasingly outlines her thoughts on the relationship between religion and poetry. Even "*doctrinal* mysteries," she asserts, are "poetical in their nature" (*BC*, 4:181), and "Christ's religion is essentially poetry—poetry glorified" (*BC*, 5:220). During these same years, she also affirms her democratic conception of the poet in poems not explicitly religious in subject. In "Mountaineer and Poet," published in 1850, she advises poets to learn from the humility of the mountaineer who understands that his giant shadow on the mountain does not result from his own stature; the mountains, not the mountaineer, are crowned in splendor. Poets, too, must pursue their work without delusions of self-grandeur. Poetry may be akin to the glories of mountains, but poets must be like "the simple" (the poem's term for the mountaineer):

> Learn from hence
> Meek morals, all ye poets that pursue
> Your way still onward up to eminence!
> Ye are not great because creation drew
> Large revelations round your earliest sense,
> Nor bright because God's glory shines for you.
>
> (WEBB, 2:144.9–14)

The poem's ambiguous conclusion (leaving open the possibility that poets are great or bright for reasons not stated) nevertheless firmly denies that poets speak on the basis of divine or prophetic revelations. Rather, patient pursuit of the splendors of truth and love should characterize their work.

Aurora Leigh and "A Curse for a Nation"

Already in 1843, Barrett had written, "If a poet be a poet, it is his business to work for the elevation & purification of the public mind" (BC, 7:21). From the mid-1840s through the end of her life, she worked for the "elevation" and "purification" of the public mind by addressing social, political, and religious issues in such poems as "The Cry of the Children," "The Runaway Slave at Pilgrim's Point," and *Casa Guidi Windows*—all of which deserve more interpretation as religious poems, or at least as poems informed by a religious imaginary. But in this last section of the chapter, I focus on *Aurora Leigh* instead, partly because of its status in Barrett Browning's oeuvre and partly because I believe the now-standard reading of it as poet-prophet discourse needs emendation. I then turn more briefly to "A Curse for a Nation" as another late poem manifesting Barrett Browning's religious imaginary.

In *Aurora Leigh*, published in 1857, Barrett Browning illustrates her mature concept of the poet-preacher and the value of the democratic and dialogic over the authoritative and visionary (*WEBB*, vol. 3). My assertion that *Aurora Leigh* figures the poet as preacher stands somewhat at odds with a substantial body of criticism that sees the poem as deploying the poet-as-prophet paradigm, especially since I differentiate between the terms *preacher* and *prophet*. Margaret Reynolds and Marjorie Stone have each argued persuasively that Elizabeth Barrett Browning's *Aurora Leigh* is a revisionary, gynocentric form of sage discourse. Stone argues, for example, that *Aurora Leigh* "enters the tradition of Victorian sage writing through its representation of a prophetic speaker, its pronounced Biblical allusions and typological patterning, its polemical sermonizing on the times, its argumentative intertextuality, its exploitation of metaphor and definition as strategies of persuasion, its quest for a sustaining 'Life Philosophy,' and its vision of a new social and spiritual order."[27] Stott, extending some aspects of Stone's approach, locates the poem more precisely within Victorian nonconformist sage discourse, arguing that it "espouses non-conformist values such as the primacy of the individual conscience, commitment to social and political reform ... and to the importance of work."[28] These and other studies, such as Linda Lewis's discussion of the Wisdom figure or prophetess in *Aurora Leigh* and Jude Nixon's analysis of Aurora as prophetic in her rendering of the apocalypse through a proliferation of biblical invocations,[29] all appropriately recognize Barrett Browning's bold interventions in the discourses of her time—and I agree that *Aurora Leigh* at times figures the poet as prophet. However, I believe the poem does not completely endorse this model of the poet.

Indeed, my argument that Barrett Browning destabilizes the prophet model in favor of an alternative she had been developing for some time actually corresponds well with several of Stone's arguments about the poet's revisionist strategies. Stone points to the poem's "defence of individualism" (*Elizabeth Barrett Browning*, 146), "'dialectical process' of persuasion and rebuttal" (153), emersion from the poet's "experimentation with dramatic speakers throughout the 1840s" (161), and refusal to present Aurora "as a sage of unquestionable authority" (162) as elements of Barrett Browning's gynocentric transformation of the sage tradition. In what follows, I do not negate this analysis, but I wish to modify it by attributing at least some of Barrett Browning's dissatisfaction with the poet-prophet paradigm to religious rather than gender formations. The image of a cultural prophet imbued with authoritative vision ultimately did not resonate well in Barrett Browning's religious imaginary. Consequently, *Aurora Leigh* depicts Aurora's shift from a naïve perspective of the poet as privileged seer to a humbler view of the poet as necessarily engaged in a communal effort to discover the right and the good. It also aligns Aurora's developing concept of the poet with Aurora's growth into biblical speech patterns. Taken together, the two movements suggest that religious knowledge increases in proportion to one's abandonment of an authoritative stance. As well, the poem endorses again the role of the emotive in knowledge by criticizing social work not based on love.

Though more frequently characterized as a verse-novel, Barrett Browning's *Aurora Leigh* is an epic-narrative-lyric hybrid, one that fits Slinn's characterization of such hybrids as shifting individual expressiveness toward social contexts and culturally produced discursive practices. The generic mixedness of the poem factors into the critical argument about its revisionary sage discourse but testifies equally well to Barrett Browning's thinking about the poet as a conversant in community.[30] In her epic-narrative, Barrett Browning breaks through the problems she confronted (or created) in her dramatic genres, where she needed prefaces and epilogues to establish self-representations that might otherwise have been damaged by the limitations of the women figures within the poems. Epic-narrative, by contrast, permits a more assertive narrative voice that need not be read biographically yet sits more comfortably with the poetic configurations Barrett Browning imagined for herself, while its hybridity replaces the usual narrative omniscience of epic with a first-person limited subjectivity that does not contradict a democratic poetics. Further, its public nature and scope accord with the imperatives of narrative, testimony, and exposition. The epic-narrative mode thus rests well within Barrett Browning's religious imaginary and serves to further her dialogic and rhetorical aims.

Aurora Leigh is structured as Aurora's narration of her own poetic growth, so that the poem contains two representations of Aurora's voice: the reflective and mature voice of the narrator looking back on her own history and the voice of the character who speaks and acts within that history. Significantly, these two voices imagine the poet in different ways. In book 1, the young Aurora thinks and speaks about poetry in exclusivist terms. Poets are the "only truth-tellers now left to God," she says, and they "thunder" to the common man to pay attention to the soul (1.859, 873–80).[31] Although poets have their "ups and downs," they are "cup-bearer[s]" to the gods (1.933, 923). Already in book 2, however, the older, narrating Aurora criticizes her earlier exalted view of the poet, calling it the proud "devil" of her "youth" that set her on "mountain-peaks" where she inappropriately demanded "empire and much tribute" from those who were below (2.532–41). As the narrative voice ceases to be retrospective and becomes autobiographical in books 5 through 9, the poet-as-prophet paradigm intermittently reappears; yet its efficacy is continually questioned, a more democratic configuration continually proposed. In book 5, Aurora remarks that poets are "called to stand up straight as demi-gods" (5.384)—but she immediately adds that one must produce a poetry that validates the claim (389–99). In book 6, she again asserts, "[W]e thunder down / We prophets, poets—Virtue's in the *word!*" (6.217–18). In protest against Romney's focus on alleviating material poverty, she insists that the poet's word can do "more for the man / Than if you dressed him in a broadcloth coat" (6.223–24). Again, though, her passionate words in defense of the poet dissipate when she remembers that Romney sees no value in her aspirations. The prospect of being the lonely prophet in the wilderness does not ultimately appeal to her. She desires dialogue, not pronouncement. Indeed, when she makes these pronouncements, she has yet to encounter the sexually violated Marian, to learn that knowledge comes not necessarily from the heights but also from those who have experienced the lowest places. By book 7, Aurora begins to acknowledge that no solitary speaker, of either sex, can ascertain truth on his or her own. She specifies, "[T]ruth is neither man's nor woman's but just God's" (7.753). Later yet, upon mature reflection she realizes that in her previous ambition, she not only demanded "no gifts / ... but God's" but also arrogantly decided she would use such gifts "[a]ccording to my pleasure and my choice, / As He and I were equals." She would even have excluded Romney "from that level of interchange" (9.631–35). Eventually, though, Aurora gives over her earlier exclusivist claims and asserts that "poet and philanthropist / (Even I and Romney) may stand side by side, / Because we both stand face to face with men" (6.199–201). Neither poetry nor philanthropy can save the world, but each needs the other in conversation, in community. Moreover, Aurora and Romney learn that they need to "stand side by side" also with the nonpoets, the nonphilanthropists, the Marians who (perhaps through bitter experience) have much to say about human existence and communal relationships. Only when Aurora and Romney acknowledge the necessity of speaking and working in community, of being humble even in independence and not arrogating to themselves prophetic or saving roles, are they able mutually to envision the heavenly city, the promise of harmony and unity. Stott calls *Aurora Leigh* "a poetry of ruminative conversation," a poetry with "*transformative conversation*" at its heart. Aurora is indeed transformed: from imagining herself as privileged seer to becoming a dialogic poet. Her more meditative moments are occasioned by her engagement in social discourse, and they return her to still further engagement. In Stott's words, "We see Aurora's strong opinions forming through conversation with herself and others, so that the views the poem champions are passionately championed, yet never held up as the *only* views."[32] Talking, inquiring, investigating her way to knowledge, Aurora can serve as an interpretive guide for others only after she has first acknowledged her own need for guidance through inquiry and conversation.

To underscore this understanding of the poet, Barrett Browning employs biblical language and poetic speech in *Aurora Leigh* more subtly and perhaps more effectively than ever before. First, her use of blank verse rather than rhymed lyrics brings her speaking voices more in line with everyday speech patterns. The long literary history of blank verse means no claim can be made that this stylistic shift by Barrett Browning was occasioned by the midcentury homiletic shift from ornamented rhetoric to simple, conversational style—though such a shift may have had a bearing. More likely, Barrett Browning replaced the grand style of her long religious poems with more natural speech here simply because she was not exploring a biblical narrative; the modern subject of her poem calls for different speech habits than did her imagined dramatic worlds. Still, the poem establishes its own link between the effective poet and appropriate religious language. It actually differentiates among speakers by their use or misuse of biblical words or images. Grimwald, for example, jibes that Lady Waldemar is a lily that "neither sews nor spins—and takes no thought / Of her garments . . . falling off" (5.664–65; cf. Matthew 6:28–30). Lady Waldemar similarly irreverently appropriates Scripture when she remarks that she will admit "No socialist within three crinolines, / To live and have his being" (9.136–37; cf. Acts 17:29). As Aurora herself notes, "Virtue's in the *word!*" (6.218), but Grimwald and Lady Waldemar do not have virtuous words.

Aurora, however, increasingly adopts biblical speech patterns that validate her integrity as she grows as a poet. She speaks approximately eighty percent of the poem's biblical allusions. However, these allusions are not evenly distributed throughout the poem. Rather, Aurora as reflective and interpretive narrator uses biblical language more often than the youthful Aurora. In book 1, Aurora as narrator incorporates biblical allusions easily and naturally into her speech, but Aurora the young girl has no biblical language, perhaps not least because her aunt had her learn

> the collects and the catechism,
> The creeds, from Athanasius back to Nice,
> The Articles, the Tracts *against* the times

> And various popular synopses of
> Inhuman doctrines never taught by John.
>
> (1.392–97)

Scripture does not appear in the list, and except for a few instances in book 2, none of Aurora's direct speech in books 1 through 5 contains biblical allusions. Aurora is not yet well versed in biblical language, so that her immature ideas about poetry and life correlate with a lack of effective biblical speech. In books 8 and 9, however, she voices at least half of her biblical references as autobiographical character and mostly in conversation with Romney, whom formerly she would have excluded from her interchange with God. By the conclusion of the poem, Aurora's conversational voice to Romney corresponds with her narrative voice to the reader. As narrator she describes the "jasper-stone as clear as glass," the "first foundations of that new, near Day / Which should be builded out of Heaven to God"; as Romney's companion, she recites aloud, "'Jasper first . . . / And second, sapphire; third, chalcedony; / The rest in order—last, an amethyst'" (9.955, 956–57, 962–64). Her two voices coalesce in subject and imagery. Although the apocalyptic vision here may evoke a poet-prophet paradigm again, the careful delineation of a mutual understanding that *precedes* Aurora's final speech again suggests a model in which the speaker is conscious of shared, rather than exclusive, knowledge. Aurora does not describe the heavenly city she envisions until she knows first that Romney also sees it spiritually: "and when / I saw his soul saw—'Jasper first,' I said" (9.961–62). She does not here capitulate to a male apocalyptic tradition or fall in step behind Romney. Rather, she waits until he catches up to her; when she sees that he also perceives, she speaks, using biblical language, of what they now mutually understand.

Not only does Aurora's religious speech develop in tandem with her better understanding of the poet, but her words also effect change in others—change of language and heart but also change of life, particularly in Romney. Romney's early biblical allusions tend to be cynical or misapplied. For example, in an early argument, he informs Aurora that (men's) social work supersedes (women's) poetry: "When Egypt's slain, I say, let Miriam sing!— / Before—where's Moses?" (2.171–72). Romney's "religious" commitment is to the socialism of Charles Fourier, whose theories Barrett Browning considered threatening to individual liberty (*LEBB*, 1:452, 467). Although Aurora early on tells Romney that his Fouriers have "failed, / Because not poets enough to understand / That life develops from within" (2.483–85), he rejects her notions of the importance of the soul. Much later, however, his spiritual eyes are opened precisely through reading her poetry (8.260–69), which he again characterizes as Miriam's singing, this time as the act that rescued him from drowning (8.334–35). Furthermore, he acknowledges that "Fourier's void," that we must "raise men's bodies still by raising souls" (9.868, 853). So while Aurora learns from experience that poet-prophets may be dangerously indistinguishable from conjurors (1.772–73) and that *if* the human soul retains some "fair, fine trace of what was written once, / Some upstroke of an alpha and omega / Expressing the old scripture" (1.830–32), much study is required to discern it, Romney learns from her poetry that social duty without love has no results and no rewards. He acknowledges that action must spring from comprehension of and empathy with the human spirit:

> "Beloved," [he] sang, "we must be here to work;
> And men who work can only work for men,
> And, not to work in vain, must comprehend
> Humanity and so work humanly."
>
> (9.849–52)

Aurora as a religious speaker brings Romney to rightly motivated action by helping him understand truth in relation, perceived in emotion. Although she uses the rhythms and diction of simple (biblical) speech instead of the passionate oratory of the Christian grand style, it is still her poetry—her cognitive-emotive work—that opens the way to God for Romney.

Aurora's effectiveness in transforming Romney returns us to the matter of the poet-preacher's gender. As observed earlier, Congregationalism's encouragement of independent religious thought did not extend so far in practice as to permit women to be preachers, in spite of the 1833 "Declaration's" ambivalence on the point. Barrett Browning never directly addressed this matter, but indirectly, of course, through *Aurora Leigh*, she does. Romney's vocation as a social worker caring for the poor and sick and Aurora's as a poet offering spiritual hope reverses Victorian assignments of domestic and hortatory roles. The poem indicates that a thoughtful woman imbued with religious understanding and possessing talents of poetic expression can function as a poet-preacher just as well as a sympathetic man can function as a caregiver. Thus, although Barrett Browning did not write directly about women as preachers, especially in her later poetic career she imagined the woman poet, including herself, as a poet-preacher whose words merited due attention.

My argument that Barrett Browning destabilizes the poet-prophet paradigm in *Aurora Leigh* might itself seem destabilized by the contemporaneous poem "A Curse for a Nation" (1856). In this poem, the speaker clearly adopts a prophetic stance. Indeed, in "A Curse for a Nation," Barrett Browning comes closest in her published works to representing the female voice as divinely authorized and prophetic. In the poem, an angel instructs a woman to pronounce a curse on an unnamed nation for its practice of slavery, and, after some objections, the woman does. The angel's instructions recall the voice that commands the apostle John to write the book of Revelation, while the woman's public and political cursing boldly contravenes convention, as Stone has shown.[33] It would seem that Barrett Browning here undercuts the democratic poetics she insisted on in *Aurora Leigh*. The poem, however, reveals a pronounced ambivalence about adopting the prophetic voice. Not only does the woman repeatedly resist the angel's command, but this resistance is given space of its own in the form of a prologue. Moreover, although the poem overtly associates this reluctance with the woman's gender, Barrett Browning's construction of the prologue along the lines of a particular biblical narrative implicitly suggests that the reluctance to prophesy goes beyond gender. In Exodus 4, Moses receives his commission from God to lead the Israelites out of their slavery in Egypt. Three times God gives the charge, and three times Moses objects. Notably, in the prologue to "A Curse for a Nation," three times the angel commands the woman to write, and three times she objects. That Moses and the woman of the poem both eventually capitulate has less to do with their willingness to be prophets, whether man or woman, than with their inability to resist the divine command, coupled with their real desire to free those who are enslaved. Barrett Browning may be suggesting that where slavery is involved, true democracy has obviously failed, so the prophetic has its place. In such situations, she experiments with a poetic mode not otherwise dominant in her religious imaginary. Nevertheless, by emphasizing the reluctance with which such a task is undertaken and the severity of the situation that necessitates it, Barrett Browning does not undercut her earlier insistence in *Aurora Leigh* that religious knowledge is best attained through democratic principles. In fact, Barrett Browning elsewhere distances herself from the prophetic, cursing voice of the poem when she writes, "In fact, *I* cursed neither England nor America— I leave such things to our Holy Father here: the poem only pointed out how the curse was involved in the action of slave-holding" (*FF*, 318). Disavowing special authority for herself, Barrett Browning here critiques papal presumption of the same, and insists that the curse of the poem proceeds from the situation, not the speaker. This remark may feel disingenuous, given the woman's cursing in the poem, but it underscores Barrett Browning's uneasiness with the prophetic mode.

Moreover, the poem has other affinities with Barrett Browning's earlier work. It again associates women's weeping with knowledge, though the speaker of the prologue deprecates her own tears. Pleading with the angel to choose a man to do the cursing, she argues, "For I, a woman, have only known / How the heart melts and the tears run down" (*WEBB*, 4:602.39–40). The angel, however, associates weeping with cursing (with power): "Some women weep and curse, I say / ... / And thou shalt take their part to-night, / Weep and write" (43, 45–46). According to the angel, emotion empowers writing, not weakens it—Barrett Browning's long-held point about the relation between emotion and knowledge. Significantly, the principle holds true for the prophetic as well as democratic voice. A (woman) poet *must* and *can* unite emotional strength with intellectual understanding; she can do so because poetic powers are not conferred from above in some preexistent (male-figured) form but developed through participation in a dialogic community.

CHAPTER THREE

"THE BELOVED ANGLICAN CHURCH OF MY BAPTISM"

Christina Rossetti's Religious Imaginary

To turn from nineteenth-century Congregationalism to Anglicanism, and especially Anglo-Catholicism, is in many ways to turn from what David Tracy, working from Paul Ricoeur, calls proclamation to what he calls manifestation, or from a dialectical toward an analogical imagination and language.[1] Congregationalism, we have seen, grounds the Christ-event as a Word-event, thus calling Christians to witness to that central experience in further, often dialectical, word and action. Anglicanism historically also values proclamation, with Scripture and sermon integral to its liturgy; as Tracy points out, the Christian faith has historically held that "Jesus Christ is both the decisive word and the decisive manifestation of God and ourselves" (215). I do not, therefore, in this chapter pitch Rossetti's Anglican/Anglo-Catholic religious imaginary as diametrically opposed to Barrett Browning's. Rossetti's several narrative poems, for example (including religious narratives such as "A Ballad of Boding"), demonstrate the impulse toward prophetic warning characteristic of religious formations serious about proclamation. Yet Rossetti approaches even such narratives differently than Barrett Browning, using a language more akin to Tracy's description of analogical language than the dialectic he associates with Protestant formations having "prophetic-ethical-historical" emphases (203). Her imaginary bends instead toward the "mystical-priestly-metaphysical-aesthetic" (203) formations Tracy finds in Catholic and Orthodox, and I would add Anglo-Catholic, Christianity. These traditions do not privilege the verbal but instead see object, ritual, and symbol as equally or more able to manifest the focal meaning of the Christ-event. Necessarily still inclusive of the verbal, these forms of Christianity yet "move in the direction of vision, image, ritual, reflection, meditation—in a word, manifestation" (377). In the present chapter, I posit that such modes of manifestation expressed—and, in reciprocal motion, formed—the deepest postures of Anglicanism and Anglo-Catholicism (its valuation of encounter, discipleship, pattern, and communion with Christ and the saints) and that these postures became formative for Rossetti's religious imaginary. I first explore how the historic Anglican liturgy shaped Rossetti's basic imaginative attunement to the world, including attention to sacrament as manifestation; the chapter then considers how the three movements that contributed to Rossetti's Anglo-Catholicism—Tractarian sacramentalism, ecclesiology, and ritualism—further formed Rossetti's deepest normative notions and images, also for her poetry.[2]

As in the Barrett Browning chapters, my attention to religious practice, formation, and poetics includes explications of both the enabling and the challenging dimensions of religious identity for a woman in the nineteenth century. Specifically, my discussion of Rossetti's religious imaginary and poetics revolves around three key issues: first, how poetry, a verbal art, might analogize worship that values manifestation (sacrament) as much as or more than proclamation (word); second, how that same verbal art might also be responsive to the visual and symbolic emphases of high ecclesiology; and third, how a woman participant in a ritualist service—one who observes rather than enacts the rituals limited to men—might respond to Anglo-Catholicism's structures of spiritual authority and its regard for the communion of saints. In the first instance, I propose that historic Anglican worship and, later, Tractarian developments shape a sensibility of encounter and discipleship that leads to a religious poetry whose central motif or force is ontological more than (not rather than) epistemological or ethical, and that takes mystery and uncertainty as a gift, not a problem. Narrowly, this orientation compels Rossetti's repeated use of a limited number of poetic genres; broadly, it effects a poetry that not only uses Tractarian analogical strategies but also is itself similarity-in-difference to the Anglican/Anglo-Catholic liturgy. In the second instance, I propose that Rossetti accepted the principle of verbal reserve but also capitalized on the rich ecclesiological tradition in her church to maximize the possibilities of poetic structure and aesthetics. Within the created, devotional space of the poem, the page, and the book, her spare verbal art paradoxically achieves a resonance that echoes the visual richness of Anglo-Catholic ecclesiology. One might expect a poetry generated by such lavish visuals to be effusive in language or symbolism, but Rossetti did not respond to her liturgical setting by reproducing it in verbal form. Instead, she multiplied the effects of seemingly simple strategies, such as slight material effects, allusive biblical phrases, and slight echoes of well-known works by predecessors, to make them yield a kind of abundance. Turning to the third question, I suggest that Rossetti's ritualist experience as an unmarked lay worshipper (a position also occupied by many men) served as an impetus to her poetic reenvisioning of the worshipping community. Such reenvisioning was made necessary by the increasing disharmony between the Anglo-Catholic ideal of the communion of saints and actual practices that led to heightened exclusivity of place and person during worship. Addressing the difficulties of community, Rossetti resembles both other Anglo-Catholic writers and non-religious Victorian writers, all of whom expressed concern with how community could be sustained in an increasingly individualistic age. Her strategy was to focus on the less visible, abstracted concept of the catholic, apostolic church rather than on the visible community, in order to critique ineffective current practices while illustrating hope for the communion of saints.

Forming the Anglican Imaginary: A Liturgy of Encounter, Discipleship, and Communion

The bare facts of Rossetti's church life are these: Rossetti was baptized as a child in the Anglican Church. She began attending Christ Church, Albany Street, London, in 1843, at age twelve, and was confirmed there two years later, at age fourteen. She continued to worship in this church until 1876, after which, having moved to Torrington Place, she attended Christ Church, Woburn Square, till her death in 1894. Her funeral and memorial service were held in this latter place. Rossetti attended services occasionally elsewhere, such as at Birchington Church when her brother Dante died in that town, or at St. Luke's in Torquay when visiting there, but essentially her worship life centered around the two Christ Churches, both deeply influenced by the nineteenth-century movements discussed later in this chapter, but both also Anglican before anything else.

Historic Anglican worship consists of three services—outlined in *The Book of Common Prayer* as Morning Prayer, Evening Prayer, and Holy Communion—but in this project I focus on the last because its inclusion of the sacrament best prepares the way for understanding Anglo-Catholicism, with its even greater emphasis on manifestation and communion. Further, because Rossetti participated in the Communion liturgy twice a week for most of her life, it can justifiably be selected from among the three services as formative for her imaginary and poetics. This Communion service can best be imagined, not as a circle with Scripture and sermon at the core, as in the Congregationalist service, but as progressing in three waves or movements, from preparation to Word to sacrament. As we will see, nineteenth-century Anglo-Catholicism disturbed the traditionally even treatment of Word and Communion in this service by emphasizing the sacrament, but the threefold movement of the historic liturgy already lent itself to the possibility of viewing Communion as the chief end of the service, the point toward which all other elements led. (In Dissenting traditions, where the Lord's Supper was inserted only occasionally into a service that more often proceeded without it, such a view was less likely to arise.) So in this chapter I discuss the Anglican Communion service as a movement toward sacrament, toward an ever-greater sense of God's manifestation.

Indeed, the Anglican construal of the church building as a holy space set apart from the world already points, if subtly, toward the sense of encounter, devotion, and communion with God that pervades the celebration of the sacrament at the end of the liturgy. Unlike Dissenters, Anglicans consecrated their buildings for religious purposes, using the Form of Consecrating Churches.[3] According to this form, consecration can occur only when the church community believes the building will be used for worship in perpetuity. In other words, once constituted as holy, it may not be put to nonsacred use. If the community has any doubt about perpetual use (for example, if the land is not free from debt), the building can only be dedicated, not consecrated. Consecration consists of a series of prayers asking that God send his presence and favor on the building "now set apart to [his] service." The prayer continues, "Let us always approach Thy holy courts with reverence and godly fear; let us behave ourselves in Thy sanctuary as mindful of Thine especial presence." Consecrated, the building represents God's dwelling among people, and worship must be performed within it on a daily basis, by the clergy if not by an entire congregation (thus the daily offices of Morning and Evening Prayer). For an Anglican to enter church, therefore, means already something significantly different from a Dissenter's entering of church. It is a stepping into God's presence. It requires a devotional orientation before the liturgy proper even commences. Later in the chapter, when I turn to the ecclesiologist agenda to heighten the sacramentality of church space, we will see how attentive Rossetti is to her devotional environment. For now, I note only that this attention is in keeping with what Diane D'Amico reveals about the close connections between the physical space of Rossetti's home in Torrington Square and the imagined space of her poetry.[4]

Having entered the consecrated church space, the Anglican worshipper engaged a liturgy comprising essentially three movements: the introit (introduction or entrance), the liturgy of the Word, and the liturgy of the Communion.[5] Traditionally, the introit consists of a psalm sung while the priest processes toward the altar; the recitation by the priest of the Lord's Prayer and the Collect (prayer) for Purity; the reading of the Ten Commandments by the priest, with the congregation responding after each commandment, "Lord, have mercy upon us, and incline our hearts to keep this law"; and, if desired, a prayer for the queen. The liturgy of the Word that then follows includes the collect (prayer) of the day; readings from two portions of Scripture (an epistle or lesson, and a gospel) with possibly another psalm or hymn between the readings; recitation or singing of the Nicene Creed by priest and people; and the sermon. The liturgy of the Communion that follows next is itself constituted by three sections: the offertory, the thanksgiving, and the communion.[6]

In the offertory, the people offer first their financial gifts for the church and the poor, while the priest places bread and wine alongside the gifts on the table for the sacrament; the people then offer prayers aloud or silently for the church universal. The priest follows with a prayer of intercession, petitioning God to accept the offerings, inspire the church to holy living, and bless the leaders of nations and churches; after this, he calls those who will communicate to come forward to the chancel area and kneel. All who do so recite a prayer of confession and receive absolution and words of comfort from Scripture.

The second movement of this section, now often named in the prayer book as "Thanksgiving and Consecration," begins with a short exchange between priest and people:

> Priest: Lift up your hearts;
> People: We lift them up unto the Lord.
> Priest: Let us give thanks unto our Lord God;
> People: It is meet and right so to do.

Thanksgiving then proceeds: the priest prays, "It is very meet, right, and our bounden duty, that we should at all times, and in all places, give thanks unto thee, O Lord, Holy Father, Almighty, Everlasting God." He then speaks the proper preface for the day (that is, the occasion for thanksgiving noted in the prayer book), followed by the words, "Therefore with Angels and Archangels, and with all the company of heaven, we laud and magnify thy glorious Name; evermore praising thee and saying Holy, holy, holy, Lord God of hosts, heaven and earth are full of thy glory. Glory be to thee, O Lord Most High." The priest then leads in the prayer of consecration for the bread and wine. During this prayer, he recites the words of institution for the sacrament from Scripture, prays that the communicants "may be partakers of [Christ's] most blessed Body and Blood," and breaks the bread, laying his hands on bread and cup.

Only then does the third and final movement of the liturgy of the Communion, and of the whole service, begin, when the bread and wine are actually distributed and consumed. The priest speaks to each kneeling communicant individually, as he gives the bread and wine to each one: "Take and eat in remembrance that Christ died for thee, and feed on him in thy heart by faith with thanksgiving"; and "Drink this in remembrance that Christ's Blood was shed for thee, and be thankful." During the communion time, a hymn or anthem may be sung, especially if there are many communicants. When all the communicants have returned to their seats in the nave, the Lord's Prayer is recited together, and the priest petitions God once more that they may all live in his grace. After the Gloria is said or sung, he speaks the parting blessing to the people: "The peace of God, which passeth all understanding, keep your hearts and minds in the knowledge and love of God, and of his son Jesus Christ our Lord: and the blessing of God Almighty, the Father, the Son, and the Holy Ghost, be amongst you and remain with you always. Amen."

This ends the Communion service, as it was conducted from the sixteenth century into the twentieth, and as Rossetti participated in it upwards of three thousand times in her life. What effect might such a liturgy have on the formation of the religious imaginary? Perhaps what strikes one first when comparing this liturgy to the ones in which Barrett Browning participated is how much less independence of language there is in the service. The prayers and Scripture readings are all assigned by the prayer book, the people's responses and even most of the priest's words are also scripted by the prayer book, and the sermon, too, is either read from a collection of approved homilies or based on the text assigned in the prayer book for that day. In this liturgy, to speak is not primarily to investigate or to discover, not even primarily to exhort, but to dwell in, to breathe life again and again into old or familiar words. The words of worship follow a set pattern because the fundamental structures of the world, the fundamental relationships between people and God, remain ever the same. The liturgy calls the participant to remember and dwell in the larger patterns of relationship.

Further, regular engagement in this threefold liturgy impresses on the participant a sense of life as a spiritual journey, a daily molding of oneself into the pattern of preparation, reception, and meditation. We might say that the essential (though not the only) question evoked for the Congregationalist liturgical participant is "What must I then do?" but the central (not the only) question evoked for the Anglican worshipper is "Who must we then be?" All the elements of the Anglican Communion liturgy encourage the believer toward communal, contemplative, and receptive modes of *shaping* and *being*. This is not to say the liturgy instills passivity or erases the individual but that its primary orientation is toward encounter with the God who manifests himself in Word and sacrament, an encounter that shapes and reshapes worshippers in their spiritual journey. In designating short periods for silence during the service, the prayer book acknowledges the importance of and preparation required for such encountering.

The attunement toward remembering and reshaping forms and is formed by the distinctive characteristics of the prayers, Scripture readings, and sermon. The prayers—or collects, as they are called in the prayer book (because they collect the people's prayers into a single expression)—form an important part of the Anglican texture of worship, their words, rhythms, patterns, and images repeatedly heard, sung, and spoken, imprinting the very body of the worshipper over time. According to David A. deSilva, the collects revolve around five themes or points of training: desire what God desires; distinguish between temporal and eternal; become more Christlike; become a unified people of God; and depend on God's grace.[7] In speaking or hearing these collects, the worshipper assumes several different postures toward God throughout the service: praise, thanksgiving, confession, petition. Each posture has its place, its appropriate moment; some of them involve the actual physical posture of kneeling, while others do not. All the collects differ qualitatively from the long, loose, and unpredictable prayers of many Dissenting ministers. For example, the Collect for Purity that begins every Communion service reads, "Almighty God, unto whom all hearts be open, all desires known, and from whom no secrets are hid: Cleanse the thoughts of our hearts by the inspiration of thy Holy Spirit, that we may perfectly love thee, and worthily magnify thy holy Name; through Christ our Lord. Amen." Invocation and petition in a single sentence, Trinitarian structure, contracted repetition, balanced prepositional phrases and clauses, stressed endings, biblical language: the collect is a model for any compressed devotional expression.

For Rossetti, the collects served as models for religious poetry in their compressed form, their biblically rich language, and their themes. Rossetti certainly wrote some long and powerful narrative poems, such as "Goblin Market" and "The Prince's Progress," but from her first publications to her last, she consistently identified her short, intense, nonnarrative poems as her devotional or religious pieces. For religious work, she most frequently chose sonnets, roundels, and other compact forms, rather than the lyrical dramas or lyric-epic-narratives that figure largely in Barrett Browning's midcareer religious poems. As concentrated moments rather than extended narratives or expositions, these more compact forms suited a religious poet who imagined God more as manifested than proclaimed and who envisioned life as a spiritual journey involving various postures of petition or praise. Victorian essayists even suggested that the sonnet (and, by implication, other compact poetic forms) required more moral discipline than dramatic or epic forms, the demand for more room being a symptom of undisciplined feelings.[8] Moreover, Alison Chapman writes, for the Victorians especially, although "the sonnet is analogous to the small and the beautiful, it transforms and transcends its small size."[9] In the collects of the liturgy, Rossetti could see just how the small and the beautiful could transcend its space. In like manner, her religious poems use mostly short, precise forms to create or re-create intense prayer-like moments in the believer's life. The next chapter examines especially sonnets and roundels in this regard, but even a poem with a less set form demonstrates the compression and biblical texture of Rossetti's prayer-poems. Indeed, the first tercet of the following poem suffices to illustrate, though I give the poem in full:

> Lord, make me pure:
> Only the pure shall see Thee as Thou art
> And shall endure.
> Lord, bring me low;
> For Thou were lowly in Thy blessed heart:
> Lord, keep me so.[10]

In this short lyric, Rossetti shifts one of the beatitudes spoken by Jesus in the Sermon on the Mount ("Blessed are the pure in heart: for they shall see God") from its original declarative form into a prayer. In extending the beatitude's second clause, she draws on 1 John 3:2–3: "[W]hen he shall appear, we shall be like him; for we shall see him as he is. And every man that hath this hope in him purifieth himself, even as he is pure." And possibly alluding to Jesus's phrase that "he that shall endure unto the end, the same shall be saved" (Matthew 24:13), she concludes the first petition of her short prayer with "And shall endure," words that recall the struggles of this life as well as the promise of a future face to face with God. In a single sentence of sixteen words, then, Rossetti blends at least three biblical texts into what might be called her own collect for purity, the whole transcending the sum of its parts.

Liturgical Scripture reading and sermon also had a formative impact on Rossetti's religious imaginary, though not the same way as in Barrett Browning's experience. For the Anglican churchgoer, there were no surprises as to the readings of the day. *The Book of Common Prayer* designated the passages to be read on each Sunday or holy day of the year; the priest did not choose his own text. There is a subtle message here: in the Anglican experience, neither priest nor people initiate a scriptural exposition; there is no seeking of a suitable message. Instead, the historic church brings Scripture to the people, who know themselves to be hearing the same Word as read that day the previous year, and the previous generation, and the one before that. Scripture reading in the Anglican service bespeaks continuity with the saints of all ages: the same people of God receiving the same comfort or instruction in the same words, for generations. While the Congregationalist approach to the Bible tended toward exegesis and application (lead out the meaning and find the significance), the Anglican approach tended toward reception (receive the truth again and again, and it will work its effects). As we will see in the second portion of this chapter, the Tractarians developed this sensibility into a hermeneutics of typology and analogy that became deeply formative for Rossetti's religious language and imagination. But the traditional Anglican sermon, though important for its further dwelling on the scriptural themes of the day, did not usually garner, from Rossetti or Anglicans generally, the kind of attention it did in Dissenting services. (John Keble's 1833 Assize sermon, a notable exception to this statement, garnered attention more for its national political import than its religious sensibility.) One does not read of an Anglican going to "hear the preacher." Indeed, the offices of Morning and Evening Prayer did not even require a sermon, as long as Scripture was read.

In addition to these models of form and method, the Anglican service, if conducted according to prayer book guidelines, also impressed upon participants a deep sense of community. Almost the only moment of individuation in the service occurs as each communicant singly accepts the bread and wine from the hand of the priest, who speaks directly to him or her at that moment; even then, the words spoken to each communicant are the same. For the rest of the service, the people participate as a group, a single body (this practice sometimes lapsed in communities of weak literacy or for other reasons, as I discuss later, but it was the norm). They plead for mercy together during the recitation of the Ten Commandments (which, James Smith writes, indicate that worship is "not just practice for eternal bliss [but] for temporal, embodied human *community*"); after the readings from Scripture, they together recite the Creed (which Smith calls a "*citizenship*-renewal ceremony");[11] they confess their sins together in the collect before Communion; they give praise together in the Sanctus and in other components of the thanksgiving movement; they recite the Lord's Prayer together before departing into the world—all of this in addition to singing together the psalms, often understood as the voice of the church rather than a single speaker. The Anglican liturgy, in short, enacts a temporal, embodied communion of saints through its patterns of communal voicing. Moreover, all of these voiced elements reinforce the historic nature of the communion of saints: not merely the people presently gathered but the worshipping community of all ages, from the Jewish people at Mount Sinai (the Ten Commandments) to the early Christian church (the Creed) to the church gathered around the first *Book of Common Prayer* in the sixteenth century.

Near the end of *The Face of the Deep*, her prose commentary on the book of Revelation, Rossetti cites a phrase from Revelation 22:16 to explain why the individual must belong to a church community and why she chose the church community she did: "It is 'in the churches' that these things [the characteristics of Christ] are testified. To myself it is in the beloved Anglican Church of my Baptism: a living branch of that one Holy Catholic Apostolic Church which is authoritatively commended and endeared to every Christian by the Word of God."[12] Rossetti evokes baptism's promise and formation of "a new person and a new people" to affirm the traditional Christian confession of the church as a community of believers,[13] and she places her present church in a historic framework. For her, for Anglicans generally, and especially for Anglo-Catholics, community-consciousness meant not only participation in a present gathering but also a belonging to a centuries-old community of men and women who, together with present believers, constituted the church of Christ. Rossetti reveals this consciousness also in the first paragraph of *The Face of the Deep:* "At the end of 1800 years we are still . . . starting in fellowship of patience with that blessed John who owns all Christians as his brethren" (FD, 9). Her poetry is imbued with a deep sense of this "fellowship of patience," of being in communion even across divides of time, place, and disposition, as these few lines attest, first from a poem in which the speaker takes courage herself from remembering the saints who have preceded her:

> Chastened not slain, cast down but not destroyed:—
> If thus Thy Saints have struggled home to peace,
> Why should not I take heart to be as they?
> They too pent passions in a house of clay.
>
> (CP, 493.9–12)

and second, from a poem in which the speaker encourages someone else to strain toward the saints with whom the speaker has dialogue:

> Strain up thy hope in glad perpetual green
> To scale the exceeding height where all saints dwell.
> —Saints, it is well with you?—Yea, it is well.—
>
> (CP, 493.3–5)

Such consciousness of spiritual community was fostered by the Anglican Communion liturgy, with its layers of communion reference: the entire service, the third portion of the service, and the sacrament itself.

In fact, community-consciousness and the sacramental act had been inextricably bound together in the Anglican imaginary since the sixteenth-century Reformation. Peter Foley explains that historically the Anglican approach to communion was part of the reformers' determination to reverse the medieval church's emphasis on the act of consecration, with its concomitant veneration of the host. Personal piety, marked by veneration of objects, wrongly overrode the sacrament's purpose of providing spiritual nourishment for the community *as* a community, according to the reformers. Thus, Anglicanism from the start emphasized the sacrament of bread and wine as an act of communion, a participation not only in Christ but in the body of Christ, the church.[14] Sacramental fellowship was (and is) as important to the

Anglican communicant as the sacramental encounter with Christ. For this reason, there is no private communion in the Anglican Church.[15] Also for this reason, Anglicans tend to use the word *communion* rather than *the Lord's Supper* to name this sacrament.

Foley continues his consideration of Anglican communion by noting that Richard Hooker's sixteenth-century explication of the sacrament long constituted the traditional Anglican approach: an emphasis on the real spiritual (not physical) presence of Christ in the bread and wine, as long as the communicant received that bread and wine in faith. Christ would not be spiritually present in the bread and wine consumed by those who lacked faith. Though God's offer of grace was unconditional, its acceptance depended on the recipient.[16] This receptionist understanding partly corresponded to the new (shifted) nineteenth-century Congregationalist theology of the sacrament, but the Anglican approach also differed significantly from the memorialist position in holding to the real presence of Christ. Thus, Rossetti's perception of the sacrament differed markedly from Barrett Browning's, even before we take into account the influence of Tractarian and ecclesiological sacramentality. Rossetti's religious poetry is saturated with the sense of communion, of both the real presence of Christ and the fellowship of all believers. Rossetti turned to this historic Anglican sense of the sacrament when the liturgical practices of Anglo-Catholicism began paradoxically to complicate its sacramental devotion. While she valued the increased sense of manifestation and the heightened reverence that the Tractarians, ecclesiologists, and ritualists brought to worship, she simultaneously envisioned a community unfractured by the distinctions increasingly being built into her Anglo-Catholic church.

In sum, the Anglican religious imaginary—and poetry generated by this imaginary—is characterized by attunement to encounter with the divine, an encounter that arises from and prompts a dwelling within the patterns of relationship; it leads to discipleship, to a spiritual journey, to formations of self that take place within community. Such dwelling in and such spiritual formations call for contemplative modes of expression, for multiple meditative moments and forms that, taken together, gesture toward spiritual progress, however fluctuating. From this groundwork on the Anglican religious imaginary, I now deepen, in turn, the three issues sketched in the opening pages of this chapter by taking up the Tractarian, ecclesiological, and ritualist movements within Anglicanism, all of which further impacted Rossetti's imaginary and poetry. The next section explores the deepening sense of manifestation and discipleship that led to an analogical imagination prompted by sacramentalism, the heightening of aesthetics encouraged by the ecclesiologists, and the communion of saints emphasized by the ritualists.

The Analogical Imagination, Aesthetics, and the Communion of Saints

To this point I have written of the Anglican liturgy as if all members of the Established Church, all of whom used *The Book of Common Prayer* in worship, experienced or understood it the same way. But, as is well known, despite this shared liturgy, the Established Church in the nineteenth century found itself increasingly divided in interpretation and practice. Philip Davis summarizes W. J. Conybeare's 1853 description of the Established Church as consisting of three parties: "[T]he Low Church Evangelicals who believed in Bible-centred literalism, enthusiastic individual conversion experiences, and plain services; the Anglican High Churchmen who believed in the Church, its formal traditions, liturgies, and sacraments; and in between the two the Broad Churchmen who, committed to a truly wide national establishment, responded to developments in contemporary biblical and scientific studies by being liberal in theology."[17] Although these parties existed before the 1830s, they did so within a consensus that accepted "the essentially Protestant nature of the Church of England."[18] This consensus disappeared in the mid- to-late nineteenth century, as Anglo-Catholics, including Rossetti, turned increasingly toward ideas and practices associated with the Roman Church and so set themselves apart from not only Dissenters but also Evangelicals within the Established Church.

The High Church party itself included three identifiable movements: Tractarianism, ecclesiology, and ritualism. Though sometimes discussed today as if synonymous, these were different, though related, movements: Tractarianism was concerned primarily with theological concepts, ecclesiology with the liturgical environment, and ritualism with liturgical practice— all of these in relation to devotion.[19] Each movement had a formative impact on Rossetti's religious imaginary, and the remainder of this chapter explores each movement's generative and/or challenging dimensions for a woman congregant's religious poetics. Organizationally, then, this section unfolds by church movement and related issue rather than strictly by liturgical element, as heretofore; but liturgical elements remain a key focus, because thematically, the section demonstrates how the formations of historic Anglican worship outlined above shifted or deepened under each religious movement to give a Tractarian and Anglo-Catholic cast to Rossetti's underlying Anglican imaginary.

Tractarianism and the Analogical Imagination

The Tractarian movement in the Anglican Church deepened the historic Anglican inclination toward manifestation as God's primary mode of communication, through its increasing emphasis on sacrament, particularly the sacrament of Communion. Because Tractarianism was a theological rather than liturgical movement, worship practices themselves did not change because of it. However much the increasing reverence for sacrament and the extended reach of sacramental interpretation might have colored the atmosphere of services conducted by Tractarian clergyman, we cannot really speak of Tractarian liturgical formations. My attention to the generative effects for poetry of Anglo-Catholic liturgy, therefore, is reserved for the sections on ecclesiology and ritualism. However, from its sacramentalism, Tractarianism fostered an analogical imagination that shaped its approach to the Bible and was powerfully generative for Rossetti's religious-poetic work.

As mentioned in an earlier chapter, the period from 1820 to 1850 saw Protestant and Roman Catholic churches alike asserting their ties to the Christian church of antiquity, not least because after Catholic Emancipation, both sides felt an increased need to defend their heritage vis-à-vis the other.[20] The Tractarian movement was part of this larger religious and cultural situation. More immediately, it was a reaction to Parliament's decision to disestablish the Church of England in Roman Catholic Ireland. The Tractarian leaders objected, asserting that the Church was not a branch of the Protestant state, to be manipulated at the state's will, but preexistent to it. Consequently, they anchored the Church of England in the apostolic age rather than in the founding of England as a Protestant nation. In Gerald Parsons's words, they "set out, consciously and deliberately . . . to deny the essentially Protestant nature, character and identity of the Church of England and asserted instead its Catholic roots, traditions and identity. They stressed the authority of the church, of the priesthood, of the sacramental system, and of the early Christian Fathers."[21] In articulating the ancient, spiritual authority of the church and the priesthood, passed on through the ages through the process of ordination, and in stressing not only the sacraments but also a sacramental system, the Tractarians did not so much create new principles in the Anglican Church as extend the reach or shift the focus of existing ones.

As perhaps their primary principle, the Tractarians affirmed that God's deepest revelation of himself lay not in the Bible or the preaching but in sacrament, "the archetypal pattern for God's communication of himself to men."[22] Consequently, Tractarians could not accept the Dissenting valuation of the sermon as the focal point of the service. Rather, they maintained that while the sermon led the hearer toward a union with Christ, actual union could be effected only in sacrament itself, since that is where God manifests himself most directly.[23] They called for greater reverence for the sacrament of Communion, especially for the bread and wine as manifestations of Christ incarnate. This led them to negate the traditional view of the real presence of Christ in the elements only for those who partook in faith in favor of the view that, during the moment of consecration, Christ became truly present in the elements, in spiritual form, and remained so, no matter who the recipient. Although God's grace would be given only to the believer, the unbelieving participant could not cancel the real presence itself. This new doctrine occasioned much debate—for example, as to whether or not the host should be venerated—but its import for the Tractarians was essentially to affirm the power of the divine presence in material objects, whether or not an individual admitted or perceived it.

As has been well recognized in literary criticism by now, from this perception of a real sacramental presence, itself built on the doctrine of the incarnation, the Tractarians developed their sense of a more widespread divine indwelling (Rowell, *Vision*, 14). That is, they understood Christ's taking on of human form, and his repeated manifestation in bread and wine at Communion, to be symbolic of a larger reality in which God was immanent in every aspect of the natural world. All material things were sacramental— embodied and able to manifest divine grace. As John Henry Newman, one of the first and leading Tractarians, put it, the sacramental system "is the doctrine that material phenomena are both the type and instruments of real things unseen."[24] Although this immanence could not be seen or touched, it could be apprehended by the devout.

Such apprehension required spiritual commitment and growth. G. B. Tennyson explains how this sensibility was expressed in the Tractarian principle of reserve: "The idea of Reserve is that since God is ultimately incomprehensible, we can know Him only indirectly; His truth is hidden and given to us only in a manner suited to our capacities for apprehending it." Further, "it is both unnecessary and undesirable that God and religious truth generally should be disclosed in their fullness at once to all regardless of the differing capacities of individuals to apprehend such things. God Himself in His economy has only gradually in time revealed such things as we know about Him." As "the disposition and understanding of the recipient mature," religious truth is gradually revealed.[25]

How does God economically and gradually reveal his incomprehensible self? The Tractarians held that he did so by analogy, both in Scripture and in the world. In Rossetti criticism, analogy remains underexplored compared to reserve, and it sometimes incorrectly slips into synonymity with typology, which the Tractarians also practiced. But the two differ subtly. To practice typology is to read the Hebrew or Old Testament as the "harbinger of the New" rather than the "history of the progressive revelation of the covenant."[26] More specifically, it is to read Christ back into the Hebrew Scriptures, such that objects and events in the earlier writings function as types for Christ (for example, manna in the wilderness is a type of Christ, the living bread). Analogy reaches further and deeper than such type-to-antitype reading. In defining analogy, James Buchanan, in his 1864 *Analogy, Considered as a Guide to Truth, and Applied as an Aid to Faith*, distinguishes the analogous from the univocal and the equivocal. Analogy, he explains, neither claims exact resemblance (univocity) nor depends on ambiguity (equivocity); instead, analogy implies "a real resemblance in some respects, while . . . a real difference in others."[27] It does not merely imagine a relation between objects of thought but observes real similarities that inhere in the objects themselves. Analogy in this sense is "intimate and radical" (57) and something other than illustration or even metaphor. It "is made manifest" (65) only to the close observer and is a legitimate ground for reasoning or even proof (57, 62). David Tracy takes up this sense of analogy in *The Analogical Imagination: Christian Theology and the Culture of Pluralism*, from which I quote at the outset of this chapter. Tracy's articulation of analogical language bears striking similarities to Buchanan's:

> [Analogical language is] a language of ordered relationships articulating similarity-in-difference. The order among the relationships is constituted by the distinct but similar relationships of each analogue to some primary focal meaning, some prime analogue. A principal aim of all properly analogical languages is the production of some order, at the limit, some harmony to the several analogues, the similarities-in-difference, constituting the whole of reality. The order is developed by explicating the analogous relationships among various realities (self, others, world, God), by clarifying the relationship of each to the primary analogue. . . . Negations of any

> claims to full adequacy (for example, any attempts at exhaustive, univocal meanings in any analogue) are negations to assure that the similarities remain similarities-in-difference . . . [and] to negate any slackening of the sense of radical mystery. (409)

Analogical language, that is, springs from an imaginary seeking harmony in the whole of reality, believing that harmony is possible because all realities tie back, in some mysterious way, to some core object or event. It is not merely that certain objects or events serve as types for something greater, as in typological interpretive practice. Rather, the analogical imagination is an entire attunement, a way of coming to the world alert, as it were, for all manifestations of order, harmony, and relationship, however veiled behind difference. Yet difference remains key to analogical thought or language. Harmony and relationship do not erase difference but bridge it by seeing it as various expressions of the same analogue—thus Tracy's expression "distinct but similar."

In the Tractarian case, the prime analogue that gives harmony to all other analogues is the incarnated Christ. This prime analogue is not merely typified in particular objects or events (though he is that, too) but is prime analogue to Scripture and the world *in their entirety*. To reverse the phrase, the Bible and the world are, in their entirety, analogues of Christ; even if they do not tell directly about him, they *are*, inherently, in all their variety, Christ manifestations. They are woven through with difference—even radical and mysterious difference—yet they ultimately cohere in Christ and manifest him. As Isaac Williams explains about the Bible in Tract 87 of *Tracts for the Times*,

> [O]ur blessed LORD is as it were, throughout the inspired writings, hiding and concealing Himself, and going about . . . seeking to whom He may disclose Himself: . . . [T]here are many things in Scripture which might appear common and ordinary accounts, relating to passing events, or words which appear to speak only of temporal wisdom; that our LORD is walking therein and concealing His divinity: in the same manner that we have supposed that in our LORD's ordinary walk and mode of life among men He very studiously and remarkably concealed His ineffable majesty under the appearance of common humanity, accompanied with great goodness. Though these two points are different yet they involve one common principle.[28]

According to Williams, Scripture, like the human body, is a form in which Christ manifests himself, but he does so as behind a veil. Nevertheless, the

Bible, the world, all subjects, are implicitly, ontologically, however veiled, part of a larger whole that always, at bottom, bespeaks God.[29] For this reason, Scripture is akin (though not equal) to sacrament. Like sacrament, it is more a manifestation than a proclamation of God. Indeed, in Tract 80, Williams uses *manifest* or *manifestation* more than twenty times to refer to God's self-communication in Scripture or world; when he uses forms of *proclaim* or *declare*, Williams does so to negate them as God's primary mode of communication. For him and other Tractarians, to read Scripture is not first of all to hear about God or to come to understand him better but to encounter him, to have contact with his being, and so to shape one's own being in response. As Samuel Leuenberger puts it, the Tractarians did not see Scripture as having primarily a "redemptive motif of the justification of sinners before God through the cross of Jesus Christ, but rather an ontological motif of the deification of man's nature as the fruit of the incarnation of God in His Son."[30] Leuenberger is not ascribing to Tractarians the belief that humans possessed some spark of the divine; his point, rather, is that they read Scripture not primarily for its *narrative* of redemption but for its *picturing* of who God is and what the individual and community should be in response.

Such a stance toward Scripture differed significantly from the Congregationalists' or, more generally, the Dissenters' conviction that the Bible progressed as a narrative of God's saving work from first creation to new creation and that it revealed God plainly to anyone who read it seriously. Indeed, whereas Congregationalists stressed that the individual believer could read and interpret Scripture responsibly, the Tractarians held that Scripture "cannot be said to possess such a clarity and plainness that the individual by himself is able to find out the doctrine hidden in it."[31] Keble, for example, in Tract 89 criticizes "the unhappy and untenable supposition, that the truth [of Scripture], if we can at all approach it, must be clear and plain to us throughout, and leave nothing unaccounted for."[32] Rossetti expresses this same stance when she writes, "Our <sole> duty towards the Bible is to obey its teaching in faith. I do *not* think we are bound to understand or account for all its utterances. I am waiting for knowledge when faith will no longer be required of me."[33] These respective beliefs about Scripture generate, I argue, different responsive practices, certainly different poetic practices. In Barrett Browning's "The Seraphim" or "A Drama of Exile," the speakers move from confusion or despair toward knowledge; in the end, they understand something about the narrative of salvation, a narrative in which they have a place, that they did not understand when the poem opened. As the next chapter demonstrates, Rossetti's religious poetry almost never moves this way. It works instead by glancing off connections, building harmonies, advancing and retreating, seeking similarity-in-difference, weaving its own fabric or veil behind which God might be now hiding, now disclosing himself. Consequently, the effusive sentimentalism that can appear in poets as critically and religiously diverse as Barrett Browning and Procter seldom, if ever, marks Rossetti's poetry. Rather, Rowan Williams's description of the late-nineteenth-century bishop B. F. Westcott's approach to the Bible could be taken instead as a description of Rossetti's poetry (Westcott delivered "An Appreciation of Christina Rossetti" at her memorial service in 1896). Westcott saw the Bible as something "like a massive canvas depicting the nature of the giver. You need to stand back again and again to see the whole; but you also need to see how that whole is constructed; you have to crawl over its surface inch by inch, not stopping to abstract and frame one section of that surface, but tracing the connections that, detail by detail, make up the whole. Interpretation for the believer is thus a shuttling between the closest possible reading of the text, with all the resources available, and the repeated attempt to find words to articulate the complex unity that is being uncovered."[34] Rossetti's religious poetry behaves this way.

Serving as a brief example are some of the ways in which Rossetti uses dove imagery across her last volume of poems. As in Matthew 3:16, where the Holy Spirit descends in the form of a dove on Jesus at his baptism as a voice speaks from heaven, the dove for Rossetti is sometimes the third person of the Trinity, as when the speaker prays in "Trinity Sunday," "O Christ the Lamb, O Holy Ghost the Dove, / Reveal the Almighty Father unto us" (CP, 443.5–6). As Holy Spirit, this was the Dove involved in the conception of Jesus: "The Lamb that indwelt by the Dove / Was spotless and holy and mild" (CP, 445.12–13). But elsewhere the dove represents for Rossetti not the third but the second person of the Trinity, the Son. In "Advent Sunday," Rossetti first uses numerous biblical images to clarify that the bridegroom and bride of the poem refer to Christ and the church. She then uses language from Song of Solomon to describe them: "His Eyes are as a Dove's, and she's Dove-eyed" (CP, 420.14; see Song of Solomon 1:15, 4:1, 5:12). Then, a few poems later, we read of John the apostle (depicted as an eagle), saying "Beloved, let us love," followed by the line, "Voice of an eagle, yea, Voice of the Dove" (CP, 424.4, 5), and we understand that now Christ is not merely being likened to a dove but *is* the Dove (that is, Christ's command to love underlies John's injunction, the Dove's behind the eagle's). Yet Rossetti does not drop the association between dove and church/bride: "Thy fainting spouse, yet still Thy spouse; / Thy trembling dove, yet still Thy dove" (CP, 416.1–2). Indeed, believers seem to be doves only because they take their pattern from the Christ-Dove, else they could not be unspotted: "Unspotted doves to wait on the one Dove / To whom Love saith, 'Be with Me where I am'" (CP, 425.2–3). But often the trembling dove refers to the speaker as an individual rather than the church as a whole, as in "O my King and my heart's own choice, / Stretch Thy Hand to Thy fluttering dove" (CP, 415.5–6)—though in low moments, the speaker might doubt her dove-ness:

> Thy lovely saints do bring Thee love,
>   Incense and joy and gold;
> Fair star with star, fair dove with dove,
>   Beloved by Thee of old.
> I, Master, neither star nor dove,
>   Have brought Thee sins and tears.
>
> (CP, 396–7.1–6)

But such doubts are usually overcome by remembering the love of Christ, his wounded hand that saved the weak analogized to Noah's hand in bringing the dove to safety (see Genesis 8:8–9):

> As the dove which found no rest
>   For the sole of her foot, flew back
> To the ark her only nest
> . . . .
> Because Noah put forth his hand,
>   Drew her in from ruin and wrack,
> . . . .
>
> So my spirit, like that dove,
>   Fleeth away to an ark
> Where dwelleth a Heart of Love,
>   A Hand pierced to save[.]
>
> (CP, 409.1–3, 5–6, 9–12)

As this gathering of dove lines from across Rossetti's religious poetry shows, Rossetti's imagery constantly shifts, though it is also constantly rooted in

Scripture. The dove in her poetry seldom means the same from use to use, yet the images interconnect, form a canvas of allusions that do make a coherent whole, because each one either is or ties back in some way to Christ, the prime analogue. Yet there is no drive to explicate. The poet need not explain how, for example, the Dove might be both Holy Spirit and Christ at the same time, not to mention both Dove-eyed church and trembling dove-individual. These multiple realities simply are, and need no accounting. The next chapter extends this example to show in more detail how, generated by an analogical imagination keyed to ontology and to similarity-in-difference, Rossetti's poetry seeks to register divine mystery rather than uncover divine meaning. It looks for and contemplates manifestations of God, valuing, even cherishing, difference yet finding everywhere the same God revealed. It enacts various postures of response to this God and dwells in various spiritual moments. In the end, it becomes its own analogue of the Anglican liturgical experience: that is, an expression of worship that is similarity-in-difference to the church liturgy Rossetti loved.

Ecclesiology and Aesthetics

The second movement in nineteenth-century Anglicanism—ecclesiology—brings us to the second key issue in Rossetti's religious imaginary and, consequently, poetry: namely, how poetry, a verbal art, might be enabled by a worship experience that so strongly emphasizes manifestation through the visual and symbolic. For while the Anglican Communion service reached its highest moment in the actual celebration of the sacrament, the Anglo-Catholic worshipper encountered God-as-manifest immediately upon entering the worship space, thanks primarily to the work of the Cambridge ecclesiologists. Prior to the ecclesiological movement, most Anglicans had a fairly orthodox ecclesiology, a concern to create an "even balance between altar and pulpit, sacrament and preaching."[35] But in the early decades of the century, the altar began to receive more attention than the pulpit, with the ecclesiologists effectively replacing the term *the Lord's Table* (per the prayer book) with the term *altar* to reinforce the sense of Christ's real presence after the consecration and especially to evoke repeatedly the sacrificial nature of Christ's act. (Altar and memorialism, by contrast, are theologically incompatible terms.) Some early-nineteenth-century innovators had already placed the "pulpit and reading-desk on opposite sides of the nave so as to permit a clear view of the altar," then raised the latter "several steps above the rest of the church."[36] But in the 1840s, the Ecclesiological Society took matters much further, determined, along with the Tractarians, to counter a felt "depreciation of the Holy Sacraments, and the undue exaltation of preaching."[37] As James Bentley writes, quoting ecclesiologists of the time, the society intended "to encourage the return of 'sacramentality' in church architecture, so that every aspect of a properly designed place of worship would speak of 'the Blessed Sacraments of the church.'"[38] Or, as Geoffrey Rowell puts it when describing the ecclesiologists' return to medieval Gothic structures as the model for contemporary worship, "Churches were to be not so much auditories for hearing sermons as windows into heaven," designed and decorated to enhance spiritual contemplation through rich visuals.[39] Ordinary parish churches must become more like cathedrals.[40]

In Christ Church, Albany Street, where she worshipped twice weekly for thirty-three years,[41] Rossetti experienced the visual richness of a worship environment attuned to sacramentality; her poetry, I demonstrate in the next chapter, attests to her attentiveness to aesthetic-religious relations. Christ Church underwent at least four major renovation projects over some thirty-five years to conform to the new sacramental vision for church architecture, and Rossetti appears to have approved of the changes. In its original form—a "bare classical galleried" design, according to Paul Thompson[42]—Christ Church was "not even correctly orientated";[43] its altar faced north instead of east (the direction favored by the ecclesiologists because of its association with the rising of the sun/Son). Neither did it have a proper chancel, so important to the ecclesiologists for its distinction of sacred space. Indeed, the *Ecclesiologist* castigated the building in 1845 as "no better than a very mediocre specimen of a modern Italianised town-church."[44] To Geoffrey Tyack's surmise that the original building must "have been austere" (35), Rossetti gives substance in her 1873 comment that "Christ Church is so improved since the old days of its plainness,—to use no stronger word" (*LCR*, 1:419). Whether she had *austerity* or *ugliness* in mind as the stronger word, she applauded the results of the renovation projects; this approval suggests an interest in sacramental aesthetics worth further exploration for its bearing on her religious poetry.

A record of the changes to Christ Church during Rossetti's period of worship there survives in the form of a historical chronicle entitled *The Half-Century of Christ Church, St. Pancras, Albany Street*. This history, written by the second incumbent of the church, Henry W. Burrows, describes the work undertaken in the 1843, 1853, 1865, 1879, and 1883 reconstruction and decoration projects, for which the church sometimes closed temporarily.

According to the *Ecclesiologist* of August 1867, leading Gothic Revival architects R. C. Carpenter and William Butterfield directed the work.[45] Both belonged to the Ecclesiological Society and functioned as "the apostles of the high-church school."[46] Under their instruction and design, laborers enlarged, elevated, and decorated Christ Church's chancel, altar, and sanctuary, respectively. First, the chancel—the area closest in proximity to the sanctuary, which held the altar—received attention. As early as 1843, only six years after Christ Church was built, the ecclesiologists created a "recess" at the ritual east end of the church to redeem the faulty chancel noted by Tyack.[47] The *Ecclesiologist* subsequently observed, "The worthy incumbent [Dodsworth] of this church has given it a more ecclesiastical character, by removing an organ and vestry which stood behind the altar, and thereby providing a chancel of inappropriate depth indeed compared with ancient ones, but still a chancel."[48] In subsequent projects, marble pavement and colored tiles enhanced the chancel further.[49] Next, the altar received attention. Christ Church's east-west interior rectangular design already had the altar in visual alignment with the seating plan, a design that made the increased frequency of Communion services easier to implement, but the pulpit stood in front of the altar.[50] The ecclesiologists did not approve of this arrangement, but they could not merely reverse the placements, since that would situate the pulpit closer to the sanctuary than the altar and thus "imply that the word was more important than the sacrament."[51] Lowering and moving the pulpit to one side and raising the altar by several steps solved the perceived imbalance by giving greater attention to the sacramental space as worthy of visual and devotional attention.[52] These renovations and decorations, in Burrows's opinion, resulted in "the enhanced beauty and dignity of the chancel" (50), now a space in which Holy Communion could be celebrated more worthily and more often than before. As noted, the pulpit received a more reserved place in the nave, to the side of the chancel. Although the pulpit, too, was decorated, it—and by implication, the liturgy of the Word—literally stood aside to the altar, or the liturgy of Communion, to the extent that one Tractarian even allowed that the sermon service might be scantily attended if only the Communion service were not.[53]

After the ecclesiologists had renovated Christ Church's chancel and altar, they paid attention to the font (water receptacle or bowl) used in the church's second sacrament. Burrows writes that this attention arose out of a desire "to express honour and reverence for Holy Baptism" (50). First, the ecclesiologists arranged the font opposite the altar, at the west end of the nave, where the congregation would pass it upon entrance from the lobby.[54] This placement "symboliz[ed] that baptism was the gateway to salvation."[55] Then, to reinforce the sacramental nature of baptism, and especially its connection to Communion, the font in Christ Church was "encased in richer marbles" and inlaid with a "large red cross."[56] When the bowl contained water, then, the font visually signified the apostle Paul's linking of baptism with Christ's death and resurrection: "Therefore we are buried with him by baptism into death: that like as Christ was raised up from the dead by the glory of the Father, even so we also should walk in newness of life." Perhaps the color red, reflected in the baptismal water, also evoked Paul's association of baptism with the Israelites' crossing of the Red Sea.[57] The font decoration, in short, was not art for art's sake but art for sacramentality's sake. Whereas baptism for Barrett Browning was nothing more than a prospective sign—an indicator of the possibility of a later acceptance of Christ as Savior—for Burrows, Anglicans generally, and Tractarians/ecclesiologists especially, baptism was a holy occasion, an entering into the family of God made possible by Christ's sacrifice. This sense of relational identity informs Rossetti's late-life description of the Church of England, already quoted, as the "beloved Anglican Church of my Baptism" (FD, 540). This is not a phrase Barrett Browning would have used, but Rossetti thinks and speaks of church in intimate terms. She uses an endearment and a possessive pronoun to mark her relationship with the church, and by capitalizing *Baptism*, she typographically elevates the sacrament to the same level as *Church*. This sacramental intimacy, reinforced through aesthetics, recurs in her poetry.

The ecclesiologists also paid attention to color and ornaments in the church at large. While the red cross in the baptismal font was permanently embedded in the marble, other decorations were temporary, as Rossetti indicates when she notes that at Christmas 1870, Christ Church "had a new and to me most delightful decoration, a large red cross reared on high in the Chancel arch." She hopes it will "reappear at Easter, though perhaps in different colours" (LCR, 1:340). As early as 1845, the *Ecclesiologist* made clear that its members' promotion of color in church distinguished their expression of Christianity from others': "We would have every inch glowing. Puritans . . . would have every inch colourless."[58] John Mason Neale, a member of the society, elaborated: "A Church is not as it should be, till *every* window is filled with stained glass, till every inch of floor is covered with encaustic tiles, till there is a Roodscreen glowing with the brightest tints and with gold, and, if we would arrive at perfection, the roof and walls must be painted and frescoed."[59] A decorated structure becomes here the necessary space holder of the devotion expressed through the liturgy. In Christ Church, Neale's opinions appear to have been influential, as color abounded in altar frontals, hangings, floor tiles, walls, windows, and ceiling.[60] From floor to ceiling, whether eyes gazed downwards, ahead, or upwards, the interior space of Christ Church was a work of carefully planned art, an appropriately beautiful and reverential environment for the sacramental worship enacted within it. At the same time, the material objects themselves functioned as "types and instruments of real things unseen." Sacramentality in visual form—that is to say, high ecclesiology—clearly shaped the worship experience at Christ Church significantly, perhaps more than any verbal practice did; certainly, the religious impulse of Anglo-Catholic ecclesiologists was deeply centered on the contemplation of space and symbol. And though Rossetti was characteristically reserved, to the point of silence, on many of the changes made in Christ Church, her few remarks indicate that she noticed and approved them.

Finally, despite what may appear as an exaggerated attention to color and design, the ecclesiologists practiced a religious-aesthetic discrimination that actually eliminated symbols or artistic practices formerly deemed appropriate by the church. Anxious to (re)establish the link between the contemporary church and historical Christianity, the ecclesiologists reevaluated the symbols used within the church. For example, while approving the tradition of stained glass windows in the church, even calling for members to commission more such windows as memorials to those who had died,[61] the ecclesiologists carefully considered the themes and subjects of these windows. An article in the *Ecclesiologist* cautioned against the use of such "allegorical figures [as] Faith, Hope, Charity, &c. All such impersonation," it declared, "is unreal and pagan."[62] This particular criticism may have reached Rossetti, for in 1873, she noted to her friend Caroline Gemmer that in Christ Church, "The far-from-beautiful faith-hope-&-charity window has been replaced by (I hope) something better" (*LCR*, 1:419). While the *Ecclesiologist*'s criticism is expressly religious and Rossetti's less apparently so, both demonstrate a willingness to assess traditional religious-aesthetic subjects and to create alternatives.

Worshipping every Sunday and Thursday in this visually rich but carefully planned church environment, Rossetti had ample opportunity to consider the aesthetic dimensions of religion. This environment must have colored her religious imaginary not merely in ways that shaped the aesthetics of her poetry but in less conscious ways as well, imprinting it with the tones of sacramentality, the postures of reverence and contemplation, and a sensibility for beauty notably absent from Barrett Browning's formulation of the ideal church as Truth and Love. From this imaginary, Rossetti created a poetics that gives attention to spatial arrangement and the material effects of the book or page. Of course, all poets pay attention to form and structure, but Rossetti paid attention to these matters for consciously religious purposes, in a way that Barrett Browning did not. The design and appearance of Rossetti's last publication of religious poems (*Verses*) to look like a prayer or hymn book, for example, is not accidental. It communicates a particular religious intention and attitude before the poems are even read, as the next chapter shows in more detail. While a medium as dependent on the word as poetry limited the visual and material effects Rossetti could create, she nevertheless devised opportunities to heighten spatial and visual effects. Just as the elaborate interior arrangements and decorated appearance of Christ Church aimed to create an environment in which the indwelling of God was everywhere signified, so the visual and material effects of Rossetti's poetry in *Verses* keep the reader ever mindful of the devotional space he or she has entered. Visual aesthetics do not merely please the eye, or spatial arrangements one's sense of proportion or balance; rather, these things make religious meaning by creating devotional, even sacramental, space. The environment itself invites the worshipper to enter a particular frame of mind and spirit. Yet Rossetti did not transfer this sensitivity toward material effect into her poetry as a repletion of named objects. In fact, Rossetti's religious poetry as a whole contains very few references to the material objects of the church space. Set against Christ Church's 1891 inventory of furnishings and ornaments—a list including illuminated scrolls, wands of office, cushions, paintings, kneeling carpets, ewers, altar books, framed engravings, ornamental flowerpots, frontals, shrouds, jeweled chalices, palls, purificators, credence table cloths, Communion plates, surplices, and jeweled flagons—Rossetti's ecclesiological (and ritualist) imagery emerges as quite spare.[63] For example, Rossetti's title "Our Church Palms are budding willow twigs" (*CP*, 437) might seem to promise a poem describing the interior of a church adorned with budding branches. A ritualist church might conceivably participate in this traditional mode of commemorating Palm Sunday. But the poem that follows describes not a church but the natural world, "widowed" at Christ's death, then resuming life on Easter morning. The palm-willows are outdoors in Rossetti's poem, their branches "willow green for hope undone" on Good Friday, then budding exactly on Easter Sunday. Though willow buds can appear quickly, this timing is unlikely. The palm rite thus seems to have prompted Rossetti to spiritual reflection, but she seems uninterested in elaborate description of church rituals. Of course, Tractarian reserve itself might preclude a linguistically ornamented poetry and an overt or excessive attention to ceremonial acts and objects. But Rossetti's attention to visual and spatial effects also operated on a different level. Rather than transferring the visual directly into the verbal, Rossetti translated the one into the other, seeking to evoke not the visuals themselves but the effects of their presence.

Further, in her poetry Rossetti imitates the ecclesiological practice of assessing long-established symbols or patterns in her selective response to the practices of religious-poetic predecessors who also pursued a relationship between church space and poetry. She demonstrates this reworking not only in her engagement with memorial windows for her brother Gabriel—the subject of many letters to designer Frederick Shields (see examples in *LCR*, vol. 3)—but also in adapting rather than adopting the poetic practices of Anglican poets such as George Herbert, Isaac Williams, and John Keble, poets whom Mary Arseneau has demonstrated were known to Rossetti.[64] Herbert in *The Temple* and Williams in *The Cathedral* had demonstrated significant architectural interests in composing and arranging their poetry, while Keble in *The Christian Year* had shown his liturgical interests by writing a volume of poetry that closely followed the church calendar.[65] The titles of these volumes disclose their interests immediately. Rossetti, however, was both more reserved in her linguistic choices—she entitled her religious volume simply *Verses*—and more subtle in her religious allusions. The church calendar served as a pattern for one section of her volume, but Rossetti was far from slavish in her inclusions; her architectural and ecclesiological interests were far less rigid than Williams's in particular, since Williams allotted a poem to every corner of the cathedral. Her choices and arrangements echo her predecessors' work but also demonstrate a selectivity and innovation in keeping with the ecclesiological practices manifested in Christ Church, where not only windows but also galleries, pews, the pulpit, and the organ were either discarded or redesigned to achieve a better religious-aesthetic effect.

Ritualism and the Communion of Saints

So far I have concentrated on Tractarian and ecclesiological sacramentality as formative for Rossetti's religious poetics. I come now to the third and most problematic aspect of Rossetti's worship experience, the question of how a woman participant in a ritualist service, one who observed rather than enacted the rituals limited to men, might have responded when ritualist structures of spiritual distinction complicated ritualist regard for the communion of saints.

Ritualism refers to "those ceremonial developments in the Church of England that were considered at the time to be making it approximate more closely to the services of the Roman Catholic Church," even though the ritualists argued that the innovations were "entirely consistent with Anglican precedent and justified by the Anglican formularies."[66] These innovations included such things as lighting altar candles, taking the eastward position at Communion (that is, the priest faces the altar rather than the congregation), mixing water with the wine in the chalice, using wafer bread, wearing vestments, burning incense, decorating the altar, having the choir wear surplices, and chanting plain-song.[67] Some of the rituals provoked more controversy than others, but the movement as a whole led to much argument and division within High Church congregations; among High, Low, and Broad Church parties; and between High Church adherents and Dissenters. Christ Church, too—one of the early leading churches in the ritualist movement—experienced internal dissent over the innovations, yet Rossetti seems to have approved them. She remained in Christ Church even when many others in the congregation departed during the turbulent years of Dodsworth's incumbency.[68] And although ritualist practices continued, even increased, during Burrows's incumbency, she stayed, even writing later that she felt "attracted" to Edmonton, Middlesex, because Burrows had become vicar there (LCR, 2:290). Perhaps she understood what the ritualist aim was in heightening ceremony in the liturgy: not to experience ritual for its own sake but to deepen the sense of the communion of saints. The ritualists were convinced that such ceremonies characterized the early church (once it moved beyond its primitive and persecuted era) and that reestablishing them in the present-day church would reinforce the sense of a spiritual community that transcended time and place.

In his study of the doctrine of the communion of saints in Anglican theology, Boniface Lautz demonstrates that, particularly in the High Church, "a definite increase of interest in the doctrine of the Communion of Saints" occurred over the years 1860 to 1900, the years of greatest ritualist fervor.[69] Perhaps because their own reverence for the consecrated bread and wine seemed to tip the historic sense of communion as a dual participation—in Christ and in a fellowship of believers—in favor of the first sense, the Tractarians, including Keble and Newman, had already reiterated the importance of the communion of saints in numerous sermons and tracts.

Newman, for example, declared members of the church to be "one and all the births and manifestations of one and the same unseen spiritual principle or power, 'living stones,' internally connected, as branches from a tree, not as the parts of a heap."[70] Gathered worshippers, Newman stressed, are not merely a conglomeration of individuals who happen to agree on doctrine or service: they are an entity, unified by a power outside themselves. They share the sap, as it were, of a single tree and so can never be alone. The title of an 1867 pamphlet makes the same point: *Alone, Yet Not Alone; or, the Communion of Saints*. Building on this groundwork, the ritualists attempted to make interconnectedness with the early saints more visible by enacting what they took to be the liturgical behaviors of the early church.

Of course, the ritualist interest in the communion of saints can also be seen as part of a larger Victorian preoccupation with the importance of human relationships in the face of industrialization, capitalism, and urbanization, all of which tended to emphasize and isolate the individual psychologically, if not also physically.[71] Besides these social factors, the Victorian interest in community also sprang from a perception of the Romantic preoccupation with the self as solipsistic.[72] Many nineteenth-century writers—George Eliot, Carlyle, and Tennyson among them—exerted themselves in poetry and prose to reconstruct society as community rather than as a conglomeration of individuals. Churches, too, responded to this cultural dynamic. Urban churches in particular felt keenly the need "to provide a sense of community to the displaced masses of the urban workers." Yet ritualists had a particular reason for valuing community, for they insisted that *only* within religious community does the individual have a relationship with God: "God conveys grace and religious knowledge not to individuals through their intellects but *to the community by means of material objects*."[73] Consequently, they attempted by rites and ceremonies to make visible the harmony that Christ had effected between God and the entire community—historical and contemporary—and to counter the tendencies of Dissenters toward independence of interpretation. Heije Faber explains why ritual and community-consciousness often coexist: "Ritual heightens the sense of belonging and of personal distinctiveness at one and the same time. In and through the rituals of the liturgy, the worshipper knows that one belongs to a worshipping community, but also that one is a separate individual."[74] Nevertheless, in the ritualist linking of community with material object lay a fracture that would eventually divide Anglo-Catholic theory from practice. In the remainder of this chapter, I investigate the ritualist vision of community and the effort to obtain this vision in practice, its less-than-ideal actualization in Christ Church and elsewhere, and Rossetti's response to this gap between religious abstraction and actual practice—her poetic effort to reconstitute the worshipping community in an ideal form that nevertheless recalls the traditional Anglican conception of sacrament as simultaneous communion with Christ and fellow believers.

The ritualists attempted to concretize their abstraction of community in several ways, the one most closely connected to the liturgy being the advancement of congregational singing. On the surface, this endeavor appears to align the ritualists with Dissenters and Evangelicals, those great proponents of congregational hymn singing, but their conceptualizations of the practice diverge. Dissenting hymn singing grew out of an urge to give voice to the wide variety of experiences encountered by the individual believer. Characterized by enthusiasm and expressiveness, it was popular in nature. Congregational singing in ritualist churches, in distinction, arose out of a desire to link the present community with the saints of the past. Encompassing a reinterpretation of the term *choral service* and a strong interest in Gregorian chant, as well as the selection and production of hymns wherein enthusiasm was moderated by reserve, it was Catholic and clerical in nature.[75]

The choral service, long a feature of the Anglican liturgy, generally meant the performance by the choir of a particular sung liturgy. The ritualists, however, gave it a new interpretation. As *The Parish Choir* observed, choral service meant "that mode of celebrating the public service by both priest and people, in which they sing all portions allotted to each respectively, so as to make it one continued psalm of praise, confession, and intercession from beginning to end."[76] Such a service, understood as participating in the "Catholic and rightful inheritance of the Anglican Church," reinforced the concept that worship has a different purpose than the personal edification which the Dissenters so valued, and which Barrett Browning insisted the sermon should provide. "Its greater aspect," writes Dale Adelmann, "was the collective binding together of the members of Christ's mystical Body to intercede for all and to join in the sacrifice of praise. In worship, . . . believers joined with the saints of all ages."[77] Choral services, ritualists felt, could recover a community-consciousness that had been partially lost in preceding years, when poor choir leadership and poor congregational singing and responsive reading had resulted in many worshippers choosing to remain silent while the appointed choir children gave out the required answers.[78] To recover further a sense of continuity and community with the early church, the ritualists also introduced the music of antiquity into these choral services.

"The Beloved Anglican Church of My Baptism"

Particularly, they chose ancient hymns in translation and Gregorian chant, which many felt to be "capable of intensifying feelings in the faithful of identification with the Church of the ages" and whose "monodic form contributed a unified musical structure to the ritual work of the congregation."[79] The revival of choral services, therefore, gave a voice to ritualist congregations, including the men and women in the pews, to deepen their sense of belonging to the communion of saints.

The principles that underlay the choral service applied also to the growing practice in Anglican churches for congregations (not only choirs) to sing hymns, which by midcentury had still not become officially recognized components of Anglican, especially Anglo-Catholic, services—not only because hymn singing was so strongly associated with the Dissenters but also because psalms seemed to many to be the more "solemn, vigorous, and manly song of the ancient Church."[80] However, the publication in 1860 and gradual widespread acceptance of a hymnal compiled by well-respected, ordained churchmen—*Hymns Ancient and Modern for Use in the Services of the Church*— more and more erased the notion that hymns belonged to either a dissenting or an "unmanly" tradition, particularly as the publishers issued the hymnbook concurrently with a collection of "solemn" and "vigorous" plainsong tunes until 1875.[81] By such association with plainsong, the hymns found their place in the Established Church. Moreover, the compilers of the hymnbook carefully included hymns with a strong catholic emphasis to forestall ritualist opposition and to distinguish Anglican hymn singing from evangelicalism's individualism. In short, more hymn singing meant more congregational participation, and when, after 1870, the use of plainsong declined in ritualist churches, the widespread use by that time of *Hymns Ancient and Modern* ensured a continued congregational participation in worship.[82]

In Christ Church specifically, choral services and congregational singing of ancient hymns probably began sometime after 1849, when Christ Church introduced its own surpliced choir. A need for this choir may have been felt because the congregation was trying to learn plainsong. Christ Church's curate from 1847 to 1849, Benjamin Webb, had introduced Gregorian chant at his previous cure,[83] and William Dyce's 1844 edition of *The Book of Common Prayer*, which explained how the principles of Latin Gregorian chant should be applied to chanting the Psalms in English, appears on Christ Church's inventory.[84] If then, for the first four to six years of Rossetti's attendance at Christ Church, the congregation's responses, or at least its songs, were still being given by the choir boys and girls mentioned by Burrows

(*Half-Century*, 11), it seems likely that by age twenty, Rossetti was participating in congregational chanting and singing, trained by the choir. Indeed, her brother William Michael observes that she did so; asserting her ignorance of music, though not insensitivity to it, he declares that she "never attempted [singing] apart from the ordinary congregational singing in church."[85] While congregational singing in ritualist churches may have been ordinary by William Michael's later standards, it was not always so. What Dissenters such as Barrett Browning took for granted, worshippers such as Rossetti in ritualist churches had only (re)gained within living memory: the opportunity to vocalize their own worship, to *hear* themselves as part of the communion of saints. Ironically, though Congregationalists cherished their individual voices, they could speak little in the worship service, because they refused to use set forms or creeds and therefore had no common text to voice; in contrast, Anglicans, attentive more to the communion of saints than to independence, spoke or—under ritualist influence—sang at regular intervals throughout the service by using a common prayer book.

While, however, the ritualists attempted to actualize their ideal of community-consciousness in part through choral services, they also found themselves increasingly confronted by difficulties and contradictions that pointed toward a gap between their religious abstractions and their actual communities. The difficulty lay in the apparently unresolvable tension between a concept of community that basically called for spiritual equality among all (internal connectedness, in Newman's terms) and an ecclesiological and ritualist practice that claimed the conveyance of grace by means of material objects—objects whose heightened status then required a differentiation among spaces and persons. Hierarchy, of course, was not new to the Established Church. The Anglican Church had always had an episcopal system that ranked clergy. Such hierarchy had its effect on Rossetti, too: she expressed elation at having shaken the bishop's hand on one occasion (LCR, 1:132). Prior to the ritualist movement, however, visible display of hierarchy featured less importantly in the worship service, and even when ritualist practices increased, Rossetti remained mostly unmoved by the prestige attached to particular clerical rankings. William Michael affirms that she "had an intense reverence for the priestly function, [but] she cared next to nothing about hierarchical distinctions: anything which assimilated the clerical order to a 'learned profession' forming part of the British constitution left her indifferent, or rather inimical."[86] Rossetti intimates this feeling herself in her 1885 devotional *Time Flies*. Dinah Roe explains that in the appendix to this work, "Rossetti is keen to stress that the 'glory' of ordained men, as with Paul, comes not from themselves, but from the grace of God." Linked to deeds rather than gender or position, such grace is available to "all Christians."[87] The ever-greater stratification of worshippers over the course of ritualism's advance, then, must have troubled Rossetti—not because she opposed the hierarchical structure of the church itself but because the new practices potentially strained the sense of *spiritual* fellowship among the saints.

The stratification of worshippers occurred as the altar became more and more the site of reverence. Its status as a holy object, and the chancel's as a holy site, increased while the nave, where the congregation sat, became correspondingly less sacred. This attention to the relative holiness of church spaces changed the rules for who could be seated where and do what. Formerly, all communicants participating in Holy Communion could be placed in the chancel during the celebration; although communicants did not literally sit around a table as Congregationalists did, they gathered and knelt in the table area. With the rise of ecclesiology and ritualism, though, celebrants no longer entered the chancel where stood the altar; instead, they approached the altar rail, at the chancel's leading edge, to receive the sacrament, then returned to their seats in the nave, while the administering clergy remained in the chancel. This stratification implicitly strained the unification efforts of the church. In addition, distinctions among the laity arose. The choir, formerly seated in the galleries (which had since been removed), sat in the chancel. In addition to being closer to the altar and the center of liturgical action than the congregation, they also wore surplices, a garment formerly worn only by the clergy (an action that led the clergy, no longer distinguished by their surplices, to begin wearing copes, stoles, chasubles, and albs for various liturgical events).[88] Requiring the congregation to stand when the clergy and choir entered in procession further distinguished the choir's privilege, marking again its difference from Congregationalist practice as described by Rev. Henry Allon in 1873: "The choir, technically so-called, is therefore only part of the singing congregation; its function is simply to lead it. It should therefore be in it, and of it—under no circumstances separated from it. It should be felt in its lead and control of the congregational song, but not seen or even heard apart from it. Hence it should be so placed as to be part of the congregation."[89] In contrast, ritualist practice emphasized choral distinction. The ritualist intent to establish continuity with the preceding saints through certain rites and ceremonies, therefore, produced in actual practice a categorization of contemporary worshippers by function.

These liturgical rankings become more troubling when one discovers that, prior to the ecclesiological and ritualist movements, parochial choirs could consist of both men and women, but under the new influences, only men and boys could join the surpliced choirs. Walter Hillsman observes that while women had few musical outlets outside of convents in the medieval period, from the late seventeenth century on, they participated in parish choirs alongside men, although not in cathedral choirs. The new movements in the High Church, however, excluded women from parish choirs on the grounds that cathedral practices should be imitated in parish churches also. In defense of the restriction, some argued that men's and boys' voices were more suitable than women's for leading congregational singing and other verbal responses; their grounds for making this argument are not clear.[90] Others were convinced that in singing, as in other acts of worship, the "duty of leading belongs to the men."[91] In Christ Church, too, prior to the construction of the choir stalls and the seating of a surpliced choir in the chancel, the choir consisted of boys from the church schools singing in the organ loft above the altar and "charity girls in mob caps, white tippets, and yellow mittens" singing around the altar below.[92] Although this children's choir located its members by gender, apparently having the girls closer to the altar than the boys presented no problem. The development of a more cathedral-like choir, however, excluded girls and women: Christ Church's inventory notes the choir surplices as either men's or boys'. Ritualist practice, therefore, also distinguished among members of the community by their gender.

Yet women made up more than half the worshippers in ritualist congregations, John Shelton Reed observes. Reed provides several reasons why this may have been so: aesthetic appeal, socially useful work, a search for accustomed figures of patristic authority, and, conversely, a challenge to authoritarian family structures as women purportedly confessed to their priests what they should speak only to their husbands.[93] None of Reed's reasons, however, allows for the possibility that Rossetti may have found ritualism heuristic for her religious poetry. Certainly, Anglo-Catholicism authorized women's social work, and Rossetti made use of this authorization in her involvement in Highgate Penitentiary as well as in her anti-vivisection campaigns;[94] but importantly, Rossetti also believed that she was called to write poetry because gifted by God to do it. She accepted the authority of the church and its understanding of the distinctions between men and women. Her well-known letter to Augusta Webster indicates that even when she found the principle of women's subservience to men's leadership problematic, she upheld it as a biblical teaching for the present world (though she could imagine differently for the hereafter).[95] Yet she did not believe in women's *inferiority*. She wrote to Caroline Gemmer that because God had given her a gift, she had to use it responsibly to teach others, including men who might (and did) read her works.[96] Within the church, she could take no leading role, for not only did ritualism turn the minister from a teacher "into a mediator between God and man, [it also] created two classes of laity, those directly involved in assisting the clergy to perform this mediatorial role and those whose function it was to be spiritually uplifted and led towards God by the events taking place within the chancel."[97] But Rossetti subtly criticized false distinctions, as in her 1865 poem "The Iniquity of the Fathers upon the Children":

> "All equal before God"—
> Our Rector has it so,
> And sundry sleepers nod:
> It may be so: I know
> All are not equal here,
> And when the sleepers wake
> They make a difference.
>
> (CP, 171.501–7)

In the context of the entire poem, the speaker, a girl born out of wedlock, is not necessarily referring to inequality within the church, but Rossetti may well be. Barred from both ordained and unordained formal participation in the ritualist liturgy, she knew firsthand that the forms of worship did not necessarily encourage a feeling of equality even though the ritualists endeavored to produce such a consciousness. But precisely this gap between theory and practice stimulated her to envision the Christian community in her final collection of poetry not in ritualist terms but with a more historic Anglican understanding of communion.

In *Verses*, the lyrical "I" predominantly represents itself as belonging to and experiencing faith and doubt within a religious community represented by the lyrical "we," a strategy that may also be the effect of long immersion in the Psalms, more particularly, in an Augustinian tradition of Psalm interpretation. As Crump's edition of Rossetti's poems reveals, the Psalms permeate Rossetti's poetry, perhaps because of their high profile in *The Book of Common Prayer*. And despite the increased use of hymns in Anglican services in the nineteenth-century, Psalms did not lose their standing as the songs of the church. Moreover, it was common to preach sermons on Psalm texts, particularly to interpret the Psalms as words to or about Christ or the church, or as the voice of Christ or the church. This tradition reaches back to (and even before) Augustine, whose expositions on the Psalms Michael Fiedrowicz analyzes. As Fiedrowicz explains, Augustine understood the "I" of many Psalms to be part of Christ's self-utterance, while in other Psalms, he took the "I" to be the voice of the church, into which "the individual who prays can and must insert himself by reason of belonging to the body of Christ."[98] The first element of traditional Psalm interpretation—the "I" as Christ's voice—does not figure strongly in Rossetti's religious poetry, where the speaker so often addresses or meditates on Christ as to make implausible the supposition that the speaker often is Christ. However, the second element of traditional Psalm interpretation pertains well to Rossetti's poetry, complicating any simple alignment of the "I" with the individual and the "we" with the community in the poems. In *Verses*, "we" may sometimes be a modulation from an "I" that is already more than one, while "I" may sometimes be an instantiation from a "we" that is somehow singular. For instance, in one sonnet, the speaker laments, "Ah Lord, Lord, if my heart were right with Thine / . . . then should I rest resigned. / . . . / Then should I stir up hope" (*CP*, 394.1, 2, 9) and remember

> How Heaven to Thee without us had been loss,
> How Heaven with us is Thy one only Heaven,
> Heaven shared with us thro' all eternity,
> With us long sought, long loved, and much forgiven.
>
> (*CP*, 394.11–14)

Here the speaker posits that were her heart more attuned to God, she would remember and be encouraged by God's desire for community with a people to whom she already belongs. The speaker senses that her personal rightness with God occurs within God's relationship with believers collectively. In fact, while her individual feelings may fluctuate, God steadfastly seeks, loves, and forgives the community as a whole—and the speaker, despite her hesitations, includes herself in that community by way of the first-person plural pronoun. More subtly, the sonnet implies that the speaker's heart is more right with God than she even realizes, since the sestet actually names what the speaker says a right heart would allow her to remember. In short, fellowship with God and believers enables the speaker to be in both the lamenting "I" and the forgiven "us" at once. Other poems, as the next chapter demonstrates, work with pronouns in slightly different though equally effective ways to present a worshipping community marked by a unified voice that yet encourages individual expression: catholicity in its most vital form. In doing so, Rossetti participated in a writerly and social community of Victorians seeking ideals of community that would accommodate individuality without giving way to individualism—or to differentiations among worshippers apparently justified by religious authority.

In this chapter I argue that Rossetti cultivated her distinctive religious imaginary within the formations of nineteenth-century Anglican worship. I have tried to show how the different orientation of Anglican from Congregationalist worship produced a deeply different orientation in Rossetti's imaginary than in Barrett Browning's. The next chapter bears out this claim still further by reading Rossetti's religious poetry as having a sense of the world as a complex web of manifestations of a nevertheless single reality; as aesthetically sensitive; and as deeply attuned to community. Taken together, these chapters remind us again that some Victorian women who chose to remain within religious institutional frameworks did so because their devotional practices stimulated their creative, intellectual work as well as their faith. Like Barrett Browning's, Rossetti's work crucially reminds us that complex religious poetry by women—poetry that questions as well as affirms—does not arise only from the religious rebel. Those deeply committed to religious tradition are not necessarily blindly committed to it; they probe its assumptions even as they treasure their participation in historic Christianity through the experience of communal worship. By embracing that which enables faith and work while subjecting to close scrutiny that which (inadvertently) hinders, these poets demonstrate that intellectual, creative, and religious commitments can coexist in the individual for the benefit of self and other.

CHAPTER FOUR

MANIFESTATION, AESTHETICS, AND COMMUNITY IN CHRISTINA ROSSETTI'S *VERSES*

In moving from a consideration of Christina Rossetti's religious imaginary as shaped within Anglican and Anglo-Catholic worship to a close reading of the religious poetry itself, this chapter focuses primarily on Rossetti's last publication. *Verses*, published in 1893, one year before Rossetti's death, is the poet's only collection of solely religious poetry. I focus on it for two reasons. First, because *Verses* concentrates on religious poetry, its liturgical associations emerge more clearly than in the shorter devotional sections or isolated religious poems scattered across other volumes; at the same time, since *Verses* is not a collection of newly written poems but a republishing of poems appearing earlier in three of Rossetti's mainly prose publications, it covers a span of poetic production that makes it representative of Rossetti's larger religious oeuvre. I focus on *Verses* secondly because it is the most neglected of Rossetti's publications in twentieth- and twenty-first-century scholarship and, I hope to demonstrate, undeservedly so. Lorraine Janzen Kooistra notes that *Verses* was "by far the best-selling poetry collection of [Rossetti's] career," and David Kent observes that 21,000 copies had been printed by 1912, but after this initial strong popular reception, *Verses* suffered a long dearth of attention that mostly continues today. As Dinah Roe notes, "There remains a critical and popular lack of interest in the poetry that postdates 1865, when [Rossetti] was only 35 years old."[1] Even the resurgence of interest in Rossetti's religious poetry and prose in recent years has brought little attention to *Verses*.

Notable exceptions include two articles by Kent in the 1970s, a discussion on the theme of love by Diane D'Amico in 1999, a defense of the volume's aesthetic reputation by Joel Westerholm in the same year, some observations on the volume as a "handbook of ritualist ceremony" by Emma Mason in 2004, and a more extensive reading by Constance Hassett in 2005.[2] Hassett assesses Rossetti's late-life poems as scrupulous in their lyric variations and their spiritual honesty but forced by their original prose contexts in *The Face of the Deep* (1892) to contribute to interpretations of prophecy instead of being free to act as poems; liberated from these contexts by being published separately in *Verses*, the poems testify "that the hard things *are* hard and that art gives repeated and time-resistant access to a necessary harmony, courage, and clarity" (237). However, apart from these analyses—some more in-depth than others—*Verses* has not garnered much attention, not even in recent monographs attentive to Rossetti's religious work (such as those by Arseneau or Roe). But as Roe observes, "Critical consensus that Rossetti's increasingly devotional post-1865 work is somehow second rate, artificially halts this poet's progress, freezing her in a post-Romantic/Pre-Raphaelite moment" (4). Perhaps its explicitly religious nature has sidelined *Verses* from critical study, or perhaps its modest subtitling of itself as a reprint of poems from previous collections has led to the conclusion that nothing can be gained from its study that was not already apparent in earlier publications. I believe, however, that understanding Rossetti's religious imaginary, indeed, perhaps her entire mature impulse as a poet, requires close attention to the volume she produced when she most strongly felt her impending face-to-face meeting with the God whom she had worshipped her entire life.

My reading of *Verses* highlights its conceptual and aesthetic features as they arise from an Anglican imaginary impacted by Tractarianism, ecclesiology, and ritualism. First in the chapter, I consider Rossetti's poetic response to the historic Anglican liturgy and Tractarian sacramentality. *Verses*, I demonstrate, is primarily attuned to manifestation and a corollary discipleship, such that the poems continually revolve around being or ontology. For example, Rossetti's St. Peter poems, especially compared to Barrett Browning's on the same subject, stress the importance of the divine look for the believer's shaping; the motif of relationship through encounter persists throughout the volume, even as it is deepened by sacramentality and its consequent practices of reserve, typology, and analogy. Further, the genres or forms that Rossetti chose to express her religious conceptions—specifically, the tightly controlled, meditative sonnets and roundels—function as poetic corollaries to the liturgical collects and repeated set forms of her worship. The demands of form became a kind of celebration, poetic and religious, as Rossetti reveled in the creative and sustaining opportunities that pattern and ritual offer. At the same time, Rossetti transcended these small spaces by creating in *Verses* as a whole the sense of a spiritual journey marked by several themes, a movement (as in liturgy) from preparation to promise to present living.

In the middle portion of the chapter, I study the material appearance of *Verses*, its sectional divisions, and its title features. Rossetti, I contend, shaped these visual and structural dimensions of the volume as integral components of its religious character. The visual features of the book illuminate its religious nature, the sectional arrangements emphasize the anticipatory and retrospective moments of the religious life—which Rossetti creatively constructed as an eightfold instead of threefold movement—and the added titles call forth new relations among and within poems. I relate these elements of *Verses* again to deep patterns of sacramental worship but also to ecclesiological attentiveness to aesthetics and arrangement. These dimensions of Rossetti's late work direct our attention to the fact that the poet did not consider *Verses* a mere reprint of earlier poems. Lastly in this section, I consider the evidence of Rossetti's discriminating choices in relation to her poetic predecessors who also undertook ecclesiological or liturgical poetic projects: her inclusions, revisions, and omissions of poems and topics in relation to George Herbert, John Keble, and Isaac Williams.

The final segment of the chapter addresses the question of community and Rossetti's attempt to revitalize and express the ritualist ideal in the face of an actual practice that failed to achieve its desired inclusiveness. Rossetti creates and develops an image of the communion of saints as a web of persons unconcerned about class, rank, or gender distinctions. Community, for her, means first of all unity, in which individual voices support rather than override each other. Building on her liturgical experience with congregational singing, she presents this notion chiefly through her representations of saintly singing. Additionally, she develops a strategic use of first-person lyrical voices, singular and plural, to communicate her sense of the ideal community among believers. She focuses not on ritualist ornaments, objects, or ceremonies but on the principles of interdependence and inclusiveness. Although *Verses* does little to rectify the immediate issues of her worshipping community, Rossetti's choice of a missionary-minded publishing house underscores the volume's point that the communion of saints lies beyond any local manifestation.

Manifestation, Aesthetics, and Community

The Liturgical Shape of Verses: Manifestation, Genre, and Journey

That Rossetti practiced reserve, typology, and analogy in her poetics because of her sacramental vision has almost become a critical commonplace.[3] However, because *Verses* remains understudied, I begin this section by establishing the appearance of these practices in this late volume as well. In a volume of over three hundred poems, for any one poem to be representative in this regard is difficult; nevertheless, I highlight five poems, two each from the early and middle pages of the collection, and one from a later page. In the sonnet beginning "Seven vials hold Thy wrath; but what can hold / Thy mercy save Thine own Infinitude . . . ?" (CP, 389–90), the second quartet elaborates on the idea of infinitude this way:

> Thy Love, of each created love the mould;
>   Thyself, of all the empty plenitude;
>   Heard of at Ephrata, found in the Wood,
> For ever One, the Same, and Manifold.

In this response, sacramentality and analogy appear first in the assertion that any form of created love carries the shape—the similarity-in-difference—of God's love and so bears witness to the higher order. But more intricately, they are woven into the third line, which alludes to Psalm 132, in which the psalmist declares that the community heard in Ephrata and the surrounding "fields of the wood" about the tabernacle that had been built for the Lord and his ark. Rossetti's poem turns the psalm's literal woods into the "Wood" of the cross, thus making manifestation out of mere setting; at the same time, it intensifies that manifestation by leading into it from Ephrata (which is Bethlehem), so that a mere eight words give us a cradle-to-cross movement. As the sonnet moves into its sestet, the sacramental vision continues. Silently developing the psalmist's reference to the ark of the covenant that signified God's presence into the ark that Noah built, the speaker asks for

> grace to tremble with that dove
> . . . .
>   Whom Noah's hand pulled in and comforted:
> For we who much more hang upon Thy Love
> Behold its shadow in the deed he did.
>
>   (9, 12–14)

Here Noah functions as a type of Christ, a shadow of God's love in reaching out and rescuing those who have no footing (the flying dove, the hanging believers). That is, Noah—in a specific instance of the more general earlier assertion—appears as a mold of God. At the same time, the believers who "hang upon Thy Love" are, in effect, not hanged, because Love (that is, Christ) is hanged (upon the Wood) in their place. Thus, similarity and difference coexist in the prime analogue that is Christ.

In the two-stanza "Judge not according to the appearance" (CP, 418), the speaker prays for such sacramental vision, for herself and others. She asks that nature's processes may be rightly understood to signify a larger, spiritual dynamic in which God might be seen in tree, bird, butterfly, just as tree, bird, butterfly might already be seen in seed, egg, cocoon:

> Lord, purge our eyes to see
> Within the seed a tree,
>   Within the glowing egg a bird,
>   Within the shroud a butterfly:
>
> Till taught by such, we see
> Beyond all creatures Thee,
>   And hearken for Thy tender word,
>   And hear it, "Fear not: it is I."

The title of the poem emphasizes a seeing that goes beyond surfaces, commanded by Christ himself.[4] Punctuation and indentation further underscore a process of deepening vision, with the third and fourth lines of each stanza literally moved inward, and the colon of stanza 1 intensifying stanza 2. Notably also, stanza 2 puts the need to see God ahead of the possibility of hearing him. For this speaker, only once we see can we hearken for and hear the Word/word.

In a pair of poems at midvolume, Rossetti turns her sacramental poetics to the subject of the Virgin Mary and her relationship to Christ, both poems arranged under the title "Feast of the Annunciation." The first poem questions how to speak of Mary:

> Lily we might call her, but Christ alone is white;
> Rose delicious, but that Jesus is the one Delight;
> Flower of women, but her Firstborn is mankind's one flower:
> He the Sun lights up all moons thro' their radiant hour.
>
> (CP, 446.3–6)

The implication throughout these lines is that Mary and Christ are too different to be spoken of with the same word, the same image. Because Christ alone is white, Mary cannot be called lily; because Christ alone is delightful, she cannot be a delicious rose; because he is mankind's one flower, she cannot be called flower of women; and so on. Therefore the speaker concludes that we can best speak of Mary by echoing the angel Gabriel's words that she is blessed among women and highly favored. In the next poem, however, the speaker seems to lose her earlier hesitation. She develops a scale of analogies whereby Mary's and Christ's relative status is signaled by upper- and lowercase letters, such that the same object becomes entirely appropriate for both Mary and Christ. It is no longer difference but similarity that marks their relationship: "Herself a rose, who bore the Rose," and "Lily herself, she bore the one / Fair Lily," and "the Sun of Righteousness her Son, / She was His morning star" (CP, 446.1, 6–7, 9–10). These type-antitype readings continue with "She gracious, He essential Grace / He was the Fountain, she the rill" (11–12). Natural objects, abstractions, and built objects all embody spiritual meaning, as the poem concludes with a mirror-image that recalls the mold-image discussed above: "Christ's mirror she of grace and love, / Of beauty and of life and death" (16–17). The mirror reflects not difference but similarity. Yet, of course, the difference remains and is even deeply noted by the two poems' proximity.[5]

Sacramentality, with its practices of analogy and reserve, appears in more subtle ways in *Verses* as well, as in a poem toward the end of the volume entitled "Balm in Gilead." Here the speaker uses aptly chosen flowers to intimate the healing power of Christ:

> Heartsease I found, where Love-lies-bleeding
>   Empurpled all the ground:
> Whatever flowers I missed unheeding,
>   Heartsease I found.
>
> (CP, 525.1–4)

In *Time Flies* (1885), where the poem first appeared, Rossetti provided nothing additional to suggest she intended a sacramental reading of these lines: no title, no commentary. But in *Verses* she points to such a reading by quoting Jeremiah 8:22 in her title. In this text, Jeremiah admonishes the Israelites for seeking physicians outside their own people: "Is there no balm in Gilead?" he asks (that is, at home). Linked with verse 19 of the same chapter, in which the prophet rebukes the Israelites for seeking false gods in other countries rather than the Lord in their own, balm in Gilead also evokes Christ as the Great Physician. Thus, Rossetti's title imputes Christ's healing power—or Christ himself—into the heartsease, unexpectedly found amid the widespread pain signified by love-lies-bleeding. Once noted, this reserved Christ-presence transforms the poem in yet another way. Suddenly, heartsease and love-lies-bleeding sound less like oppositions than similarity-in-difference, for Christ-bleeding enables the believer to find heart-peace. Because of the prime analogue (Christ), one is no longer surprised to find heartsease among love-lies-bleeding; rather, one finds heartsease because love-lies-bleeding. Yet the two flowers as flowers remain unlike.

Such close readings of a sacramental and analogical aesthetic in *Verses* may merely reinforce what other scholars have already asserted about Rossetti's poetics, but if we step slightly back from the practices of reserve, typology, and analogy, we can observe a broader liturgical presence in *Verses* also, specifically, the sense of encounter and response so deeply embedded in Rossetti's imaginary through liturgical experience. For while the poems in *Verses* certainly depend on a sacramental aesthetic that sees the material as invested with spiritual meaning, what strikes the reader also is how often the poems revolve around some kind of formative contact between God and speaker. It is not simply that the speaker sees Christ sacramentally manifested in natural or ecclesial objects but that the speaker continually encounters (or seeks to encounter) God more directly and personally: through a look, by a hand, through the heart. The poems become spaces where divine encounter happens and human discipleship begins. The encounter between speaker and God within poems can be so intense as to compel the reader's prolonged attention, even participation—an effect Rossetti may have envisioned as her poetry's iconic potential. As religious-aesthetic objects, the poems, she perhaps hoped, would draw also their viewer-readers into lingering encounter with the Christ within them.

Rossetti's St. Peter poems provide an excellent starting point for examining these assertions. As Esther Hu has observed, these poems all involve the gesture of turning and looking, which then becomes a sustained encounter, a gaze.[6] In "Vigil of St. Peter," the speaker implores Jesus to look on her and make her his penitent as he did with Peter, who denied knowing him but then broke down and wept when Jesus looked at him. The poem reads,

> O Jesu, gone so far apart
>   Only my heart can follow Thee,
> That look which pierced St. Peter's heart
>   Turn now on me.
>
> Thou Who dost search me thro' and thro'
>   And mark the crooked ways I went,
> Look on me, Lord, and make me too
>   Thy penitent.
>
> (CP, 448)

Noting the possessive pronoun in the final appeal to Christ, Hu writes, "Rossetti's speaker invites Christ to bring her, compassionately, to a state of repentance which leaves her vulnerable and exposed, but also divinely protected" (178). The distance between speaker and Jesu is overcome by the relationship that follows from the divine look. In the second St. Peter sonnet, Hu continues, it is Christ who urges the encounter, calling on the human speaker (who has aligned herself with Peter in her disbelief) to look on him, that he might teach her love:

> "Open to Me, look on Me eye to eye,
>   That I may wring thy heart and make it whole;
> And teach thee love because I hold thee dear,
>   And sup with thee in gladness soul with soul,
> And sup with thee in glory by and by."
>
> (CP, 449.10–14)

Here, to look on Christ eye to eye again causes penitence (heart-wringing) but again, restoratively so. "Christ's look," writes Hu in reference to yet another poem with a St. Peter allusion, "restores the fallible believer to continued faith" (184). All the St. Peter poems, she concludes, foreground the "possibility of personhood in relationship" through the mode of prayer (185, 186).

Rossetti's focus on "personhood in relationship" contrasts strikingly with Barrett Browning's three consecutive sonnets on the same subject of Christ's look at Peter. Even though Barrett Browning also chose the sonnet form, her approach differs substantially from Rossetti's: her sonnets do not pray but explicate and suppose; her speaker does not align herself with Peter but becomes an interpreter of Scripture. The titles of the three sonnets already gesture in this direction: "The Two Sayings," "The Look," and "The Meaning of the Look." In the first sonnet, the speaker identifies two sayings of Scripture that provide rest and encouragement for the church to entreat God's fellowship: "Jesus wept" and "Looked upon Peter." But in spite of this reference to God's fellowship, the impulse of the first sonnet is already toward explication, as evident in its concluding lines: "Oh, to render plain / By help of having loved a little, and mourned, / That look of Sovran love and Sovran pain" (WEBB, 2:98.10–12). Drawing on her own experience, the speaker will attempt to "render plain" that look, that is, to unpack its meaning, to translate the look into language. In the second sonnet, the speaker observes that Christ made no gesture of reproach but only looked on Peter. She then notes, "None record / What that look was, none guess" (WEBB, 2:100.5–6); all we know is that Peter, receiving the look, straightway knew God in it and went out weeping. Astonishingly then, the third sonnet opens with the line, "I think that look of Christ might seem to say" (WEBB, 2:102)—as if this speaker can record or guess meanings that others have not found or dared. The remaining lines of the poem consist of Christ's imagined words to Peter: first of rebuke, then of instruction to repent, then of encouragement and promise that Christ will not deny Peter before God and the angels. In contrast with Rossetti's poems, for this poetic speaker Christ's look is apparently *not* enough: it must be explained, translated into language; it needs proclamation. Indeed, the three sonnets taken together sound remarkably like a sermon: the speaker moves from stating the text to explaining the historical circumstances to interpreting the meaning. She remains outside the Peter experience, except to say up front that the church may be comforted by the message. Though Barrett Browning also envisions fellowship between church and Lord, such fellowship comes for her through an explanation of the Word. It is therefore somewhat ironic that Rossetti's poems on Peter compel more sustained and repeated readings—and have potentially more iconic power—than Barrett Browning's.

Rossetti might well have composed her St. Peter poems in response to Barrett Browning's. She certainly knew the earlier poet's work, and certain elements of her Peter poems echo Barrett Browning's closely: they both refer to Christ's washing of Peter's feet, to the crowing of the cock, to an eschatological conclusion. But the similarities do not go much deeper than that, for unlike Barrett Browning, Rossetti makes no attempt to "render plain" the meaning of the look. Rather, her speaker, as a kind of Peter, enters into the look or entreats Christ to bestow such a look upon her. She desires not only that the Peter episode have meaning for her—as does Barrett Browning's speaker—but that it actually recur for and in her. She asks for encounter, not for explication. Christ's look, she believes, will make her the kind of devoted worshipper she longs to be. In these poems, when Christ speaks, he does not explain what things mean; he calls the hardened heart to encounter him, and that encounter, by its very nature, leads to fellowship.

This alertness to radical encounter is typical of *Verses* broadly, and especially its opening sonnet section. The poems seldom try to make plain; instead, they maintain the mystery of a God who always remains veiled, even in manifestation, yet nevertheless brings about relationship, not distance. In the first poem, the speaker opens the motif of turning and looking (or looking for): "We turn to Thee; as on an eastern slope / Wheat feels the dawn beneath night's lingering cope / Bending and stretching sunward ere it sees" (*CP*, 389.7–9). Five poems later, the voice becomes individual as it pleads for God to "turn from those Thy lovers, look on me / . . . / Till I too taste Thy hidden Sweetness, see / Thy hidden Beauty in the holy place" (*CP*, 391.3, 7–8). Three poems later, the speaker asks God to "be mindful how out of the dust / I look to Thee while Thou dost look on me, / Thou Face to face with me and Eye to eye" (*CP*, 393.12–14).

And in the following poem, the speaker spells out the sequence that follows from looking: "Increase our faith that gazing we may see, / And seeing love, and loving worship Thee" (*CP*, 393.2–3). In all these poems, it is not words that bring relationship but a penetrating visual contact, a sustained gaze that signifies an embodied encounter formative for the human speaker. In other poems, of course, the embodied encounter may involve dialogue between God and a human speaker, such that the speaker poses questions and Christ answers. For example, the poems beginning "Lord, carry me" (*CP*, 402) and "Lord, I am here" (*CP*, 402–3) both consist of six questions or fears expressed by the believer and six responses from Christ. But this verbal exchange is not, in Rossetti's poetry, required for intimate knowledge or relationship. Because "the Creator [is] still the Same / For ever and for ever" and because "[w]e too are still the same" and because "[Jesus] still the Same regards us" ("New creatures," *CP*, 403.1–2, 5, 7), neither Creator nor creature need always speak in order to know or make known. Bodily knowing often suffices: "We know Thy wounded Hands: and Thou dost know / Our praying hands" (9–10).

Actually, praying hands, or postures of prayer more broadly, characterize *Verses* as a whole. The poems bear witness to the multiple spiritual conditions that make up the journey of faith. They do so in a variety of compact forms consonant with the concision, pattern, yet variety of the Anglican collects. These collects, to be sure, do not in themselves generate specific poetic forms, but they might be said to tilt the Anglican-Tractarian imaginary toward such forms as the sonnet and roundel as best for religious expression. In earlier chapters I argue that Elizabeth Barrett Browning developed a strong narrative or dramatic voice in her religious poetry out of a religious imaginary attuned to language, dialogue, and democracy. I do not suggest that Barrett Browning eschewed compact lyric forms in her midcareer or later religious poetry, only that increasingly her poetics revolves around forms that allow greater discursiveness and greater opportunity for dialogue and democratic exchange. Although, for example, her *Sonnets from the Portuguese* attests to her success with the sonnet form, and although she did use the sonnet occasionally to explore religious subjects, generally speaking, Barrett Browning was not as certain as Rossetti that the lyric "I" could articulate the depths and intricacies of religious thought and feeling adequately. As Alison Chapman observes, Barrett Browning enacts this hesitation in her sonnet "The Soul's Expression," where the solitary speaker draws back in fear from complete self-utterance:

> This song of soul I struggle to outbear
> Through portals of the sense, sublime and whole,
> And utter all myself into the air:
> But if I did it,—as the thunder-roll
> Breaks its own cloud, my flesh would perish there,
> Before that dread apocalypse of soul.
>
> (WEBB, 2:62.9–14)

In Chapman's words, Barrett Browning was "cautious of the cost of the sonnet epiphany. She describes it here as a self-immolation."[7] The poem's religious vocabulary—mystic depth, infinite, soul, apocalypse—suggests that Barrett Browning had in mind specifically the difficulty of religious utterance within the pressured confines of the sonnet and similar compact forms.

Rossetti, in contrast, turned increasingly toward forms for her religious poetry that require this brief but intense lyricism, this utterance of religious thought or feeling in an absolutely concentrated moment. Her choices of religious-poetic genres show the reverse process to Barrett Browning's over time. While she produced short lyric forms of many kinds from her earliest volumes onward, the ratio of longer narrative forms to shorter, purely lyric forms changed over the course of her life and publication history. Sonnets of any kind, for example, appear minimally in her early publications; when they do begin to multiply, more of them are religious than not. Roundels, another compact form, are absent from the early volumes altogether, only beginning to appear after *A Pageant and Other Poems* (1881). In contrast, the powerful narrative poems that have absorbed so much critical attention ("Goblin Market" [1862], "The Prince's Progress" [1866], "The Iniquity of the Fathers upon the Children" [1866], "The Lowest Room" [1875]) dominate the early volumes. As Rossetti turned more and more to specifically religious poetry, however, the number of sonnets, roundels, and other compact forms increased while the number of longer, narrative forms decreased. Indeed, they disappeared almost completely from *Verses*, even though Rossetti had earlier experimented with narrative forms for religious subjects, as in "A Ballad of Boding." Instead, sonnets constitute almost one-fifth of the poems in *Verses*, with roundels also figuring significantly.

Rossetti commented in her poetry on both forms. "Sonnets," she writes in the sonnet to her mother that opens her 1881 volume, "are full of love, and this my tome / Has many sonnets" (*CP*, 267.1–2). Whereas Barrett Browning feels the threat of self-immolation in the soul's expression of itself in a sonnet, Rossetti views the sonnet as having presence and fullness. Sonnets in general, she asserts, are full of love—not only sonnets to her mother, not even only her own sonnets. The sonnet tradition is, of course, an amatory one, but by the nineteenth century, it had been used to comment on everything from social and political issues (Wordsworth's "The world is too much with us" and Shelley's "England in 1819") to the dissolution of marriages (George Meredith's *Modern Love*). On the one hand, Rossetti frequently participates in the amatory sonnet tradition by using sonnets to speak about love (for example, "Monna Innominata"). On the other hand, not all her sonnets have love as their subject matter (for example, "A Thread of Life"). The clue to Rossetti's meaning in "sonnets are full of love," therefore, lies not in the subject matter of her sonnets but in her attitude toward the sonnet form and toward the process of sonnet writing itself. Although I cannot give detailed readings of Rossetti's major sonnet sequences here, it may suffice to say that both "Monna Innominata" and "Later Life," though not religious poems, portray Rossetti's sense of the sonnet as being rich and full of possibility. "Monna Innominata" is a sequence of fourteen sonnets, one for every line of the sonnet form, and "Later Life" is a double sonnet of sonnets: twenty-eight sonnets, one for every line of the sonnet form doubled. Clearly, for Rossetti, the small space of the sonnet offers concentrated power.

Rossetti highlights this potential in her manipulation of the form in the sixty-four sonnets of *Verses*. Although the octaves of these sixty-four sonnets have few variations on the conventional *abba abba* rhyme scheme of the Petrarchan sonnet (ten out of sixty-four differ), the sestets have an astonishing sixteen variations on the *c*, *d*, and *e* rhymes, even though *cd* almost always forms the first two rhymes. In section one alone, for example—a section comprising seventeen sonnets, thereby highlighting the form's significance to the volume—the sestet always begins with *cd* but the remaining four lines vary in nine ways, one pattern being used four times, one pattern three times, three patterns twice each, and four patterns once each.[8] Even then, Rossetti has not exhausted the possibilities: in the remaining sonnets of the volume, she creates seven more sestet patterns.[9] Her most unusual arrangement occurs in the sonnet whose first line reads "O Christ our All in each, our All in all!" (CP, 415), where the sestet incorporates the *a* of the octave to give *cdcaac*. To compensate for this unusual scheme, the octave receives the *d* rhyme usually appearing in the sestet: *abba cdad*. This scheme attracts attention by occurring in the very sonnet whose first line echoes the title of the entire section: CHRIST OUR ALL IN ALL. Whereas Victorian essayists and critics frequently condemned experimental sonnets as impure or illegitimate,[10] Rossetti clearly delighted in and maximized the sonnet's potential for variation and fullness. Taking up little space, these sonnets nevertheless draw attention to that space (even more pointedly, to the sestet's space) as being rich in possibility, so that their abundant appearance in *Verses* matches the poetic abundance within them.

This principle of potential or fullness or abundance also accords well with Tractarian principles of reserve and sacramentality. Rossetti's Anglican poetic predecessors had made much use of the sonnet: John Donne and George Herbert in an earlier century, and the Tractarians John Keble and Isaac Williams in Rossetti's own. In his lectures on poetry, for example, Keble had claimed that the sonnet's "unusually stringent" form enables the expression of "deepest emotions and longings without violating a true reserve."[11] But the sonnet relates to sacrament in another way as well. The very nature of a sacrament, particularly Communion and particularly to the Tractarians, requires it to be repeatedly celebrated. The words and actions that belong to the ritual are prescribed, fixed in print and in memory. Although the priest speaks the words, the words are not his per se; they belong to the form, to the sacrament itself. Unlike preaching, where the words are not prescribed, sacrament follows pattern. Yet despite its sameness from celebration to celebration, the sacrament's effect does not wear thin. On the contrary, its ritual sameness turns attention away from the form itself to what is occasioned when the form is activated: the metaphorical presence of Christ, experience of grace, confirmation of faith, assurance in doubt, commitment to service, renewal of love, awareness of the faithful community. In this sense, the sonnet is also a ritual evoking fullness of presence. The form rests in a long-standing tradition, but properly effected, it never lapses into mere recital, mere echo. The required structures or patterns encourage an exploration of the multiple effects possible within the mode. For Rossetti, writing sonnets is also a celebration of ritual—ritual not for its own sake but for its affirmation of creative renewal, whether poetic or religious.

The second major form dominating *Verses* is the roundel, with fifty-four appearing through all sections but the first. Four of eight times, a roundel concludes a section, and the number of roundels per section increases as the volume progresses. As with the sonnet, Rossetti commented on the roundel—*in* a roundel. A light-hearted and self-deprecating poem intended as a birthday gift but possibly never sent because of the poet's skepticism about its reception,[12] Rossetti indicates in the poem's opening line the key relationship she sees between its form and content: "A roundel seems to fit a round of days" (CP, 871). That is, a roundel's form suitably suggests such things as the passing of time, change, and human mutability. It does so because the form itself is, in a sense, round: it consists of three stanzas (of four lines, three lines, and four lines, respectively), is built on two rhymes, and has the opening phrase of the poem repeated as its fourth and eleventh (final) lines. Recurrence and circularity are thus integral to the form. While Kent asserts that the roundel "fosters a sense of inevitability—the inevitability Rossetti thought appropriate to human powerlessness before providential will," I suggest that Rossetti's roundel on the roundel builds on a more positive, or, at least, a more versatile, conception of the form.[13] The occasion for the roundel is celebratory, a birthday. While the round of days might be for "upright man or scoundrel" (CP, 871.2), in this particular case, the roundel functions as a token of love to pay tribute to the passing of another year. Thus, while inevitability and powerlessness do not inhere in the roundel, the passing of time does.

Kent rightly acknowledges, however, that Rossetti's frequent use of the roundel gives her poetry a "ceremonial and liturgical flavor," a description that underscores how repetition in liturgy is not powerlessness but effectiveness: as Gordon Lathrop observes, liturgy repeats the old to evoke an "utterly new thing."[14] Just as every celebration of Communion arises from

Christ's injunction to remember him yet every celebration evokes anew its own moment of grace, so the roundel's opening phrase acquires new meaning when remembered or repeated as the fourth, and again the final, line. In the following roundel, for example, the opening phrase points to weakness. Its repetition at the close, however, points to hope.

> We are of those who tremble at Thy word;
> > Who faltering walk in darkness toward our close
> Of mortal life, by terrors curbed and spurred:
> > We are of those.
>
> > We journey to that land which no man knows
> Who any more can make his voice be heard
> > Above the clamour of our wants and woes.
>
> Not ours the hearts Thy loftiest love hath stirred,
> > Not such as we Thy lily and thy rose:—
> Yet, Hope of those who hope with hope deferred,
> > We are of those.
>
> > > (CP, 478)

The speaker's key phrase remains the same, but its meaning shifts as it passes through different moments of the poem: confronted with death, the speaker is among those who tremble; yet once she names God's lily and rose—here again metaphors for the Virgin Mary (even if only to describe her unlikeness from them)—her key phrase modulates toward another meaning: she is now among those who hope. A poetic form that remembers and reuses its own phrases this way fits well with a religious tradition that believes so strongly in remembering its past through frequent repetition of a centuries-old liturgy.

Admittedly, Rossetti's interest in the roundel was also spurred by a nonreligious source. In 1883 Algernon Charles Swinburne had published his *A Century of Roundels*, a collection of one hundred roundels of both a serious and a lighthearted nature. Swinburne dedicated the volume to Christina Rossetti, with her permission. It sold well and, in Flowers's words, "popularized the form" (CP, 1169), after which Rossetti, too, took it up. She published twenty-four roundels—one of which she noted as her first—in the 1885 *Time Flies*, and thirty-two more in the 1892 *The Face of the Deep*. Clearly Swinburne's collection prompted her toward expanding her poetic repertoire in this form. But as clearly, she adapted it toward religious ends. Ultimately she came to view the popular poetic form of the roundel, as much as the elitist tradition of the sonnet, as suitable for expressing the multiple postures of prayer in the believer's spiritual journey. While the sonnet as a ritual celebrates grace and creative fullness, the roundel presents ritual as an opportunity for reflection and growth.[15]

For the poems in *Verses* are not a mere conglomeration of concentrated spiritual moments. Rather, Rossetti arranged them so as to convey the progress of the spiritual life. Not imitating but creatively analogizing the movement of the liturgy, she designed *Verses* with an anticipatory-retrospective oscillation that also accords with the trans-temporality of liturgy. She divided her work into eight sections with the following titles:"Out of the Deep Have I Called unto Thee, O Lord"; "Christ Our All in All"; "Some Feasts and Fasts"; "Gifts and Graces"; "The World. Self-Destruction"; "Divers Worlds. Time and Eternity"; "New Jerusalem and Its Citizens"; and "Songs for Strangers and Pilgrims." Kent describes these sections as falling into two major movements: "The first four sections center on the speaker's personal growth, while the second quatrain of sections shifts to a more cosmic, impersonal vantage point." He then describes what he sees as the key theme or tone of each section. Taken together, he asserts, the sections "dramatize the spiritual pilgrimage of the poet-speaker."[16] I draw much from Kent's insightful analysis and concur with his sense of the speaker's spiritual pilgrimage across the sections, but I also feel that the trajectory of *Verses* is not quite so divided into the personal and cosmic (not least because of the pervasive sense of the communion of saints, discussed in the final portion of this chapter). Instead, it loosely echoes the liturgical pattern of entering to encounter God (section 1), moving through the modes of confession, comfort, and renewal after Christ (sections 2-4), and going out again for further living in the present (sections 5-8). At the same time, it evokes throughout its sections the sense that, in Christ, past, present, and future are simultaneous moments.

In discussing *Verses* earlier as attentive to manifestation, I have already shown section 1 to be a kind of introit to the volume, with a preponderance of poems on the motif of turning and looking, of encountering God. Sections 2 through 4 express various moments in the discipleship of the speaker (and community) that follow from and are supported by the encounter with God.[17] In section 2, the theme of human insufficiency and Christ's sufficiency predominates, with opening lines such as "Lord Jesus, who would think that I am Thine?" (CP, 399) offset by opening lines such as "Thy Name,

O Christ, as incense streaming forth / Sweetens our names before God's Holy Face" (CP, 404). Penitence and comfort are interwoven throughout the section, which ends on a rising note. The penultimate poem reads in part, "A chill blank world. Yet over the utmost sea / The light of a coming dawn is rising to me" (CP, 418.1–2), and the final poem declares, "O Jesu, better than Thy gifts / Art Thou Thine only Self to us!" (CP, 419.1–2). Section 3 both builds on this rising note and remembers the chill blank world, as it observes some feasts and fasts of the liturgical year, communal commemorations that support the individual's spiritual growth. Section 4 dwells especially on the resultant formations of the believers, who are marked as new beings by the gifts and graces received from God. Love, patience, hope, peace, purity, innocence, grace, cheer, contentment, and faithfulness—all characterize and, at the same time, are more and more desired by the speaker who has been made new in Christ.

As liturgical renewal prepares the believer/community for entering the world again, so too do sections 5–8 of *Verses* function for the speaker as a renewed orientation toward the temporal and eternal. Section 5, the shortest, ponders the vanities and evils of the present world, while section 6 provides the contrast by variously imagining the world to come. As the seventh poem here puts it, "This near-at-hand land breeds pain by measure: / That far-away land overflows with treasure" (CP, 475.1–2). The speaker reflects particularly on time, urging wisdom for present living: "Time lengthening, in the lengthening seemeth long: / But ended Time will seem a little space" (CP, 483.1–2); "So brief a life, and then an endless life / Or an endless death" (CP, 484.1–2); "Short is time, and only time is bleak; / . . . / Long eternity is nigh to seek: / . . . / Pray and watch" (CP, 486–87.1, 3, 6). Moving from these general observations about the passing of one world into the next, the speaker meditates variously in section 7 on the place and community of heaven (New Jerusalem and its citizens, as the section title puts it) and in section 8 on the spiritual pilgrimage that must yet precede the New Jerusalem. This arrangement of the final two sections may at first seem surprising: should not the record of a spiritual pilgrimage conclude with reflections on the New Jerusalem, the point of arrival and heavenly reward? Not according to liturgical pattern. Anglican service ends with a parting blessing that implicitly acknowledges a between time. After the eschatological promise of communion, the participants still depart into a world in which they consider themselves but pilgrims. Similarly in *Verses*, the placement of "New Jerusalem and Its Citizens" *before* the record of the pilgrims' songs along the way suggests that the goal of a New Jerusalem gives purpose to the pilgrimage and motivates the pilgrims' songs. The "strangers and pilgrims on the earth" press forward to the heavenly city, but the idea of that city lies behind their everyday walk of life with its triumphs and sorrows.[18] The future is alive in the present.

Thus *Verses* embeds anticipation and retrospection not only in the form and subject of its roundels but also in its overall teleology, and even within sections. In "Songs for Strangers and Pilgrims," for instance, the first poem title comes from Genesis and refers specifically to the fall into sin that made the spiritual pilgrimage necessary: "Her Seed; It shall bruise thy head" (*CP,* 503; see Genesis 3:15, God's words to the snake). However, the next two titles allude to the Last Day, even as a present moment: "Judge nothing before the time" and "The day is at hand" (*CP,* 503, 505). Only after this past-future-present framework is set do the rest of the songs of pilgrimage follow. The section ends with similar anticipatory and retrospective gestures. "The goal in sight! Look up and sing," begins the penultimate poem (*CP,* 542), while the final poem begins, "Looking back along life's trodden way" (*CP,* 543). Importantly, the looking ahead does not counteract the looking back, for the looking back is an act of retrospection, not of longing: "Yesterday we sighed, but not today / Looking back." Although the final poem is not a roundel, as is the penultimate poem, in both poems the final lines reinforce their opening gestures: "The goal in sight" and "Looking back." The two poems conclude not only section 8 but also the entire volume. Their deliberate juxtaposition in this important, final position recapitulates the point that the spiritual life involves many points of return and reflection as well as anticipation and projection. Taken together, the two poems—and the entire volume—suggest that the spiritual journey, or liturgical life, for all its apparent temporal movement, is not sequentially remembering the past, scrutinizing the present, anticipating the future. Rather, in Christ it is trans-temporal, a living in past, present, and future simultaneously.

At the same time, as the reader has perhaps already observed, across these eight sections Rossetti's themes correspond to the five themes of the collects identified by deSilva: godly desire, the distinction between temporal and eternal, discipleship after Christ, the communion of saints, and dependence on God's grace.[19] The section headings do not align neatly with specific collect themes—Rossetti's work is not so constrained—but section 4, "Gifts and Graces," closely echoes the theme of dependence on God's grace, and sections 6 and 7, the theme of the distinction between temporal and eternal.

The themes of godly desire, discipleship after Christ, and harmony among believers, less identifiable with section titles, certainly characterize many of the poems across the volume. Given the prayer-like mode of most of the poems, this thematic correspondence with the prayers of the Anglican liturgy deepens the overall impression that *Verses* is kin to liturgy.

One might be tempted at this point to suggest that, given the ways in which *Verses* mirrors liturgical movement and effect, Rossetti must have been subversively seeking to supplant the authoritative liturgy of the church with a private, woman-authored devotional liturgy. But such an assertion would, of course, undercut Rossetti's whole understanding and practice of analogy. For analogy exists first of all because of difference, from which it seeks to establish relationship and harmony by orienting all objects, practices, and languages first to the prime analogue and then to each other. Consequently, although *Verses* is sacramental, it does not struggle to be sacrament. Although it is rich in language, it does not aim to be the Word. And though it enacts a spiritual journey, it does not duplicate all the embodied practices of public worship. Rather, it stands alongside liturgy, facing Christ, and testifying to order and harmony among various realities by its analogous relationship to liturgy and to Christ. Like heartsease and love-lies-bleeding, like fountain and rill, Rossetti's liturgical experience and religious poetry share a focal meaning but are not thereby substitutes for each other. Rather, Rossetti's poetic analogue to liturgy makes liturgy's relationship to Christ more evident, which it could not do if it merely replaced or echoed that liturgy. The creative work of analogy is what enriches both the liturgy and the poetry.

Aesthetics and Structure

The religious-aesthetic features of *Verses* include its material appearance and internal structures. Rossetti's attention to physical space as an important part of the total religious experience is first of all evident in the material concerns of the book *Verses*, the original edition of which manifests a strong visual-verbal aesthetic not evident in the modern Crump edition, with its focus on text. While certainly the actual production of the book lay in the publisher's hands, not in the poet's, Rossetti was fully attuned to its physical appearance and effects (*LCR*, 4:328, 343). Moreover, she had the precedents of her prose volumes to assure her of her religious publisher's meticulous attention to appearance. The 1893 edition presents a black exterior with relatively small gold lettering and no additional adornment. Inside, red lines frame the pages into four generous margins and a rectangular room in which the poems are centrally set, each corner of this room being thus marked by a red cross where the lines intersect. At the top of each page, the red line is doubled, with the sectional title printed within the space thus created. Each section also receives its own entrance page, its title centered within the red-ruled room. Each poem begins with an elaborately styled drop letter (one of the few features already modified in the 1896 edition), and a printer's stock mark separates all poems. Lorraine Janzen Kooistra observes that some of these features were standard to works published by the Society for Promoting Christian Knowledge (SPCK), the publisher for *Verses*, but she also argues persuasively for Rossetti's lifelong interest in joining image with text, even when the two are not a literal match: "'To illustrate' retained, for both Christina and Dante Gabriel, its primary etymological meaning of 'to light up' or 'to illuminate' a text rather than 'to reflect' it as in popular contemporary usage."[20] Although *Verses* is not illustrated in the conventional sense, its visual features certainly illuminate its religious nature.

True, such spaces and fonts also obtained in secular poetry. Jay A. Gertzman observes that for businessmen attuned to the upwardly mobile middle class's desire to appear as refined readers, "Fashionable book design ... was a business necessity as well as an aesthetic pleasure." An 1887 publication of Robert Herrick's poems, for instance, has each poem beginning on a separate red-bordered page with generous remains of white space; and Chapman notes that Victorian sonnet anthologies typically emphasize the sonnet's aesthetic value by situating each sonnet on a red-bordered page of its own.[21] However, as the Herrick example most clearly demonstrates, publishers usually compensated for the high costs of such book production by selecting only poets of earlier eras for these aesthetic editions—"a Chaucer, a Milton, or a Herrick," who "presented no problems of copyright."[22] In this way, aesthetically pleasing collections of poetry (including sonnet anthologies) could be priced affordably. Contemporary poets, by contrast, could seldom find publishers able to produce a book having both high aesthetic appeal and a reasonable price—unless such publishers had strong reason to subject profit margins to other motives, such as religious ends. The High Church–oriented SPCK, Rossetti's publisher, arguably had such a motive. Quite possibly, it featured rich visual effects in its publications in response to High Church aesthetics rather than middle-class social aspirations.

Such ecclesiological aesthetics certainly obtain in *Verses*, where the physical spaces that mark the end of one section and beginning of the next seem akin to pauses in the liturgical service or to the entrance and exit moments between lobby, nave, and chancel. They magnify the opportunities for retrospection and anticipation that poetry usually offers. The running titles at the top of each page remind the reader of the larger frame in which the immediate poem stands, giving a sense of placement and relational meaning rather than overwhelming accumulation, much as different moments of the liturgy are anchored in different spaces within the church. The red lines that frame the page and draw the eye around its perimeter may operate as do the colors in floor, walls, windows, and ceilings, reminding the viewer that religious words are suitably uttered in beautiful and consecrated spaces. Indeed, the red lines form window frames that may encourage the viewer's upward gaze to heaven, their cross-corners serving as a reminder of what makes the gaze possible. In short, the visual-verbal aesthetic of *Verses* is a determinedly *religious* aesthetic, one not likely to be missed by the regular readers of SPCK publications. It may well, of course, be missed by other readers less attuned to Rossetti's religious experiences. For such readers, the visual details may relapse into a peculiarity of late-nineteenth-century book production or perhaps suggest a visual-verbal aesthetic traceable only to Pre-Raphaelite influence. No doubt these factors contributed to Rossetti's aesthetic interests, but her creative practice also certainly inclined toward the strong, religious dimension I have outlined.

These claims for Rossetti's attention to a visual-verbal relationship in *Verses* are substantiated by a consideration of the poet's knowledge of a Tractarian emblematic tradition and illustrative habits. Isaac Williams's *The Cathedral*, for example, demonstrates a commitment to making visible the association between ecclesiology and poetry: his book opens with a floor plan of a cathedral, from which the parts of his book then develop. The detailed table of contents associates the various church parts with particular liturgical elements, and each sectional title page reiterates the relationship by linking the ecclesiastical space to a Bible text. Running titles and fonts receive special attention, while each of the "Ecclesiastical Sonnets" takes its own page. Although the scattering of Rossetti's library after her death prevents us from knowing for certain that she owned a copy of this particular book, Rossetti did own Williams's *The Altar*, a series of twenty sonnets considering the events from Gethsemane to Pentecost. This book and others, including John Keble's *The Christian Year* (1827), Rossetti illustrated with marginal drawings, showing again her interest in the relationship between the verbal and the visual.[23] Kent has also argued that Rossetti almost surely knew George

Herbert's *The Temple*, which features bordered pages, framed running titles, unusual visual representations of key words and lines, and an ecclesiological or liturgical division of poems into sections titled "The Church-Porch," "The Church," and "The Church Militant."[24] Rossetti's visual-verbal religious aesthetic had solid Anglican and Tractarian ground on which to build.

In addition to this visual appeal, *Verses* manifests its concern with structure, arrangement, and symbolic meaning in other ways. Rossetti's offhand reference to her "slavish copying" (LCR, 4:313) of these poems out of her earlier prose-poem volumes, and the knowledge that William Michael first suggested the scheme of reprinting them (LCR, 4:301n), may lead to the conclusion that Rossetti produced *Verses* with little creative thought. Nothing is less likely for a poet so meticulous in habit and so conscious that "each volume heaps up [her] responsibility" (LCR, 3:100). In fact, Rossetti referred to *Verses* as her "revise" as well as her "reprint" (LCR, 4:328, 316), the former term indicating an active critical engagement rather than mere copying—a suggestion borne out by the expansion of the poem beginning "Life that was born today" from eight lines to twenty-four (CP, 457), the inclusion of one poem not originally appearing in the prose volumes ("Good Friday Morning," CP, 435), and the exclusion of four poems that appear in *Time Flies* and eleven in *The Face of the Deep* (of which only three are unsuitable for *Verses*). Actually, *Verses* can be viewed as a renovation or restoration project, rather than a new construction. Like Christ Church itself, it shapes existing material into new forms and relationships in ways that have significant religious meaning.

The arrangement of poems into eight sections, discussed above, is one element of this shaping process. The addition of titles to many poems untitled in their original prose publications is another. Although William Michael asserted that Rossetti wrote poetry without "making any great difference in the first from the latest form of the verses," Kent estimates that Rossetti made about eight hundred revisions to the poems included in *Verses*, most of them rather minor, such as changes in line indentation, capitalization, and punctuation.[25] However, her addition of two hundred titles to poems and sequences of poems cannot be considered a minor revision. It is as though, having removed the poems from the prose contexts of their first appearance, Rossetti felt the need, or perhaps seized the opportunity, to build some other meaningful framework for them. As William Michael observes in several instances in his notes to *The Poetical Works of Christina Rossetti*, the added titles often have little to do with the original prose contexts of the poems. Instead, in the renovation project of *Verses*, Rossetti built new scaffolding around her poems, drawing their meanings upward to a more visible site and marking off spaces in the text according to the movement of her themes. Indeed, the titles often serve as the "face of the deep," surface clues to the depths underneath. In a way, they become illustrations in the volume as their mostly scriptural phrases illuminate the rooms of poetry. They contribute to a community of poems all manifesting the same spiritual principle or power, to use Newman's phrases, quoted in the previous chapter, again.

For example, the fourth poem of *Verses* is entitled "As the sparks fly upward" (CP, 390), a quotation from Job 5:7. In the source text, one of Job's friends asserts to Job after calamity has struck him, "Yet man is born unto trouble, as the sparks fly upward." Here, a principle of nature (sparks do not fly downward but upward) confirms a human experience of distress as inevitable. In the poem, however, the speaker associates sparks' upward flight with the aspiration of saints to mount toward heaven. This turns the meaning of the source text on its head but becomes a key image throughout *Verses*. In subsequent poems, the title phrase with its reconfigured meaning at first reverberates strongly, then modifies into slightly new shapes. In "I will come and heal him" (CP, 393), the speaker pleads that God not allow "blazing Seraphs utterly to outflame / The spark that flies up from each earthly coal" (7–8). A few poems later, the speaker seems yet more despondent, calling herself "a spark upon the wane" ("Lord, grant me grace," CP, 395.5). But soon thereafter, in a poem already quoted ("New creatures," CP, 403), the speaker regains assurance and declares, now more faintly echoing the original image, "still we / Mount toward Him in old love's accustomed flame" (7–8). Later yet, she urges Christ to "Kindle my burning / From thine unkindled Fire" (CP, 417.11–12). Of St. John, she asserts, "Earth cannot bar flame from ascending" ("St. John, Apostle," CP, 423.1). By the time we come to the lines "Lo! like a stream of incense launched on flame / Fresh Saints stream up from death to life above" ("All Saints," CP, 453.9–10), "The joy of Saints, like incense turned to fire / In golden censers, soars acceptable" (CP, 497.1–2), and "O foolish Soul! to make thy count / For languid falls and much forgiven, / When like a flame thou mightest mount / To storm and carry heaven" (CP, 542.1–4), the image, in whatever modulated form—like that of the dove examined in the previous chapter—has become an inextricable thread in the overall canvas of *Verses*, a canvas over which we must crawl inch by inch, not stopping too long anywhere but tracing the connections that make up the whole. We must move among the poems as much as move forward in the volume to discover how words and images echo each other, "keeping the poet's meaning in motion."[26]

The section entitled "Christ Our All in All" serves as an example of how the poem titles also help the reader trace out connections across a single section. The section heading sets out the general theme of Christ's sufficiency, while the twenty-one internal titles break down this theme into component understandings. The first few titles describe the people to whom Christ is All. The titles then turn to Christ and lay out his fullness by his names, followed by descriptors of his person and activity. The sufficiency of Christ evokes in the believer(s) a response of trust. Christ then assures the believers of their belonging to him and of his supremacy. Selected titles can even be arranged to form a sentence that summarizes the section: "The ransomed of the Lord," who know that their "King of kings and Lord of lords" was "slain from the foundation of the world" for their sake, believe Christ's assurance "that where I am, there ye may be also," for they understand that he is "chiefest among ten thousand." Thus although the section consists of one poem from *Called to Be Saints*, twelve from *Time Flies*, and thirty-seven from *The Face of the Deep*, Rossetti underscores their new and meaningful relationship with each other in *Verses* by inserting carefully chosen titles.

While the titles taken collectively serve as structural guides within the sections, individually they often bear elusive relationships to the poems they precede. The sometimes tenuous relationship between title and poem, however, forms part of Rossetti's effort to add new dimensions to the poems' spiritual meanings. The phrase "subject to like passions as we are," for example, is the apostle James's description of the Old Testament prophet Elijah as an ordinary man whose earnest prayers had powerful effects.[27] James highlights Elijah's ordinariness to give his readers confidence in the effects of their own prayers. Rossetti's poem turns the apostle's words to a different end. The poem is not about the power of prayer but about religious anguish as evidence of spiritual desire: "Anguish is anguish, yet potential bliss" (*CP*, 458.9). The speaker asserts that other heavenly "citizens felt such who [now] walk in white" (11), and only this assertion holds the poem to its title. Rossetti seems to be considering how Elijah's spiritual anguish and occasional lack of faith did not prevent him from entering heaven.[28] In Rossetti's poem, the title appears as a gesture of comfort for the spiritually weak and fearful rather than as proof of the power of prayer. The elusive title reference, absent from the poem in its original appearance in *The Face of the Deep*, gives historical specificity to an otherwise potential platitude. This is but one example of a process repeated dozens of times in *Verses*. Such title additions indicate that Rossetti seriously occupied herself with creative revision and enrichment, not just reprinting, when she prepared *Verses* for publication.

Finally, besides its formative impact on Rossetti's sacramental imaginary, poetic genres, and aesthetics, High Church ecclesiology also contributed to Rossetti's participation in a religious-poetic practice that valued both tradition and innovation. I return briefly to George Herbert, John Keble, and Isaac Williams. Each of these Anglican devotional poets had set precedents for how ecclesiology and liturgy might be engaged poetically. I have already considered the religious-aesthetic features of Herbert's and Williams's books of poetry, so I will here concentrate on Keble's *The Christian Year*, with its strongly liturgical focus. Keble's volume includes a poem for every day in the church calendar as identified in the 1549 *Book of Common Prayer*. Like other Tractarians seeking to return to the church's earliest formulations, Keble does not recognize the days added to the 1662 *Book of Common Prayer*, namely, those for St. Mary Magdalene and the Transfiguration of our Lord.[39] Like Williams, he is also quite methodical and literal in his approach. Frequently his subject matter relates explicitly to the biblical narrative associated with the day.

Keble's liturgical collection undoubtedly influenced Rossetti's inclusion of a liturgical cycle of poems in *Verses*. Unlike Keble, however, Rossetti did not write the poems included in section 3 of *Verses*—"Some Feasts and Fasts"—with the church calendar in mind. Indeed, *The Face of the Deep* reveals her dissatisfaction with the church calendar, for she writes, "Our solemn feasts languish, and our fasts where are they?" (FD, 243). She chose instead to work out some associations between poems already written and selected liturgical days. Sometimes her association between poem and day is obvious and natural, such as the assignation of her *Called to Be Saints* poems to the liturgical days of those saints. Sometimes her association is less clear: her poem "Palm Sunday," for example, presents a dialogue between a frightened speaker and Christ on the cross rather than Christ on the road to Jerusalem, as the title would suggest. Some might argue that the nature of the collection inevitably produces these weaker associations, but the sectional title makes clear that Rossetti did not feel obliged to find a poem for every liturgical day. When she had no suitable poem, she simply omitted that day. Moreover, Rossetti also divided some liturgical days into morning, day, and eve, which neither the prayer book nor Keble's collection does. Keble followed the prayer book exactly in supplying one poem for each of Christmas, Epiphany, Good Friday, Ascension Day, and Whitsunday. Rossetti, by contrast, divided these days into parts, which she indicates in her titles: "Christmas Eve," "Christmas

Day," and "Christmas Tide," for example; or "Epiphany" and "Epiphany Tide." Again, Keble provided one poem for each of the additional holy days in the calendar. Rossetti omitted some days, while for others she gave both a poem of vigil and a poem of feasting—to correspond with her section title, no doubt. Further, she did not necessarily limit herself to one poem per heading. The day for St. Peter she observes by setting one poem under the heading "Vigil of St. Peter" and three poems under "St. Peter." And whereas Keble faithfully provided a poem for each of the twenty-four Sundays after Trinity designated in the church calendar, Rossetti provided one for "Trinity Sunday" and then skipped the twenty-four Sundays after. Again, had she wished to follow the calendar slavishly, she could easily have taken poems out of the other sections of *Verses* and assigned them to these Sundays, but she did not do so. Neither, however, did she break with the Tractarian preference for the earliest version of the prayer book, which did not recognize days for Mary Magdalene or the Transfiguration—even though she had written at least one such poem earlier in her life (see *CP*, 385).

Clearly, Rossetti allowed tradition and innovation to stand side by side in her collection, much as the ecclesiologists renovating Christ Church had done. She studied her predecessors, but far from reproducing their strategies, she devised her own. Actually, while situating herself firmly within the contexts of Anglo-Catholicism, she went considerably beyond Keble's and Williams's affirmations of the High Church's liturgical and ecclesiological practices. Her arrangement of poems in "Some Feasts and Fasts" addresses, at least partially, her own critical question in *The Face of the Deep*. It is not enough to observe St. Bartholomew's Day. We must have a vigil (a watching, a fast) and a feast of St. Bartholomew. The same is true for the Presentation, the Annunciation, St. Peter's Day, and All Saints' Day. Whereas in Keble's *The Christian Year*, poetry serves to invigorate the liturgical observances of the church, in Rossetti's *Verses*, poetry *considers* liturgy, advises it, stands as analogue to it—and it does so from within, with an obvious appreciation for the importance of liturgy. The point bears repeating: Rossetti's gathering and republishing of the poems in *Verses* constitute much more than an act of reprinting, despite the volume's modest subtitle. Jennifer Wagner believes that Wordsworth's rearrangement of his early sonnets into the long sequence titled *Miscellaneous Sonnets* turns them into a kind of autobiographical long poem, a collection of small moments that open out to a "larger conception of his own life history," even though Wordsworth had not originally planned this when writing the separate sonnets.[30] Rossetti, I conclude, engaged in a similar act: reviewing much of her mature life's work, she arranged her poems in *Verses* to reflect the multidimensionality of the religious life and—my focus in these past paragraphs—the ways in which liturgy might be restructured to enhance that life still more. From the vantage point of her sixty-third year of life, Rossetti produced a volume that surveys the religious life comprehensively. Formerly each poem stood alone within its prose context; now the poems together attest to the religious life in its entirety. In its focus on manifestation, lyric concentration, and aesthetics, *Verses* speaks to Rossetti's accomplishment as a mature poet working from an Anglican/Anglo-Catholic religious imaginary.

Envisioning the Communion of Saints

The characteristics of *Verses* discussed so far form important dimensions of Rossetti's poetic response to her chosen experience of worship, but there is one more to consider: her powerful envisioning of the worshiping community as a harmonious whole that supports and encourages the individual believer. This vision is, in part, Rossetti's response to the liturgical stratifications of Anglo-Catholic worship that sat so oddly with the Tractarian and ritualist emphases on a communion of saints; further, it is a participation in a long history of reading the biblical psalms—so valued by the prayer book—as Christocentric and communal.

Tractarian and ritualist theologians discussed the concept of the communion of saints extensively, with differences of opinion as to the role of the departed saints in this communion. Newman, for example, hesitated to say whether departed saints still worked actively for the church; Henry Edward Manning considered it logical that the saints in heaven would remember those whom they had known on earth.[31] The discussion continued through most of the century. Rossetti's awareness of the topic but uncertainty as to which theological direction to take appears in her poem beginning "Our Mothers, lovely women pitiful":

> I know not if they see us or can see;
>   But if they see us in our painful day,
>   How looking back to earth from Paradise
>   Do tears not gather in those loving eyes?—
>   Ah, happy eyes! Whose tears are wiped away
> Whether or not you bear to look on me.
>
> (*CP*, 500.9–14)

The speaker's wistfulness combines with hesitation on this foremost theological debate. If her mother, presumably now a saint in heaven, can see her daughter on earth, would she not weep to do so? the speaker asks, and then responds with the comfort that, even so, her mother's tears would be wiped away (an allusion to Revelation 21:4). If this poem represents her uncertainty as to the exact role of the saints in heaven, however, Rossetti was confident that a real bond of fellowship exists among all saints, whether living or departed. In *The Face of the Deep*, she presents an intriguing image for her understanding of this bond: "The acts of all saints from the beginning to the end" form "one fair unbroken web"; when "held up to that light which manifests all works," this web reveals itself to be "a perfect whole" made by the "interweaving of cross threads, of *crosses*" (FD, 437; original italics). In this image, Rossetti refers to the catholic community of believers not with the term *church*, which can be mistaken to mean the institution, but with the term *saints*, the people of God. She values the individual acts of the saints, even the bearing of their individual burdens, as necessary for the fullness of the community. The unity of this catholic community may not be immediately visible to the individual saints, whose struggles and crosses preoccupy their hearts and minds, but a larger, or more divine, perspective reveals its interlace. The saints include, yet surpass, any single worshipping community. This understanding prevents an overpreoccupation with the faults of actual communities, which form only small parts of a larger picture. At the same time, the image compels each worshipping community to acknowledge the significance of its individual members for its own existence and for the entire communion of saints, which cannot be complete until every thread receives recognition and takes its place. The latter thought implies also that the community, for its own well-being, should seek out and bring in any missing threads.

In *Verses*, Rossetti expresses the catholic and egalitarian nature of the worshipping community by again using the term *saints* rather than *church* to mean the people of God, whether on earth or in heaven. Although she acknowledges their different locations and spiritual conditions along the pilgrimage, Rossetti uses the word *saints* to reinforce the imagined link between the earthly and heavenly worshipping communities. On earth, "tired saints press on" toward their heavenly goal ("The gold of that land is good," CP, 394.12). They are "saints who mount" "onward and upward" "toward that blessèd place" where numerous fellow-saints already rest ("As the sparks fly upwards," CP, 391.9, 11). The saints in heaven likewise long for the arrival of the saints yet on earth, so that they may obtain "[l]oves to their love and fires to flank their fire" from that "oncoming host" ("All Saints: Martyrs," *CP*, 453.12, 11). Separated for the present, the saints all long to be one in place, as they are essentially one in spirit and devotion. In sonnet 16 of section 1, for example, Rossetti's speaker longs to be at one with those who give alms, toil, and yearn for a future union (that is, the saints on earth) and with those who already gather around the crystal sea, waiting for the end of time (that is, the saints in heaven; see Revelation 15:2):

> Lord, make me one with Thine own faithful ones,
>   Thy Saints who love Thee and are loved by Thee;
>   Till the day break and till the shadows flee,
> At one with them in alms and orisons;
> At one with him who toils and him who runs,
>   And him who yearns for union yet to be;
> At one with all who throng the crystal sea
> And wait the setting of our moons and suns.
>
> (*CP*, 395.1–8)

Rossetti's concept of the community of saints, then, envisions unity and harmony among all believing communities, past, present, and future; it is transtemporal and Christocentric. Within this frame, Rossetti works to depict how unity within a single worshipping community might operate—that is, how the individual participates fully within the community without losing his or her individuality.

Rossetti represents this relation between earthly and heavenly communities, and of individual within community, by capitalizing on the ritualist understanding of congregational, or communal, singing as an expression of the apostolicity and catholicity of the church. Choirs seldom get notice in *Verses*, but when they do, they appear as all-inclusive. Unlike an earlier poem in which choir singing occurs when "white-robed men and boys stand up to sing" ("St. Andrew's Church," *CP*, 690.4)—a poem written in 1848 and never published in Rossetti's lifetime—*Verses* explicitly states that all the "Saints flock to fill thy choir" ("Jerusalem of fire," *CP*, 489.3). More frequently, however, the word *choir* does not appear, for when the entire community sings, the need for a choir lessens, if not disappears altogether. Instead, Rossetti pictures the saints as continually engaged in song. Moreover, this engagement recognizes the contributions of individual voices but not as isolated singers. In "What hath God wrought!" the song of the saints is "One thunder of manifold voices harmonious and strong, / ... one shout of one worshipping throng" (CP, 495.5–6). Individuality of voice is not erased ("manifold voices")—indeed, it cannot be erased, since the saints are "multi-fashioned" ("Behold, it was very good," CP, 474–75.6)—but the conjoined voices make a single harmony. Repeatedly, Rossetti highlights these two dimensions of the vocal unison of the saints: "As the voice of many waters all saints sing as one" ("Before the Throne, and before the Lamb," CP, 495.1); "While they all at once rejoice, while all sing and while each one sings" ("So great a cloud of Witnesses," CP, 499.6). Linked with depictions of saintly activity in the book of Revelation, the saintly, singing community of *Verses* is, of course, often idealized. Nevertheless, Rossetti is also realistic. She recognizes that the earthly saints do not always wish to sing, for example, when faced with troubles or doubts. She does not rebuke them for this lack, but she marks it as a temporary situation, as also the title of the following poem indicates:

"Then shall ye shout."

It seems an easy thing
Mayhap one day to sing
Yet the next day
We cannot sing or say.

Keep silence with good heart,
While silence fits our part:
Another day
We shall both sing and say.

Keep silence, counting time
To strike in at the chime:
Prepare to sound,—
Our part is coming round.

Can we not sing or say?
In silence let us pray,
And meditate
Our love-song while we wait.

(CP, 536)

Elsewhere Rossetti's speaker reflects on dying as a believer, and concludes, "Death is not death, and therefore do I hope: / Nor silence silence; and I therefore sing / A very humble hopeful quiet psalm" ("It is not death, O Christ, to die for Thee," *CP,* 392.9–11). For Rossetti, the musical metaphor works in multiple ways. It signifies unity of purpose and devotion among believers and at least temporarily overrides the class and gender distinctions often made among them. It also signifies unity with God, as an untitled poem in the section "Gifts and Graces" indicates in its first two lines: "Tune me, O Lord, into one harmony / With Thee, one full responsive vibrant chord" (*CP,* 455). In this concentration on the songs of the saints, Rossetti shows herself fully attuned to ritualist principles, while at the same time she works—herself humbly and quietly (or, we might say, reservedly)—to counter the notion of a ranked and limited choir participation. For if in the communion of saints no separate choir is required, the congregation itself becomes the choir, with all its attendant privileges and responsibilities. While this idealized choir might not don surplices or walk in procession, it does step into a role formerly held by a select few. True, such idealization obscures faults that would be better addressed openly, but it also turns attention to a principle equally in danger of being obscured: that of the universality of the Church of Christ (as opposed to the particularity of Christ Church). *Verses* draws attention to the former.

Rossetti secondly figures the individual and the communal as interdependent through her strategic use of singular and plural lyrical voices. We have already seen her careful pronoun modulation in "Ah Lord," the poem discussed at the end of the previous chapter, where the praying individual inserts herself into the voice of the church. Such subtle pronoun change appears again in, for instance, the untitled poem beginning "O Christ our All in each, our All in all!" (*CP,* 415). In this line, "each" and "all" stand juxtaposed but also superposed, with "Christ-All-All" holding them apart-yet-together, and "our" making communal and possessive what "the" would render abstract and distant. Midway through the poem, the line recurs, transfigured to "O Christ mine All in all" (8). In the reverse move to that of "Ah Lord," the voice of the church here modulates into the voice of the praying individual: "our" becomes "mine." *Verses* constantly makes such pronoun moves within a single poem to envision the individual as belonging to the body of Christ. Without discussing the pronouns of the poems, Kent recognizes this balance of individual with communal voices, especially in the third section of *Verses,* when he writes that the section places "the personal relationship with God within the larger context of the church's corporate life of worship because, for Rossetti, it is there that the pilgrim receives the necessary nourishment to carry on in the world."[32] In the third poem, for instance, the speaker, referring to the symbolic river of death, asserts, "We all must pass that way," then immediately adds, "Each man, each woman" "alone, alone," even "I, rated to the full amount, / Must render mine account" (*CP*, 420–21.8, 9, 12, 17–18). Similarly, "Passiontide" opens with a communal voice—"It is the greatness of Thy love, dear Lord, that we would celebrate"—but ends with individual voices responding to Christ's call: "I come—and I—and I" (*CP*, 432.1, 17). But other poems beyond the third section also situate individual within community, or the community as constituted by individuals. Late in the volume, for instance, appears the poem entitled "One of the Soldiers with a Spear pierced His Side." The speaker fixes no blame on the soldier but immediately laments, "Ah, Lord, we all have pierced Thee: wilt Thou be / Wroth with us all to slay us all?" She then pleads that God "spare one"—and having done so, to spare "Another, and another," till his "mercy overrun" (*CP*, 530.1–2, 6, 9, 10). Here the "all" are rescued precisely because they are each recognized as "one."

These poems work internally to distinguish-yet-fuse the "I" and the "we," but more frequently, Rossetti works across poems to build the individual-community relationship in Christ. Constance Hassett observes that Rossetti clustered the poems in *Verses* "in thematic groups that call attention to their differences *as* poems and to the virtuosity prompted by successive new formal ideas."[33] Sonnets 8, 9, and 10 of section 1 demonstrate this primacy of attention to difference and virtuosity through the strategic employment of "I" and "we." The lyrical "I" speaks in sonnet 9, expressing penitence and humble petition by drawing on Old and New Testament phraseology: "Lord, I believe, help Thou mine unbelief: / Lord, I repent, help mine impenitence: / Hide not Thy Face from me" ("Cried out with Tears," *CP*, 392.1–3). It ends with the speaker's plea that the Lord be mindful of how "I look to Thee while Thou dost look on me, / Thou Face to face with me and Eye to eye" (12–13). Here the speaker is strongly aware of being in individual encounter with God. Indeed, Rossetti's lyrical "I" always senses (and often rejoices) that membership in the community neither shields nor bars one from this individual encountering. At the same time, in the sonnet under discussion, a simultaneous communal encounter with God in the surrounding poems encompasses the single speaker's face-to-face meeting with him. Rossetti uses similar body images in the three poems, yet she also makes room for difference through her shifting prepositions: heart *in* heart, face *to* face, hand *in* hand. The plural voice of sonnet 8 prays,

> Lord, grant us eyes to see and ears to hear,
>> And souls to love and minds to understand,
>> And steadfast faces toward the Holy Land,
> And confidence of hope, and filial fear,
> And citizenship where Thy saints appear
> Before Thee heart in heart and hand in hand,
>
> (CP, 392.1–6)

while the plural voice of sonnet ten concludes confidently, "Yet art Thou with us, Thou to Whom we run, / We hand in hand with Thee and heart in heart" (CP, 393.13–14). The three sonnets, therefore, move from a communal prayer seeking intimacy with God, to an individual petition pleading for grace in the personal encounter with God, to a communal assertion that fellowship with God already graciously exists, also for the participating individual. The individual speaker, by participating in community, likewise moves from facing God, looking at God, to being with God, being in God.

Actually, the plural voice entirely frames section 1 of *Verses*, despite a title that seems to prioritize the individual ("Out of the Deep Have I Called unto Thee, O Lord"). The lyrical "we" speaks sonnets 1–5 as well as the concluding sonnet. Indeed, the sense of community arises as soon as the section (and volume) opens. Although the first word of the first poem is "Alone," it refers not to a lonely speaker or a lonely God but to God as the one-and-only to whom the believing community turns:

> Alone Lord God, in Whom our trust and peace,
>> Our love and our desire, glow bright with hope;
>> Lift us above this transitory scope
> Of earth.
>
> (CP, 389.1–4)

The individual "I" does not appear until sonnet 6. Yet even then, the speaker measures her relationship with God against what she sees in the wider community: "O Lord, I am ashamed to seek Thy Face / As tho' I loved Thee as Thy saints love Thee" (CP, 391.1–2); and she still hopes for the grace that will allow her "too"—that is, along with others—to taste God's "hidden sweetness" (7). In short, these poems show that in Rossetti's work, the lyrical "I" is a universal Christian voice, unmarked by gender, rank, or office, but not an independently constituted voice. Free to speak its individual experience, it nevertheless surrounds itself with the plural lyrical voice of a community, a communion of saints. This lyrical "we" likewise testifies to a range of religious experience: faith, hope, doubt, fear, awe. But though it is the catholic voice of the church, it is always the voice of the people of God, the body of Christ, not the institution or the episcopacy.

By thus focusing on this interdependence of individual and community in *Verses*, Rossetti's poetry avoids adopting either the ecclesiastical aura of Keble's and Williams's work or the singularity of Gerard Manley Hopkins's voice, with its often painful awareness of the individual in relation to God. It is neither church poetry nor exclusively private poetry. Instead, it harmonizes what is often represented as being in competition or discord. Elevating neither above the other, *Verses* reminds readers that individual and community can coexist—more than that, they can only flourish when brought together, when it is understood that they exist *within* each other *because of* Christ. Thus *Verses* implicitly upholds a pre-Anglo-Catholic, balanced, historic Anglican understanding of communion as both a fellowship with Christ and a fellowship with all believers. Communion with Christ, though a sacred encounter with the divine who manifests himself in bread and wine, does not lead to segregation of worshippers or even of spaces. Rather, when Christ shines his light on the fair unbroken web that is the lives of the saints, he reveals it as a perfect whole, interwoven with crosses that are themselves but lowly statured beside his own tall Cross (see "A bundle of myrrh," *CP,* 436.3, 4).

As a volume of poetry attuned to manifestation, replete with the postures of prayer, sensitive to visual-verbal aesthetics, and attentive to communion with Christ and the fellowship of all believers, *Verses* may truly be read as similarity-in-difference to the imaginal character of Anglo-Catholic liturgy. Rossetti's religious imaginary produces not merely a certain reading method or poetic strategy but, to return to Tennyson's phrase cited in chapter 3, a poetic collection that is itself an act of worship—particularly of Anglican-sacramental-ecclesiological-ritualist worship.

It may be that under this lengthy discussion of the "I" and "we" lurks the question of whether Rossetti's activity in *Verses* is so abstracted as to be ineffective. No doubt the lyrical "I" is in many ways universalized. It has no rank, gender, or class and seems unengaged with particularized situations. Only once does *Verses* refer to a specific clerical position, for example, even though sixty-nine poems deal with the liturgical calendar of feast or fast days. This single reference, moreover, occurs in "The General Assembly and Church of the Firstborn" (CP, 497–98), a poem centrally concerned with unity among diversity—or, in the poem's words, "one while manifold" (5). This poem describes the wide variety of people in the "ransomed race" (6), itemized by Rossetti as mitred priests, kings, patriarchs, matrons, mothers, virgins, little ones, home-comers, hermits, and life-losers. All, the speaker concludes, are "[f]riends, brethren, sisters, of Lord Jesus Christ" (19). Certainly no privilege to men or mitred priests can be found here, not even an implication that their task on earth in any way distinguishes them from little ones or life-losers. We might legitimately ask, therefore, whether Rossetti's representation of a singing and interdependent community remains too abstracted to address sufficiently the actual problems of her worshipping community. Was Rossetti perhaps avoiding real engagement with the issues? Or, if we understand her poems as implicit critique, is that critique so muted as to be virtually ineffective? May not her notion of a web made of crosses imply that we need not work to remove *particular* crosses (burdens), since they necessarily make the web?

It is fairly easy to conclude that Rossetti's approach in *Verses* is too renunciatory and otherworldly: this world must simply be borne while one waits for the next and better to arrive. There are at least two replies to this accusation. First, an otherworldly focus need not be escapist, as C. S. Lewis recognizes in *Mere Christianity* when he writes, "If you read history, you will find that the Christians who did most for the present world were just those who thought most about the next." Citing examples of activity by apostles and missionaries as well as by English evangelicals opposed to the slave trade, Lewis continues, "All left their mark on earth, precisely because their minds were occupied with heaven."[34] Lewis's remarks suggest that Rossetti's abstractions and otherworldly interests are not a priori ineffective in addressing present realities. I think also of John Tropman's assertion that a community ethic with an "otherworldly focus" usually recognizes "the process of change to be long term and systemic, rather than short term and individualistic."[35] Such an ethic does not absolve the individual of responsibility to work toward change, but by emphasizing an "ensemble self" rather than a "solo self," it lays no burdens on individuals to engender change single-handedly. Whereas an individualistic ethic might see change as beginning with the immediate and working toward the conceptual, a community ethic sees change as beginning with conceptual agreement and working toward the particular. Rossetti's *Verses* fits well within such an understanding, for it revitalizes a concept of community in danger of fading under the pressures of actual situations, even while its effacement of such particular situations potentially delays resolution of local and immediate issues. But with her understanding of the catholic, universal nature of the church, Rossetti could be patient with local situations. Renewing attention to the meaning and purpose of important concepts could, in her view, lead to systemic change in due time.

Secondly, though, Roe's recent reading of Rossetti's last devotional prose work seriously challenges a long-standing critical belief in Rossetti's renunciatory aesthetic. In a careful study of *The Face of the Deep*, Roe shows that Rossetti believed Scripture "teaches mankind to redeem the earth and itself," to "experience God through the medium of the world," though it be both "obstacle and gateway to heaven." Moreover, Roe argues that Rossetti, far from failing to see contradictions in religious texts or readings, identified and tried to reconcile them in her work. Roe writes, "Rossetti posits God as the answer to contradiction, and heaven as the place where all contradictions will be resolved.... [B]ut she arrives at this answer, not through the assertion of blind faith, but via complex literary strategies involving a combination of two other great contradictory forces: intellect and feeling."[36] As we have seen, intellect, feeling, and complex literary strategies also combine in *Verses* to depict God's community as resolving the problems of human community.

Nevertheless, if *Verses* does not engage with the actual contentious situations of Christ Church in the subject matter of its poems, might its engagement with the world appear in some other form? As mentioned in the previous chapter, Rossetti believed herself to have received the gift of poetry for the purpose of teaching; she also felt her responsibility to grow with each volume she published. Perhaps this sense accounts for the increasing number of devotional pieces included in, or later added to, each volume she published over her lifetime. In her earlier years, she accompanied her poetry writing with more direct and physically demanding ways of reaching the troubled or untaught—in, for example, her work at Highgate Penitentiary, her campaigning against pew rents, or her teaching in Sunday school (*LCR*, 4:413).[37] But as she grew older and struggled increasingly with health issues, she may have relied more on writing as her sole means of drawing people to the Christian faith. Her publications after 1881 are almost exclusively religious. Certainly in 1893, at age sixty-three, having just survived surgery for breast cancer and on the brink of her final, terminal illness, Rossetti could not afford to expend precious energy on a vigorous assault on ritualist practices, even if such an approach were in keeping with her character. Besides, she was not writing new poems for this volume. She was reshaping existing material from a variety of sources into a new, coherent text—one that she probably knew would be her last publication, her last opportunity to teach through poetry.

Perhaps she also felt that, collected as an independent volume, her late-career religious poems would reach a wider audience than one inclined to buy, say, a commentary on the book of Revelation. Likely, not all of Rossetti's usual readers had read all the poems in *Verses* in their original prose contexts. *Called to Be Saints*, *Time Flies*, and particularly *The Face of the Deep* (from which the majority of poems in *Verses* come) were devotionals and commentaries designed for thoughtful meditation and theological analysis. *The Face of the Deep* especially requires patient, even studious, attention to its complexities of thought, centered on each verse in the book of Revelation. Though it went into seven editions and seems to have been purchased for devotional as well as theological purposes, its poems probably reached a limited audience, perhaps mostly a clerical one willing to expend seven shillings sixpence on a scriptural commentary.[38] At three shillings sixpence, *Verses* was certainly a more affordable devotional option, even compared to *Called to Be Saints*, priced at five shillings. In producing this new context for her poems, Rossetti, I suggest, endeavored to reach a wider lay audience with her meditations on the Christian faith—specifically, as I have shown, on a relationship with Christ that involves both the individual and the worshipping community.

I want to consider lastly, then, how Rossetti's choice of the Society for Promoting Christian Knowledge (SPCK) as the publisher for *Verses* may have been an attempt to broaden the horizons of the religious community. In Rossetti scholarship, the devotional prose and poetry published by the SPCK has frequently been taken to have a primarily middle-class religious female readership, but as D'Amico observes, "With *Verses*, Rossetti most likely reached a wider audience than she had with the volumes in which the poems were first printed, for as one reviewer noted, *Verses* 'addresses itself definitely to the general public.'"[39] Kooistra gives substance to this possibility by examining the SPCK's records. She concludes, "The history of the SPCK suggests that these books were in fact principally distributed according to a class rather than a gender system of market differentiation."[40] A brief survey of the economics of book production for the mass market in the late

1800s situates this SPCK system within its broader context. In the 1870s and 1880s, the three-decker novel's first one-volume reissue (usually appearing twelve months after the first edition) was generally priced at five shillings, and its second, more densely worded reissue at three shillings sixpence.[41] The latter price quickly established itself as a cheaper, mass-market price—not a shilling shocker price, to be sure, but a price equated with patient waiting for a third printing. Moreover, even though the price band of five to seven shillings accounted for more titles in *Bookseller's* 1875 listings than the price band of three shillings sixpence to five shillings[42]—presumably indicating that many readers were willing to pay the higher of the cheap-range prices— Rossetti and the SPCK still marketed *Verses* at three shillings sixpence. Given the aesthetic features of the book, the SPCK could probably not go lower, but reaching a wide readership appears to have been a significant factor in pricing *Verses*. I conclude, therefore, that by removing her poems from their surrounding prose contexts, especially the complex *The Face of the Deep*, and by choosing the SPCK as publisher and marketer, Rossetti made her religious poetry more accessible to readers with modest disposable funds.

In short, I am suggesting that *Verses* was intended, in some ways, as an outreach effort. We have already seen that Rossetti may have envisioned her poems as iconic, perhaps even as having conversionary effect. She certainly expresses more directly as well a strong awareness of and concern for the spiritually lost. "Come," the speaker of one poem calls. "Come from your famine, your failure, your fighting; / come to full wrong-righting" ("This near-at-hand land breeds pain by measure," *CP*, 475–76.29–30). "Can man make haste who toils beneath a load?" asks another poem, and answers, "Out of himself, Lord, lift him up to Thee" ("Let Patience have her perfect work," *CP*, 461.2, 10). The sections "The World. Self-Destruction" and "Divers Worlds. Time and Eternity" both lament the world of sin and darkness and call for sleepers to awake ("Awake, thou that sleepest," *CP*, 478). Rossetti was by no means preoccupied with her own situation in the liturgical practices of ritualist churches. As her web image suggests, she felt the need to find and weave in the missing threads of the web.

For this reason, Rossetti's choice of the SPCK as publisher was particularly well-considered. From its inception in the late seventeenth century, the SPCK, as its name implies, had definite, missionary aims. "From the very first," write W. Allen and Edmund McClure—the latter the SPCK's editorial secretary in the late nineteenth century—"the Society has been forward in working for the evangelization of the poor.... [I]t devoted special efforts to particular classes of the community."[43] In 1815, it gave as its threefold object "the distribution of the Scriptures, the Prayer Book, and religious tracts; the education of the poor in the principles of our faith; and missions."[44] Allen and McClure observe that much of the financial resources needed to carry out these aims came from the annual subscriptions of the society's members (494), Rossetti among them. Indeed, Rossetti corresponded closely with Edmund McClure about her publications and issues in the society at large (see, for example, LCR, 4:264, 279, 352, 359, 373). She writes in one letter to him, "Thank you for your valued address, all the more welcome to my feelings because it sends rich and poor together to that Central Influence which undermines all selfishness without respect of persons." The letter continues with a revealing glimpse of Rossetti's concern over class relations and her desire that the working classes be addressed compassionately and the mercenary reprovingly: "It is so easy from an armchair to exhort a man on a bench: I wish the scene could be varied occasionally, and that instead of a roomfull [sic] of 'Labour' to appease, some heart and tongue of fire faced a roomful of 'Capital' to abate" (LCR, 4:164). If Rossetti was not able, either by opportunity or by character, to achieve the latter, she could and did support the former goal through her affiliation with the SPCK. In 1892, the SPCK reiterated again its goal of reaching the masses with religious literature; it called for "the increased support of all members of the Church" in this aim.[45] Both in her annual subscriptions to the SPCK and in her publications, Rossetti responded to this call. While not even the mass-market price of *Verses* made the book affordable for the working classes, Rossetti gave over to the SPCK her copyright on the book, so that all the profit of its sale went to promote the SPCK's missionary work.[46]

And *Verses* successfully reached a wide audience, becoming Rossetti's most popular volume of poems. Determining who, exactly, bought and read *Verses* is difficult, but even if Rossetti's and the SPCK's hopes of reaching the unchurched with high-quality, High Church religious poetry did not materialize in this case, Rossetti's purposes would not have been defeated. The communion of saints, after all, exceeds class boundaries, and the reading of her poetry by members of any class could, in Rossetti's view, only contribute to the well-being of the Church and its individual members. As we have seen, Rossetti also understood the communion of saints to supersede time barriers. The SPCK's decision after 1925 to cease publishing new editions of *Verses* suggests, at first glance, the failure of Rossetti's effort to produce a poetry transcending the local and particular. But as Kooistra makes clear, the failure of *Verses* to sell well in the mid-twentieth century lies not so much in a depreciation of the poetry as in the limited appeal of the "sweetly sad and saintly Rossetti" that the SPCK marketed when it issued *Verses* with frontispieces and plates highlighting the "ethereal spirituality" of the poet instead of the "technical achievement and aesthetic merit" of the poetry.[47] Consequently, *Verses* as a distinct volume dropped from sight for well over half a century.

Its poems, however, did not drop from sight. While Rossetti's last volume may not have projected its vision of the communion of saints into the twentieth century in quite the manner Rossetti may have intended, her effort to envision a communion of saints surpassing perceived boundaries met with a different mode of success. Several of her poems became well-known as hymns in the Anglican Church, with two of them being sung at her funeral at Christ Church, Woburn Square,[48] and others later gathered into new editions of *Hymns Ancient and Modern*. In light of Rossetti's status as a religious poet, it is not surprising that her own denomination should adopt some of her poems as hymns. But in the twentieth century, several of Rossetti's poems also began appearing in Presbyterian, Methodist, and Baptist hymnals, as well as in the nondenominational American *The Hymnal: Army and Navy*[49]—a tantalizing suggestion that *Verses* may have been among the books distributed at discounted prices to army and navy chaplains at home and overseas.[50] Five of the six most frequently included poems in these hymnals derive from *Verses*—a cross-denominational acceptance that unexpectedly testifies to the vision of *Verses*.[51] Quite likely, Rossetti would have approved such universality of religious expression, however much she identified herself with the beloved Anglican church of her baptism.

CHAPTER FIVE

"THE ONE DIVINE INFLUENCE AT WORK IN THE WORLD"

Adelaide Procter's Religious Imaginary

This chapter once again suggests that sustained practices have a powerful formative effect on how we imagine the world and our place in it and, consequently, on how we talk or write about it. As did Barrett Browning and Rossetti within their respective traditions, Adelaide Procter developed a poetic aesthetic and practice deeply informed by her worship. While the few critics to take up study of Procter's poetry in recent years have noted Procter's commitment to Roman Catholicism and its importance for her poetry, no one has thoroughly investigated the precise configurations of this Catholicism or considered it as generating a religious imaginary crucial to the poet's aesthetic and thematic choices.[1] Even those who wish to do justice to Procter's religious commitments tend to be selective in their treatment of the poet's last publication, the 1862 *A Chaplet of Verses*, preferring to discuss the few poems of social critique in that volume over, for example, the many paeans to Mary. To address this imbalance, I attend in the next chapter extensively, though not exclusively, to *A Chaplet of Verses*, arguing that it reveals Procter's Roman Catholic imaginary in diverse, often subtle ways. That *A Chaplet of Verses* has drawn such twentieth-century judgments as Susan Drain's—"This volume is the repository of [Procter's] worst verse, showing all the sentimental excesses of the Roman Catholic convert"—results, I believe, from a failure to recognize Procter's engagement with the complexities of nineteenth-century Roman Catholicism in England.[2] The present chapter investigates these complexities, showing that Procter's religious imaginary enabled a multidimensional religious-poetic voice and a serious engagement with religious, social, and political issues.

Readers might expect that I would again draw on David Tracy's concept of the analogical imagination to discuss Procter, since Tracy names Roman Catholicism among the strands of Christianity that lean toward manifestation more than proclamation. However, despite her Roman Catholic orientation, Procter does not fit Tracy's paradigm as well as Rossetti, not because the liturgy of the Mass was not formative for her but because it was not exclusively formative. From age twenty-five to her death at thirty-eight, Procter participated in worship at both St. James's Church, formerly the Spanish Embassy chapel and commonly called Spanish Place, and the Brompton or London Oratory. In both places, she observed the traditional Tridentine Mass, while in the latter, she also participated in the extraliturgical services of the revivalist movement. Tridentine Mass involved the solemn rituals of an ancient Latin liturgy. From her participation in this liturgy, Procter derived an attunement to reserve, mystery, and adoration of the divine; to the operations of parallel devotional texts; and to structures of moral authority. Revivalist services, by contrast, were not guided by ancient rubrics. They involved a new, fervent devotional style that included a hymnic musical orientation and an association with the poor and immigrant classes. Spurred initially by the (for Anglicans, shocking) conversion of leading Tractarian John Henry Newman to Romanism, it was characterized by expressiveness, enthusiasm, and an optimism that, if Newman, then all of England could be brought over to Rome. From this liturgy, Procter derived an appreciation for devotional expressiveness, apparent spontaneity and deliberate simplicity, and a moral concern for the poor and Irish. However, she resisted the revivalist enthusiasm for religious authority structures, instead quietly criticizing such structures as potentially hampering devotion and moral activity. Procter thus developed an imaginary not sufficiently captured in a single term such as either *proclamation* or *manifestation*. Rather, she became attuned to the power of both affect and reserve, spontaneity and control, lay devotion and moral authority—and used them strategically in her poetry. For example, on the one hand, she shifted the grounds for her use of an emotive, sentimental voice from the supposedly feminine aesthetic typically prescribed for Victorian women writers to a religious aesthetic much favored by important revivalist male figures, who co-opted it for their own ends—thus enabling her to cast her poetry alongside texts perhaps considered more authoritative. On the other hand, she also developed a less emotive style characterized more by subtlety than expressiveness. When we so understand Procter's poetics as evolving from her varied liturgical experiences, we can move beyond the perception that Procter's religious work consists only of a few late-life, excessively sentimental poems that do not warrant critical attention.

Procter's Liturgical Experiences

As her correspondence with her friend Bessie Parkes reveals, Procter chose not one but two locations for her regular worship life. After her entry into the Roman Catholic Church on August 15, 1851, on the Feast of the Assumption of Mary, she and her sister Edith (who, along with a third sister, Agnes, also left Anglicanism for Catholicism) took a pew in St. James's Church in Spanish Place, and Procter regularly invited Parkes to join them in worship there.[3] Spanish Place traced its roots and its name to the days of Elizabeth I, when its chapel was let to the Spanish ambassador. It relinquished its official connection with Spain in 1827 but continued to display the personal standard of King Alfonso XIII, thus keeping visible its former Continental connection. Long a site of public worship for English Catholics as well as Spanish dignitaries, in the 1840s Spanish Place swelled to a "very large congregation [that included] the principal members of the aristocracy and gentry professing the Popish faith"; in the 1850s, a "vast crowd … [still] thronged the church."[4] To accommodate these numbers, Spanish Place expanded the number of masses offered on Sundays and during the week; under the influence of revivalism, it also added such services as Benediction and Compline, though not the evening exercises offered at the Oratory.[5] In the years of Procter's attendance there, Spanish Place was a worship community in flux, open to new practices, yet chiefly committed to the historic Tridentine Mass. The latter is the only liturgical service there that Procter names in her correspondence with Parkes.

Procter also regularly attended the London Oratory.[6] As a Roman Catholic church, the Oratory, like Spanish Place, naturally observed Tridentine Mass, on Sundays and Wednesdays, as well as Benediction; but it also offered other worship exercises. Officially deemed extraliturgical because they were not prescribed in the *Roman Missal* but essentially still liturgical in nature, these exercises were shaped by nineteenth-century Catholic revivalism, not by the Sacred Congregation of Propaganda, the administrative body in Rome that regulated the Church's ecclesiastical affairs. Procter frequently attended these revivalist exercises centered on preaching and vernacular hymn singing rather than Mass, and she urged Parkes to accompany her, often mentioning as incentive the preaching of the Superior, Father Faber. Faber, who converted to Roman Catholicism shortly after Newman in 1845, had returned from his postconversion trip to Rome with a dedication unrivalled by his English contemporaries to an "Italian devotional school" of worship.[7] Along with Newman, he committed himself to establishing in England a Congregation of the Oratory of St. Philip Neri. Because of his fundamentally different temperament from Newman, Faber departed in 1849 from Newman's oratory in Birmingham to establish an oratory in London (first located in King William Street, the Strand, and then later in Brompton). Although the two houses remained in friendly contact, Newman did not favor the Roman devotions so important to Faber, whose "baroque spirituality and extravagant emotions" set the Oratory apart even from other Catholic churches in London.[8]

Worshipping in two churches thus bound by a common liturgical celebration of Mass, though differentiated by the Oratory's additional exercises, Procter did not so much experience conflict as diversity in her worship life. The basic tenets of the Roman faith held in each place, most significantly, the interpretation of the Mass as a sacrifice the "same in substance with that which Christ offered . . . upon the cross," that is, as a ritual in which, at every celebration, "Christ is mystically immolated" in the consecrated bread and wine, truly present in body as well as spirit;[9] just as significantly, the leading London Catholic clergyman in the 1850s—Henry Edward Manning, himself an 1851 convert from Anglicanism—could preach in each place without opposition. Like Faber, Manning had gone to Rome for his training in the priesthood. Although never adopting Faber's devotional style, he became a committed revivalist. Shortly after returning to London, and to the dismay of many English Catholics who did not favor the Italianate influence, he was appointed provost of the Chapter of Westminster. The position gave him access to all established Catholic churches, including Spanish Place, while his revivalist devotional interests led him to accept invitations by Faber to preach also in the Oratory—as, at least on one occasion, Faber did in Spanish Place.[10] Admiring Manning's preaching as much as she did Faber's (GCPP Parkes 8.37), Procter could easily interpret Faber's and Manning's crossings-over as an affirmation of her own multiple liturgical engagements within a larger Roman Catholic context.

That Procter and others might engage simultaneously in these diverse forms of Roman Catholic worship might seem unlikely if measured by the dominant twentieth-century historical construct of a sharp nineteenth-century divide between old English Roman Catholicism (which traced its heritage to the sixteenth-century refusal to join Anglicanism) and revivalist Catholicism. But as Mary Heimann has shown in *Catholic Devotion in Victorian England*, nineteenth-century English Catholicism had a much more blended character than this construct allows; the different forms of Catholicism were not truly oppositional. Yes, there were different approaches to devotion, with the Oratory adopting the most elaborate practices, and sometimes denounced because of them; but the differences do not fall into the neat categories the earlier historiography supposed. Rather, the debate in English Roman Catholicism—as across Victorian culture—centered on "how much importance ought to be attributed to feeling."[11] By participating in two forms of worship, Procter entered this debate; though I believe ultimately she saw how its tensions cohered in its commitments, no doubt there were times when the differences proved challenging to the formation of her religious imaginary.

The conviction that outward differences could be overcome by an inner cohesion was seemingly borne out by the architecture and interior arrangement of Procter's two Roman Catholic churches. Spanish Place and the Oratory had very different exteriors but quite similar interiors. *Survey of London* indicates that the original embassy chapel was built in 1791 in the neoclassical style by Italian-born-and-educated Roman Catholic architect Joseph Bonomi.[12] Its original architecture, therefore, signified balance, simplicity, and purity. By contrast, the Oratory as first constructed (1853–54) was a long, low structure in plain brick with an ordinary peaked roof.[13] It was designed by Roman Catholic architect Joseph John Scoles and externally resembled, as some have said, a warehouse. Perhaps because the structure was meant to be temporary, the Oratorians did not consider its external form critical to their work of devotion and service. Temporary or not, these external differences between the Oratory and Spanish Place disappeared from view once one stepped inside the buildings. The interior of the Oratory from the start conveyed an Italianate sensibility. Faber brought in pictures of the Virgin Mary and of St. Philip of Neri to flank the altar. Crucifixes and statues proliferated, as did crimson damask, lace, flowers, candles, and chandeliers, while carved columns, niches, and chapels further marked the interior.[14] The overall effect was baroque. Likewise, the interior of Spanish Place grew markedly more elaborate at midcentury. As the editor of *The Lamp* observed in 1852, it was "one of the most richly decorated places of worship in the metropolis. The Lady chapel, forming a new aisle the whole length of the church, and the altars of St. James and of St. Vincent de Paul have all been opened within the last three years.... [A] splendid new high-altar in the decorated 'Renaissance' (semi-Italian) style has just been completed."[15] Apparently, neoclassicism was replaced by an Italianate style here, so that the visual aesthetic inside both Spanish Place and the Oratory inclined toward the elaborate, with the Oratory perhaps the more extravagant and Spanish Place the more formally designed of the two. No doubt Procter, though not developing a Rossetti-like verbal-visual aesthetic (the revivalists as a whole seemed not to theorize their ecclesiology), observed that differences in exterior form did not preclude an inner compatibility—or, to extrapolate, that different modes of Catholic worship did not preclude (though perhaps they challenged) a unified imaginary. Certainly in her letters, Procter never pits one liturgical environment or experience against the other. In her religious poetry, too, she crosses formations, blending and critiquing different liturgical voices, interests, and forms to create a distinctive religious-poetic voice.

The remainder of this chapter investigates more precisely the characteristic features of the traditional and revivalist Catholic liturgies to discover how they impacted the imaginary, and, subsequently, how that imaginary opened into the poetry (although, as with the previous poets, the close readings of poetry occur mainly in the subsequent chapter). The discussion considers Procter's religious imaginary as constituted by and participating in a diverse Catholicism, and it presupposes that Procter gave the same degree of critical and creative attention to her religious poetry as she did to her poems that scrutinize gender or society, poems that have received the greater share of critical attention to date.

The Mass-Inflected Imaginary

Because I have discussed the Anglican liturgy first in this book, the historic Roman liturgy described next might sound as an echo of the Anglican; it is, of course, the precursor, its basic pattern existing even before its rubrics were set by the Council of Trent (from which derives the term *Tridentine*) in 1570. The Roman and Anglican liturgies share basic structures (such as the pattern of Epistle reading, Gospel reading, sermon, and creed; the use of collects; the exchanges between priest and people/servers), but there are important differences between them, differences that affect the imaginary of the worshipper. Whereas, for example, the Anglican service identifies its main components by liturgical element (liturgy of the Word, liturgy of the Communion), the rite of Mass historically identifies its components by who is to benefit from them (the Mass of the Catechumens, the Mass of the Faithful). Further, whereas the Anglican liturgy, in its verbal structures, emphasizes an (individual and communal) encounter with God, the historic Roman liturgy, in its verbal patterns, stresses a mysterious act of God that occurs apart from an individual's reception of him. Thirdly—and connected to the preceding idea—whereas Anglican communion, especially in High Church thought, is premised on the spiritual presence of the resurrected Christ, Tridentine Mass is premised on the physical sacrifice of the re-suffering Christ, the Victim in each consecration. The first, therefore, is oriented toward the future; it looks toward the heavenly supper with the glorified Christ. The second has no counterpart in the next world, since Christ will never again be Victim there; it therefore urges adoration for Christ's sacrifice in the present more than joyful yearning toward the future. To unpack these assertions, I next outline the pattern of the Roman liturgy, then take up further its impact on the imaginary and the poetry.[16]

Although sometimes prefaced by a penitential rite called the Asperges, the Mass proper begins with the first of two halves, namely, the Mass of the Catechumens, or those under instruction.[17] Priest and servers process toward the altar and make the sign of the cross. They recite Psalm verses and pray with bowed heads at the foot of the altar, the chief prayer being the priest's Confiteor, or confession of sin, afterwards repeated by the servers. Then the priest alone moves closer to the altar and, having gained assurance through prayer, speaks the Introit (a Psalm), followed by the Kyrie Eleison ("Lord, have mercy") and the Gloria ("Glory to God in the highest"), both of which the choir also sings, though not in time with the priest, who speaks at his own pace and usually finishes before the choir does. Next comes an exchange between priest and servers ("The Lord be with you." "And with thy spirit."), after which the priest speaks the collect of the day. The liturgical language so far is Latin, and most of the service is inaudible to the people in the pew, though certain beginning and ending phrases are spoken loudly enough that they may know where in the service the priest and servers are. Latin continues in most of the Instruction that follows, except for the sermon: an Epistle reading (from the letters of Paul), choir responses (a Gradual and an Alleluia), a Gospel reading, the sermon, and the Nicene Creed (the sermon may be preceded by a second reading of the Scripture passages in English). Historically, the catechumens were dismissed at this point, though no longer by the nineteenth century. But even without dismissal, they know by the nomenclature of the second half of the liturgy that they are to see themselves as spiritually separate from it.

The Mass of the Faithful, which comes next, has four main components: offertory, consecration, communion, and conclusion, all of them also spoken in mostly inaudible Latin, with the priest and servers mostly facing the altar, not the people. The offertory here refers not to the people's gifts but to the priest's offering of the sacramental elements to God. It begins with a designated Scripture verse; moves to the priest's extension of bread and wine in his hands over the altar as he prays for God's acceptance of the "spotless host" for his own and others' sins; includes an incensing of the offerings and people, the priest's washing of hands, and a prayer that the Trinity might receive the offering being made in remembrance of Jesus's passion and in honor of Mary and the saints; and concludes with the Orate Fratres spoken by the priest ("Pray, brethren, that my sacrifice and yours be acceptable to God the Father almighty"), the Suscipiat spoken by the servers ("May the Lord accept this sacrifice at your hands, to the praise and glory of his name, for our good and the good of all his Holy Church"), the Secret (a designated prayer whose name suggests mystery, though it was printed in the *Missal*) spoken by the priest, and the Amen response by the servers.

The canon or rule of consecration begins with another exchange between priest and servers ("Lift up your hearts." "We lift them up unto the Lord." "Let us give thanks to the Lord our God." "It is meet and right."), continues with the Sanctus ("Holy, holy, holy") and Benedictus ("Blessed is he who comes in the name of the Lord"), and peaks with the actual consecration or transubstantiation of the elements, in which, according to the Roman faith, at the moment that the priest speaks Christ's words of Luke 22:19–20, Christ voluntarily undergoes "a destructive change" by the "apparent separation of the body from the blood" (that is, the bread and wine), and becomes again the Victim for sin.[18] Then the Victim (formerly the host) is again offered to God—or, more properly, offers himself—through elevation above the altar. The priest then prays for the dead and others (for example, saints and the living), and a doxology concludes the consecration.

The communion begins when the priest speaks the Lord's Prayer and the Libera Nos (prayer to Mary for freedom), after which he breaks the Victim/host, recites the Agnus Dei three times ("Lamb of God, who takest away the sins of the world, have mercy on us, grant us peace"), prays that he be not judged or condemned when he partakes of Christ's body, strikes his breast while reciting three times, "Lord, I am not worthy," then receives the bread and wine himself. If he also gives communion to others—and it is not required—he turns to the people, makes the sign of the cross over each person kneeling at the altar rail, and says to each, while placing the host on the person's tongue, "May the Body of our Lord Jesus Christ preserve your soul for eternal life. Amen." The people do not receive the wine. The Mass of the Faithful concludes with ablutions, postcommunion psalms and prayers, the dismissal blessing (*Ite Missa est*, from which the word *Mass* derives), and the reading of John 1:1–14, an account of the incarnation.

This liturgical pattern Procter engaged in weekly—perhaps more often—for some thirteen years (eleven of them before the publication of *A Chaplet of Verses*). Marie Belloc Lowndes (daughter of Bessie Parkes) records, "Until it was quite impossible for her to do so, [Procter] went to Mass every morning" (GCPP Parkes 16.1.6). The Catholic registries I was able to consult list regular Mass services at Spanish Place and the Oratory only on Sundays and Wednesdays, so Lowndes may be inaccurate in stating "every morning," but there is no doubt that Procter went as often as she could, even when ill, for in a note to Parkes dated January 1, 1859, she writes, "Tho' I have crawled to an early mass I can not drag myself to you I fear" (GCPP Parkes 8.8).[19] How might participation in this liturgy have shaped her religious imaginary? What does Tridentine Mass impress upon the Catholic worshipper?

Two formations it does *not* impress are the dialogic and the communal. Unlike either the Congregationalist or the Anglican service, the Mass is not a dialogue between God and people, at least not laypeople; neither is it a memorial, nor an encounter between God and gathered community. Rather, in Tridentine Mass the people in the pew are distanced from the prayers, exchanges, and actions at the altar. They do not participate orally (or even aurally) in the service, not even to sing or to speak the creed. As a result, while the Catholic Church stresses its universality *as a church*, the liturgy construes the gathered people less as a body of believers, a congregation, than as individuals making their private devotions to God alongside the church's official act. Not a call to independence, the liturgy nevertheless expects individuals to keep their own focus during the Mass, in appropriate parallel step with the Latin forms. The church even encouraged laypeople to use additional supports for this purpose. Since 1740, English Roman Catholics had, in fact, often attended Mass with Bishop Richard Challoner's *The Garden of the Soul*, a manual of spiritual exercises and devotions, in hand.[20] This devotional book provided alternative English texts for the pew-person to pray while the Latin Mass proceeded. For example, the manual instructed the layperson, when the priest says his Confiteor in Latin, "You may either say the Confiteor, according to the form [provided earlier], or you may pray as follows: [then follows an alternative prayer]."[21] As T. E. Muir writes, while such "parallel reflections on the text" might be called participation, they "could easily spill over into personal devotions that were only loosely connected with the public action"—a possibility seemingly recognized by the required ringing of a bell to attract attention at important moments in the service.[22]

Procter never mentions *The Garden of the Soul* in her correspondence with Parkes, but she still may have used the manual at Spanish Place, where Challoner had been a "familiar figure."[23] Even if she did not, she must have been aware that vernacular devotions were permitted, even encouraged, as parallel texts to the Latin liturgy. Many of her poems seem just such parallel texts, built as they are on phrases from the fixed portions of the Latin liturgy. Procter seems to have emulated Bishop Challoner in providing vernacular (poetic) meditations to benefit the lay worshipper. Because many of these poems are dispersed throughout her two *Legends and Lyrics* collections (published in 1858 and 1861), their liturgical nature has gone unremarked. But gathered together as in the next chapter, they reveal Procter's creative engagement with formal worship patterns. Quite possibly, they also reveal her sense of disjunction from the Latin liturgy of the church; that is, her creative engagement with liturgy may have been compelled by a sense of dislocation or even frustration, one that the Latin-speaking clergy may not feel. Whether or not this is the case, the liturgy of the Mass, in spite of its potentially isolating effects, does not intend to frustrate or exclude but to liberate the worshipper, a point emphasized by Cardinal Ratzinger (now Pope Benedict XVI): "In the liturgy, we are all given the freedom to appropriate, in our own personal way, the mystery which addresses us."[24] Ratzinger does not encourage creativity in the liturgy itself (as pope, he encouraged the return of the traditional Mass after it had fallen into disuse), but he views Tridentine Mass as freeing each worshipper to be active in the necessary way. One activity Procter clearly felt freed into was the writing of devotional poems built on liturgical phrases from the Mass.

If the Mass is non-community-oriented and nondialogic between God and people, Ratzinger's phrasing—"the mystery which addresses us"—helpfully alerts us to what the Mass does convey about its fundamental presuppositions. First, what happens at the altar is *not* an act of the people, not even of the clergy, but an act of God. The people are addressed; they do not address. Christ does not arrive in actual bodily form under the bread and wine because a person calls him forth. Rather, when the priest repeats the words recorded in Luke ("This is my body"; "this is my blood"), he speaks *in persona Christi*, and Christ then acts on his own words. Second, though this act cannot be explained, it does communicate (the mystery addresses us). It imparts itself as mystery "to impress upon the mind, that some things are clearly known and distinctly understood, and that other things are now hidden from us for the trial of our obedience and faith."[25] For this reason, Latin remains suitable for the liturgy, as does inaudibility. The Bible readings and sermon, being for the instruction of the catechumens, need be in the vernacular, but the rest of the service, being for God and even by God, may (should) be spoken in a universal, unchanging language, even if the people cannot understand or hear it.[26] As Thomas Woods, defender of Tridentine Mass, explains, "the instruction or edification of the people is not . . . [Mass's] primary function."[27] Rather, Mass's primary function is to enable the mystery of Christ's repeated offering of himself to God for human sin. At Mass, worshippers are, in effect, again at the foot of the cross. Indeed, in a Roman Catholic church, they are typically at the foot of a crucifix, not a cross, the passionate Christ being more the focus than the resurrected Christ represented by the empty cross. Therefore, in the Mass, the action of God calls the worshipper not primarily to verbal celebration but to silent penitence and a sorrowful but simultaneously adoring heart, receptive to Christ's renewed giving of himself. And because in Mass, Christ is again present on earth, the sacrament conjures no future heavenly banquet but instead stirs one to adoration in the present, to living in the consciousness of this sacrifice. In short, Tridentine Mass does not cultivate the power of the Word/word or the communion of saints or the sense of a heavenly future but instead reinforces the propriety of quiet, penitent waiting for the mysterious arrival of the Christ who will work again to redeem the sinner. His mysterious coming cannot be spoken, but his presence can be adored, even when not actually received.[28] On the one hand, then, reserve is an appropriate response to the deepest mysteries of faith enacted by God; on the other hand, so is (underspoken or silent) adoration of the passionate Christ incarnate in the sacrament.[29]

Procter's poems alluding to Mass carry both these inflections, as even a few lines from "Our Daily Bread" demonstrate. In this poem, the speaker prays to receive bread of strength, bread of healing grief, and bread of comfort in the first three stanzas, then in the final stanza moves to the bread of Mass:

> Give us our daily Bread,
>   The Bread of Angels, Lord,
> By us, so many times,
>   Broken, betrayed, adored:
> His Body and His Blood;—
>   The feast that Jesus spread:
> Give him—our life, our all—
>   To be our daily bread!"[30]

Though the poem has been building toward this point, once it is reached, reserve takes over in the form of a dash. The body and blood on the left of the dash are silently transmuted into the bread and wine of the feast on the right; nothing can be spoken during the actual process of immolation. But afterwards, the speaker's adoration bursts out, though briefly. Her final petition contains an escalating acknowledgment of Jesus as bread, life, all (and "Jesus" here bears the Mass-weight of the one sacrificed, not the one risen). But the line, stanza, and poem also end here. As another of Procter's speakers says, "What words can speak the joy" of union with Jesus? "Silence and tears are best / For things divine" ("The Sacred Heart," *PAAP*, 365–66.90, 94–95).

In addition to its formative impressions regarding the value of mystery, reserve, and adoration, Tridentine Mass attunes the imaginary toward distinctions that, on the one hand, require a submissive attitude and, on the other hand, endorse an instructive impulse. Most obviously, the Mass distinguishes between clergy and laity, with the clergy and assistants conducting the liturgy almost as if no one else were present. Whereas the Anglican priest always uses the first-person plural pronoun, placing himself among the people, the Roman Catholic priest, guided by the *Missal*, not only uses the first-person singular pronoun quite often but sometimes even highlights his mediating role between God and people: "[G]rant that the sacrifice which I, unworthy as I am, have offered to the eyes of thy majesty, may be acceptable to thee, and, by thy mercy, be a propitiation for me, *and for all for whom I have offered it.*"[31] Phrases such as these mark the spiritual authority that the church confers on the priest. The principle of spiritual distinction also reaches beyond Mass to the larger structures of the Roman Church; when, after centuries of governance by vicars, the hierarchy of the Roman Church was restored in England in 1850, revivalist Catholics readopted it with enthusiasm and posited deference to papal authority as a virtue. Manning, for example, expressed his submission to the pope in such published statements as "If anything I have written needs correction or suppression . . . I should rejoice in the opportunity of giving an example of docility in opinion."[32] Faber declared similar sentiments, while both men preached sermons on the temporal power and authority of the pope and the Roman Church. In addition, Manning—critical of English injustices inflicted on Ireland, though opposed to Irish autonomy—held up Irish loyalty to the Roman faith as evidence that the Catholic principle of submission creates strong civic virtues. Good Catholics, Manning argued, make good subjects when treated justly, because they believe in authoritative structures.[33] From the perspective of a Congregationalist, such praise of and willing deference to authority would be counterproductive to genuine intellectual investigation and the pursuit of religious truth. Faber and Manning, however, found the principle of submission to authority liberating, as Robert Gray's analysis of the effect of submission to Rome on Manning indicates: "There need be no more questions; the answers were all determined in Rome."[34] Shifting the weight of ultimate responsibility to a higher power freed Manning from an anxiety that had crippled his productivity as an Anglican. In turn, he willingly assumed responsibility for instructing those beneath him in the hierarchy. It was an exchange system that worked well for those for whom moral, religious, and intellectual independence seemed insufficiently humble as well as threatening.

As a Catholic, Procter had to have concurred with the principle of spiritual authority—indeed, in her poetry she adopts it—but as she also knew, women's lives and writing could be profoundly circumscribed by the assumptions that authoritative systems sometimes generated. As Gill Gregory demonstrates in her book on Procter's life and work, Procter felt constrained to negotiate with male authority in many areas: with the spiritual weight of John Keble, the poetic influence of Robert Browning, the paternal pressure of Bryan Procter, and the editorial demands of Charles Dickens. Given these already present demands, it is perhaps not surprising that Procter never declared the kind of papal allegiance that Faber and Manning did. While deference to authority—in the sense of willingness to abide by tradition to a degree—might have freed her from the compulsion to produce independent interpretations of scriptural passages or to create new generic forms, ultimately it may have been too threatening a principle for a woman poet to endorse. Consequently, Procter made no mention, in either correspondence or poetry, of the pope or of subjecting her work to scrutiny by religious authorities. Indeed, unlike Rossetti, whose devotional writings were reviewed by a panel of Anglo-Catholic priests before being accepted for publication by the SPCK, Procter selected nonreligious publishing houses for all her work, including *A Chaplet of Verses*.

Oddly, this resistance to authority did not translate into truly democratic exchanges or forms in Procter's poetry, perhaps because the Mass-formed imaginary deeply feels what the very structure of Mass impresses, namely, a division among laypeople too.[35] The distinction between catechumens and faithful implicitly validates, on the one hand, the need for instruction in the move toward faith (for the catechumens) and, on the other hand, the instructive impulse itself (in the faithful). That is, the structure of the Mass justifies the voice of moral authority, or at least the felt burden to reach via teaching those yet outside the church. In this sense, the Mass legitimizes what might negatively be called didacticism but might positively be seen as a catechumenical effort to draw the less knowledgeable or less committed toward greater spiritual benefits through direct instruction, even rebuke. Procter's speakers often adopt a morally instructive voice, while the listener receives, or possibly requests, the instruction. Sometimes, this stance becomes problematic, as when the poetic persona's supposed moral authority prevents a truly democratic exchange of ideas with speakers of supposedly less developed moral or religious fiber. Procter's poetic auditors seldom get to offer their own stories or experiences, and Procter makes little use of, for example, dramatic monologues, which would permit lower-class speakers to voice their own perspectives on the interventions of religious authorities in their lives. Instead, in almost all of Procter's poems involving conversation, the exchange takes a question-and-answer form in which the main speaker answers the concerns, worries, or doubts of another. In "Comfort," for example, the speaker not only offers comfort but also poses the potential circumstances the auditor might have experienced to necessitate receiving this comfort:

> Has Fate o'erwhelmed thee with some sudden blow?
>   Let thy tears flow;
> But know when storms are past, the heavens appear
>   More pure, more clear;
> ....
> Has thy soul bent beneath earth's heavy bond?
>   Look thou beyond;
> If life is bitter—*there* forever shine
>   Hopes more divine.
>
>   (*PAAP*, 187.19–22, 27–30)

For this reason, there is not much difference between Procter's conversational and monologic lyric poems: in both cases, the moral pedagogy goes all one way. Notably, though, Procter does not limit her moral pedagogy to lower-class audiences. Many of her poems of social and religious critique assume middle-class readers whom she wishes to galvanize into charitable action. Speaking to the less privileged listeners within her poems, Procter adopts a kindly, almost patronizing voice; speaking to complacent middle- or upper-class readers, she takes a much sharper tone. In other words, her moral authority cuts across class divisions, although it is shaped in different ways, depending on her audience. For a woman poet, then, the distinctions implied by the Mass and extended throughout the church's ecclesiastical structure could prove both opportunity and threat. As one of the faithful, Procter could legitimately instruct, even chide, others. As nonclergy and female, she could do so to a limited extent, even more limited than less hierarchically organized denominations (such as Congregationalism) might permit. Yet Procter seems in her poetry to thrive on the opportunity more than worry about the restriction.

Finally, Tridentine Mass offered to Procter's imaginary a rich sacred music that informs the musical consciousness in some of her poems—a point I shall explore here and not carry over to the next chapter. Both Spanish Place and the Oratory drew acclaim for their sacred music, which drew on Renaissance polyphony as well as baroque and classical compositions. Muir notes that the embassy chapels were "centers of musical excellence" constituting a "crucial link with Catholic music on the Continent"; they included in their choirs "professional singers from the London opera scene"—so much so that by the 1840s "music originally designed for the liturgy was transformed into concert oratorios appealing to religious and non-religious alike."[36] Likewise, liturgical music at the Oratory drew from the start on well-established European musical settings for Mass, using a choir, not lay participation, and Latin, not English, text.[37] Organists at Spanish Place and the Oratory drew on works from the Renaissance Palestrina to the baroque Scarlatti to the classical Mozart—as did Procter in her poetry, most directly in "A Tomb in Ghent" (*PAAP,* 75–84). In this poem, the maiden whose singing arouses the narrator's attention in the opening verse paragraph—a girl whose musical formation has occurred under her father's masterful organ playing in (the Roman Catholic) St. Bavon's Cathedral in Ghent—does not sing "as village maidens sing, and few / The framers of her changing music knew" (14–15). Instead, this young girl sings "Chants such as heaven and earth first heard of when /

The master Palestrina held the pen" (16–17).[38] The narrator, her own musical ear "not quite unskilled," has often thrilled with "heart and soul to the grand echo" of such music, and she now marvels, as the maiden's "cadence fell / From the Laudate" (a musical setting of the opening phrase of Psalm 117, "Praise the Lord") and moved "[i]nto Scarlatti's minor fugue, how she / Had learned such deep and solemn harmony" (20, 21, 22–23, 24–25), including, we learn later, "Mozart's Sanctus" (200). The composers Procter chose in this poem as formative for the girl's musical life were all Roman Catholics; Procter did not, for instance, include Bach, the famous Lutheran organ composer of the baroque era, but did name his near-contemporary, the Catholic Alessandro Scarlatti.[39] No doubt church organists, also in Spanish Place and the Oratory, did not choose their music according to the church affiliation of the composers, but all the same, Procter's choices here imply that England's richest sacred music derives from a European Roman Catholic heritage—or at least, that the Ghent-born (Roman Catholic) maiden's musical life involves deeper and more solemn harmony than does that of the English village maidens.

Procter's experience with sophisticated church music seems also to lie behind the poem's descriptions of the power, indeed, what she often calls the soul, of the organ, which can "thrill with master-power the breathless throng" (167):

> Only the organ's voice, with peal on peal,
> Can mount to where those far-off angels kneel [in the buttresses]
> . . . .
> Bearing on eagle-wings the great desire
> Of all the kneeling throng, and piercing higher
> Than aught but love and prayer can reach, until
> Only the silence seemed to listen still;
> Or gathering like a sea still more and more,
> Break in melodious waves at Heaven's door,
> And then fall, slow and soft, in tender rain,
> Upon the pleading, longing hearts again.
>
> (71–72, 79–86)

One can imagine Procter composing such lines with Oratorian and Spanish Place organ music resounding in her memory. Perhaps more significantly, though, these lines—and their counterpart, Procter's famous "A Lost Chord"—connect organ music to religious feeling. In "A Tomb in Ghent," organ music rolls to the heights of its expressive reach but then falls back again upon its hearers. In this surge and fade of sound, music parallels feeling, the lines imply: great desires surge upward too, but in the end the hearts are still longing after the inexpressible. Similarly, in "A Lost Chord," the speaker relates how she inadvertently struck a "chord divine" that she could not afterwards find again, though it calmed her "fevered spirit" and "linked all perplexéd meanings / Into one perfect peace" (*PAAP*, 224.22, ll, 17–18). As Mason notes, this poem "betrays a troubled mix of reserve and expressivity" in which the speaker suggests that feeling, like music, can have both "consolatory and replenishing" effects; yet in the end it, like the chord, "slip[s] away or become[s] unobtainable" so that the speaker ends up "bearing the weight of emotion internally rather than externalizing it aesthetically on the page."[40] Both poems, then, draw on Procter's experience with sophisticated church music to query how the "soul" (of organ or of person) might speak, how it might address us. In considering such problems of expression, these poems may also testify to a certain tension in Procter's religious imaginary as the poet works to resolve the quite different formations that the reserved Mass and the expressive devotional exercises supply. But as the next section and chapter reveal, this tension does not color all Procter's poems. Rather, Catholic revivalism also enabled Procter to shape a poetics in which her speakers externalize feeling on the page rather than bear its weight internally. To the formation of this imaginary we now turn.

The Revivalist Imaginary

Procter likely attended Mass more often at Spanish Place, her parish church, than the Oratory. It is unlikely, for instance, that she was referring to the Oratory when she describes how she "crawled to an early mass" in very poor health (GCPP Parkes 8.8), because the Oratory was farther from her home than was Spanish Place. However, she seems to have attended Mass at least occasionally at the Oratory, for she twice notes to Parkes a significant difference in liturgical order there: "[T]he sermon is preached before mass instead of as usual in the middle of the service" (GCPP Parkes 8.36); "The *sermon* is at 11" (GCPP Parkes 8.35).[41] The Oratorian foregrounding of the sermon, I argue next, functions as one mark of a revivalist Catholicism that played significantly on and sometimes against the Mass-inflected imaginary described so far, potentially enriching it, perhaps sometimes confusing it. This revivalist spirit spilled over into the devotional exercises that deeply shaped certain key features of Procter's religious poetics: florid expressiveness, apparent spontaneity of composition and delivery, and privileging of an apparently simple, emotional faith over intellectual or theological complexity. As we shall see, while modern neuroscientific and philosophical examinations may discredit the emotion-intellect divide that the Victorians endorsed (and assigned to gender), revivalist Catholics, including Procter, seem to have played it up for their own purposes.

That the Oratorians relocated the vernacular sermon to the opening of the liturgy points to revivalist Catholicism's determination to make Roman Catholicism accessible to the masses. The Latin Mass might draw catechumens and faithful, but for mission work to succeed—and the revivalists, remember, believed the conversion of all England possible—a fervent vernacular mode had to lead the way. The Oratory's two key preachers, Faber and Manning, both rejected a scripted sermon text in favor of spontaneous delivery from prepared notes. Scripted versus extemporaneous preaching (and praying) was much debated across denominations at the time, but these men notably shifted their methods after their conversions from Anglicanism to Roman Catholicism, with Manning commenting after his conversion that his Anglican sermons were too studied and monotonous.[42] It would seem that the new Catholic practices fostered a deeper regard than Tridentine Mass for spontaneity, or at least, for spontaneous effect. Faber preached in what his biographers and contemporaries describe as a florid or ornate style—"warm, enthusiastic, romantic . . . essentially evangelical"—while Manning gave the impression of having "an effortless flow of language."[43] Manning even deprecated as improper for preachers forms that required too much craft-consciousness; such forms hampered the more pressing business of preaching the gospel. Referring to Jesus's words in Luke 10:1–4 that the disciples should go out and preach without pause, Manning declared, "If we are to 'salute no one by the way,' certainly we are not intended to write sonnets"— or, apparently, sermons too obviously attentive to their own craft.[44] Certainly, the extemporaneous method worked well for both Faber and Manning. The Oratory quickly became known as "a center of great preachings," with Faber as the central figure,[45] while Manning drew crowds in whatever church he preached: the Oratory, Spanish Place, and elsewhere.

Such devotional expressiveness and trust in the power of spontaneity sprang, I suggest, from the revivalist movement's privileging of the emotive dimension of faith over the cognitive. Though they understood faith to embrace both elements, revivalists nevertheless strategically valued the work of affect—at least, of effusion—more highly than Tridentine Mass seemed to do. An emphasis on affect allowed them, for instance, to create (or imagine) unity in a worshipping community comprising people with widely disparate socioeconomic and educational backgrounds. The revivalists may also have seen affect as useful in refuting accusations of mere political machination: filling people's emotive spiritual needs could hardly be equated with attempting to reinstate Rome's power in England (the accusation arose anyway). Certainly for both Faber and Manning, emotion and devotion always superseded theological explication. Upon learning, for example, that Newman had obtained for his Birmingham Oratory an exemption from the clause in St. Philip's rule that cautioned against theological education, Faber reiterated his intention to maintain the rule. An oratory, he wrote to Newman, was called to "primaeval simplicity."[46] Following the Rule of St. Philip, the London Fathers contented themselves with simple and familiar preaching on some spiritual reading, a text of Scripture, a point of church history, or the lives of the saints. Not that they considered theology unimportant—Faber's colleague and early biographer John Bowden asserts that under Faber's "familiar and ardent language ... lies an extreme accuracy of theological statement; so that passages which are seemingly written with carelessness of exuberant eloquence will bear the closest examination as simple statements of doctrine."[47] Nevertheless, Faber tended to privilege emotive more than intellectual forms of knowing, as Cardinal Wiseman's comparison of Newman and Faber makes clear: "[Newman] has brought the resources of the most varied learning, and the vigor of a keenly accurate mind, power of argument, and grace of language, to grapple with the intellectual difficulties, and break down the strongly-built prejudices of strangers to the church. [Faber] has gathered within her gardens sweet flowers of devotion for her children, and taught them, in thoughts that glow and words that burn, to prize the banquet which love has spread for their refreshment."[48] Wiseman's portrait of Faber, itself rather effusive and metaphorical, pays tribute to the power of Faber's language, not the power of his intellect. Manning also preferred an emotionally grounded faith over an intellectually derived one. For instance, while Newman detested Wesley, Manning never tired of expressing admiration for him. Wesley, Robert Gray explains, "had touched men's hearts, and that, for Manning, was the first condition of all charitable activity." "Emotion not logic was always at the root of Manning's attitudes," Gray adds.[49] Manning's sermons, another biographer notes, displayed "high moral courage and zeal" rather than "close thought."[50]

These testimonies point to the type of sermon, the kind of religious language, that Procter frequently heard: a discourse not at all troubled to downplay exegesis in favor of emotion, or logical structure in favor of apparent spontaneity. While Faber's books (produced from the notes for his extemporaneously delivered sermons) seem to have toned down the drama of his devotional language, they reveal how he explained Catholic dogma in the simplest terms possible. *The Blessed Sacrament*, for example, asserts about Mary that "1. Jesus did not come without her. 2. When He came, He made the access to Him lie through her. 3. When He went He left her to be to the Church what she had been to Him, and in fact always works in the Church by her and never without her."[51] Here, Faber outlines a complete Marian theology in three short statements, using almost all one-syllable words. If Faber's theology did not become more complicated in the pulpit (though by all accounts it was more colorfully expressed there), Procter certainly had no need to echo Barrett Browning's desire for more emotion and less intellect in the sermons of her experience.

Such preaching was not, however, limited to Sunday morning Mass. At the Oratory, preaching services continued through the week. Procter notes in 1855 that "Father Faber is preaching a great deal this May. Every Wednesday and Friday at 4 o'clock on the Dolours of the Blessed Virgin—and next Sunday (the 6th) and the Sunday after (the 13th)." In the next sentence, she reveals that she attended these additional preaching services, perhaps even preferring them to the Sunday Mass: "Today I know you are engaged or should try if you were [relieved?] to accompany us. Perhaps the Sunday sermons will please you better. I don't think I shall go on Sunday" (GCPP Parkes 8.35). The letter reveals Procter's interest in the extraliturgical exercises at the Oratory. These exercises were decidedly popular in character, using Faber's hymns and other devotional materials prepared by the Oratorians, such as sequences of prayers arranged for recitation with prayer beads called chaplets: "A Chaplet of Acts of the Love of God," "Chaplet of the Sacred Heart," and "Chaplet of the Twelve Mysteries of the Sacred Infancy."[52] Some of these were crafted in response to new devotional themes in the Catholic Church, such as the "cult of the Sacred Heart," which reached its highest following in the nineteenth century, its feast declared a "day of universal observance in 1856."[53] According to Ronald Chapman, Faber may himself have preferred the weekly devotions on these themes over Sunday services; he is thought to have said "that Vespers and the High Mass could go" but not the popular exercises.[54] With Spanish Place as her home church, Procter may have had a similar attraction to the popular devotions. Certainly it appears that when she visited the Oratory, she attended those exercises that provided an alternative experience from Tridentine Mass, one with more unrestrained devotion and spontaneous language and form. One component of this experience was the singing of vernacular hymns, which were excluded from Tridentine Mass.[55]

Faber, conscious from his own background of the growing resources of Anglican hymnody, longed for a vernacular Catholic hymnody for the extraliturgical exercises. He wrote in 1849 that the hymns in *The Garden of the Soul* were too few and unvaried, that translations "do not express Saxon thoughts and feelings, and consequently the poor do not seem to take to them," and that the "domestic wants of the Oratory" required more hymns.[56] From this rationale, he set out to produce a Catholic hymnody. In contrast to Newman, who translated hymns from the Latin Breviary for his Birmingham Oratory, Faber wrote his own hymns for the London Oratory and its missions. His first collection (1848) was relatively small, but it was succeeded by numerous enlarged editions: *Jesus and Mary, or Catholic Hymns for Singing and Reading*, 1849 and 1852; *The Oratory Hymn Book*, with its penny version, *Hymns for the People*, 1854; and a new collected edition, *Hymns*, 1861 (from which citations in this chapter are taken).

Although Faber's hymns became part of both the Oratory's domestic life and its public services, where they were taken up with "animation," they garnered some criticism.[57] Even the Oratory's 1949 centennial booklet characterizes some of them as "shocking" and "unfortunate."[58] Some objected that the hymns "suggested the ways of the Methodists," meaning they were too popular in nature;[59] while the Roman Catholic Pugin complained, "By their music you shall know them, and I lost all faith in the Oratorians when I found they were opposed to the old song"—that is, plainchant.[60] Others found the hymns excessively sentimental or deficient in literary quality. Unlike Keble, whose hymns adopt a quietly reflective language, Faber employs in his hymns "a rhetoric of repetitive exclamations" such as *Ah* and *O* and a "highly florid ... use of adjectives" such as *sweetest* and *dearest*.[61] The nine stanzas of "Corpus Christi" (Faber, *Hymns*, 107–9), for example, all end with "Sweet Sacrament! we Thee adore! / Oh make us love Thee more and more!" while stanza 1 of "The Immaculate Conception"—a hymn fervently supportive of the newly declared dogma that Mary was free from original sin—reads,

> O purest of creatures! sweet Mother! sweet Maid!
> The one spotless womb wherein Jesus was laid!
> Dark night hath come down on us, Mother! and we
> Look out for thy shining, sweet Star of the Sea![62]

As this stanza suggests, Faber's hymns abound with an almost ecstatic devotion, especially to Mary. Indeed, Faber's devotion to Mary and his Marian rhetoric were notorious. Even in a period "in which Marian devotions reached their highest peak in recent history," Faber disturbed many by referring to Mary as "Mama."[63] His Marian and other hymns are rarely restrained in thought or form even when their titles suggest a single focus. "The Thought of God," for example, runs to fourteen stanzas (*Hymns*, 267–70). Whatever Manning thought of sonnets, he certainly could not accuse Faber's seemingly unsophisticated hymns of being improperly self-conscious.

Yet such fervor and simplicity were (ironically) deliberate choices, underscoring Martha Nussbaum's argument—discussed in chapter 2—that emotions always involve appraisal. To all his detractors, Faber replied that "less than moderate literary excellence, a very tame versification, indeed often the simple recurrence of a rhyme [are] sufficient" to help people take hold upon religion (*Hymns*, xv). He wished to depict the "different states of heart and conscience . . . in easy verse," in meters "of the simplest and least intricate sort" (xvii). As with his sermons, Faber did not want his hymns to appear cultivated or sophisticated in either form or language. According to R. S. Edgecombe, Faber, in his preconversion poetry, which was modeled "on the sober idiom of Wordsworth" and the Tractarians, exhibited "neither extravagance nor credulity," nor expressed dogma; but after his conversion, Faber "cast aside the reticence and chastity of his earlier verse in trying to decorate and concretize the abstractions of dogma."[64] That is, Faber's self-declared easy verse deliberately eschews subtlety in its service to the new Catholic cause, even though he was capable of such subtlety. Because of his commitment to Italianate devotions, his practices as a preacher and hymnist show little reserve. Indeed, in a completely un-Tractarian statement, he declares in *Growth in Holiness*, "The Spirit in which we serve [God] should be entirely without reserve. . . . Can there be reserves with God?"[65]—a stance that must have been occasionally difficult to reconcile with the solemnities of the reserved Latin Mass.

The revivalist promotion of emotion and expressiveness prompts here a momentary return to the Victorian association of such characteristics with femininity. As previous chapters have already stated, period critics tended to assign emotional work to women writers and critical work to male writers. Yet male revivalist Catholics such as Faber exalted sentimental rhetoric in their efforts to revitalize the Roman faith in England. Why? In the absence of liturgical studies based on neurological data, or of analyses of emotion such as Nussbaum's, they could not explicate the contributions of embodied practice to the imaginary, or emotive knowledge to critical appraisal. Nevertheless, they seemed to value emotion as an indicator of good judgment, consequently challenging the contemporary association of emotion with nonrationality. Isobel Armstrong warns that the so-called gush of the feminine in much nineteenth-century women's poetry ought not to be interpreted "as a special feminine discourse or censured as nonrational" but should be understood instead as having analytical power. Affective discourse, Armstrong contends, allowed women writers to present their experience in accepted modes so that they could then use such forms and languages "to *think* with. . . . A subtext of women's poetry is the question of how far the affective *is* knowledge and how far it may just be affect."[66] Elsewhere, she argues that Victorian women writers, enjoined to use the culture and language of affect, put to work its "double imperative": they both assuage the wounds of society and probe what caused those wounds, so that their writings heal and analyze.[67] Revivalist Catholics, I suggest, understood what Armstrong explains, namely, that "gush" need not be "of the feminine" at all; gush might simply be good to think with, good for work. So they turned the double imperative of affect to their own ends. As Catholics, they could not (and did not wish to) eschew the Roman faith itself; yet the ancient Roman faith had, to their minds, failed to permeate the English nation in satisfactory ways. Unable to fault the church's dogma for the dearth of conversions to the Roman faith in England, the revivalists (implicitly) faulted the language and practice of traditional forms of worship instead. Characterizing that mode as austere, dry, and ineffective (to a degree that it was not), they adopted a linguistic mode so distinct from that of the Latin liturgy as to make clear to Catholics and non-Catholics alike that the Roman faith was truly being revitalized in England. Renewed, it could potentially draw into its communities those who felt no attraction to the solemnities of the Latin rites. Emotive language, sufficiently augmented with devotional terms, could be associated not only with the feminine but also with vigorous faith for all people.

To this perception of gush—of simple, emotive, and apparently spontaneously produced speech as best suited for religious ends—Procter responded by shaping most of her religious poems as didactic (catechumenical) lyrics or narratives in which affective devotion is privileged over intellectualism. It is worth quoting at length her description of her own conversion process to note how she elevates bodily and emotive images over cognitive issues (that is, new dogma). The movement from Anglicanism to Roman Catholicism certainly involved her general perception of where the "revelation of God's

Truth" lies, but she names not a single theological precept as important to her decision, not even the ones frequently named by other converts (such as historical roots of the church or interpretations of sacrament):

> My fight was a hand to hand one. I could not attend to the general disposition of the troops. I could only struggle out to find which was the right camp—and having done so, get into it thro' a very heavy fire and take breath. You know there is a sin which we call spiritual selfishness. It was not that I hope, but the mere instinct of self preservation. . . . My way was perhaps Is [sic] this a revelation of God's Truth—if so—it must do good even though it should seem to do evil—it must give health, though its first effect may be to redouble the ailment. Mind I don't say it does—far from it—but if it did it would not shake me in the least—and though I believe it to be the one divine influence at work in the world, I believe also that for that reason it meets with opposition from the princes of this world—or the powers of darkness—which no other benevolent efforts do—which attack the mind and the body, or leave the soul in the chains that hold it, so that to begin with we might even differ as to what is the good to be effected—perhaps more in words than in fact (don't all differences reside more in the way of expressing ideas than in the ideas themselves). (GCPP Parkes 8.38)

Although late in the passage Procter mentions the mind as vulnerable to attack, she first names a bodily knowing that has nothing to do with cognition ("instinct of self preservation"). Further, her metaphors have mostly to do with breath and body. Her images invoke, on the one hand, battle (fight, troops, camp, fire, attack, chains) and, on the other hand, illness (health, ailment). Though in the nineteenth century the latter might be associated with the feminine, the former definitely conjures the masculine. Against anti-Catholic perceptions of revivalist Roman Catholicism as an effeminate faith, Procter casts her conversion process as a strong, physical effort. In other words, an emotionally grounded faith involves its own exertions; these may even be of heroic proportions. Procter here defends affect and body as vital, not subordinate, components of faith. Though not entirely discounted, intellectual acuity figures minimally in her narrative. Indeed, her parenthetical remark indicates a greater faith in the power of expression than in the importance of precise thought.

In her religious poems, Procter similarly represents the struggle to discover religious truth and express faith as a matter of the spirit or heart (and also of the body) more than of the mind. And while such an affective mode situates Procter among other Victorian women poets who were expected to write "from the heart," espousing devotion over intellect also aligns Procter's poetry with (male) revivalist Catholic modes of speech and writing felt to be necessary for the conversion of the English masses to the Roman faith. As with Faber's hymns, many of Procter's lyric verses—especially in her overtly Catholic collection, *A Chaplet of Verses*—read easily, the emotive elements unreserved. Repetition and exclamation occur regularly, as do florid adjectives and devotional expansiveness—as a glance at "Evening Chant" reveals. In this poem, the speaker urges an auditor to strew flowers with her before a picture of Mary, then to leave a prayer in each blossom so that as they sleep, the fragrances might carry the prayers up to Mary. Here are the central five of the nine stanzas:

> Strew white Lilies, pure and spotless,
>   Bending on their stalks of green,
> Bending down with tender pity,—
>   Like our Holy Queen.
>
> Let the flowers spend their fragrance
>   On our Lady's own dear shrine,
> While we claim her gracious helping
>   Near her Son divine.
>
> Strew before our Lady's picture
>   Gentle flowers, fair and sweet;
> Hope, and Fear, and Joy, and sorrow,
>   Place, too, at her feet.
>
> Hark! the Angelus is ringing,—
>   Ringing through the fading light,
> In the heart of every Blossom
>   Leave a prayer to-night.
>
> All night long will Mary listen,
>   While our pleadings fond and deep
> On their scented breath are rising
>   For us—while we sleep.
>
>   (*PAAP*, 395.9–28)

Flowers, shrines, bells, fragrances; pity, fondness, fairness, sweetness; chants, prayers: these objects and sentiments proliferate in Procter's affective poetry, especially poems to Mary. Such poems seem uninterested in intellectual rigor or scrutiny of doctrine or even the logic of practice. They care first about the expression of devotion, the release of feeling. Moreover, these poems in their very forms avoid any sense of studied self-consciousness. Whereas Rossetti multiplied sonnets and roundels, Procter, in a corpus of over 150 poems, produced only one sonnet. She preferred loose lyric forms in which predetermined line counts or rhythmic patterns do not constrain religious expression. Procter certainly paid attention to form in her religious poems: stanzas and rhymed lines predominate, and the poems cast as parallels to liturgical moments build carefully on key phrases. But the poems might have few or many stanzas, and the rhyme patterns might be regular, irregular, or both. This flexibility of form often creates the impression of spontaneity, natural expression, and unself-consciousness. In form, in language, and in subject, then, many of Procter's poems reveal an imaginary significantly shaped by the liturgy of Catholic revivalism. These poems have sometimes been taken as the sum of the religious poetics that Procter undertook, but they are actually only one component of her larger aesthetic. And though they have sometimes been dismissed for easy sentiment and simple form, they actually perform a labor of their own, as the next chapter argues more closely.

Beyond the Liturgy Proper: Catholic Devotional Reading and Social Activity

The revivalist Catholics imagined themselves as the rescuers of the Roman faith in a nation where its present adherents had, so they thought, been too long unconcerned with the unconverted or with pressing social issues. While revivalist rhetoric was likely exaggerated on these points—Spanish Place, for example, had conducted mission work since the early nineteenth century—it seems true enough that many older Catholic communities did not have a mission mentality.[68] Perhaps these Catholics gave little attention to converting the nation because they accepted the "plurality of religious belief [in England] as a natural consequence of historical developments and the exercise of rational choice." They may have felt the revivalists were simply wrong to desire and pray for what was "morally impossible."[69] But the revivalists, fuelled by a conviction brought over by the converts from Anglicanism that any form of dissent could not be accepted, made the conversion of England one of their primary goals. As Manning represented it,

"Our mission ... is not to a section or to a fraction who may be approaching nearer to us, but to the whole mass of the English people."[70] To that end, the revivalists adopted several trademark endeavors or attitudes, each of which contributed to Procter's religious poetics as well: an effort to produce or provide devotional reading material for new Catholics, a moral concern for the poor, and an (ambiguous) association with the Irish.

The determination to provide reading material for lay devotions spurred what has been called a Catholic literary revival.[71] Faber envisioned his hymns as reading material for the laity in addition to songs for service (*Hymns*, xviii), but the literary revival went beyond such devotional verse. Many of the converts endorsed a literature of "folk-based devotions" and "pious legends [such as] tales of early Christian martyrs."[72] Newman wrote his own such tale of martyrdom, in *Callista*; other leaders in the movement felt early Italian and other Continental devotional writers could supply the necessary material to infuse renewed spirituality into Catholics of all walks of life.[73] Soon after his conversion, Faber began the project of translating many of these Continental writings into English. For example, from the Italian, he translated a series of works depicting various saints as models of holy living. When a number of Catholics protested the "un-English" tone and frequent descriptions of unauthenticated miracles in these *Lives of the Modern Saints*, the bishop ordered the series discontinued, so instead Faber preached regularly on the lives of the saints and encouraged his listeners to read St. Francis de Sales, St. Theresa, St. Ignatius, Lallemant, Rodriguez, Lombez, and others.[74] These writers, as the titles of their works often demonstrate, instruct their readers how to grow in devotion or Christian perfection while living in the world. St. Francis de Sales's *Introduction to the Devout Life* (1619), for example, gives as its purpose, "to guide individual souls on the way to devotion"—not those who seek to enter the religious life but "those who have to live in the world and who, according to their state, to all outward appearances have to lead an ordinary life." The devotional life, de Sales insists, is possible in any situation, not just the monastic: "It is not only erroneous, but a heresy, to hold that life in the army, the workshop, the court, or the home is incompatible with devotion."[75] Alphonsus Rodriguez's *On Christian Perfection for Persons Living in the World* (1614) similarly gives instructions on how to increase in virtue in ordinary life. "Advancement in perfection," Rodriguez writes, depends on our ordinary actions being performed well."[76] This perspective also informed the traditional *Garden of the Soul*—whose subtitle reads *A Manual of Spiritual Exercises and Instructions for Christians Who (Living in the World)*

Aspire to Devotion—so the revivalists were not introducing a new concept. But they were suggesting that lay Catholics needed more accounts of saints' lives and more guidebooks or encouragements to devotional living, and they worked first to create and then to fulfill this need.

An enthusiastic reader of Faber's books, Procter may or may not have read selections from *Lives of the Modern Saints*, but she owned and presumably read many of the books Faber recommended. After Procter died, her sister Edith wrote out a list of Procter's books of spiritual guidance, from which she encouraged Parkes to choose some for herself (GCPP Parkes 8.101). As this list reveals, Procter's personal library included, among other titles, works by de Sales, Rodriguez, and Lallemant, as well as Newman's *Callista*.[77] At a minimum, Procter read de Sales closely, for in a letter to Parkes, she chides herself for the slowness of her spiritual improvement, then adds, "and here I am quite wrong for St. Francis of Sales says you should be just as patient with yourself as with your neighbour and discontent at yr own slow progress is not humility but pride" (GCPP Parkes 8.37; compare de Sales: "In any case, this sort of annoyance and bitterness with ourselves springs from self-love and leads to pride, for we are merely upset and disturbed at finding ourselves imperfect. Displeasure over our faults must be peaceful, unemotional and sincere"[78]). In another letter Procter encourages Parkes to read *St. Philip in England* (GCPP Parkes 8.38), not part of Faber's series but nevertheless a hagiographic book. Procter also seems to have valued religious narratives and instructive guides wherein devotion is seen to penetrate both religious communities and the ordinary world. In addition to her many lyrics that encourage or even instruct the reader in devotional living—poems such as "Evening Chant"—she casts several poems as legends, an important genre for transmitting communal values. According to Timothy R. Tangherlini, "By constructing a symbolic reality which encompasses [a community's] values and beliefs, the legend not only maintains its vitality in tradition, but also reinforces those very beliefs it makes use of."[79] Procter created her own legends rather than revitalizing existing ones, but the different "symbolic realities" she constructed do encompass values and beliefs that she intended the legends to reinforce. Further, she narrated episodes in the lives of ordinary, even humble, people (not saints of the church), so that, as in her lyrics, she might encourage ordinary Christians living in the world to aspire to perfection. Perhaps to remind English Catholic converts of their Continental heritage, perhaps because Faber and other revivalist leaders also turned to Continental writings, perhaps because the Spanish associations of her home church prompted her imagination, she set her three best known legends in Europe, not England: "A Tomb in Ghent," already briefly discussed; and "A Legend of Bregenz" and "A Legend of Provence," discussed in the next chapter. These poems can all be read as part of Procter's contribution to the Catholic literary revival (though as legends they could also be admired—and safely relegated to the past—by Protestant readers). Further, though *A Chaplet of Verses* contains few legends ("Milly's Expiation" might be read as one), its entire devotional nature casts it also within the larger revivalist project of providing reading material for (newly converted) lay Catholics—not to mention the yet unconverted poor.

For despite Manning's statement about not focusing on any sector of the population to the exclusion of any other, the revivalists appear to have given special attention to the poor and the Irish. To a large extent *poor* and *Irish* meant the same thing—the thousands of Irish immigrants to England in the wake of the potato famine lacked almost all the necessities of life—but the English poor also numbered in the thousands. Whether conflated as one group or distinguished as two, though, the poor and the Irish figured significantly in the overall revivalist agenda of converting more people to the Roman faith. In fact, when Faber and Manning chose for a fluently expressive but simple language and for spontaneous forms of delivery, they did so under the impression that such choices enabled them to reach the poor with their message more effectively than if they had used highly sophisticated language or rhetorical forms. Manning purposefully used the fewest and simplest words possible, that poor people might understand, and Faber gave out in the preface to his hymns that the "simplest and least intricate" meters were necessary so as "not to stand in the way of the understanding or enjoyment of the poor."[80] Faber's remark links poverty rather unequivocally with lack of intellectual ability or at least lack of education; while both Faber and Manning worked to alleviate the conditions of poverty, neither thought it necessary to provide greater intellectual opportunities for the poor for their own sake. Both viewed education for the poor as necessary only to the extent that it served religion and saved souls. Faber supported the establishment of a Catholic Ragged School for the Irish Catholic children in London only because without such schools, he wrote, "Conclamatum est [It is all over] with Catholicism among the poor Irish in London." He and the other London Fathers began the Catholic Ragged School only because no one else would. Having established it, he felt the Oratorians "should be allowed to retire from it" and leave it to a committee, since "it was not the direct work of [the Oratorian] Institute."[81] Manning, too, worked to establish schools for the poor to prevent the children from "being lost to the Church for want of any proper Catholic education."[82] To these men, the Roman Church in England needed the influx of numbers that the conversion of the poor could bring. But the mass of good Catholics need not be intellectual; they need only be devotionally committed to effect the transformation of England into a Roman Catholic nation.[83]

To make this influx of the poor into the church more attractive, revivalist leaders idealized the poor as having a holy simplicity that all Catholics should emulate. Theoretically, this idealization would encourage well-to-do Catholics to mingle with poor Catholics, and Heimann argues that such mingling did actually occur in the Roman Catholic confraternities, which combined devotional and social work. That is, revivalist confraternities established to combat poverty sought also to channel the supposedly natural and holy simplicity of the poor toward a devotional purpose.[84] But paradoxically, the perception of a holy simplicity in the poor gave the lower classes a moral edge that the middle classes could not fully acknowledge without endangering their own moral and social status; therefore, the holiness of the poor was perceived as latent until activated through the instruction and moral example of the more educated middle class. This constellation of conflicting impulses was part of what Lauren Goodlad has described as a Victorian charitable pastorship in which altruistic motives—not systems of law—propelled the wealthy or economically comfortable classes to care for the underprivileged. Such pastorship would purportedly "unite individuals" of different classes into a social family, which state-managed programs could not do. Again, though, these idealized pastoral relations "depended on intrinsically unequal relations between rich and poor, educated and uneducated. [They were] thus structured around a hallowed but contradictory concept of the social bond." Goodlad further observes that despite the rhetoric of familial models and bonding among classes, many Victorians saw charitable pastorship as "woefully insufficient"; perhaps the wealthier classes were less altruistic than supposed, or perhaps the poor were so desperate or so numerous that the pastorship model could not adequately meet their needs.[85] The Catholic revivalists, however, did not give up their view of the essentially holy nature of the poor. Indeed, Heimann, still speaking of the poor, notes, "If we were to single out one aspect of a Victorian and Edwardian Christian sensibility which united Catholics where it divided Protestants, we might suggest a particularly English Catholic stress on the value and holiness of simplicity."[86]

Yet despite their enthusiasm for assisting (and converting) the poor, the revivalists did not escape the contradictions outlined by Goodlad. On the one hand, as Josef Altholz argues, the revival of the medieval ideal of holy poverty allowed "English Catholics to overcome the contemporary Protestant distinction between the 'deserving' and the 'undeserving' poor and ultimately to accept the Irish poor as proper objects of charity, not to be forced to mirror a middle-class respectability but to be accepted within their own context";[87] on the other hand, it appears to have been difficult for middle-class, revivalist Catholics to remember that they were also to learn something from the poor, especially when the experience of working among them was not always pleasant. Faber himself was not above lamenting the "propinquity of stink and dirt" among the poor who attended the first, King William Street Oratory; he at times felt sure that "a great part of our mission ought to be [to] the higher classes; and yet the poor turn them out even from the afternoon lectures which are specially directed to the educated."[88] In this remark, Faber ignores the possibility that the poor might have come to the lectures for the educated because they, too, desired (religious) knowledge. Instead, he distinguishes between what is necessary for the educated and what is necessary for the poor/uneducated. One cannot help but wonder whether such opinions lay behind the relocating of the Oratory from its first "self-conscious attempt at class unity" in the Strand to the upper-class Brompton neighborhood after some five years.[89] Clearly, revivalist attitudes toward the poor were much conflicted: while revivalist rhetoric targeted the poor for inclusion in the church, and poor people did actually attend revivalist services and seek help at revivalist confraternities, middle-class standards and attitudes made it difficult even for genuine religious impulses to bridge the gap between classes. Still, the revivalist determination to view the poor in a positive light contrasts significantly with other contemporary discourses, which cast the poor as a diseased body, a social threat, or a source of criminal impulses.[90] It also contrasts with an older Catholic view that politics or social reform was "not a legitimate concern of the Church."[91] Whatever the contradictions in their own attitude, revivalists viewed the poor as worthy of spiritual and physical attention: as needing assistance rather than elimination or governance or neglect.

Like Faber and Manning, Procter deprecates the need for education of the poor, except as it serves religion. In the same letter in which she describes to Parkes her own difficulties in finding out "God's Truth," she expresses reluctance to teach "every man woman and child in England" to read, lest such education "give them the means of reading books they had better let alone"

(GCPP Parkes 8.38)—the context indicating that she means Protestant books. But since they *will* have education, "bad or good," she adds, "they had better have it good so we must all help." Education, she continues, holds no particular interest for her, "except as [it] affects the salvation of the many or the few."[92] But also like the revivalists, Procter echoes in her poetry the notion of an idealized holiness among the poor, and—through her poetic activity on behalf of the Providence Row Night Refuge—she marks her participation in the revivalist project of combining devotional instruction with social charity. As we will see, her commitments are also marked by the contradictions within charitable pastorship approaches to the poor.

The question of the Irish was likewise a troubled one for the revivalists. Catholics of aristocratic or gentrified background tended to disparage the Irish influx on the grounds that it impoverished England economically and culturally and that it awakened the unwelcome interest of Rome in parishes where their own influence had long reigned.[93] They were not alone in their opinions: broadly, the middle and upper classes perceived the Irish as social delinquents who disproportionately filled the prisons.[94] Even the working classes resented the Irish willingness to work for cheap wages and so break the strikes intended to improve wages and working conditions.[95] The revivalists, however, welcomed the Irish: not only had their presence drawn the papal attention that led to the restoration of the Roman hierarchy in England in 1850, but it also "gave rise to the second-spring account of the Irish appearing as holy reinforcements just at the critical moment."[96] Never having forsaken their allegiance to Rome, the Irish provided an image of and a discursive means for bolstering the presence of the Roman Church in England (of course the revivalists had to ignore the possibility of the Irish being nonpracticing Catholics, or not Catholics at all). Conversely, the actual presence of the Irish presented the revivalists with a problem, for if the success of an English Roman Catholic Church depended on the presence of the Irish, could they claim to present to Rome a specifically English nation restored to its ancient faith? The revivalists, therefore, had to minimize the Irish presence in the church while at the same time imagining the Irish as the second spring or new birth of that church. What they wanted but could not have was Irish Catholics without Irish-ness. The Irish immigrants, therefore, were both the basis of and barriers to the revivalist agenda.

For this reason, Faber sometimes wrote slightly different hymns for English and Irish singers/readers. He reformulated his famous "Faith of Our Fathers" into "The Same Hymn for Ireland" by altering significant words, as these juxtaposed stanzas show:

Mary's prayers	Mary's prayers
Shall win our country back to thee;	Shall keep our country fast to thee;
And through the truth that comes from God	And through the truth that comes from God
England shall then indeed be free	Oh we shall prosper and be free

(Hymns, 265, 266)

Similarly, the lines "Ye sons of dear England, your Saviour is calling / You back to His Fold and your forefathers' faith" in "Invitation to the Mission" become "Ye sons of Saint Patrick! Dear children of Erin! / 'Tis God that hath kept you your wonderful faith" in "The Same Hymn for Ireland" (*Hymns*, 292, 293). One wonders whether Faber meant the paired hymns to be sung simultaneously, with English and Irish voices choosing their appropriate version. Even if not, their side-by-side inclusion in his hymnal highlights difference rather than unity among English and Irish Catholics. In fact, the Irish versions of the hymns imply a moral or religious superiority of Irish over English Catholics. Clearly, in light of the social and political problems confronting England with regard to the Irish, this positioning was problematic—also because, as missionary work quickly proved, many of the Irish were Catholic by birth, national origin, or politics only, not by devotional feeling or intellectual appreciation.[97] As a result, despite their rhetoric, the revivalists often found it easier to idealize Irish Catholicism than to deal with its presence among them.

Procter's poems on Ireland express a similar ambivalence toward that country and its people. By dealing in her poetry with the so-called Irish question mainly through her constructions of the Irish in Ireland and not the people on her doorstep in London, Procter participates in this inclination to keep Irish Catholics distinct from English Catholics. Intriguingly, like Faber, her poetic speakers both align themselves with and distance themselves from Irish Catholics. Such ambiguity may be easy to disapprove, but Procter's social-poetic activism, however inflected with paradox, is itself significant. As Hoxie Neale Fairchild points out, most of Procter's contemporary Catholic poets remained disengaged from political questions.[98] By considering the plight of the Irish at all, Procter engages in her poetry with one of the most pressing Roman Catholic concerns of her day.

Unlike Barrett Browning, then, whose word-oriented and democratic religious imaginary led to a dialogic poetics that yet demanded action, or Rossetti, whose manifestation-oriented imaginary led to a verbal-visual, contemplative, and sacramental poetics, Procter developed an imaginary so multifaceted that it may at first be difficult to recognize *as* an imaginary. Indeed, Procter's imaginary may at first appear fragmented, with the poet vacillating between social and feminist critique and religious submissiveness; or between thoughtful reserve and weak effusion; or between creative form and simple imitation. Upon first acquaintance with Procter's liturgical practice and poetics, one might wonder whether such multidimensionality might undermine rather than enrich the religious-poetic project. Might there be a point at which diversity of experience hinders rather than helps the formation of an imaginary? Conceivably, yes—just as narrowness of experience might do. But in this chapter I have argued that Procter threaded her way astutely through the complexities of her chosen devotional life, bringing many elements of her liturgical formations to bear successfully in her religious poetry. Perhaps she did not succeed in fully integrating the diverse components of her imaginary before she died. After all, she had a relatively short Catholic life, and it fell mostly during the period when English Catholicism as a whole was still searching out its postrestoration identity. Moreover, given the greater authoritative structures of the Roman Church, Procter probably faced even more challenges than Barrett Browning or Rossetti in their respective traditions to work out which aspects of her faith served a woman poet well and which warranted wariness or critique. It may even be that Procter was less gifted than her now-more-famous contemporaries. Yet once we see how her liturgical life generated her religious-poetic voice, formed in and complicated by a certain historical moment, we might no longer dismiss her religious poetry as inferior work but instead accept it as the creative output of a distinctive religious imaginary.

CHAPTER SIX

RELIGIOUS-POETIC STRATEGIES IN ADELAIDE PROCTER'S LYRICS, LEGENDS, AND CHAPLETS

In contrast to the long publishing careers of Barrett Browning and Rossetti, Adelaide Procter's public poetic career spanned only nine years: it began in 1853 with a poem printed in Dickens's *Household Words* and concluded in 1862 with *A Chaplet of Verses*, which Procter prepared as a fund-raiser for the Providence Row Night Refuge, a shelter for homeless women and children managed by the Sisters of Mercy.[1] The poetry published over this decade voices Procter's Roman Catholic imaginary in different ways: sometimes subtly, sometimes overtly. Procter's poetry of the earliest years after her conversion from Anglicanism does not yet manifest a Catholic imaginary. Much of this early poetry has a general moralistic quality satisfying to the mainstream, middle-class readership of Dickens's *Household Words* and other such journals but not identifiable with a particular Christian formation. In her last collection, Procter's poetry proclaims a specific religious commitment so overt that the volume seems intended mainly for a Roman Catholic readership. Between these ends of her career, Procter's religious poetics gradually emerges, as the Catholic liturgies that the poet chose to engage increasingly shape the way she encounters or imagines the world.[2]

The first part of this chapter studies poems from across *Legends and Lyrics, Series 1* (1858), *Legends and Lyrics, Series 2* (1861), and *A Chaplet of Verses* (1862). It seeks to reveal the Mass-inflected imaginary in many of the lyric poems. Reading such poems as "Our Titles," "A Desire," and "Give Me Thy

Heart," it first explores how meditations on the Mass inevitably produce a reserve that leaves mystery unspoken. Speakers in these poems cast themselves, as it were, at the foot of the cross, adoring Jesus the Victim, seeking heart-union with him, often imagined as present on earth, dwelling among them, rather than as glorified in heaven, awaiting future full communion. Reverence for mystery also permeates poems about artistic production, such as "Unseen" and "Unexpressed"—and at least one poem, "The Inner Chamber," imagines disastrous consequences for artistic production when the holy is not respected. The Mass-inflected imaginary also appears in Procter's many lyric poems built on liturgical phrases, particularly "The Pilgrims," "A Chant," "Kyrie Eleison," and "Ora Pro Me." These poems, though fully independent as poems, both support the liturgical context from which they are drawn and imagine new contexts or dimensions to the expressions they echo. More obviously generated by the liturgy than any other poems in Procter's oeuvre, they have drawn almost no critical attention to date; yet they demonstrate Procter's creative engagement with her faith practices.

The second section of the chapter focuses mainly on *A Chaplet of Verses* as revelatory of Procter's more revivalist imaginary and aims, particularly in the effusive rhetoric, popular form, and Marian devotion of many of the poems. I posit that because Procter intended *A Chaplet of Verses* as a fund-raiser for the Providence Row Night Refuge—a revivalist cause—she crafted her collection alert to the probability that her main buyers would be new Catholics attracted to the effusive language and simple forms of the animated revivalist services. Most of the poems in the volume privilege affect over intellect, the spirit and heart over the mind. Particularly the Mary poems adopt a devotional expressiveness and apparent spontaneity of worship, adoration, or supplication after the manner of Faber's hymns and Oratorian chaplets. Such a mode runs the risk of appearing collusive with prescriptions for women's writing, but it also participates in the revivalist liturgical effort to represent the new Roman faith as more vibrant than the old. *A Chaplet of Verses* functions quite obviously as lay devotional material, but the latter part of this section also examines two of Procter's earlier legends as more subtly part of the Catholic literary revival. "A Legend of Bregenz" and "A Legend of Provence" reaffirm the values and beliefs held by the community with which Procter identified not least by reaching to Catholic Continental locations and the medieval past to bring to English readers' attention the heritage of the Catholic faith and the effort of ordinary but devout people to aspire to right living in the world.

Procter also pursued revivalist interests on the thematic front by including in *A Chaplet of Verses* several poems about the poor and the Irish, who simultaneously advanced and complicated the mid-nineteenth-century Roman Catholic agenda. These poems are explored in the third part of the chapter. Idealizing the poor as holy, Procter calls on the principle of charitable pastorship to demand justice for the poor; implicitly acknowledging the insufficiencies of the idealized social bond, she criticizes middle-class moral laxity and social inactivity in poems such as "The Homeless Poor," "Homeless," "An Appeal," "Milly's Expiation," and "The Beggar." Procter's speakers, however, typically assume a didactic, moral authority that denies agency to the subjects of the poems, and Procter consistently chose lyric forms that do not give voice to the poor themselves. Rather, a middle-class narrator always mediates the experience of the lower classes, even in the one poem ("The Beggar") constructed as a poor man's speech. Similarly, Procter idealized the Irish, as a people laudably faithful to the Roman Church; but as "An Appeal" reveals, she found it easier to empathize with English ideals of Catholics in Ireland than with the Irish in England. While, therefore, she complemented her poetic concern for the poor with active contributions to the Providence Row Night Refuge, her concern for the Irish could not escape the political, social, and religious entanglements that accompanied the Irish presence in England. This struggle to negotiate between the ideal and the real, with regard to both the poor and the Irish, recalls Rossetti's project of envisioning a saintly community that exceeds the limits of the actual worshipping congregation; within her shorter writing career, however, Procter did not formulate as successful a literary project as Rossetti's to address the tensions between the actual and the envisioned. Her geographical dislocation of the Irish rests uneasily alongside her idealizations of their Catholic faith.

While questions of gender and authority percolate throughout these discussions about language and social issues, they come most to the fore when we consider in the final portion of the chapter how Procter, in her most overt Roman Catholic volume, resists the explicit subservience toward authority that some male revivalist leaders found liberating; no doubt she was aware that such authority structures could be problematic for a woman religious poet. Procter, therefore, never directly acknowledges the presence of hierarchical religious structures in the (literary) Catholic community. Unlike many writings by prominent revivalist leaders, not a single poem or prefatory remark in *A Chaplet of Verses* mentions Rome or the authority of the pope. On the contrary, even the poems of religious-political orientation, such as "The Church of 1849" and "The Jubilee of 1850," prioritize other points of discussion. Procter simply does her own work, in all its diversity.

"Silence and tears are best / For things divine": Reserve, Adoration—and Experimentation

Procter's poetry as a whole does not suggest that silence and tears are always best, but in the poetry most deeply informed by the experience of Tridentine Mass, silence and tears—or, put differently, reserve and emotive-bodily response—frequently do appear as best for things divine, and sometimes as best for other mysteries as well. To attune ourselves to the Mass-inflected imaginary that produces reserve in Procter's early religious poetry, we can begin our poetic readings with a later poem that refers quite openly to the experience of Mass—though even here, much is unsaid. In "Our Titles," published in *A Chaplet of Verses* (PAAP, 398–99), the speaker considers the various names by which believers may be called, coming at last to "Temple." As a biblical metaphor for the person/body in whom resides the spirit of God, *temple* prompts the speaker to think of food, particularly spiritual food; yet reserve cuts the prompt short so that the mystery of the consecrated bread of Mass is not articulated but adored in silence instead:

> Are we not holy? Do not start[;]
>   It is God's sacred will
> To call us Temples set apart
>   His Holy Ghost may fill:
> Our very food.... O hush, my Heart,
>   Adore IT and be still!
>
>   (19–24)

While the auditor has clearly been startled by the speaker's assertion (rhetorical question) that believers are holy, the speaker readily affirms that God has made them temples. She does not hesitate to say so. Neither does she hesitate to speak of the Holy Spirit who fills these believers-temples. These mysteries may be asserted confidently. But when she begins to speak of the food that nourishes the temple-body, she breaks off. She cannot name what the ellipses bespeak, namely, that the believer's food requires Jesus's renewed sacrifice. Instead, the capitalized *IT* carries all the weight of the consecration of the elements and the immolation of Christ's body and blood into bread and wine. *IT* equals host/Victim, before which the heart can only be stilled into adoration. This adoration leads, in the next stanza, to a heart-union with "Dear Jesus": "Adoring in Thy Heart, I see / Such blood as beats in mine" (28, 29–30). That is, heart-union enables the speaker to see Jesus present in the host as a beating heart, and so to know the efficacy of the sacrifice just repeated. In this image, Jesus is again present on earth, his heart beating alongside the speaker's. Whereas Rossetti's speaker in "After Communion" wonders,

> how will it be
> When Thou for good wine settest forth the best?
> Now Thou dost bid me come and sup with Thee,
> Now Thou dost make me lean upon Thy breast:
> How will it be with me in time of love?
>
> (*CP*, 222.10–14),

Procter's speaker in "Our Titles" is not prompted by Mass to think of a future heavenly banquet. Instead, she turns somewhat anxiously to the present: "Shall we upon such Titles bring / The taint of sin and shame?" (37–38). She pleads for God's help for worthy living in the present, exchanging, as in other Procter poems, a "heavenly focus for an entirely present, practical focus on immediate, individual acts of engagement with God."[3]

Moving back in Procter's oeuvre, we see similar evocations in the final stanza of "A Desire," also published in *A Chaplet of Verses*. In this poem, a penitent repeatedly longs to have known Jesus in his earthly life—to have been in Bethlehem or to have sat at his feet or to have stood at the cross. After each longing, the speaker is told by an unidentified respondent to hush, for service to others in Jesus's name remains possible. The penitent finally dares to suggest that even the experience of Mass does not match up to having known Jesus on earth:

> O to have seen what we now adore,
>   And, though veiled to faithless sight,
> To have known, in the form that Jesus wore,
>   The Lord of Life and Light!
>
> (*PAAP*, 385.51–54)

These lines cast an interesting, implicit parallel between Jesus's earthly experience and the Mass—in both instances, the faithful can see beyond the surface (bread, human body) to the "Lord of Life and Light" who is "veiled to faithless sight"—but the respondent again quickly tells the first speaker to hush. The longing is misguided, says the respondent, because "He dwells among us still," in a very real and physical sense:

> Jesus is with his children yet,
> for His word ["This is my body"] can never deceive;
> Go where His lowly Altars rise
> And worship and believe.
>
> (59–62)

The poem ends here, both instructing and chiding the first speaker for not realizing that in Mass, at the earthly altar, one is as close to the divine presence as one can get.

Toward an earthly altar is precisely where the speaker of "Give Me Thy Heart" goes (*PAAP*, 92–94). In this poem, Mass has concluded, and all worshippers but one have departed. Lingering, this speaker notes that "One lamp alone, with trembling ray / Told of the Presence" remaining on the altar (that is, the unconsumed host), and to that Presence she speaks. The speaker four times reminds the Victim what she has done to gain divine favor: shunned sin, given up wealth, aided the poor, fasted and wept.[4] After each plea for recognition, a voice replies, "*My child, give me thy Heart!*" (original italics). After the fourth reply, the voice/Presence continues,

> "When pierced and wounded on the Cross,
>   Man's sin and doom were mine,
> I loved thee with undying love,
>   Immortal and divine!
> . . . .
> To gain thy love my sacred Heart
>   In earthly shrines remains."
>
> (45–48, 51–52)

The poem is silent about the mysterious process by which the Sacred Heart entered the earthly shrine, so that a reader unattuned to this one line might even miss the Catholic substrate of the poem (which Procter published in *Legends and Lyrics, Series 1*). But the speaker—overcome by the reminder that the Sacred Heart is at that very moment, to gain her love, in the earthly shrine marked out by the one lamp with trembling ray—pleads for "sacred fire" to cleanse her sin so that her heart may be "Thine alone" (65, 63). Her prayer granted, she leaves the Presence purified and at peace.

Yet despite longings for heart-union between speaker and Jesus, Procter's speakers, in both late and early poems, demonstrate restraint, or recognition of mysteries that ought not to be violated. As the speaker of "The Inner Chamber" (from *Legends and Lyrics, Series 2*) learns, it is forgotten at one's peril. As this poem opens, the speaker is singing in an outer court, her music grown immortal as its echoes ring back to her from an inner chamber. Curiosity as to who or what resides in the inner chamber at last overcomes the singer, with disastrous results:

> Long I trembled and paused,—then parted
>   The curtains with heavy fringe;
> And, half fearing, yet eager-hearted,
>   Turned the door on its golden hinge.
>
> Now I sing in the court once more,
>   I sing and I weep all day,
> As I kneel by the close-shut door,
>   For I know what the echoes say.
>
> Yet I sing not the song of old,
>   Ere I knew whence the echo came,
> Ere I opened the door of gold;
>   But the music sounds just the same.
>
> Then take warning, and turn away;
>   Do not ask of that hidden thing,
> Do not guess what the echoes say,
>   Or the meaning of what I sing.
>
> (*PAAP*, 337.21–36)

What was in the inner chamber? The speaker does not share the mystery, only the consequences for her music of having probed into it. But in evoking several biblical passages, the poem indirectly suggests what kind of mystery must not be probed, even by artist-singers. Both the tabernacle and the temple had inner and outer areas, the Holy of Holies being the innermost area. It was secluded by a curtain or golden door and forbidden to all except the high priest, and he gained admittance only once a year. In this inner chamber stood the ark of the covenant, representing God's presence. Irreverence toward this ark could result in death.[5] These allusions imply that what the curtain in the poem hides, what the inner chamber holds, is the holy, the divine. When the speaker breaks through to the holy, she is thrown out, shut against, unable to sing the former songs. She now knows what the echoes say, but the knowledge has destroyed her music. Respect the hidden things, she warns others in grief, and do not try to guess the meaning even of these stanzas. Thus the poem, though evocative of Mass only in its allusions to the temple as a place of God's presence, makes clear that mystery enriches, makes poetry "immortal" (5), while inquisitiveness destroys. Heart-unity with the holy one must not slide into spiritual familiarity. Reserve and a submissive, adoring heart remain the best responses to the divine.

This theme also appears in numerous *Legends and Lyrics* poems not typically seen as religious. "Unseen," for example, concludes,

> But, though a veil of shadow hangs between
> That hidden life and what we see and hear,
> Let us revere the power of the unseen,
> And know a world of mystery is near.

(PAAP, 298.17–20)

"Unexpressed," its precursor in publication, carries the same conviction, this time strongly linked to the work of the poet and the theme of love:

> No real Poet ever wove in numbers
> All his dream; but the diviner part,
> Hidden from all the world, spake to him only
> In the voiceless silence of his heart.
>
> So with Love: for Love and Art united
> Are twin mysteries; different, yet the same:
> Poor indeed would be the love of any
> Who could find its full and perfect name.
>
> Love may strive, but vain is the endeavor
> All its boundless riches to unfold;

Still its tenderest, truest secret lingers
Ever in its deepest depths untold.

(*PAAP*, 190–91.21–32)

Critics have noted the reserve in these two poems, Isobel Armstrong observing that the message in "Unexpressed" (as in "A Lost Chord") is the "ephemeral nature of language," and Emma Mason noting that the poem implies "only God has access to the full resonance of what the artist endeavours to fix in form."[6] But both poems could be linked also to the imprint of Mass, with its sense that "some things are clearly known and distinctly understood, and that other things are now hidden from us for the trial of our obedience and faith."[7] The Roman Catholic undertones may be muted (perhaps even purposefully, for publication to a general audience), but it is hard not to associate these poems with a Mass-inflected imaginary when they are read alongside the ones examined earlier. References in "Unexpressed" to "the deepest beauty / [that] Cannot be unveiled to mortal eyes" (7–8); to the "holier message that is sent" (10); to the "diviner part / Hidden from all the world, [that] spake to him only / In the voiceless silence of his heart" (22–24): these all evoke the sense of Christ's presence in the host, veiled from sight but addressing the listener with a holy message. Of course, the poem is not *about* Mass. But Procter's sense that "sacred mysteries" (6)—even those not directly related to worship—cannot be fully articulated surely arises from an imaginary shaped by the Mass, where "Poor indeed would be the love of any / Who could find its full and perfect name" (27–28). This underlying sense is what allows the poem to resolve. Whereas early stanzas speak of "noble discontent" (12) at inarticulateness, the last stanzas decide that despite failure, "Still [Love's] tenderest, truest secret lingers / Ever in its deepest depths untold" (31–32). Untold, in other words, does not mean unpresent; what is untold still lingers. Indeed, the speaker goes on, Art and Love "must be" (34) like wind and waves that do not speak clearly. Perhaps "must be" ought not to be taken here as lamenting the fact, but acknowledging it as the better way. For something greater to happen, "words *must* be / Like sighings of illimitable forests / And waves of an unfathomable sea" (34–36; my italics). Even as it considers nonliturgical subjects such as love and art, then, "Unexpressed" relies on formations of the religious imaginary to explore and then resolve the tensions of those who seek to approach the mysteries of the world.

Religious-Poetic Strategies

If the Mass-inflected imaginary emerges in Procter's poetry partly through an attunement to mystery and adoration, it also appears in many poems through a creative engagement with the liturgy itself. Procter wrote a number of poems that present as alternative, English texts for parallel reading during the Latin service. She built these poems on liturgical phrases from the fixed portions of the liturgy, not exerting her poetic efforts on phrases that would not regularly appear in the service (that is, the varying introits or graduals or collects). Of the poems I study here, the first three were published in the *Legend and Lyrics* series without first appearing in a Dickens (or other) periodical; the others appeared in *A Chaplet of Verses*. Most of the poems could have been comfortably received by Protestant readers of Dickens's periodicals, since the liturgical phrases that shape them also appear in the Anglican liturgy (where they are often translated); but perhaps for Procter the phrasal associations with the Catholic liturgy were strong enough that she chose not to publish any of them in a (Protestant) periodical. Or perhaps Procter submitted them but Dickens rejected them as too church-like rather than popularly moralistic. Certainly the poems carry the resonance of church liturgy, even specifically of the Tridentine Mass liturgy, as their collected presence in this section of the chapter reveals.

"The Pilgrims" (*Legends and Lyrics, Series 1*) reads as a parallel text for the communion portion of the Mass of the Faithful, specifically the "Agnus Dei" portion of the liturgy in which the priest twice prays, "Lamb of God, who takest away the sins of the world, have mercy on us," and then varies this line with "Lamb of God, who takest away the sins of the world, grant us peace." Procter's poem imagines a situation not directly represented in the liturgy of Mass but common in Christian thinking: the spiritual life as a pilgrimage. In the poem, the pilgrims speak, in each stanza bearing their suffering by remembering Christ's greater trials, then echoing in their last three lines the liturgical prayer for mercy and peace:

> The way is long and dreary,
> The path is bleak and bare;
> Our feet are worn and weary,
> But we will not despair:
> More heavy was Thy burden,
> More desolate Thy way;—
> O Lamb of God who takest
> The sin of the world away,
> *Have mercy on us.*

> The snows lie thick around us
> In the dark and gloomy night;
> And the tempest wails above us,
> And the stars have hid their light;
> But blacker was the darkness
> Round Calvary's Cross that day;—
> O Lamb of God who takest
> The sin of the world away,
> > *Have mercy on us.*
>
> Our hearts are faint with sorrow,
> Heavy and hard to bear;
> For we dread the bitter morrow,
> But we will not despair:
> Thou knowest all our anguish,
> And Thou wilt bid it cease,—
> O Lamb of God who takest
> The sin of the world away,
> > *Give us peace.*
>
> > (*PAAP*, 113.1–27; original italics)

The stanzas of this poem not only plead that Christ, as the sacrificial lamb, have mercy on the pilgrims but also express conviction that he will hear the plea ("But we will not despair") and certainty that he will respond to it ("And Thou wilt bid [our anguish] cease"). Elaborating where the liturgy does not, the poem moves from what might be taken as a plea for mere physical relief to what is clearly a call for spiritual support. Yet each stanza is anchored in its midsection by the recollection of Christ's suffering (burden, darkness, cross, anguish), the Lamb-becoming that Mass continually recalls. Indeed, the poem's suitability as a liturgical text for Mass was recognized by Arthur Sullivan, who published the poem with a musical setting in 1871, giving the first six lines of each stanza to combined alto, bass, and tenor voices, and highlighting each Agnus Dei refrain by giving it alone to soprano voices.[8]

The "Lord, have mercy" theme of the Agnus Dei continues in "The Storm," also published in *Legends and Lyrics, Series 1*. This poem briefly narrates the story of a ship struggling at sea during a storm while a frightened child prays for the lives of the sailors. Morning arrives with the ship in the bay and the child at play, so the prayer has been answered. Such a narrative could probably not function as a liturgical text, yet its devotional underpinnings emerge in the liturgical phrases that conclude each stanza. These phrases, the Kyrie Eleison and the Gloria, occur in the early portion of the Mass and mean, respectively, "Lord, have mercy" and "Glory to God." Procter chooses the Latin parallel of the Kyrie Eleison, "Miserere Domine," as the final phrase of each of the first six tercets, the ones that express distress. The seventh and final tercet, the resolution, concludes with "Gloria tibi Domine," or "Glory be to Thee, O Lord." Consequently, the poem reads as an expansion of the liturgy into daily living: the phrases of worship extend beyond the formal worship setting into a child's evening prayer. The poem could be taken, therefore, as an indirect form of instruction, an example of how one might turn to God in distress and know that he answers prayer. As such, it suits well the catechumenal portion of the Mass from which its liturgical phrases are actually drawn, even though it seems less imaginable than "The Pilgrims" as a poem to appear in a prayer manual.

"A Chant," however—appearing in *Legends and Lyrics, Series 2*—has again the devotional texture of "The Pilgrims" and might be imagined as a parallel liturgical text, this time to the Benedictus, which immediately precedes the arrival of Christ in the bread and wine. Procter gives the Latin text of the Benedictus as her epigraph, then provides the English parallel as the refrain of each stanza. Catholics long familiar with Tridentine Mass would hear the liturgical resonance of the epigraph and refrain, perhaps more than others would, and the poem's title—"A Chant"—might also reinforce its association with liturgy. (It might even imply that Procter imagines the poem as the choir's text rather than the layperson's, since in traditional Mass only the choir actually chanted.) As with "The Pilgrims," though, Procter both uses the liturgy and imagines beyond it. Instead of naming Christ as the one who comes in the name of the Lord, as the Benedictus intends, she figures different angels as coming in the Lord's name, so that the faithful ought to accept whatever they bring as the Lord's will, whether Life and Joy (stanzas 1 and 2) or Pain and Death (stanzas 3 and 4):

"Benedictus qui venit in nomine Domini."

I.

Who is the Angel that cometh?
Life!
Let us not question what he brings,

  Peace or Strife;
Under the shade of his mighty wings,
   One by one,
Are his secrets told;
   One by one,
Lit by the rays of each morning sun,
   Shall a new flower its petals unfold,
   With the mystery hid in its heart of gold.
We will arise and go forth to greet him,
   Singly, gladly, with one accord;—
"Blessed is he that cometh
  In the name of the Lord!"

. . . .

    IV.

Who is the Angel that cometh?
   Death!
But do not shudder and do not fear;
  Hold your breath,
For a kingly presence is drawing near,
   Cold and bright
Is his flashing steel,
   Cold and bright
The smile that comes like a starry light
   To calm the terror and grief we feel;
   He comes to help and to save and heal:
Then let us, baring our hearts and kneeling,
   Sing, while we wait this Angel's sword;—
"Blessed is he that cometh
  In the name of the Lord!"

     (*PAAP*, 247–50.1–15, 46–60)

The willingness of Procter's speaker to accept Pain and Death as angels to be welcomed in the name of the Lord can seem morbid, even masochistic, to modern readers. But as Esther Hu writes in relation to Rossetti's poetry of suffering, for certain Christians, "A corollary to trusting in the ultimate goodness of divine will is approaching suffering with a grateful attitude."⁹ If not exactly grateful, Procter's speaker certainly is accepting, as she says, "[I]n that shadow [of Pain] our crowns are won" (41). Given that the liturgical phrase at work in the poem occurs in the Mass at the moment approaching Christ's greatest suffering under the divine will, the speaker's attitude carries the knowledge of Christ's impending re-destruction of body for her sake, and this knowledge enables her trust that human pain and death are also subservient to the divine will. Procter does not make direct scriptural-textual connections that would facilitate our seeing these associations, as perhaps Barrett Browning might have done; she does not, for example, link "let us, baring our hearts and kneeling, / Sing, while we wait this Angel's sword" with the prophecy Mary remembers in "The Virgin Mary to the Child Jesus":"[T]he dread sense of things which shall be done, / Doth smite me inly, like a sword—a sword?— / (That 'smites the Shepherd!')" (*WEBB*, 1:485.143–45). But perhaps Procter's reserve is also at play in these poems of liturgical exploration.

When Procter publishes her more overtly Roman Catholic collection of poetry, she continues to echo the liturgy in a few poems, sometimes directly, sometimes subtly. In "Kyrie Eleison" (*PAAP*, 372–73), she returns to the theme "Lord, have mercy." In the Mass of the Catechumens, the appeal for mercy follows the introit and is addressed first to the Lord, then Christ, then the Lord again: "Kyrie, eleison; Christe, eleison; Kyrie, eleison." Procter emulates this pattern in a poem conscious of the catechumenal context of these phrases. The poem is a prayer for those "among Thy children [who] / Deny this faith and Thee" (3–4). Though these deniers "will not ask Thy mercy," the faithful, who see the Father's hand everywhere, "kneel for them in prayer" (5, 6) and plead "Kyrie Eleison!" (12). But the unbelievers do not see that nature itself praises God and that life goes on beyond death, and so again the faithful plead, "Kyrie Eleison!" (24). The speaker then appeals directly to Christ's passion:

> By thy bitter death and passion,
>   And the Cross which they deride;
> By the anguish Thou hast suffered,
>   And the glory Thou hast won;
> By Thy love and by thy pity—
>   Christe Eleison!

(31–36)

Finally, the speaker asks seraphs, Mary, and saints in heaven to "Call them ere life is done, / For His sake who died to save them, / Kyrie Eleison!" (46–48). The poem ends here. That is, unlike "The Storm," which resolves into "Gloria tibi Domine," "Kyrie Eleison" stands independently as a parallel devotional text to the Kyrie of the Mass. It could easily be read by the layperson while the priest and choir carried on their Latin versions of the same, its Mass-orientation particularly evident in its foregrounding of Christ's suffering and death in the third stanza, the only one, appropriately, that concludes with "Christe eleison."

Although not echoing a liturgical phrase from the Mass, "Ora Pro Me" (*PAAP*, 389–90) also reads as a parallel devotional text, this time to the Libera Nos prayer that the priest offers to Mary before breaking the bread. This prayer for deliverance asks Mary to intercede for the faithful to obtain peace in the present time. Procter's poem shifts theme but similarly pleads for Mary's intercession, "ora pro me" meaning "pray for me." A liturgical quality is again evoked in this poem by closing each stanza with the Latin phrase, as in the first and last of the five stanzas, given here:

> Ave Maria! bright and pure,
>   Hear, O hear me when I pray!
> Pains and pleasures try the pilgrim
>   On his long and weary way;
> Fears and perils are around me,
>   Ora pro me.
>
> (*PAAP*, 389.1–6)

> When my eyes are slowly closing,
>   And I face from earth away,
> And when Death, the stern destroyer,
>   Claims my body as his prey,—
> Claim my soul, and then, sweet Mary,
>   Ora pro me.
>
> (*PAAP*, 390.25–30)

Again, a layperson might conceivably pray these stanzas during the priest's recitation of the Libera Nos.

Less tied to a particular moment in the liturgy, "Confido et Conquiesco" continues to evoke the Latin heritage of the church, as does "Per Pacem ad

Lucem." The first of these less explicitly Roman Catholic poems—which appear in the more explicitly Roman Catholic volume—still retains a liturgical association in working with a Latin phrase from St. Ignatius, ten of whose meditations appear in Richard Challoner's prayer manual *The Garden of the Soul* (1843). "Confido et Conquiesco" (*PAAP*, 388–89) might, therefore, be read as an additional meditation for such a prayer manual. After the title, which means "I trust and am at peace"—and which is echoed in the concluding line of each stanza, "Trust and rest"—Procter gives this epigraph: "*Scit; potest; vult: quid est quod timeasmus*," which translates as "Knowledge (or wisdom); power; will: what is there to fear?" As with the title, the epigraph serves as a building block for the subject and structure of the poem. In successive stanzas, the poem urges a poor soul not to fret, plan, strive, or desire, for God sees, calms, and loves. Stanza 2 urges trust and rest because God's "*wisdom* sees and judges right" (9; my italics); stanza 3 recommends trust and rest because all "*power* is His alone" (14; my italics); stanza 4 advocates trust and rest because God always "do[es] His loving *will*" (19; my italics); and stanza 5 pulls this *scit*, *potest*, and *vult* (even though Procter shifts *vult* from *will* to *love* via the "loving will" of line 19) together with the epigraph's question and the poem's title into this conclusion:

> What dost thou fear? His wisdom reigns
>   Supreme confessed;
> His power is infinite; His love
> Thy deepest, fondest dreams above;
>   So Trust and Rest.
>
> (21–25)

The poem's linguistic and formal discipline indicates that the more revivalist-oriented poems in the same volume—to be discussed shortly—result not from religious-poetic failure but from choice. Clearly Procter could and did sustain her poetic experiments with the traditional liturgy, even after she chose to expand into the new, more effusive style also. As Kirstie Blair argues in regard to Keble's meter in *The Christian Year*, Procter's attention to form in "Confido et Conquiesco" may be a method of controlling the very feeling she was elsewhere displaying to different ends.[10]

Procter's interest in writing parallel texts, even apart from the liturgy, may, finally, be supported by a reading of "Per Pacem ad Lucem" (the only Procter poem to become a widely known hymn outside Roman Catholic circles)¹¹ alongside John Henry Newman's well-known hymn, "The Pillar of the Cloud."¹² Although I can find no evidence that Procter actually read Newman's poem, the associations between her poem and Newman's are too strong to dismiss; and because Procter owned *Callista* (GCPP Parkes 8.101), the novel Newman published in 1856, it seems reasonable to assume that she read some of his poetry as well. To compare Newman's poem (more commonly known by its opening phrase than its actual title) to Procter's "Per Pacem ad Lucem" is to see how closely yet creatively Procter could respond to existing devotional texts. Newman's poem opens as follows:

> Lead, Kindly Light, amid th'encircling gloom
>   Lead Thou me on!
> The night is dark, and I am far from home—
>   Lead Thou me on!
> Keep Thou my feet; I do not ask to see
> The distant scene—one step enough for me.¹³

Writing this poem while at sea, Newman envisions life as a journey; the speaker prays for guidance from the divine Light through the gloom of life. With Newman's phrases and metaphors in mind, we turn to Procter's poem, from whose six stanzas I give the first, third, and fifth:

> *I do not ask*, O Lord, that life may be
>   A pleasant road;
> *I do not ask* that thou wouldst take from me
>   Aught of its load;
>
> . . . .
>
> For one thing only, Lord, dear Lord, I plead,
>   *Lead me aright*—
> Though strength should falter, and though heart should bleed—
>   Through *Peace to Light*.
>
> . . . .
>
> *I do not ask* my cross to understand,
>   *My way to see*;
> Better *in darkness just to feel Thy hand*
>   And follow Thee.
>
>   (*PAAP*, 430.1–4, 9–12, 17–20; my italics)

Newman's phrases and images fairly leap from Procter's lines, as the italicized portions show. The speaker does not ask to see her way on the road of life, to know the destination, but only to follow God's guiding hand, to be led to Light (here representative of the destination rather than the Guide). The poem could hardly echo Newman's more closely in its subject and language while still remaining a distinct creation. Moreover, the resemblance between the poems extends to meter: Newman's sestets alternate iambic pentameter with iambic dimeter in the first four lines, then close with an iambic pentameter couplet. Procter's quatrains have no closing couplet but still alternate iambic pentameter and dimeter lines. Given the parallels in phrasing and theme, the parallels in meter can hardly be coincidental. Procter seems to have quite consciously experimented, in this poem and across the poems I have studied so far, with respected devotional material within an established Catholic tradition.

Revivalist Devotion: Affect and Legend as Religious Work

The language, form, and emotive quality of most of the poems in *A Chaplet of Verses*, including the many Mary poems frequently elided in anthologies and critical studies, manifest an aesthetic in the spirit of Rome that prevailed in the Oratory and appealed to the revivalist reading community. I deduce Procter's appeal to such a primary readership from the promotion and publishing history of *A Chaplet of Verses*. Both *Legends and Lyrics* series had been published by Bell and Daldy and had garnered favorable reviews in such literary journals as the *Athenaeum*, *Literary Gazette*, *Saturday Review*, and the *Spectator*. The volumes had gone quickly into multiple editions, including morocco-bound editions priced at more than double that of the original. Such success did not, however, persuade Bell and Daldy to take on Procter's *A Chaplet of Verses*. Marjorie Lang links Bell's reluctance with religious bias, concluding that "because of his professional and personal connections to theologians and his own fervent commitment to the Church of England, Bell refused to publish the verses that reflected Procter's crossing to Roman Catholicism."[14] Bell must have known that Procter had already become Catholic when he published *Legends and Lyrics*, as the literary world frequented the Procter household; he obviously did not object to moral verse or even religious verse—only to explicitly Roman Catholic verse. So for *A Chaplet of Verses*, Procter found a new publisher in Longman, Green, Longman and Roberts, but papers such as *Notes and Queries*—which had lauded each new edition of Procter's *Legends and Lyrics*—gave scant notice to her new work and offered none of the earlier encomiums.[15] Yet *A Chaplet of Verses* sold well. Two editions appeared in 1862 and a third in 1868, the lack of conventional advertisement perhaps being offset by the distribution of promotional cards bearing the lead poem of the volume.[16] According to Parkes, the volume generated such profit for Providence Row that "Monsignor Gilbert founded a bed in the Refuge called the 'Adelaide Procter Bed,' a permanent memento and reminder of prayer for her soul"; the book was still selling in 1895.[17]

It may be that Procter's established readership did not need reviewers' endorsements to encourage their purchasing of the new volume. But it seems equally if not more likely that the buyers of *A Chaplet of Verses* were not the earlier or ongoing buyers of *Legends and Lyrics*, at least not in the main. To buy an edition of *Legends and Lyrics* was to show oneself a reader of populist literature first made respectable through appearances in Dickens's periodicals. To own a gift edition of *Legends and Lyrics* marked one as middle class, moral, and literate.[18] To buy *A Chaplet of Verses*, in distinction, was to declare oneself unashamedly Roman Catholic. Never appearing as a gift edition, the book could not be displayed as a class status symbol. It could only ever be a religious purchase, both as reading matter and in the cause its production supported. That Procter intended it as such is suggested also by the fact that, though she had written some poems in the volume some twenty years before, she had not published them in periodicals or included them in *Legends and Lyrics*.[19] With a separate publication, however, she had confidence that there were readers willing to spend funds on a particular kind of poetry to benefit the refuge. The volume's sales proved her right.

Procter's astuteness in determining who would be the likely purchasers of a benefit volume for the refuge and the poet's willingness to craft the poems to appeal primarily to these readers' devotional preferences does not mean, however, that *only* economic motives fuelled the writing of the poems, as earlier portions of this chapter have already shown. *A Chaplet of Verses* also presents as lay Catholic reading material to support a devotional life in the ordinary world. For example, the book may have found use as a devotional text within Providence Row Night Refuge itself. Procter's introduction to *A Chaplet of Verses* reveals how Providence Row pursued the revivalist dual agenda of social relief and religious instruction: homeless women and children received food and a night's lodging, and the Catholics among them were given "simple instructions on the Catechism" (*PAAP*, 353). The first noun of the frontispiece inscription to the book ("for the Benefit of the Providence Row Night Refuge for Homeless Women and Children") no doubt refers primarily to the financial benefit Procter hoped would accrue to the refuge through the book's sales, but Procter may also have had in mind a spiritual benefit: a reading of her poems to the homeless women and children, if not during the periods of catechetical instruction, then perhaps during other periods of rest and reflection. Actually, it is hard to imagine that *A Chaplet of Verses* would not have been readily available for reading in Providence Row, because the board of governors valued the work highly enough to insert one of its poems in the refuge's annual report for several years.[20] Moreover, as the naming of the Procter bed reveals, the founders of the refuge valued Procter's effort, and using her poems as spiritual exercises for homeless Catholic women and children, many of whom would not likely have had access to devotional reading material, would have been one way of showing their gratitude.

Whether or not the book appeared in the refuge, *A Chaplet of Verses* reads as Procter's contribution to the Catholic literary revival, with its linguistic and formal choices successfully emulating the affective mode of Oratorian devotional texts. The various Mary poems, for example, correspond closely to Faber's Marian hymns in their effusiveness, exclamatory nature, and exaltation of Mary. Here again is stanza 1 of Faber's "The Immaculate Conception":

> O purest of creatures! sweet Mother! sweet Maid!
> The one spotless womb wherein Jesus was laid!
> Dark night hath come down on us, Mother! and we
> Look out for thy shining, sweet Star of the Sea!
>
> (*Hymns*, 120)

Faber, writes Carol Engelhardt Herringer, believed that Mary "was so intimately connected with her son throughout his earthly life that she became the central figure—after the Trinity—in the story of salvation," such that there was, in Faber's words, "no possibility of excess" in devotion to her.[21] Though most Victorians were uncomfortable with the authority and influence Faber ascribed to Mary (either because her supremacy sat uneasily with Victorian notions of female submission or because Protestants took Victoria as their only queen), Procter clearly endorses Faber's views in many of her Marian poems. "The Names of Our Lady," for example, echoes Faber's emotionalism and promotes Mary's ascendancy and influence over the Church and individual believers, whom Procter, like Faber, figures as children. Procter's adjectival choices—dearest, dear, sweet, holiest, best—recall Faber's highly wrought expressions; her featured names for Mary, Faber's laudations. Yet the poem does not merely echo Faber's hymn. It considers the various names of Mary in turn and eventually draws a conclusion that answers the question posed in stanza 2 as to which name is "dearest" and "most worthy." To demonstrate this, I give the poem in full:

> Through the wide world thy children raise
>   Their prayers, and still we see
> Calm are the nights and bright the days
>   Of those who trust in thee.
>
> Around thy starry crown are wreathed
>   So many names divine:
> Which is the dearest to my heart,
>   And the most worthy thine?
>
> *Star of the Sea:* we kneel and pray
>   When tempests raise their voice;
> Star of the Sea! The haven reached,
>   We call thee and rejoice.
>
> *Help of the Christian:* in our need
>   Thy mighty aid we claim;
> If we are faint and weary, then
>   We trust in that dear name.
>
> *Our Lady of the Rosary:*
>   What name can be so sweet
> As what we call thee when we place
>   Our chaplets at thy feet.
>
> *Bright Queen of Heaven:* when we are sad,
>   Best solace of our pains;—
> It tells us, though on earth we toil,
>   Our Mother lives and reigns.
>
> *Our Lady of Mount Carmel:* thus
>   Sometimes thy name is known;

It tells us of the badge we wear,
    To live and die thine own.

Our Lady dear of Victories:
    We see our faith oppressed,
And, praying for our erring land,
    We love that name the best.

Refuge of Sinners: many a soul,
    By guilt cast down, and sin,
Has learned through this dear name of thine
    Pardon and peace to win.

Health of the Sick: when anxious hearts
    Watch by the sufferer's bed,
On this sweet name of thine they lean,
    Consoled and comforted.

Mother of Sorrows: many a heart
    Half broken by despair
Has laid its burden by the cross
    And found a mother there.

Queen of all Saints: the Church appeals
    For her loved dead to thee;
She knows they wait in patient pain
    A bright eternity.

Fair Queen of Virgins: thy pure band,
    The lilies round thy throne,
Love the dear title which they bear
    Most that it is thine own.

True Queen of Martyrs: if we shrink
    From want, or pain, or woe,
We think of the sharp sword that pierced
    Thy heart, and call thee so.

Mary: the dearest name of all,
    The holiest and the best;
The first low word that Jesus lisped
    Laid on His mother's breast.

Mary, the name that Gabriel spoke,
    The name that conquers hell:
Mary, the name that through high heaven
    The angels love so well.

Mary,—our comfort and our hope,—
    O may that word be given
To be the last we sigh on earth,—
    The first we breathe in heaven.

(*PAAP,* 366–68)

Is this the gush of the feminine, negatively construed, the consent to nonrational and emotional experience? Certainly in the poem, affect predominates over intellect, as the speaker articulates the various emotional conditions in which the devout approach Mary: in distress, weariness, sadness, oppression, guilt, anxiety, despair, pain, fear. Whatever the emotional condition, hearts, spirits, and bodies assume the proper attitude of humility: bodies kneel, spirits trust, hearts love. As with Manning's and Faber's sermons, emotion prevails over logic, zeal over close thought (for example, is it likely that the infant Jesus's first word was "Mary"?). Procter's poem is neither hermeneutical (like Barrett Browning's "The Virgin Mary to the Child Jesus") nor meditative (like Rossetti's "Herself a rose who bore the Rose").

But as noted earlier, affect does its own kind of work, and emotion is not necessarily dislodged from cognition. This poem actually accomplishes much. While its primary appeal may be to revivalist readers, it is careful not to alienate whatever Catholics of a more reserved bent may also have purchased the volume. First, more than half the names for Mary that Procter selects appear also in the Litany of Loretto included in *The Garden of the Soul*—though without the superlatives already noted—so that the tributes offered have as much traditional as new Catholic resonance.[22] Second, in the accumulation of names, one hardly notices the omission of any title reflective of Mary's lately proclaimed Immaculate Conception, so enthusiastically endorsed in Faber's hymn. Given that not all Roman Catholics of the period fully endorsed this dogmatic point, proclaimed in 1854, Procter's omission seems strategic—and strategically disguised. By capitalizing on revivalist rhetoric, Procter appeals to revivalist readers familiar with the language of affect, but that same language allows her to avoid alienating a potential other audience. While certain Catholics might not approve the poem's rhetoric, they could not actually fault its subject. Further, as Cheri Larsen Hoeckley points out, the catalogue of names for Mary is strategic also in its refusal to value Mary's virginity or purity above any other virtue. The list conveys Procter's belief "that holiness extends well beyond female chastity to include courage for sailors, justice in ruling powers, consolation for the sick, and compassion in sorrow"; by not repeatedly underscoring Mary's purity above all else, Procter shows in this poem and throughout *A Chaplet of Verses* that "her moral concerns are with economic justice and mercy, rather than with sexual surveillance."[23] In more than one way, then, "The Names of Our Lady" relies on affect to do subtle, cognitive work—once again, to make the judgments of value that Martha Nussbaum associates with emotion (see chapter 2).

Formally, the poem corresponds to the standard set out by Faber in the preface to his hymns: "tame versification" to help people grasp religion without having to decipher poetic complexities. "The Names of Our Lady" follows a simple quatrain structure with alternating tetrameter and trimeter lines in an *abab* rhyme scheme: the common measure Barrett Browning avoided in her later, more intricate hymns. In keeping with the idea of spontaneous and effusive worship, Procter's poem runs to multiple stanzas, considering many names in a rapid succession of stanzas rather than a single name in a tightly controlled form. Compilation displaces concentration, with each devotional epithet having scant time to register before being supplanted by the next—a strategy evocative of the interior arrangements of Procter's churches, where elaborate decoration and freedom from restraint indicate a certain trust in the effects of compilation. Yet seventeen poetic stanzas of exactly the same rhyme scheme and meter might also be viewed as an "excessive structuredness" or "overdetermined formalism" illustrative of great care.[24] As Elizabeth Gray notes, if one proceeds slowly enough, the poem can operate much as a good chaplet, a string of prayer beads.[25] More specifically, it offers thirteen prayers to our Lady, each chaplet/prayer clearly distinguished from the preceding and the next by an italicized name, a bead marker in the recitation. The final stanzas form the chaplet's *Ave Maria* conclusion, dwelling as they do on Mary as the best name of all. Actually, the poem imitates a standard chaplet for Marian devotion. Although I could not find among the Oratorian devotional books that I examined a chaplet specifically designated for Mary, the traditional chaplet for Mary, "Our Lady, Star of the Sea," consists of twelve beads corresponding to the twelve stars of Mary's crown. Discounting the stanzas that dwell on the name Mary itself, Procter's poem echoes this traditional chaplet by eulogizing twelve names for Mary. As a survey of Faber's hymns indicates, "Star of the Sea" was a much used term for Mary in Oratorian liturgy, and a twelve-bead chaplet may have been familiar to Procter. In any case, "The Names of Our Lady," though reading much like "sentimental excess" (to use Susan Drain's words cited at the start of chapter 5) to twenty-first-century readers, echoes the language and structure of Oratorian devotional material in ways comfortable to revivalist Catholics. Its gush does quite knowing work.

The term *chaplet* may be itself an indicator that Procter aimed in her volume toward a lay readership. Typically, members of a religious house used the rosary (fifteen decades of aves) for devotions, while lay Catholics used a chaplet (fewer beads, for shorter devotions). Procter's term, therefore, signals her intention to be populist rather than elitist or exclusive in her linguistic and structural practices. Further, unlike the rosary, chaplet bead numbers vary to suit the devotion at hand: the Chaplet of the Infant Jesus has either three (representing the Holy Family) or twelve (representing the twelve years of Jesus's infancy), the Chaplet of Our Lord has thirty-three (representing his years on earth), and chaplets for saints have any number corresponding to the virtues to be remembered.[26] The Oratorian devotional books reflect this diversity. The book *Devotions to the Infant Jesus, as Practised in the Oratory* (1849) contains the "Chaplet of the Twelve Mysteries of the Sacred Infancy," and *The Prayer-Book of the Oratory* (c. 1850) gives ten recitations in its "Chaplet of Acts of the Love of God." Thus, Procter knew the chaplet form to be versatile as well as populist—an appealing combination for a poet looking to be creative as well as religious. In several poems, she experiments with the form as well as the devotional association of the chaplet. In "The Sacred Heart"—perhaps Procter's contribution to the aforementioned "cult of the Sacred Heart"—a weary, trembling, and mournful soul is three times questioned about its distress and is correspondingly instructed to find rest, strength, and comfort in the Sacred Heart of Jesus. Each question, response, and direction forms its own verse paragraph, with the soul being directed three times to the Heart of Jesus. The "Chaplet of the Sacred Heart" in *The Prayer-Book of the Oratory* similarly begins with a *venite*, or call to come near, and a response to the call, followed by six statements of remorse or praise and then a second *venite* and response; the whole concludes with a prayer to the Sacred Heart of Jesus. The similarities of pattern and content between the Oratorian chaplet and Procter's poem suggest how familiar Procter was with revivalist extraliturgical materials, how deliberately she constructed her own poem as a similar prayer that her readers would feel comfortable using (as with the poems paralleling the Latin liturgy), and yet how creatively she departed from the model in form and content. Likewise, in "A Chaplet of Flowers" (*PAAP*, 369–72), a fairly conventional opening, wherein an ailing speaker instructs a younger person to gather and weave flowers on her behalf, quickly shifts into an instructive-devotional mode as each flower carries a religious meaning that must be passed on to the chaplet maker:

> First, take those crimson roses,—
>   How red their petals glow!
> Red as the blood of Jesus,
>   Which heals our sin and woe.
>
> (21–24)

The eventual wreath, laid on Mary's altar, becomes the prayer of the speaker in absentia. If, therefore, the volume title, *A Chaplet of Verses*, first appears to signify merely a wreath of poems, a more religious connotation of the word *chaplet* soon emerges, to support the deliberate Roman Catholic character of the volume.

The instructive-devotional mode of "A Chaplet of Flowers" actually characterizes quite a few of the Marian poems in the volume, with one of the faithful gently teaching a potential catechumen by what name and in what manner to address Mary. Sometimes the fact that this instruction is happening does not become clear to the reader until the end of the poem, as in "The Annunciation" (*PAAP*, 374–76). The poem opens with a quatrain that indeed uses an imperative, but one that could be self-directed:

> How pure, and frail, and white,
>   The snowdrops shine!
> Gather a garland bright
>   For Mary's shrine.
>
> (1–4)

Then follow six stanzas that explain why Mary deserves a gift this day: it is a day of recognition for her, in memory of the angel Gabriel's appearance with the news that she will bear the Christ. His "Hail, Mary!" becomes the focus of the last five stanzas of the poem, which describe how the angelic greeting has been taken up by the faithful of all ages, in all circumstances of life. The final stanza then reveals that the speaker all along has been addressing someone nearby, the person earlier instructed, it turns out, to make a garland of snowdrops:

> "Hail, Mary!" lo, it rings
>   Through the ages on;
> "Hail, Mary!" it shall sound
>   Till time is done.
>
> "Hail, Mary!" infant lips
>   Lisp it today;
> "Hail, Mary!" with faint smile
>   The dying say.
>
> "Hail, Mary!" many a heart
>   Broken with grief
> In that angelic prayer
>   Has found relief.
>
> And many a half lost soul
>   When turned at bay,
> With those triumphant words
>   Has won the day.
>
> "Hail, Mary, Queen of Heaven!"
>   Let us repeat.
> And place our snowdrop wreath
>   Here at her feet.
>
> (29–48)

Given the explanatory tone of the preceding stanzas, the "us" in this last stanza does not carry quite the tone of shared experience that Rossetti's "we" usually does. Instead, it suggests that the speaker places herself alongside the auditor as a gentle teacher-model. She explains both the origins and significance of a common expression among the Catholic devout—"Hail,

Mary"—and the value of making a gift for the one so addressed. Indeed, the instruction seems to have arisen naturally and proceeded throughout the wreath's being made and the pair's approaching a shrine or statue of Mary, for the poem moves from "Gather a garland" to "And place our snowdrop wreath / Here at her feet." The circumstances within the poem therefore call for a simple poetic form, one that adds to the feeling of spontaneity or extemporaneity. Short lines, short stanzas, and a shifting rhyme scheme (some stanzas rhyme *abab*, others *abcb*) help convey this apparent unconcern with exact craft. As a result, the poem keeps attention on its devotional lesson. The pupil enters further into the devotional life through the example of the speaker-model—and readers of the poem and *A Chaplet of Verses* as a whole might do the same.

That Procter was attentive to the project of rejuvenating the Roman Catholic community in England even before composing *A Chaplet of Verses* appears also in her creation of poetic legends that encompass and reinforce the values and beliefs of Catholicism. "A Legend of Bregenz" (*PAAP*, 115–21) first appeared in the 1854 Christmas issue of *Household Words* and was republished in *Legends and Lyrics* in 1858. It is structured as twenty-three octets in rhymed iambic trimeter, a form reminiscent of the ballad and thus well suited for its medieval subject. The poem opens as legends often do, with the narrator providing a context for the tale that will follow—in this case, a description of the "quaint" city of Bregenz on Lake Constance, whose quietude and beauty suggest "a piece of Heaven / Lies on our earth below" (13, 7–8), and about which

> Mountain, and lake, and valley,
>   A sacred legend know,
> Of how the town was saved, one night,
>   Three hundred years ago.
>
>   (21–24)

The narrative then commences, telling of how a maiden of Bregenz once fled to the Swiss valleys—for reasons unstated in the poem—where she served kind masters and grew into the community:

> Her friends seemed no more new ones,
>   Their speech seemed no more strange;
> . . . .
> She spoke no more of Bregenz,
>   With longing and with tears;
> Her Tyrol home seemed faded
>   In a deep mist of years.
>
>   (35–36, 41–44)

But when war arises and her present community threatens to destroy Bregenz, suddenly

> The faces of her kinsfolk,
>   The days of childhood flown,
> The echoes of her mountains,
>   Reclaimed her as their own!
>
>   (101–4)

She looses "the strong, white charger" (117) and rides through dark and danger to warn—and thereby save—her beloved first home. Arriving at midnight, she is ever afterwards honored both in the town's "quaint old carving [of] / The Charger and the Maid" and in the midnight call of the warder, who, instead of calling the hour of twelve, "calls the maiden's name!" (184). Thus an artistic object and a ritual practice—and a poem—preserve and retell the past, the story of one person's loyalty to the place of birth, to a "piece of Heaven" that has also been blessed with the peace of heaven.

    But the poem does more. The seventh stanza relates that despite her fading "memory of the Past" (32), whenever the maiden sings to her master's children, what she sings are "ancient ballads / Of her own native land" (51–52). And whenever she kneels "before God's throne," what rises to her lips are the "accents of her childhood" (54, 55). That is to say, although the maiden in the Swiss valleys no longer has any conscious thought of Bregenz, deeply embedded in her mind and body are the formative songs and prayers of her past practice. These cannot be erased, however much they might appear forgotten. In the critical moment, everything these ballads and prayers have preserved within her returns most vividly. Her first home rises before her again as her only home, and she risks her life to save it. The ballads and prayers do not, of course, embody a Catholicism that has been forgotten or repressed in her new home and that now returns in full force to spur her action. The poem's medieval setting means that the Catholic faith has been her religious frame in both Austria and Switzerland; the maiden's sudden kinship with Bregenz arises when its existence, not its religion, is threatened. But read in the context of the Catholic effort to bring the pious legends of the Continent to English readers, this stanza implies something remarkable about Procter's belief in the power of "ancient ballads" or legends. Because the poem is itself a legend in ballad form, it, too, has the potential to imprint in its readers systems of belief or patterns of behavior that produce deep commitments, commitments that last even through periods of displacement. As a legend, the poem could place its readers within *their* true home, within a community of readers eager to retain (or regain) deep loyalties with their spiritual past. One of Procter's earliest published legends, "A Legend of Bregenz" is somewhat muted in its Catholic commitments, but it joins Faber's translations and Newman's *Callista* as an effort to enrich the Catholic lay community with literary material that models heroic commitment to traditional values while also deepening the sense of connection to a past in which the Catholic Church was everyman's/everywoman's spiritual home. Further, in Procter's "sacred legend," the maiden's not being named, not being made a saint in either the world of the poem or the world of the reader, affirms what the Continental spiritual manuals said, that ordinary Christians living in the world could also aspire to perfection. It is not their names but their actions that inspire others to similar commitments.

Constructed as verse paragraphs in rhymed couplets of iambic pentameter, "A Legend of Provence" (*PAAP*, 203–14) moves away from ballad form, though it retains a medieval setting and becomes more explicitly Roman Catholic in subject. In brief, the legend tells of devout Angela, a convent novice who, assigned to tend a young, wounded knight, falls in love and departs the convent secretly with him, is ruined, and returns many years later, broken-hearted and spiritually exhausted, only to discover that the Virgin Mary has kept her place in the convent all those years, so that her absence has not been noted; Angela resumes her place humbly and with great love, till she dies. On one level, the poem is, like many of Procter's other religious poems, a tribute to Mary, who welcomes the penitent woman home without judgment, the mother of the prodigal daughter. Mary reveals herself and God as more truly forgiving than humans, even nuns, would be:

> "Didst thou not know, poor child, *thy place was kept?*
> Kind hearts are here; yet would the tenderest one
> Have limits to its mercy: God has none.
> And man's forgiveness may be true and sweet,
> But yet he stoops to give it. More complete
> Is Love that lays forgiveness at thy feet,
> And pleads with thee to raise it. Only Heaven
> Means *crowned*, not *vanquished*, when it says, 'Forgiven!'"
>
> (271–78)

As Christine A. Colón notes, Procter here challenges Victorian assumptions that the fallen woman could never be fully restored: "Angela does not enter a penitentiary where she gradually learns to reform. Her reformation is immediate, dependent solely upon God's grace.... For Procter, then, the convent is ... a symbol of the perfect forgiveness offered by God to everyone through the Virgin Mary." In this reading, Procter embraces medieval Catholicism in part for its "remarkable redemption offered to everyone."[27] Medieval Catholicism, I would add, also enables Procter to picture devotion to Mary without being criticized of devotional excess; the placing of "fresh garlands sweet, / ... before the shrine at Mary's feet" (83–84), the singing of "Ave, Maris Stella" (106), the strewing of the garden path with hawthorn blossoms during "Our Lady's last procession" (151)—these all seem acceptable when enacted by medieval nuns instead of modern lyric speakers, but the Marian devotions in "A Legend of Provence" are essentially the same as those in "A Chaplet of Flowers" or "The Names of Our Lady."

Colón enriches her reading of the poem by observing that another part of what Procter found attractive in medieval Catholicism is "its central role in society, its communal values, and its acceptance of the miraculous." The convent nuns in "A Legend of Provence" have important social functions; they settle village brawls, comfort wronged lovers, shelter pilgrims and beggars, heal the sick in the surrounding area, and take in orphans. They do all this, not as embittered but inspired women: "Their joyful devotion to God reveals both the force that empowers their social action and the joy that they receive from enacting it." For Procter, such devout women and the Catholic faith more broadly are the agents not only of individual redemption but also of social reform—and they are not restricted to the nuns of her poem. In her introduction to *A Chaplet of Verses*, Procter highlights both the religious and social work of the Sisters of Mercy working at Providence Row Night

Refuge. These women "become the model for the rest of society who are then challenged to enact these same values of community in their own lives, thereby broadening the influence from the cloister to the rest of Victorian society." Catholicism, for Procter, breaks through Victorian domestic ideology to model "the type of action that needs to be taken in Victorian society: action that is based on love, forgiveness, spiritual equality, and a sense of community that extends beyond the nuclear family."[28]

To this reading of the poem's affirmation of Catholic communal values and social reform, I add that "A Legend of Provence" also suggests that Procter saw legend itself as able to shape a community's values. Indeed, this particular legend exists only because its chief characters were themselves narrators who knew the power of story to shape people's beliefs and actions. The poem opens with the narrator's recollection of being told the legend, which she recalls after seeing a portrait of a nun; it closes with the narrator's moral reflections and attempts to interpret the tale. Within this frame narrative, an old nun "spake thus to [her], and told / The Convent's treasured Legend, quaint and old" (41–42). This nun, it turns out, knows the legend in the first place only because long ago, the chief character, Angela, herself told the story that no one else knew. In the story that Angela told, the pivotal moment arose also through storytelling. So stories, tellers of stories, and interpretations of stories all require attention in this legend.

For "A Legend of Provence" is, on another level than the ones already discussed, a poem about what kinds of stories best shape good (moral and social) lives, and why such stories should be transmitted. We may begin with the innermost stories: to soothe the wounded knight in her care, Angela tells him "legends of the martyred Saints"; she describes "the pangs, which, through God's plenteous grace, / Had gained their souls so high and bright a place" (136, 137–38). To Angela, these are healing stories—spiritually healing, primarily, but able also to calm the agitated, wounded knight and so contribute to physical healing. Angela has, of course, learned these legends from the nuns in the convent, who obviously encourage each other to spiritual and material sacrifice by looking ahead to their souls' reward. Legends help them remember that God's grace turns "pangs" into profit. Till this moment in her life, Angela has been well served by these legends of martyrdom, and she has no reason to believe they will not have the same effect on the wounded knight. Indeed, they do quiet the knight, but, we later learn, they do not affect his life, which has been shaped by other stories instead—stories that he, in turn, tells Angela. The knight's stories are not, however, of martyred saints but of "the glories of his past; / Tourney, and joust, and pageant bright and fair, / And all the lovely ladies who were there" (158–60). He enchants Angela with a world "of love and bliss," a "glorious world of joy, all joys above, / Transfigured in the golden mist of love" (162, 167–68). So skilled is his telling that Angela does not note the possessive adjective that betrays the self-centered direction of his stories: the glories of *his* past. Enraptured, she secretly leaves the convent with him, to learn eventually that the knight has upended what she once knew to be true: that martyred saints really do gain a higher and brighter place than that promised by this "glorious world of joy." She has mistakenly believed and followed the wrong story.

But in the process, Angela has learned the power of life stories to affect people's beliefs and behaviors. She could have died silent to the end about the sins of her past, since Mary herself was silent about them. But she does not. On her deathbed, she relates what none in the convent have known about her. To the sisters kneeling round her bed, "Angela told her life: / Her sin, her flight; the sorrow and the strife, / And the return" (306–8). Further, she makes clear the point of her so doing: "Praise God for me, my sisters" (309). The sisters understand her meaning. They do not praise *her*; they raise a "psalm" to heaven (309). In telling her story, then, Angela allows praise to be directed to God; but she also releases what becomes the legend, thus adding her own life story to the legends of martyred saints whose telling helps the faithful maintain their own spiritual path.

The frame narrator of the poem understands the first point, the one about God's mercy. Taking over the narrative again, this speaker ponders "the lesson of God's pardon" (318). She even extrapolates from Mary's keeping of Angela's place in the convent to God's keeping of the believer's place in heaven: we have all lost the "pure ideal of a noble life" (321)

> in this daily jar and fret,
> And now live idle in a vague regret.
> But still *our place is kept*, and it will wait,
> Ready for us to fill it, soon or late.
>
> (325–28)

But she does not, it seems, grasp what Angela has further understood, namely, that the didactic point to be gained from the story may actually be less important than the recognition that story itself may shape what one values—and consequently, how one lives. As we know from the frame narrative, Angela's story is told and retold by the nuns through the generations; perhaps it becomes the legend par excellence for helping other novices in conflicted situations make the right choices. Certainly, the memory of the legend changes even the frame narrator, though she may not realize it. When the poem opens, she is "[h]alf weary with a listless discontent" (2). At the poem's close, this lethargy and gloom have vanished, and the narrator formulates an interpretation of Angela's legend—"We always may be what we might have been" (330)—that seems also to have sparked her own new, more hopeful mood. Though she is busy with interpreting the legend for the benefit of others (her tone becomes explanatory as well as meditative), she has, in fact, been substantially changed by it. Its values have shifted her stance.

As a contribution to the Catholic project of recovering Continental legends that would help form the values and beliefs of the growing Catholic community in England, Procter's poem, then, goes beyond its frame narrator's spoken conclusions. It becomes its own legend, wider than the one it tells (because it includes the nun-teller and the narrator), carrying its own spiritual weight. In addition to espousing Catholic devotion and communal values, it warns its readers not to be beguiled by mere fables, by life stories filled with the "glories" of a world detached from religious devotion. Rather, it prompts readers toward legends of the martyred saints, or legends of Provence, or legends of Bregenz, as aids in the formation of their spiritual and social lives. These legends, Procter implies, give readers the right kind of story (we might say the right kind of imaginary) to live by. Rooted in a Catholic era, set in still-Catholic countries, but brought to England to help shape a new Catholic community, these legends work to restore the values of a past so far back in memory as to appear forgotten but ready to revive and save the nation in a crisis.

Idealizing the Poor and Irish

While Procter had already manifested a social conscience in her poems about the poor in *Legends and Lyrics*, her critique sharpened in the later volume with the more overt religious character. By directing the financial recompense for her poems of social critique toward the refuge, she forestalls potential accusations that she would benefit from the very condition of the poor that her poems lament; from this morally secure position, she criticizes those who failed to do their part in establishing the social bond between classes. Her critique is the sharper for her perception of this bond as ultimately a religious one. At the same time, her idealization of the poor as holy is accompanied by an assumption that such holiness can only be activated or properly directed through the spiritual intercession of people like herself. That is, the poor always wait for the social or religious bond to be activated by others; in Procter's poems, the poor do not exhibit spiritual initiative.

The complexities of Procter's engagement with the poor emerge strongly in her longest poem on this topic, "The Homeless Poor" (*PAAP*, 407–13). In this poem, as in others, Procter criticizes the failure of devout Christians to translate their love for Jesus into concern for the poor whom Jesus loves. The poem portrays an Angel of Prayers, who rejoices in gathering tender words of devotion from homes and churches, being rebuked by an Angel of Deeds, who insists Jesus will not "prize mere words of love and honour / While His Homeless Poor are left to die" (69–70). Tears and prayers do much, this second angel insists, but "[b]etter still would be the food and shelter, / Given for Him and given to His own" (131–32). The Angel of Prayers, acknowledging the truth of these words, throws away the wreaths of prayers. After the vision of this celestial exchange fades, the narrator addresses the listeners/readers of the poem with words that recall the birth of Jesus in lowly circumstances and that insist on his continuing presence:

> Jesus, then, and Mary still are with us,—
>   Night will find the Child and Mother near,
> Waiting for the shelter we deny them,
>   While we tell them that we hold them dear.
>
> (145–48)

In this stanza, Procter attributes the gap between religious words and action that the angels have been discussing to a failure to perceive the presence of Jesus and Mary in the poor of the earth, particularly the children and women. Procter seeks to motivate the middle classes to intervene on behalf of the poor, not because the poor might otherwise spread disease in the social body or because lack of intervention might produce social or political instability but because the bond of fellowship between classes is the natural extension of Christian devotion to Jesus and Mary, the paradigmatic homeless child and mother who relied on strangers for basic accommodation. By consistently using the names "Jesus," "Child," or "Infant" rather than "Lord," "Christ," or other alternatives, Procter accentuates the humanity and dependence of the holy child and, by implication, his kinship with the helpless poor. Given this closer kinship with the poor than with any other class, the middle classes ought to seek fellowship with the poor as a way of devoting themselves to Jesus.

But this call to fellowship is complicated by the poem's assumptions and structures. On the one hand, Procter adds weight to her middle-class narrator's rebuke by portraying the narrator's words as the account of a heavenly vision—a rebuke authorized by angels. On the other hand, whereas Barrett Browning's seraphim are alike confused and wondering, Procter's angels duplicate the morally unequal relationship between the didactic (catechumenical) middle-class narrator and the presumably devout but socially inactive listeners. Ignoring the problem created by casting a heavenly being as unable to detect superficiality in devotion, Procter depicts the Angel of Prayers as simple, almost naïve, and the Angel of Deeds as perceptive, knowing and, consequently, the better angel. Despite the Angel of Prayers's sincerity, the Angel of Deeds must guide that sincerity into proper channels; the Angel of Prayers offers no reciprocal comment, such as the insufficiency of deeds without prayers. Intentionally or not, this unequal celestial relationship mirrors not only the relationship between the narrator and her audience but also Procter's perception of the relationship between classes. In the poem, the vision does not come to one of the poor. That is, no homeless persons—despite their supposed close kinship to Jesus and Mary—overhear the angelic exchange and carry the message of instruction to the middle classes. Instead, a middle-class narrator receives the vision. For Procter, the call to action cannot arise from the poor, who have no authority to address their superiors. In fact, the poor—to retain their holiness and special kinship with Jesus—must remain poor and simple. Only the middle classes must become more knowing. Moral authority also divides the generalized middle class from the narrator. The didactic narrator has no qualms about addressing moral laxity in others, though she humbly (or strategically) includes herself among those who need help:

> Help us, Lord! not these Thy poor ones only,
>   They are with us always, and shall be:—
> Help the blindness of our hearts, and teach us
>   In Thy homeless ones to succor Thee.
>
> (149–52)

In spite of this apparent self-inclusion, by framing the angelic conversation with the interpretive words of the narrator, the poem leaves no doubt as to the narrator's moral authority. The narrator functions as the mediator between heavenly wisdom and middle-class blindness.

Procter's next poem about the poor approaches the question of the social-religious bond from a somewhat different angle. If in "The Homeless Poor" Procter represents the lowest class as the holiest, in "Homeless" (*PAAP*, 441–42) she represents the highest class as the most callous, the least devotional. Dropping the celestial voices of "The Homeless Poor" (much as Barrett Browning did when moving from "The Seraphim" to "A Drama of Exile"), she imagines a dialogue between a "lady" and what again appears to be a middle-class narrator. But the dialogue again lacks genuine exchange. The lady responds to her middle-class interrogator but hardly grasps the point of the questions or the hypocrisy of her answers. The ellipsis between the lady's final response and the middle-class instructor's moral conclusion reinforces the gap between the two speakers. Taking a stronger position than in "The Homeless Poor," where she partly aligns her speaker with the middle classes being chastised for their narrowness of religious commitment, Procter has her questioner now appear to rebuke the upper classes without any indication of self-chastisement. In the poem, the inquirer repeatedly draws the lady's attention to the sounds and sights of the street at night, only to be repeatedly dismayed at the lady's responses: what the inquirer takes to be lost pets, lurking criminals, or neglected goods needing attention, the lady dismisses as "only" homeless children and women. In "Christian England" (9), the lady asserts, our dogs, criminals, and goods receive good care; she has no regard for the homeless, who have neither moral nor market value for her. Taken together, "The Homeless Poor" and "Homeless" imply that the further one moves away from being (associated with the) poor, the less truly Christian one can be. The lady in "Homeless," for example, empties the term "sister-woman" (21) of all its potential meanings. She recognizes neither a social bond (sisterliness) nor a religious bond (Sister-woman) between herself and the homeless woman she ignores outside her door. Procter implicitly contrasts superficial Christianity with true religion; her term "sister-woman" calls to mind other Sisters who do give homeless women food and shelter—at the Providence Row Night Refuge, for example, where Catholic devotion and social activity combine in the practice of charitable pastorship. Moreover, by including in a volume intended for middle-class readers a poem that figures the higher classes as absolutely callous toward the poor, Procter implicitly exhorts the middle classes to action on the grounds that they are more feeling.[29]

In addition to representing the spiritual relationship between the poor and other classes through conversations involving angels, middle-class narrators, and a lady, Procter also experiments with giving voice to a poor man himself, in "The Beggar" (*PAAP*, 437–38)—the only time she does so. Again, she idealizes. If actual beggars who came to Oratorian exercises drove out the educated by their stink (I am recalling Faber's words mentioned in the previous chapter), there is no acknowledgment of it in Procter's poem. Her beggar does not betray her notion of a holy poor. Indeed, he displays concern for his spiritual well-being, not his economic or social status, demonstrating that while middle-class narrators might call for material aid for the poor, the poor themselves, revealing their deep strain of holiness, place the well-being of their souls ahead of the needs of their bodies. Yet despite Procter's laudable effort to give voice directly to the poor here, the poem actually reinforces middle-class moral superiority once again. The beggar pleads "Not for gold and not for silver" but "for something even more," namely, pity and prayer (3, 4). Turning to various parties (adults, children, laypeople, clergy), the beggar repeatedly and insistently pleads, "Pray for me." Despite his supposed holiness, he stands only on the doorstep, while others, to whom he pleads, "stand before the Altar" with "anointed hands" (25, 26):

> I am standing on your doorstep as a Beggar
>   Who will not be turned away,
> And the Charity you give my soul shall be—
>   Pray for me!
>
> (39–42)

This is puzzling. Why, given Procter's insistence in other poems that prayer without deeds merits nothing and that the poor desperately need food and shelter, does she envision the beggar here turning impatiently away from the gold and silver he obviously needs to ask instead for prayers for his soul? Why does he not pray himself for his soul? The answer, it seems to me, lies in the paradox that, despite their apparent holiness, the poor are less exemplars of moral action than the occasion for such middle-class conduct. Whether or not Procter notices the paradox she creates, the very holiness that compels the beggar to show concern for his soul does not actually suffice for his spiritual well-being. He needs (and knows he needs) the intercession of people whose (material, moral) advantages seemingly give them an influence with God that he does not possess. Had Procter envisioned the beggar asking for food and shelter or even demanding them on the grounds of religious equality before God, she might have avoided this ultimately patronizing note. Instead, while the interventions of the revivalists on behalf of the poor inform Procter's poetic endeavors, so do the paradoxes that accompany their idealist visions.

These same paradoxes emerge in Procter's poems about the Irish, who seem a conceptually distinct group from the poor for Procter, perhaps because for the revivalists the identifying feature of the Irish was not their poverty but their (assumed) faith. Procter makes no mention of the Irish in her poems about the poor, though she did write two separate poems about the Irish themselves. The first of these, "An Appeal: 'The Irish Church Mission for Converting the Catholics'" (*PAAP*, 376–79), offers a fiercely political and religious critique of English attitudes toward Ireland and Irish Roman Catholicism. It exposes the inhumane methods of Anglican England's attempt to convert the Irish Catholics. The poem calls Ireland England's "Sister" and praises the Irish for holding to the "ancient worship" (that is, Catholicism) that "prosperous England" has "cast aside" (2, 27, 68, 69). The Irish here are morally superior to the English. The same is true in "Milly's Expiation" (*PAAP*, 414–28). In this poem, Procter turns from lyric to narrative as she attempts to evoke sympathy and regard for Irish Catholic Milly, who, though she commits perjury and so becomes a morally fallen woman, expiates her sin through lifelong devotion and acts of kindness to those in need. Though hardly an ideal religious figure, Milly exemplifies Catholic virtue, as does her family generally in their steady commitment to the Roman faith in the face of many trials. Much like Faber's hymns about the Irish, both poems represent Ireland as an example to England in its loyalty to the Catholic faith.

As with the poems about the poor, however, "An Appeal" seems ambivalent about adopting a full commitment to the Irish cause and so undercuts the strength of its critique of England. The speaker has significant trouble aligning her voice consistently with the Irish. The first-person-plural alignment that gives the narrator initial sympathy of tone melts away, reappears, then melts away again. "We ask not" (5) slips into "They ask not" (11); later, the recovered "we" becomes "them" precisely when inclusion becomes too threatening:

> Then, then, *we* plead for mercy,
> Then, Sister, hear *our* cry!
> For all *we* ask, O England,
> Is—leave *them* there to die!
>
> (38–41; my italics)

The speaker wishes to both stand alongside the Irish and be distanced from them. The problematic nature of the narrating voice also appears in such lines as the ones that bid England to "Take all the scanty produce / That grows on Irish soil" as long as Ireland's "ancient worship" remains untouched (19–20, 27). Would an Irish narrator accept these terms? Or is an English narrator again idealizing the Catholic commitment of the starving poor/Irish? The latter seems the case, both in "An Appeal" and in "Milly's Expiation." Given that Procter must have had the opportunity to hear (or been able to discover) the stories of Irish Catholic women in London, perhaps via her visits to the refuge, why did she produce a poem that imagines a Catholic woman in Ireland? I suspect that these ambivalences and difficulties arose from Procter's actual experience with the Irish presence in London, specifically, in revivalist missionary efforts—a presence and activity neither poem acknowledges. After all, despite the "Second Spring" rhetoric, it had become increasingly clear that many Irish immigrants were Catholic in name but not in practice and that many of them were more attached to their local Irish priests than to the English revivalist movement. Procter seems to have avoided dealing with these contradictions between the revivalist idealized vision of the Irish as an asset to the English Catholic church and the actual facts of the Irish immigrant community. By imaginatively confining the Irish to Ireland, she applauds the Catholicism rather than the Irish-ness of Irish Catholics.

Negotiating Catholic Authority

As a Catholic woman poet, Procter did not make the kinds of claims to authority or to hermeneutical importance that Barrett Browning did quite boldly as a Dissenting woman poet or that Rossetti did less overtly as an Anglican woman devotional writer. Roman Catholicism, after all, acknowledges hierarchy as part of its history and faith, and by converting into the denomination, Procter accepted such structures to a degree. Had she lived longer, she might have offered the kinds of resistance to male exclusivity that Rossetti (whose Anglicanism also acknowledges a system of religious hierarchy) produced in her prose devotional writings as well as in her poetry. Instead, Procter's claims for the religious woman poet remain more muted than Rossetti's or Barrett Browning's. Nevertheless, in at least two poems in *A Chaplet of Verses*, Procter privileges lay devotion over clerical pronouncement.

Procter's method for reasserting a measure of independence begins in the composition of two poems as present-tense meditations even though they were written some years after the declared dates in their titles. Both "The Church in 1849" (*PAAP,* 390–91) and "The Jubilee of 1850" (*PAAP,* 379–81) deal with the status of the Roman Catholic Church in England at midcentury. However, as Procter did not convert to Catholicism until 1851, and as the poems lament the loss of the Catholic faith in England, it is highly probable that she wrote the poems not in 1849 or in 1850, as their present-tense constructions would indicate, but sometime after 1851—quite possibly sometime near the publication date of *A Chaplet of Verses.* This poses the question, why produce after 1851 and publish in 1862 poems that purport to have been written in 1849 and 1850? The answer may lie in Procter's sense that revivalist enthusiasm for new directions needed some balance. By calling to mind the experience of the Catholic Church in England in 1849 and 1850, Procter reminds her primarily revivalist readers that what they have gained arose from the bedrock of an older Catholicism (the revivalist movement did not truly establish itself as a force to be reckoned with until the establishment of the Oratory in Brompton, in 1854). Procter's poems, therefore, assert the continuing importance and value of traditional Catholicism even for revivalist Catholics. As if to emphasize the importance of heritage, Procter reserves her sole use of the sonnet form for "The Church in 1849." With its lengthy literary tradition, the sonnet appropriately reflects her attention to the history of English Catholicism.

Procter's ambivalence toward religious authority emerges when we read "The Church in 1849" and "The Jubilee of 1850" in the context of national and international events pertaining to midcentury Roman Catholicism. In 1849 the Roman Church in England had gained notice through the reception of prominent figures such as Newman, but it had not yet achieved the status that arrived with the restoration of the hierarchy the subsequent year. "The Church in 1849" offers the beleaguered Roman Church in England the consolation of remembering that its "first and greatest Prince" appeared for a time as a "fisher on the Lake of Galilee" (13, 14); analogously, the midcentury Church appears dim in glory but is and will reveal itself again to be a "Mighty Mother" (1). Though the "foes" of the Roman Church "exulting cry / That [her] old strength is gone," the speaker asks bracingly, "And is it so? The raging whirlwind blows / No stronger now than it has done of yore" (1, 2–3, 5–6). Not even "Hell's gates [can] prevail to conquer" the Church; even in 1849, the speaker declares, "We [can] rejoice" (11, 9). By imagining this spiritual vibrancy as existing already in 1849, Procter disassociates the Church's strength from the reestablishment of the hierarchical system in

1850. The restoration of systems does not figure in Procter's account of a revitalized Church.

Equally subtly, "The Jubilee of 1850" declares the importance of lay devotion apart from clerical pronouncements by turning attention to a significant event in the international Roman Catholic community—or rather, to a nonevent. From the medieval period onward, on a more or less regular basis, the pope officially declared every twenty-fifth year as a Jubilee for the faithful, a year of spiritual celebration and pardon. According to the liturgical calendar, 1850 should have been a Jubilee year. However, because of the political turmoil in Italy, which drove the pope temporarily out of Rome, Pius IX did not declare the Jubilee that year. Strikingly, however, Procter's poem asserts the Jubilee year as an actual occurrence despite the lack of papal declaration. The speaker laments England's denial of the Catholic faith once held and pleads that Catholic nations pray for England in "this most happy hour" of the Jubilee (34):

> While, with united joy,
>   This day you all adore,
> Remember what she was,
>   Though her voice is heard no more.
>
> (5–8)

Taking "The Church in 1849" and "The Jubilee of 1850" together, we see Procter virtually ignoring the event that *did* occur in 1850—the restoration of the hierarchy—and constituting as actual an event that did *not* occur that year—the Jubilee. In other words, she invests the year with spiritual significance according to what *she* perceives as its key event, not according to what religious authorities decide. Political-religious structures of authority, she implies, neither make nor break the occasions by which ordinary Catholics engage in devotion. As "Our Titles" (*PAAP*, 398–99) asserts more openly in the form of rhetorical questions, are not ordinary Catholics all nobles, princes, and kings? They carry their own glories. Consequently, Procter did not feel the need to pass *A Chaplet of Verses* through the hands of clerical examiners before publishing it, nor did she seek a religious publishing house such as the Catholic Publishing and Book-selling Company, which published a wide range of Catholic materials from tracts to saints' lives to fiction from the 1850s onwards. Bell and Daldy having declined her manuscript, she turned to Longmans as if to assert that the Catholic woman poet can seek a measure of independence from explicitly religious structures while still fully subscribing to the Catholic faith. Moreover, in this final publication decision, Procter implied that however much her poetry had emerged from her own religious engagements, she saw no reason why it should not also capture the attention of those beyond her faith tradition. It has, after all, not only religious but also imaginative and even critical merit.

CONCLUSION

THE INTRICACY OF THE SUBJECT

> There are three great inlets of human knowledge....
> The first is sense, or the senses.... The second inlet
> of knowledge is intellect, understanding, mind, with
> all the mental faculties; the will, the memory, the
> judgment, and the imagination.... The third inlet, and
> the greatest of all, is faith.
>
> James Stratten, 1862

In his sermon entitled "Increase of Faith," the Reverend James Stratten of Paddington Chapel identifies three avenues by which "conviction and enjoyment [are] realized in the mind."[1] His identification of the senses as an inlet of knowledge is both Lockean and Romantic; his extended valuation of intellect is both Augustinian and Enlightenment-inflected; and his naming of faith as the third and greatest inlet of knowledge reaches as far back as the biblical proverb "The fear of the Lord is the beginning of knowledge" (where "fear" means reverence). Actually, not just the latter but all three "inlets of knowledge" are affirmed in the Hebraic and Christian Scriptures: the Pentateuch imperative "Love the Lord thy God with all thine heart, and with all thy soul, and with all thy might" is echoed in the Gospels as "Love the Lord thy God with all thy heart, and with all thy soul, and with all thy strength, and with all thy mind."[2] Perhaps for this reason as much as any other, Stratten's tripled avenue of knowledge can be found in any number of nineteenth-century and earlier writings.

For much of the twentieth century, though, this body-mind-spirit triangulation of knowledge did not have much purchase. The religious skepticism of the modern period led to a privileging of cognitive functions as the way to knowledge also in literary criticism. But as the introduction to this book shows, in the past one or two decades we have again become alert to the senses and emotions as instructive components of being. We are now also poised to restore to our serious criticism an acknowledgment of faith commitments and practices as formative for knowledge and creativity. If such religious commitments were often taken earlier as failures in critical thinking or as restrictions on creativity, the advent of philosophical, sociological, neuroscientific, feminist, and other analyses explored in the introduction to this book requires that we reexamine those assumptions.

For some readers it may be easier to allow for the formative impact of religious sensibility privately held than for the generative power of church practice. It may even be that many participants in church today do not find its practices transformative in any way. In a 2006 article in *Religion and Literature*, Stanley Hauerwas and Ralph Wood indirectly address this point. From their survey of American literature, they conclude that America, despite being "'a nation with the soul of a church,' [has produced] few writers who are Christian in any substantive sense of the word." Intriguingly, they then identify as a cause the "cultural establishment" of Protestant churches in America—the churches' too-close identification with the American liberal project. In other words, mainstream churches in America are not sufficiently distinctive from their surrounding culture and so do not offer even Christian writers any deep alternative ways of imagining the world. This failure of the churches to offer distinctive religious imaginaries to their adherents has resulted in the church being "nearly everywhere . . . occluded from our imaginative vision."[3] In Hauerwas and Wood's judgment, private religious sensibility, however much it might contribute to literary work in some ways, cannot generate a religious imaginary as powerfully transformative as that shaped by long participation in distinctive church practices. Implicitly, this argument suggests that in a culture or time when churches *were* still or increasingly at odds with the secularizing project—for example, in Victorian England—those same churches might have had more to offer for literary work than we have been accustomed to believe.

I began this book by identifying along with James K. A. Smith the significance of practices to the formation and expression of the imaginary. I do not wish to assert the primacy of the affective over the cognitive, or of practice over proposition, but their equivalent power. We operate in the world as thinkers-feelers-doers; we are shaped by propositions, emotions, and actions; we are cognitive-affective-practicing people. Religious identity and expression arise also from this complex constellation of ideas, feelings, and actions. The religious poetry of Elizabeth Barrett Browning, Christina Rossetti, and Adelaide Procter, I argue in this book, can best be read in light of their intellectual, affective, and habitual engagements with Christianity, because these dimensions taken together constitute a religious imaginary or way of approaching the world. My emphasis on these women's liturgical practice is not, I hope it is clear, intended to minimize the critical and creative dimensions of these poets' work or to reduce it to some kind of "natural" output of unarticulated subconscious formations, as if the poets had no choice but to produce what they were programmed by habit formations to produce. If I have leaned heavily on liturgical practice, it is because I feel it so useful for enlarging our perception of the individuality of each woman's religious work. F. Elizabeth Gray has shown us some of the shared dimensions of Victorian women's devotional poetry—for example, its focus on a personal relationship between Christ and poet-speaker, and its insistent linguistic ornamentation—but I have tried to show what distinguishes some of these poets from each other.

Perhaps a juxtaposed reading of the three poets working with a common theme may reinforce here the thesis I develop throughout this book about distinctive religious imaginaries. Barrett Browning, Rossetti, and Procter all wrote Christmas poems at advanced stages of their poetic careers. These poems, which mutually recognize a major Christian celebration and associate it with gift giving, diverge in their representations of the best way to respond to that event. Barrett Browning's "Christmas Gifts" situates religious freedom as the desired outcome of political freedom; Rossetti's "A Christmas Carol" meditates first on the character of Almighty Christ, then on the appropriate response of the worshipper who recognizes the disjunction between Christ's rightful glory and willing humility; Procter's "Christmas Flowers" considers love as an appropriate gift for the sympathizing Mother and Child who remain present among the worshippers.

"Christmas Gifts," published in 1860, confirms that Barrett Browning's sensibility about individual freedom as a religious matter continued to resonate late in the poet's life. Briefly, the poem laments the usurpation by the pope of the devotion due to Christ on Christmas Day. It speaks directly to the Italian religious-political situation in which Pope Pius IX exerts temporal control, such that, from the narrator's perspective, "The magi kneel at his foot, / Kings of the east and west" (*WEBB*, 4:591.13–14), and he puts the gifts of gold, incense, and myrrh they bring toward the cause "of a sword" (33). Meanwhile the people cry out, "[W]ho will show us where / Is the stable where Christ was born?" (5–6). When "a king of the west" arrives with "gifts" of red, green, and white representing the Italian flag (37–42; that is, when Napoleon III aids Italian efforts to throw off Austrian aggression, a liberty effort that will also threaten the rule of the papal states), the people hail him as a kind of savior, exclaiming, "Now blessed be he who has brought / These gifts" (50–51; compare Mark 11:9 about Jesus's entry to Jerusalem, "Blessed be he that comes"), not because he will replace the pope but because the flag he brings them "is the star we sought / To show us where Christ was born!" (53–54). Political liberty, in other words, will effect a greater, spiritual liberty, so that the people can direct their worship to the end identified in the poem's epigraph. Given in Greek, that epigraph comes—fittingly for a sort of nativity poem—from Gregory of Nazianzus's "Oration on the Nativity," notably from that section of the oration that Barrett had identified in 1832 as especially fine, the bringing of the magi's gifts to the Christ-child (see *BC*, 3:12). In Barrett's 1824 translation, the epigraph reads, "[A]s unto thy King, as unto thy God, as unto Him who was a corpse for thee" (*WEBB*, 5:467). Taken in conjunction with the title "Christmas Gifts," the epigraph clearly calls for a right orientation of worship, and the poem makes clear that such orientation should not be obstructed by political or temporal pursuits. In her life in Italy, Barrett Browning had seen firsthand the threat of arrest for Italians who owned their own Bible and were suspected of Protestant leanings (*LA*, 2:32). In this poem she imagines the spiritual hunger such deprivation causes, for the people's desire to find Christ in his stable metaphorically represents their longing for the Word. So although the poem contains no dialogue, foregrounds no poet-figure, and narrates no growth toward balanced intellectual-emotive knowledge, it bespeaks the most basic principle of all in Barrett Browning's religious imaginary: the right of every individual to seek out the Word without interference from human authority.

Rossetti's well-known "A Christmas Carol" (*CP*, 210–11), beginning "In the bleak mid-winter" and first published in 1872, grows not from a religious-political orientation but from an attunement toward the manifested Christ of glory. After an opening stanza that seems as much about an unreceptivity toward Christ as about winter weather conditions ("Earth stood hard as iron, / Water like a stone" [3–4]), the second stanza pivots around an important midway colon:

Conclusion

> Our God, Heaven cannot hold Him
> > Nor earth sustain;
> Heaven and earth shall flee away
> > When He comes to reign:
> In the bleak mid-winter
> > A stable-place sufficed
> The Lord God Almighty
> > Jesus Christ.
>
> > > (9–16)

The stanza begins by acknowledging Christ's second coming, not his first, in order to deepen what is actually unspoken in the stanza, namely, that Christ's first coming, his birth in a stable, is utterly unfathomable. The one who is a king so powerful that heaven and earth are insufficient to hold him (an allusion to 1 Kings 8:27) and who will come in such glory that heaven and earth will flee from him (an allusion to Revelation 20:11) actually deemed a "stable-place" as sufficient for his entry into the world—even though he remained Lord God Almighty while doing so. The speaker can hardly believe it, can only contrast the majestic worthiness of Christ with his condescending action and leave the incredible disjunction between the two hanging in the air behind that colon for our amazement. That juxtaposition between what Christ deserves and what he accepts continues through the next stanza (where in place of angel worship, Christ accepts as "[e]nough" "[t]he ox and ass and camel / Which adore" [21, 23–24]) and leads the speaker to wonder about the appropriate human response to such an incredible act of self-giving. She notes that angels may have thronged around the stable,

> But only His mother
> > In her maiden bliss
> Worshipped the Beloved
> > With a kiss.
>
> > > (29–32)

Her point is not that Mary (reservedly identified only in her relation to Christ, as mother) alone worshipped, but that Mary alone worshipped with a kiss, that is, with a human, embodied gesture of love. And the one she kissed is not here a helpless infant (and not ever named with his earthly name alone, Jesus) but the Beloved, with all the biblical resonance of that term (such as in the

Song of Songs, where the beloved bridegroom is usually read typologically as Christ, and in the Gospel accounts of Christ's baptism, where a voice from heaven says, "This is my beloved Son"). This speaker is completely conscious of the Christ in the child. So it is a question not of what one offers as a gift to the infant Jesus but of how one responds to the first step of the saving work of the "Lord God Almighty / Jesus Christ." The speaker has nothing to offer by way of material object (no shepherd's lamb, no wise man's gift), but she can do as Mary did, that is, respond with a human, embodied gesture: "what I can I give Him, / Give my heart" (39–40). In this poem, then, the speaker pulls on numerous biblical threads to consider who actually manifested himself at Christmas. Her response is to orient her heart into relationship with the one whom she has reencountered through her meditation. Unlike the iron earth and stony water, she acknowledges and responds to the Beloved, not effusively but in stripped poetic lines "[e]nough for Him" who reserved his fullness by becoming a child. In short, then, this poem demonstrates that for Rossetti, a Christmas poem necessarily becomes a place for yet another underspoken yet deeply personal response to the Christ of glory everywhere manifested in Scripture. It speaks to the discipleship of living in communion.

Like the two poems studied above, Procter's poem "Christmas Flowers" (*PAAP,* 381–83), published in *A Chaplet of Verses,* is built on the theme of gift giving. Like Rossetti's "A Christmas Carol," it opens with attention to the bleak weather (but without subtle analogy to cold hearts) that prevents any flowers from blooming. As subsequent stanzas reveal, the lack of flowers presents a problem in that the speaker has no blossoms to offer Mary at Christmas. May, August, October, February—in these festal Marian months, flowers abound to decorate Mary's shrines, but in December, "We seek all in vain: / Not the tiniest blossom is coming / Till Spring breathes again" (34–36). The poem continues to its end with these five stanzas:

> And the bright feast of Christmas is dawning,
>   And Mary is blest;
> For now she will give us her Jesus,
>   Our dearest, our best,
> And see where she stands, the Maid Mother,
>   Her babe on her breast!
>
> And not one poor garland to give her,
>   And yet now, behold,

Conclusion

> How the Kings bring their gifts,—myrrh, and incense,
>   And bars of pure gold:
> And the Shepherds have brought for the Baby
>   Some lambs from their folds.
>
> He stretches His tiny hands towards us,
>   He brings us all grace;
> And look at His Mother who holds Him,—
>   The smile on her face
> Says they welcome the humblest gifts
>   In the manger we place.
>
> Where love takes, let love give; and so doubt not:
>   Love counts but the will,
> And the heart has its flowers of devotion
>   No winter can chill;
> They who cared for "good-will" the first Christmas
>   Will care for it still.
>
> In the Chaplet on Jesus and Mary,
>   From our hearts let us call,
> At each Ave Maria we whisper
>   A rosebud shall fall,
> And at each Gloria Patri a lily,
>   The crown of them all!
>
>   (37–66)

These stanzas, like Rossetti's, lament the lack of traditional gifts to offer the child born in Bethlehem—no myrrh, incense, gold, lamb (or flowers)—and they come to the same conclusion: offer the heart instead. But the poems nevertheless differ significantly. Most obviously, as a Roman Catholic devotional poem, Procter's foregrounds devotion to Mary, which Rossetti's does not (indeed, Procter's poem almost elevates Mary to equal status with Jesus in the "they" of the penultimate stanza). Procter's is also more obviously linked to devotional practice, in its survey of Marian feasts and its concluding reference to the Chaplet on Jesus and Mary. Procter's is also more effusive than reserved, with its accumulation of flowers, superlatives, and fourteen beginning "And" clauses. But the more significant difference between the two poems resides in the way the speakers imagine the incarnation and the nature of Christ. Whereas Rossetti's poem considers the incarnation as a completed event ("In the bleak mid-winter / Long ago" [7–8]), which nevertheless still prompts a present relationship, Procter's speaker contemplates the incarnation both as upcoming event ("For now she will give us her Jesus") and ongoing occasion ("He stretches His tiny hands towards us"). On the one hand, of course, the present tense is a natural choice here, since the speaker appears to be contemplating a Madonna sculpture or painting in which the infant hands are always stretching. On the other hand, the tense also reveals an imaginary that holds to the perpetual presence of the Savior on earth. Just as he enters bread and wine at every Mass, so too at every viewing of his depicted infancy, he "brings us all grace" through his tiny stretching hands. As with all Procter's poems about Jesus, this one has a solid present orientation—Jesus among us, sympathizing with us, yearning toward us. This Jesus is not primarily in heaven but on earth. Procter's speaker therefore emphasizes the human, not the divine nature of Christ. Whereas Rossetti's poem carefully remembers even the incarnated Christ as Almighty God, Procter's poem unhesitatingly casts the child as a child, heaping possessives and endearments on him, emphasizing his "tiny hands," and calling him "Jesus, / Our dearest, our best."[4] As in "The Homeless Poor," there is no Lord God Almighty here. Rather, the sympathetic *human* nature of Jesus (and Mary) draws the speaker's love. The speaker gives her heart to the "Baby," not the "Beloved." This is not to say, of course, that the Catholic imaginary does not honor Jesus as God; rather, at least in Procter's case, its basic attunement to him is to his sympathizing, loving, generous, beating Sacred Heart (to recall another Procter poem), present on earth. Neither kingdoms on earth nor kingdoms in heaven factor into Christmas devotion here. Instead, "Christmas Flowers" reiterates the aspiration to heart-union with Jesus that reverberates in "Our Titles," "A Desire," "Give Me Thy Heart," and other poems shaped by the Mass-inflected imaginary; and it adopts the instructive-devotional mode and affective aesthetic common to much of Procter's religious poetry.

In asserting that these poems arose from the distinctive religious imaginaries of their respective authors, as shaped by their liturgical lives in particular denominations, I do not claim that other poets whose faith lives were constituted in the same denominations would or did necessarily write poetry in exactly the same way as these women. In keeping with this project's overall attention to distinctive voices, I do not rule out individuality within a single religious community. No two people respond to the same liturgical practices or theological positions the same way; they may not even experience them the same way. For example, we have seen that the priest and servers in Tridentine Mass play a very different role in the liturgy than do the people in the pew; conceivably the imaginary takes a somewhat different shape for them and may, in the case of writers, lead to a somewhat different poetics. Further, the imaginary may take shape more slowly for some people than for others, depending perhaps on whether the individual wholly engages or rote performs the liturgy; on whether the person has spent a lifetime in the tradition or has come to it from another background; or on whether the person has chosen the tradition or been compelled to join or remain in it. An individual might also habitually engage in other practices that counter or compete with liturgical practice in the formation of an imaginary. Any number of circumstances or attitudes might lead one person's imaginary to differ from another's in the same community, so that their religious poetics might take somewhat different forms.

Yet I believe there would be certain strong similarities in the imaginaries and poetic voices that take shape within given denominations. At least with regard to the Victorian period, this belief is supported by existing critical alignments of Rossetti's work with John Keble's. In the introductory chapter, I suggested that religious affiliation might be as formative as gender for the period's poetry. More studies of men and women poets with a shared church affiliation might support (or challenge) this suggestion. It would be instructive to examine together the poetry of Victorian men and women writers who shared a particular denominational commitment: Adelaide Procter alongside Alice Meynell and Gerard Manley Hopkins, for example; Elizabeth Barrett Browning alongside her contemporaries, preacher-poet Thomas Binney (Congregationalist), Horatius Bonar (Free Church of Scotland), or Robert Browning; or even a cross-century reading of Christina Rossetti alongside Anglo-Catholic poet T. S. Eliot, whose religious commitments have been newly examined.[5]

Perhaps as pressing for further consideration would be a study that integrates the explicitly religious poetry studied here with other poems in Barrett Browning's, Rossetti's, and Procter's oeuvres: how might the religious imaginaries detailed here inform the poems not typically seen as religious? Primarily for reasons of space, I have examined only a few such poems, but if the religious imaginary shapes poetic voice, as I have argued, then presumably that shaping should be evident in a poet's work more widely. How, then, might Barrett's ballads or *Sonnets from the Portuguese* be read alongside the religious dramas written in the same decades? Or how might we read Rossetti's "The Princess" alongside the devotional lyrics? How might more of Procter's *Legends and Lyrics* be read alongside *A Chaplet of Verses*? We need to find ways of reading the religious poetry as part of rather than distinct from the other forms of work these women produced.

Religious-literary criticism with a cognitive-affective-practices focus might also exceed the present book's period, genre, and national boundaries. Congregationalism, for example, has been a powerful formative influence in fiction as well as poetry, in the eighteenth and twentieth centuries as well as the nineteenth century. We might better understand the reach of this religious formation by studying Barrett Browning within a Congregationalist literary history that includes John Adams, George MacDonald, and Marilynne Robinson.

Whatever lines of inquiry develop from the ones I have pursued, I hope this book has opened a way for thinking further about the intricacy of the subject of religion in the nineteenth century, for recognizing that nineteenth-century commitments to public worship were understood to characterize "serious thoughtful persons" (to return to Samuel Palmer's words with which I begin the introduction to this volume)—persons who took liturgical practices as formative for their understanding of God, the world, and their own living and working. For the women studied here, such working primarily meant writing poetry that, like "the public service of the Almighty," would be "most conformable to [God's] nature and will, most honourable to religion, and most conducive to genuine edification." That these women produced such distinctive bodies of religious poetry shows how deeply their differing church lives shaped their respective Christian imaginaries.

NOTES

Introduction

1. Samuel Palmer, *A New Directory for Nonconformist Churches: Containing Free Remarks on Their Mode of Public Worship, and a Plan for the Improvement of It* (London, 1812), 1–2.

2. Dennis Taylor, "The Need for a Religious Literary Criticism," in *Seeing into the Life of Things: Essays on Literature and Religious Experience*, ed. John L. Mahoney (New York: Fordham University Press, 1998), 3.

3. See Bruce Holsinger, ed., "Literary History and the Religious Turn: Announcing the New ELN," *ELN* 44, no. 1 (2006), particularly essays by William A. Johnson (p. 5), Jennifer Hardy Williams (67), James Simpson (121), Julia Reinhard Lupton (147), and Kenneth S. Jackson (151–52).

4. Jude V. Nixon, "Framing Victorian Religious Discourse: An Introduction," in *Victorian Religious Discourse: New Directions*, ed. Jude V. Nixon (New York: Palgrave, 2004), 14.

5. Cynthia Scheinberg, *Women's Poetry and Religion in Victorian England: Jewish Identity and Christian Culture* (Cambridge: Cambridge University Press, 2002), 9.

6. F. Elizabeth Gray, *Christian and Lyric Tradition in Victorian Women's Poetry* (New York: Routledge, 2010), 1.

7. Scheinberg, *Women's Poetry and Religion*, 7; Gray, *Christian and Lyric Tradition*, 228.

8. Roger Lundin, *Believing Again: Doubt and Faith in a Secular Age* (Grand Rapids, MI: Eerdmans, 2009), 198, 194.

9. Charles Taylor, *Modern Social Imaginaries* (Durham, NC: Duke University Press, 2004), 25; James K. A. Smith, *Desiring the Kingdom: Worship, Worldview and Cultural Formation* (Grand Rapids, MI: Baker, 2009), 28.

10. Charles Taylor, *A Secular Age* (Cambridge, MA: Belknap Press of Harvard University Press, 2007), 171, 173, 387.

11. Smith, *Desiring the Kingdom*, 139.

12. Pierre Bourdieu, *The Logic of Practice*, trans. Richard Nice (Stanford: Stanford University Press, 1990), 57, 53.

13. Ibid., 64.

14. Taylor, *Secular Age*, 173.

15. E. Byron Anderson, "Liturgical Catechesis: Congregational Practice as Formation," *Religious Education* 92, no. 3 (1997): 352, 359.

16. Fred P. Edie, "Liturgy, Emotion, and the Poetics of Being Human," *Religious Education* 96, no. 4 (2001): 483, 478, 475.

17. David A. Hogue, "Sensing the Other in Worship: Mirror Neurons and the Empathizing Brain," *Liturgy* 21, no. 3 (2006): 37.

18. Elizabeth A. Wilson, *Psychosomatic: Feminism and the Neurological Body* (Durham, NC: Duke University Press, 2004), 91, 93.

19. Suzanne Nalbantian and Jean-Pierre Changeux, "Neuroaesthetics: Neuroscientific Theory and Illustration from the Arts," *Interdisciplinary Science Reviews* 33, no. 4 (2008): 361.

20. Cliff Guthrie, "Neurology, Ritual, and Religion: An Initial Exploration," *Proceedings of the North American Academy of Liturgy* (2000), 121.

21. Gregory Tate, "Tennyson and the Embodied Mind," *Victorian Poetry* 47, no. 1 (2009): 71, 78.

22. Marie Banfield, "From Sentiment to Sentimentality: A Nineteenth-Century Lexigraphical Search," *19: Interdisciplinary Studies in the Long Nineteenth Century* 4 (2007): 4.

23. William A. Cohen, *Embodied: Victorian Literature and the Senses* (Minneapolis: University of Minnesota Press, 2009), xiii, 2.

24. James K. A. Smith, *Introducing Radical Orthodoxy: Mapping a Post-secular Theology* (Grand Rapids, MI: Baker, 2004), 225, 226.

25. G. B. Tennyson, *Victorian Devotional Poetry: The Tractarian Mode* (Cambridge, MA: Harvard University Press, 1981), 4, 6.

26. Peter Elbow, *Everyone Can Write: Essays Toward a Hopeful Theory of Writing and Teaching Writing* (New York: Oxford University Press, 2000), 193, 206.

27. Kevin Irwin, *Liturgy, Prayer and Spirituality* (New York: Paulist Press, 1984), 14, 16.

28. See the etymology of liturgy (noun) as well as definition 2, *Oxford English Dictionary*, online edition, dated November 2010. Oxford: Oxford University Press.

29. Jan M. van der Lans and Henri Geerts, "The Impact of the Liturgical Setting: An Empirical Study from the Perspective of Environmental Psychology," in *Current Studies on Rituals: Perspectives for the Psychology of Religion*, ed. Hans-Günter Heimbrock and H. Barbara Boudewijnse (Amsterdam: Rodopi, 1990), 88.

30. Tyron Inbody, *The Faith of the Christian Church: An Introduction to Theology* (Grand Rapids, MI: Eerdmans, 2005), 293–94.

31. *The Congregational Service Book: A Form of Public Worship Designed for the Use of the Independent and Other Nonconformist Bodies in Great Britain* (London, 1847), n.p.; Samuel Clarkson, *Form or Freedom: Five Colloquies on Liturgies, Reported by a Manchester Congregationalist* (London, 1856), vi.

32. See Williston Walker, *The Creeds and Platforms of Congregationalism* (Boston: Pilgrim, 1960), 550.

33. Clarkson, *Form or Freedom*, 50.

34. Elizabeth Barrett Browning and Robert Browning, *Florentine Friends: The Letters of Elizabeth Barrett Browning and Robert Browning to Isa Blagden, 1850–1861*, ed. Philip Kelley and Sandra Donaldson (Winfield, KS: Wedgestone; Waco, TX: Armstrong Browning Library, 2009), 401. Hereafter cited in the text as *FF*.

Chapter 1: Truth and Love Anchored in the Word

1. Rather than aim for continuity of nomenclature through the pre- and postmarriage years by referring to the poet as "EBB" throughout (Elizabeth Barrett Barrett; Elizabeth Barrett Browning), I designate the poet as "Barrett" in premarriage contexts and as "Barrett Browning" in postmarriage or comprehensive contexts.

2. For Hope End references, see Elizabeth Barrett Barrett, *Diary by E.B.B.: The Unpublished Diary of Elizabeth Barrett Barrett, 1831–1832*, ed. Philip Kelley and Ronald Hudson (Athens: Ohio University Press, 1969), 4, 12–13, 41, 131, 225. Hereafter cited in the text as *Diary*. For Sidmouth references, see Elizabeth Barrett Browning and Robert Browning, *The Brownings' Correspondence*, vols. 1–18, ed. Phillip Kelley, Ronald Hudson, and Scott Lewis (Winfield, KS: Wedgestone, 1984–); 3:65, 79, 122; 5:278. Hereafter cited in the text as *BC*. For London references, see *BC*, 4:93; 8:150; 11:10; 13:315; 14:357–60.

3. Simon Avery and Rebecca Stott, *Elizabeth Barrett Browning* (London: Longman, 2003), 38.

4. See W. B. Selbie, *Congregationalism* (London: Methuen, 1927).

5. For a short history of this occurrence, see Kenneth Scott Latourette, *A History of Christianity*, rev. ed. (New York: Harper, 1975), 2:1190–96.

6. James A. Wylie, *Disruption Worthies: A Memorial of 1843* (Edinburgh: Grange, 1881), xvi, xxi, xxv.

7. Andrew L. Drummond and James Bulloch, *The Church in Victorian Scotland, 1843–1874* (Edinburgh: Saint Andrew, 1975), 53–54.

8. George G. Cameron, *The Scots Kirk in London* (Oxford: Becket, 1979), 133.

9. Harmony later led to unity. When the Presbyterian Church of England emerged in the mid- to later nineteenth century, the Free Churches there first joined it, then together united with the Congregationalists in the twentieth century to form the United Reformed Church of England and Wales. For accounts of these various denominational developments, see Latourette, *History of Christianity*, 1194; also Yngve Brilioth, *A Brief History of Preaching*, trans. Karl E. Mattson (Philadelphia: Fortress, 1965), 162; and Bryan D. Spinks, *Freedom or Order: The Eucharistic Liturgy in English Congregationalism, 1645–1980* (Allison Park, PA: Pickwick, 1984), 12–14, 72. The Free Church of Scotland had a presbyterian system of church government: local churches organized themselves into larger groups called presbyteries. This made the merger with the Presbyterian Church logical, particularly given the doctrinal similarities between the two. Congregationalists declined this organizational system but concurred on the principles of spiritual and legislative independence. This concurrence proved strong enough for the 1972 union of all three.

10. The Continental Committee of the Free Church of Scotland had a mandate "to establish and support fully equipped Presbyterian congregations in various Continental cities, which become for many months in winter and spring the homes of English-speaking

residents"; these cities include "Rome, Florence, Naples, Genoa and Leghorn." See George Buchanan Ryley and John M. McCandlish, *Scotland's Free Church* (Westminster, UK: Constable, 1893), 364. See the previous note also.

11. Elizabeth Barrett Browning, *The Letters of Elizabeth Barrett Browning to Her Sister Arabella*, 2 vols., ed. Scott Lewis (Waco, TX: Wedgestone, 2002), 1:53. Hereafter cited in the text as *LA*.

12. See William Ewing, ed., *Annals of the Free Church of Scotland, 1843–1900*, 2 vols. (Edinburgh: Clark, 1914), 1:181; 2:54.

13. For this last belief, see Elizabeth Barrett Browning, *The Letters of Elizabeth Barrett Browning*, 2 vols., ed. Frederic G. Kenyon (New York: Macmillan, 1898), 2:426. Hereafter cited in the text as *LEBB*.

14. Gerald Parsons, "From Dissenters to Free Churchmen: The Transitions of Victorian Nonconformity," in *Religion in Victorian Britain*, vol. 1, *Traditions*, ed. Gerald Parsons (Manchester: Manchester University Press, 1988), 71, 103, 105.

15. Dale quoted in J. H. Y. Briggs, "Image and Appearance: Some Sources for the History of Nineteenth Century Nonconformity (1)," *Baptist Quarterly* 23, no. 1 (1969): 24.

16. Ibid., 28.

17. Albert Peel, *These Hundred Years: A History of the Congregational Union of England and Wales, 1831–1931* (London: Congregational Union of England and Wales, 1931), 54.

18. John Roxborough, "The Legacy of Thomas Chalmers," *International Bulletin of Missionary Research* 23, no. 4 (1999): 176.

19. Elizabeth Barrett Browning, *Elizabeth Barrett Browning's Letters to Mrs. David Ogilvy, 1849–1861*, ed. Peter N. Heydon and Philip Kelley (London: John Murray, 1973), 117. Hereafter cited in the text as *LO*.

20. John Blackburn, *Congregational Year Book* (London: Congregational Union of England and Wales, 1847), 157. For the drawing, see Percy Green, *Paddington Chapel, 1813–1963* (London: Farmer, 1965), plate 1.

21. Wylie, *Disruption Worthies*, xxxviii, xxxix.

22. For these changes in Congregationalist chapel architecture, see Parsons, "From Dissenters," 100; and R. Tudor Jones, *Congregationalism in England, 1662–1962* (London: Independent, 1962), 230.

23. Elizabeth Barrett Browning, *Works of Elizabeth Barrett Browning*, vols. 1–5, gen. ed. Sandra Donaldson (London: Pickering and Chatto, 2010), 4:99.631–32, 643, 669–70. Hereafter cited in the text as *WEBB*.

24. See James F. White, "The Spatial Setting," in *The Oxford History of Christian Worship*, ed. Geoffrey Wainwright and Karen B. Westerfield Tucker (Oxford: Oxford University Press, 2006), 808.

25. Spinks, *Freedom or Order*, 95–97.

26. Quoted in Williston Walker, *The Creeds and Platforms of Congregationalism* (Boston: Pilgrim, 1960), 550–51.

27. Quoted in Spinks, *Freedom or Order*, 95.

28. Tyron Inbody, *The Faith of the Christian Church: An Introduction to Theology* (Grand Rapids, MI: Eerdmans, 2005), 293.

29. Wylie, *Disruption Worthies*, xxxix.

30. Elizabeth Barrett Browning, *Aurora Leigh*, vol. 3 of *WEBB*, book 7, lines 821–22. Hereafter cited in the text by book and line number(s).

31. Lundin, *Believing Again*, 208, 27.

32. Nathan Camp, "The Christian Poetics of *Aurora Leigh* (with Considerable Help from Emanuel Swedenborg)," *Studies in Browning and His Circle* 26 (2005): 62–72.

33. Emmanuel Swedenborg, *True Christian Religion*, trans. John C. Ager (New York: American Swedenborg Printing and Publishing Society, 1906), section 706. Available through Internet Sacred Text Archive, http://www.sacred-texts.com/swd/tcr/index.htm.

34. Maria LaMonaca, *Masked Atheism: Catholicism and the Secular Victorian Home* (Columbus: Ohio State University Press, 2008), 141.

35. Samuel Palmer, *A New Directory for Nonconformist Churches: Containing Free Remarks on Their Mode of Public Worship, and a Plan for the Improvement of It* (London, 1812), 56. Geo. Wm. Conder noted that Congregationalist prayers ran twenty to forty-five minutes (*Intelligent and True Worship: A Sermon Preached in the Congregational Church, Cheetham Hill, Aug. 22nd, 1869* [London, 1869]), 5–6.

36. See Spinks, *Freedom or Order*, 88–89.

37. Some argued that free prayer was open to error and poor choice of words, while defendants of free prayer called it more scriptural and more likely to be sincere. The proponents of form prayer said it, too, could be sincere, but their detractors said forms solved nothing, because they could be as poorly read as extemporary prayers were poorly spoken. See Colloquy 1 in Samuel Clarkson, *Form or Freedom: Five Colloquies on Liturgies, Reported by a Manchester Congregationalist* (London, 1856).

38. Palmer, *New Directory*, 140.

39. Josiah Conder, ed., *The Congregational Hymn Book* (London: Congregational Union of England and Wales, 1836), iv.

40. Ibid., xi.

41. This declaration is reprinted in Walker, *Creeds and Platforms*, 548–52. The first two quotations in this paragraph come from 549, the next two from 551 and 548, respectively.

42. Although Barrett does not refer to the declaration in her correspondence, she may well have read it. In 1833, she was living in Sidmouth, East Devon, a county invited to join the Congregational Union and eventually doing so in 1837 (Peel, *These Hundred Years*, 82). Shortly thereafter, she began attending Paddington Chapel, whose minister had supported the founding of the London Congregational Union in 1826 and the Congregational Library in 1830 and, being thus in favor of cooperation among Independent churches, was most likely among the many London ministers who supported the establishment of a National Union with its accompanying declaration (ibid., 42, 47, 62). It seems fair to surmise that Paddington Chapel-goers would have been acquainted with the declaration. Yet even if Barrett did not read it, the liturgical practices in which she participated embodied the stated principles as much before the declaration was written as after it.

43. Elizabeth Barrett Browning and Robert Browning, *Letters of the Brownings to George Barrett*, ed. Paul Landis with the assistance of Ronald E. Freeman (Urbana: University of Illinois Press, 1958), 214. Hereafter cited in the text as *LGB*. When Barrett remarks, "[A]s this Christian Church universal differs widely with regard to the signification & bearing of the word, my belief is that the full meaning of it is not revealed or intended to

be understood by us" (BC, 7:370), she refers to the particular word *predestination*, not to the Word of Scripture. An earlier sentence in her paragraph makes this clear: "I do not understand ... what is the revealed doctrine upon predestination, neither do I believe ... that anybody else understands it." Then follows the sentence first quoted. For an analysis of Barrett Browning's spiritualist interests—the context of this quote—see my article "Elizabeth Barrett Browning, Congregationalism, and Spirit Manifestation," *Victorians Institute Journal* 36 (2008): 103–22.

44. Richard Arnold, *The English Hymn: Studies in a Genre* (New York: Lang, 1995).

45. Susan S. Tamke, *Make a Joyful Noise Unto the Lord: Hymns as a Reflection of Victorian Social Attitudes* (Athens: Ohio University Press, 1978), 22.

46. For the description of Wesley's hymns, see Erik Routley, *A Panorama of Christian Hymnody* (Collegeville, MN: Liturgical, 1979), 25. For the description of Watts's hymns, see J. R. Watson, *The English Hymn: A Critical and Historical Study* (Oxford: Clarendon, 1997), 149.

47. See Peel, *These Hundred Years*, 221–35.

48. Quoted in Tamke, *Make a Joyful Noise*, 6.

49. Conder, *Congregational Hymn Book*, xiv.

50. See note 42.

51. John Ruskin, *The Works of John Ruskin*, vol. 18, ed. E. T. Cook and Alexander Wedderburn (London: Allen, 1905), 121–22, 125. For similar declarations by Ruskin's contemporaries, see Carol Bauer and Lawrence Ritt, eds., *Free and Ennobled: Source Readings in the Development of Victorian Feminism* (Oxford: Pergamon, 1979).

52. Susan Drain, *The Anglican Church in Nineteenth-Century Britain: Hymns Ancient and Modern (1860–1875)* (Lewiston, NY: Mellen, 1989), 3.

53. Briggs, "Image and Appearance," 22.

54. John A. Broadus, *A Treatise on the Preparation and Delivery of Sermons* (New York, 1898), 15.

55. Owen Chadwick, *The Victorian Church*, vol. 1, *1829–1859*, 3rd ed. (London: Black, 1971), 408.

56. On this point, for Congregationalists see Rosemary O'Day, "The Men from the Ministry," in *Religion in Victorian Britain*, vol. 2, *Controversies*, ed. Gerald Parsons (Manchester: Manchester University Press, 1988), 272; for the Free Church of Scotland, see James Lachlan MacLeod, "Race Theory and the Free Church of Scotland: A Nineteenth-Century Case Study," *Perspectives in Religious Studies* 25, no. 3 (1998): 228.

57. Henry Allon, "Scriptural Idea of a Christian Church," in *Services Connected with the Ordination of the Rev. Theophilus Lessey to the Pastoral Office over the Congregational Church at Barnsbury Chapel, Islington, on Tuesday, Dec. 7th, 1852* (London, 1853), 6.

58. Ibid., 7–8.

59. See Walker, *Creeds and Platforms*, 552.

60. See O'Day, "Men from the Ministry," 258–79.

61. David Ives, *The Principles of Dissent from Church Establishments; with a Comparative View of the Modes of Worship of Churchmen and Orthodox Dissenters*, 3rd ed. (London, 1833), 16.

62. Paddington Chapel's centenary booklet quotes such a motion made at a congregational meeting on September 2, 1818, at which the man who was to become one of

Barrett Browning's most respected preachers was called: "The Rev. James Stratten having laboured amongst us for nine weeks in compliance with our request, we feel perfectly satisfied that he possesses competent gifts and abilities for this important station, a zeal for God and universal holiness, skill to divide the word aright so as to give to each his portion in due season, tender compassion for the souls of men, and learning and talents to disarm and confute error—Resolved that he be respectfully and affectionately invited to the Pastoral office to take the oversight of us in the Lord." See *Paddington Chapel, Marylebone Road, London: Centenary, 1813–1913* (London: Morton, [1913]), 21. The booklet mentions that ninety-nine people signed the letter. Although I was not able to trace this particular letter, I did find (tucked into the register of Paddington Chapel's members in the London Metropolitan Archives) the letter of invitation to the chapel's next minister, the Rev. Anderson. Several women signed it. In addition, the letter is addressed to "Rev. and Mrs. Anderson." Equally attentive to women's voices in the church, the Free Church of Scotland, in its first year of existence, changed historic practice in Scottish Presbyterianism, which had restricted voting on church matters to male heads of households, by extending the vote to women "as, in the fullest sense, members of the Church." See Norman L. Walker, *Chapters from the History of the Free Church of Scotland* (Edinburgh: Oliphant, 1895), 67.

63. Conder, *Intelligent and True Worship*, 6–7.

64. Walker, *Creeds and Platforms*, 552.

65. Barbara MacHaffie, *Her Story: Women in Christian Tradition* (Philadelphia: Fortress, 1986), 107–12.

66. See Margaret Forster, *Elizabeth Barrett Browning: A Biography* (London: Chatto, 1988), 33, 313.

67. R. W. Dale, *Essays and Addresses*, 3rd ed. (London: Hodder, 1891), 127.

68. John Holloway, *The Victorian Sage: Studies in Argument* (Hamden, CT: Archon, 1962), 2.

69. Thomas Carlyle, "The Hero as Poet," reprinted in *The Victorian Poet: Poetics and Persona*, ed. Joseph Bristow (London: Croon, 1987), 66.

70. Thaïs E. Morgan, "Victorian Sage Discourse and the Feminine: An Introduction," in *Victorian Sages and Cultural Discourses: Renegotiating Gender and Power*, ed. Thaïs E. Morgan (New Brunswick, NJ: Rutgers University Press, 1990), 6.

71. Stephanie L. Johnson, "*Aurora Leigh*'s Radical Youth: Derridean *Parergon* and the Narrative Frame in 'A Vision of Poets,'" *Victorian Poetry* 44, no. 4 (2006): 427, 435.

72. For the teaching functions of priests, see Nehemiah 8:2–9; 2 Kings 17:27–28; Ezekiel 44:23. For Moses's reliance on Aaron, see Exodus 4:10–16. For the "priesthood of all believers," see Peter 2:9.

73. Antony H. Harrison, *Victorian Poets and the Politics of Culture: Discourse and Ideology* (Charlottesville: University Press of Virginia, 1998), 89. See also BC, 3:162–63.

74. Richard A. Lanham, *Analyzing Prose*, 2nd ed. (New York: Continuum, 2003), 8.

75. Debora K. Shuger, *Sacred Rhetoric: The Christian Grand Style in the English Renaissance* (Princeton: Princeton University Press, 1988), 8, 7, 10, 8, 10, 8.

76. O. C. Edwards, *A History of Preaching* (Nashville, TN: Abingdon Press, 2004).

77. *Sacred Rhetoric; or, The Art of Rhetoric as Applied to the Preaching of the Word of God* (Dublin: Browne and Nolan, 1881), 59.

78. Julie Melnyk, "'Mighty Victims': Women Writers and the Feminization of Christ," *Victorian Literature and Culture* 31, no. 1 (2003): 133.

79. Chadwick, *Victorian Church*, 408.

80. Michael Wheeler, *The Old Enemies: Catholic and Protestant in Nineteenth-Century English Culture* (Cambridge: Cambridge University Press, 2006).

81. The editors of WEBB state: "A characteristic of the manuscript [of Barrett's translation of Gregory's Oration 38] is its presentation of alternative wording, the choices being placed one above the other on a line. To represent this technique typographically, we [the editors of WEBB] have inserted a slash between the two choices, giving first the word or words that appear on the line, and the alternative that appears above the line second. In some cases, one of the choices is underlined [italicized].... In a number of instances, one word is overwritten on another (indicated by o/w)" (*WEBB*, 5:457–58).

82. *Sacred Rhetoric*, 47.

83. Henry Clay Fish, *History and Repository of Pulpit Eloquence* (New York: Dodd, 1856), 24.

84. James Stratten, "The Titles and Offices of Christ," in *The Pastoral Echo: Nineteen Sermons by Eminent Dissenting Ministers and Others* (London: W. Harding, 1837), 112.

85. Avery and Stott, *Elizabeth Barrett Browning*, 77.

86. Robert H. Ellison, *The Victorian Pulpit: Spoken and Written Sermons in Nineteenth-Century Britain* (Selinsgrove, PA: Susquehanna University Press, 1998), 28, 32.

Chapter 2: "Truth in Relation, Perceived in Emotion"

1. Martha Nussbaum, *Upheavals of Thought: The Intelligence of Emotions* (New York: Cambridge University Press, 2001), 23.

2. Glennis Stephenson, *Elizabeth Barrett Browning and the Poetry of Love* (Ann Arbor: UMI, 1989), 15; Dorothy Mermin, *Elizabeth Barrett Browning: The Origins of a New Poetry* (Chicago: University of Chicago Press, 1989), 56, 69.

3. The two stanzas from Watts can be found in Selma L. Bishop, ed., *Isaac Watts: Hymns and Spiritual Songs, 1707–1748; A Study in Early Eighteenth Century Language Changes* (London: Faith, 1962), 156, 290.

4. The manuscript—held at Syracuse University Library—is undated. The editors of BC posit an 1824 composition date, which the editors of WEBB echo (BC, 2:166n1; WEBB, 5:443), though their grounds for doing so are unclear. Philip Kelley and Betty A. Coley, in *The Browning Collections: A Reconstruction with Other Memorabilia* (Waco, TX: Armstrong Browning Library of Baylor University; Browning Institute; Mansell; Wedgestone, 1984), do not date the poems (see entry D0363).

5. Barbauld quoted in William McCarthy and Elizabeth Draft, eds., *Anna Letitia Barbauld: Selected Poetry and Prose* (Peterborough, ON: Broadview, 2002), 237.

6. Ibid., 11, 234–36.

7. See Kelley and Coley, *Browning Collections*, entries D1106, D528, D912, D1105.

8. J. R. Watson, *The English Hymn: A Critical and Historical Study* (Oxford: Clarendon, 1997), 19.

9. See William Hendrikson, *New Testament Commentary: Exposition of the Gospel According to John* (Grand Rapids, MI: Baker, 1953), 155–56.

10. Scheinberg, *Women's Poetry and Religion*, 70, 65.

11. See Romans 8:31–39; 9:19–26; 10:14–21; 11:1–12.

12. Amy Christine Billone argues in *Little Songs: Women, Silence, and the Nineteenth-Century Sonnet* (Columbus: Ohio State University Press, 2007) that Barrett turned increasingly toward the sonnet form in the years 1838 to 1850, because this form allowed her to explore the difficulties of articulation. Billone correctly points out that Barrett published three sonnets in 1838, twenty-eight in 1844, and fifty in 1850. However, the forty-four *Sonnets from the Portuguese* printed in 1850 were actually written in 1845–46, so the twelve-year exploration of silence that Billone pictures is better described as a three-year concentration on the sonnet that afterwards diminished. Essentially, I agree with Billone that Barrett eventually showed less interest in tightly controlled poetic forms such as sonnets and hymns, but I believe this shift occurred prior to 1850. From the mid-1840s on, Barrett's self-assertions were accomplished less "through rhetorical constructions that [insist] on the stifling of assertion" (Billone, *Little Songs*, 156) than through quite expansive forms.

13. E. Warwick Slinn, "Experimental Form in Victorian Poetry," in *The Cambridge Companion to Victorian Poetry*, ed. Joseph Bristow (Cambridge: Cambridge University Press, 2000), 52.

14. Philip Davis, *The Oxford English Literary History*, vol. 8, *1830–1880: The Victorians* (Oxford: Oxford University Press, 2002), 463; Slinn, "Experimental Form," 59.

15. James Stratten, "Spiritual Declension," in *The Pastoral Echo: Nineteen Sermons by Eminent Dissenting Ministers and Others* (London: W. Harding, 1837), 195.

16. Linda M. Lewis. *Elizabeth Barrett Browning's Spiritual Progress* (Columbia: University of Missouri Press, 1998), 37.

17. James Stratten, "Entrance to the Holiest by the Blood of Jesus," in *The Intermediate State and Other Discourses* (London: James Nisbet, 1867), 88–120.

18. For *WEBB* editors' treatment of alternative wording, see note 81 to chapter 1.

19. Heather Shippen Cianciola, "'Mine Earthly Heart Should Dare': Elizabeth Barrett's Devotional Poetry," *Christianity and Literature* 58, no. 3 (2009): 372, 373.

20. Scheinberg, *Women's Poetry and Religion*, 77–83; Marjorie Stone, "A Heretic Believer: Victorian Religious Doubt and New Contexts for Elizabeth Barrett Browning's 'A Drama of Exile,' 'The Virgin Mary,' and 'The Runaway Slave at Pilgrim's Point,'" *Studies in Browning and His Circle* 26 (2005): 27.

21. Scheinberg, *Women's Poetry and Religion*, 81.

22. Ingrid Hotz-Davies, *The Creation of Religious Identities by English Women Poets from the Seventeenth to the Early Twentieth Century* (Queenston, ON: Mellen, 2001), 300.

23. Marjorie Stone, *Elizabeth Barrett Browning* (New York: St. Martin's, 1995), 81.

24. Alexandra M. B. Wörn, "'Poetry is where God is': The Importance of Christian Faith and Theology in Elizabeth Barrett Browning's Life and Work," in *Victorian Religious Discourse: New Directions in Criticism*, ed. Jude V. Nixon (Basingstoke, UK: Palgrave Macmillan, 2004), 235–52. For Eve as acquiescent and silent, respectively, see Helen Cooper, *Elizabeth Barrett Browning: Woman and Artist* (Chapel Hill: University of North Carolina Press, 1988), 124; and Deirdre David, *Intellectual Women and Victorian Patriarchy: Harriet*

Martineau, *Elizabeth Barrett Browning, George Eliot* (London: Macmillan, 1987), 101. For Eve as challenging gender norms, see Mermin, *Elizabeth Barrett Browning*, 91; Stone, *Elizabeth Barrett Browning*, 80; and Lewis, *Spiritual Progress*, 63.

25. See Stone, "Heretic Believer," 23.

26. Mary Charles Murray, "The Christian Zodiac on a Font at Hook Norton: Theology, Church, and Art," in *The Church and the Arts: Papers Read at the 1990 Summer Meeting and the 1991 Winter Meeting of the Ecclesiastical History Society*, ed. Diana Wood (Oxford: Blackwell, 1992), 90, 94, 95.

27. Margaret Reynolds, "Critical Introduction," in *Aurora Leigh*, ed. Margaret Reynolds (Athens: Ohio University Press, 1992), 12–15; Stone, *Elizabeth Barrett Browning*, 138.

28. Avery and Stott, *Elizabeth Barrett Browning*, 206–7.

29. Lewis, *Spiritual Progress*, 173, 188; Jude V. Nixon, "[S]he shall make all new: *Aurora Leigh* and Elizabeth Barrett Browning's Re-Gendering of the Apocalypse," *Studies in Browning and His Circle* 26 (2006): 72–93.

30. On *Aurora Leigh*'s revisionary sage discourse, see Marjorie Stone, "Genre Subversion and Gender Inversion: *The Princess* and *Aurora Leigh*," *Victorian Poetry* 25, no. 2 (1987): 101–27. Reprinted in *Aurora Leigh*, ed. Margaret Reynolds (Athens: Ohio University Press, 1990), 494–505.

31. Elizabeth Barrett Browning, *Aurora Leigh*, vol. 3 of *WEBB*, book 1, lines 859 and 873–80. This edition is cited in the text by book and line number(s).

32. Avery and Stott, *Elizabeth Barrett Browning*, 133, 121.

33. Marjorie Stone, "Cursing as One of the Fine Arts: Elizabeth Barrett Browning's Political Poems," *Dalhousie Review* 66, no. 1–2 (1986): 155–73.

Chapter 3: "The Beloved Anglican Church of My Baptism"

1. David Tracy, *The Analogical Imagination: Christian Theology and the Culture of Pluralism* (New York: Crossroad, 1991), 203–15, 408–16.

2. In focusing on the relationship between Rossetti's poetry and liturgical experiences, I develop G. B. Tennyson's assertion that Rossetti's poetry grew "out of the act of worship" (Tennyson, *Victorian Devotional Poetry: The Tractarian Mode* [Cambridge, MA: Harvard University Press, 1981], 199). Few critics have yet investigated or elaborated on this claim, perhaps because Tennyson's book as a whole encourages readers to think about poetry in terms of Tractarian principles rather than liturgical experiences; certainly, Rossetti's religious poetry and, more recently, her prose have garnered extensive commentary as to their Tractarian nature. I concur with critics including David Kent, Diane D'Amico, Mary Arseneau, and Dinah Roe that Rossetti's aesthetics cannot be separated from Rossetti's religious commitment and practice and that Rossetti's hermeneutics derive largely from the Tractarian principle of reserve and the return to a medieval hermeneutics relying on typology and analogy. I concur also with critics such as Emma Mason that Rossetti's poetry shows the influence of Anglo-Catholic ritualism. But these Tractarian and ritualist readings of Rossetti, important as they are, do not delineate Rossetti's religious imaginary fully because they examine new, nineteenth-century Anglican developments without sufficient attention to Anglicanism itself.

3. Because the Form of Consecrating Churches that was passed in Convocation (the assembly of the Church of England) in 1712 never received royal assent, it did not become an official service in the Church of England. Bishops could, therefore, formulate their own prayers for a church consecration. However, in this paragraph, I cite the Convocation form, which can be found at http://justus.anglican.org/resources/bcp/Consecration_Church1712.htm.

4. Diane D'Amico, "The House of Christina Rossetti: Domestic and Poetic Spaces," *Journal of Pre-Raphaelite Studies*, n.s., 19 (2010): 31–54.

5. The service of Holy Communion is, of course, printed in *The Book of Common Prayer*. The 1549, 1552, and 1662 versions of *The Book of Common Prayer*—as well as multiple nineteenth-century editions—can be found at http://justus.anglican.org/resources/bcp/england.htm. In this volume I primarily I refer to the 1880 edition printed by Cambridge University Press for the SPCK.

6. Among Anglican theologians today, it is common to speak of the liturgy of the Communion as having a fourfold shape. Leonel Mitchell observes that since Gregory Dix described the pattern in *The Shape of the Liturgy* (1945), there has been an "almost universal recognition" that it goes back to the first *Book of Common Prayer* (Leonel L. Mitchell, *Praying Shapes Believing: A Theological Commentary on the* Book of Common Prayer [Harrisburg, PA: Morehouse, 1991], 146). The four actions consist of the offertory, the thanksgiving prayer, the breaking of the bread, and the communion. Mitchell further observes, however, that the breaking of the bread, though a significant action, is secondary to the thanksgiving and communion (147). In the prayer book, in fact, the instructions for the breaking of the bread are printed in the margins of the text of the thanksgiving or consecration prayer. It is appropriate, therefore, to speak of a threefold rather than fourfold shape to the third movement as well as to the Communion service as a whole.

7. David A. deSilva, *Sacramental Life: Spiritual Formation through the* Book of Common Prayer (Downers Grove, IL: IVP, 2008), 118–20.

8. Jennifer Ann Wagner, *A Moment's Monument: Revisionary Poetics and the Nineteenth-Century English Sonnet* (Madison, NJ: Fairleigh Dickinson University Press, 1996), 119.

9. Alison Chapman, "Sonnet and Sonnet Sequence," in *A Companion to Victorian Poetry*, ed. Richard Cronin, Alison Chapman, and Antony H. Harrison (Oxford: Blackwell, 2002), 101.

10. Christina Rossetti, *The Complete Poems*, ed. R. W. Crump, with notes and introduction by Betty S. Flowers (Harmondsworth, UK: Penguin, 2001), 462. Hereafter cited in the text as CP.

11. James K. A. Smith, *Desiring the Kingdom: Worship, Worldview and Cultural Formation* (Grand Rapids, MI: Baker, 2009), 174, 191 (my italics).

12. Christina Rossetti, *The Face of the Deep: A Devotional Commentary on the Apocalypse* (London: SPCK, 1892), 540. Hereafter cited in the text as FD.

13. Smith, *Desiring the Kingdom*, 183.

14. Peter Foley, "Anglican Communion: A Theological Consideration," in *Challenge and Hope: Epiphanies for Our Age* (Epiphany Study 2007, www.msgr.ca/msgr-3/Challenge_and_Hope 00.htm).

15. DeSilva, *Sacramental Life*, 91.

16. Foley, "Anglican Communion," 3.

17. Philip Davis, *The Oxford English Literary History*, vol. 8, *1830–1880: The Victorians* (Oxford: Oxford University Press, 2002), 103.

18. Gerald Parsons, "Reform, Revival and Realignment: The Experience of Victorian Anglicanism," in *Religion in Victorian Britain*, vol. 1, *Traditions*, ed. Gerald Parsons (Manchester: Manchester University Press, 1988), 32.

19. See Nigel Yates, *Buildings, Faith, and Worship: The Liturgical Arrangement of Anglican Churches, 1600–1900* (Oxford: Clarendon, 1991), 143; Nigel Yates, *Anglican Ritualism in Victorian Britain, 1830–1910* (Oxford: Oxford University Press, 1999), 36; Parsons, "Reform, Revival and Realignment," 17.

20. The Roman Catholic Relief Act, which allowed Roman Catholics to sit in Parliament, was passed by Parliament in 1829, a signal moment in the process of Catholic political, social, and religious emancipation that had begun in the late eighteenth century.

21. Parsons, "Reform, Revival and Realignment," 32.

22. Geoffrey Rowell, *The Vision Glorious: Themes and Personalities of the Catholic Revival in Anglicanism* (Oxford: Oxford University Press, 1983), 77.

23. Alf Härdelin, *The Tractarian Understanding of the Eucharist* (Uppsala, Sweden: Almquist, 1965), 305, 303.

24. John Henry Newman, *Apologia Pro Vita Sua*, ed. David J. DeLaura (New York: Norton, 1968), 28. See also Rowell, *Vision Glorious*, 14.

25. Tennyson, *Victorian Devotional Poetry*, 45.

26. Murray Roston, *Prophet and Poet: The Bible and the Growth of Romanticism* (London: Faber, 1965), 45, 47.

27. James Buchanan, *Analogy, Considered as a Guide to Truth, and Applied as an Aid to Faith* (Edinburgh, 1864), 55.

28. Isaac Williams, "On Reserve in Communicating Religious Knowledge (continued)," Tract 87 of *Tracts for the Times*, Project Canterbury, http://anglicanhistory.org/tracts/tract87/.

29. Maria Keaton has shown this analogical mode at work even in Rossetti's poetry for children, published as *Sing-Song* in 1872. See Keaton, "Mystic, Madwoman or Metaphysic? The Analogical Theodicy of Christina Rossetti," in *Outsiders Looking In: The Rossettis, Then and Now*, ed. David Clifford and Laurence Roussillon (London: Anthem, 2004), 145–54.

30. Samuel Leuenberger, *Archbishop Cranmer's Immortal Bequest: The Book of Common Prayer of the Church of England: An Evangelistic Liturgy* (Grand Rapids, MI: Eerdmans, 1990), 237–38.

31. Härdelin, *Tractarian Understanding*, 36.

32. John Keble, "On the Mysticism Attributed to the Fathers of the Church," Tract 89 of *Tracts for the Times*, Project Canterbury, http://anglicanhistory.org/tracts/tract89/.

33. Christina Rossetti, *The Letters of Christina Rossetti*, 4 vols., ed. Antony H. Harrison (Charlottesville: University Press of Virginia, 2004), 4:259. The angle brackets indicate that Rossetti struck out the word after writing it. Hereafter cited in the text as *LCR*.

34. Rowan Williams, *Anglican Identities* (Cambridge, MA: Cowley, 2003), 75.

35. Yates, *Buildings, Faith and Worship*, 108.

36. Ibid., 16.

37. *Ecclesiologist* 1, nos. 12–13 (August 1842): 204.

38. James Bentley, *Ritualism and Politics in Victorian Britain: The Attempt to Legislate for Belief* (Oxford: Oxford University Press, 1978), 14.

39. Rowell, *Vision Glorious*, 104.

40. Owen Chadwick, *The Victorian Church*, vol. 1, *1829–1859*, 3rd ed. (London: Black, 1971), 213.

41. See William Michael Rossetti, "Memoir," in *The Poetical Works of Christina Georgina Rossetti: With Memoir and Notes* (New York: Georg Olms Verlag, 1970), lvii.

42. Paul Thompson, *William Butterfield* (London: Routledge, 1971), 243.

43. Geoffrey Tyack, *Sir James Pennethorne and the Making of Victorian London* (Cambridge: Cambridge University Press, 1992), 35.

44. *Ecclesiologist*, n.s., 1, no. 1 (January 1845): 54.

45. *Ecclesiologist*, n.s., 25 (August 1847): 234. Butterfield had an especially close connection with Christ Church: he designed the 1883 choir stall screen, the windows for one aisle, the stone pulpit built between 1882 and 1885, the jewelled candlesticks, and the eagle lectern (Thompson, *William Butterfield*, 90, 471, 473, 496, 497).

46. Quoted in Kenneth Clark, *The Gothic Revival: An Essay in the History of Taste* (London: Murray, 1973), 176.

47. Henry W. Burrows, *The Half-Century of Christ Church, St. Pancras, Albany Street* (London: Harrison and Sons, 1887), 21.

48. *Ecclesiologist*, n.s., 1, no. 1 (January 1845): 54.

49. Burrows, *Half-Century of Christ Church*, 47, 72.

50. The word *interior* is important here. Christ Church, Albany Street, did not actually open up toward Albany Street, the usual feature that determines a building's address. Rather, Albany Street ran along the west side of the church, so that from the exterior the church had a north–south orientation, that is, its lobby or vestibule entrance faced geographically south, and its altar was located on the building's north wall. However, liturgical practice of long standing was to situate the altar to the east, in relation to the rising of the sun (Son), and churches "arranged with the chancel not to the east are nevertheless described as though orientated correctly" (James Stevens Curl, *A Dictionary of Architecture* [Oxford University Press, 1999], e3249, available at http://www.oxfordreference.com). Thus, on the (unfortunately undated) renovation plans of Christ Church housed in the London Metropolitan Archives (P90/CTC2), geographic north is clearly labelled "Ritual East" and its opposite is labelled "west," resulting in a conceptually east–west interior arrangement. This is significant because in a north–south interior arrangement, the pulpit and reading desk are situated either at the north or south end with the pews facing them and the altar to the left or right of the congregation. This arrangement "accepted the notion of the Eucharist as an occasional service for which the altar-space or chancel could be effectively cut off from the rest of the church" (Yates, *Buildings, Faith and Worship*, 77). An east–west rectangular interior, by contrast, "gave the whole building an aesthetic unity" (Yates, *Buildings, Faith and Worship*, 89) because pulpit, reading desk, and altar were all arranged at the geographically north but conceptually east end, with the pews facing them. That is, Christ Church

overcame its exterior positioning by reconceptualizing its interior geography to meet ritualist requirements.

51. Yates, *Buildings, Faith and Worship*, 85.

52. Burrows, *Half-Century of Christ Church*, 47.

53. See Härdelin, *Tractarian Understanding*, 270, 273. Other changes to the physical arrangements in Christ Church included removing several galleries, which the ecclesiologists "denounced as ugly and post-medieval innovations" (Yates, *Buildings, Faith and Worship*, 159), replacing pews with open benches (in 1866), and erecting a screen in front of the choir stalls to more completely distinguish the chancel from the nave where the congregation sat (in 1883).

54. See the renovation plans for Christ Church described in note 49.

55. Yates, *Buildings, Faith and Worship*, 159.

56. Burrows, *Half-Century of Christ Church*, 50, 51.

57. See Romans 6:4 and 1 Corinthians 10:1-2.

58. Quoted in Thompson, *William Butterfield*, 229.

59. Quoted in Rowell, *Vision Glorious*, 104.

60. Besides the reds, greens, and blues that infused the copy of Raphael's "Transfiguration" hanging above the altar, and the white and crimson altar frontals mentioned by Thompson (*William Butterfield*, 493), an 1891 inventory of Christ Church's furnishings and ornaments (see note 63) lists white, green, violet, and red alms bags; white and red hangings for the litany stool; and a red hanging for the choir stalls. In addition, Christ Church's enhancements involved structural polychromy, in which "colour is not applied after construction but is provided by the brick, stones, or tiles used in the building: it was a feature of the mature Gothic Revival" (Curl, *Dictionary of Architecture*, e3586). In 1879, "the dado of tiles in the church and vestibule was put up, and ... tiles were laid in the floor of the latter. More colour was also introduced in the walls and ceiling of the church, and the vestibule was coloured" (Burrows, *Half-Century of Christ Church*, 72). In the London Metropolitan Archives are the colored drawings of the six different tile patterns that were introduced into different areas of the church, each made with colored marble and Portland stone paving. Paul Thompson, relying on William Butterfield's notebooks, describes Christ Church after the 1860s as "completely redecorated, the side walls with a dado of pink tiles, the middle section brown, and the uppermost part slate grey; pilasters a slightly lighter grey, with the spandrels of the chancel arch a greyish red, and the imposts a warmer red; and the panelled ceiling grey, with ribs picked out in gold and blue" (*William Butterfield*, 243-45).

61. *Ecclesiologist* 2, no. 18 (January 1843): 72.

62. *Ecclesiologist* 2, nos. 19-20 (February 1843): 109.

63. The inventory is in the London Metropolitan Archives, P90/CTC2/119a.

64. Mary Arseneau, *Recovering Christina Rossetti: Female Community and Incarnational Poetics* (London: Palgrave, 2004), 99; also David A. Kent, "'By thought, word, and deed': George Herbert and Christina Rossetti," in *The Achievement of Christina Rossetti*, ed. David A. Kent (Ithaca, NY: Cornell University Press, 1987), 250-73.

65. For more on Williams and Keble as writers who "uphold the view that poetry is architectural just as architecture is poetical" (130), see Kirstie Blair, "Church Architecture,

Tractarian Poetry and the Forms of Faith," in *Shaping Belief: Culture, Politics and Religion in Nineteenth-Century Writing*, ed. Victoria Morgan and Clare Williams (Liverpool: Liverpool University Press, 2008), 129–45.

66. Yates, *Anglican Ritualism*, 1.

67. Ibid., 334.

68. Burrows, *Half-Century of Christ Church*, 23.

69. Boniface Lautz, *The Doctrine of the Communion of Saints in Anglican Theology, 1833–1963* (Ottawa: University of Ottawa Press, 1967), 81.

70. John Henry Newman, "The Communion of Saints," in *Parochial and Plain Sermons*, vol. 4 (London: Longmans, 1909), 170.

71. Matthew Arnold, for example, writes in *Culture and Anarchy* (1869), "Perfection, as culture conceives it, is not possible while the individual remains isolated: the individual is obliged, under pain of being stunted and enfeebled in his own development if he disobeys, to carry others along with him in his march towards perfection, to be continually doing all he can to enlarge and increase the volume of the human stream sweeping thitherward; … And this function [of culture] is particularly important in our modern world, of which the whole civilisation is, to a much greater degree than the civilisation of Greece and Rome, mechanical and external, and tends constantly to become more so" (*Culture and Anarchy and Other Writings*, ed. Stefan Collini [Cambridge: Cambridge University Press, 1993], 13–15).

72. Thomas Carlyle, for example, in 1843 wrote, "Think it not thy business, this of knowing thyself; thou art an unknowable individual: know what thou canst work at; and work at it, like a Hercules! That will be thy better plan" (*Past and Present*, ed. Richard D. Altick [Boston: Houghton, 1965], 196).

73. R. W. Franklin, *Nineteenth-Century Churches: The History of a New Catholicism in Württemberg, England, and France* (New York: Garland, 1987), 27, 35 (my italics).

74. Heije Faber, "The Meaning of Ritual in the Liturgy," in *Current Studies on Rituals: Perspectives for the Psychology of Religion*, ed. Hans-Günter Heimbrock and H. Barbara Boudewijnse (Amsterdam: Rodopi, 1990), 48.

75. Härdelin, *Tractarian Understanding*, 297; Susan Drain, *The Anglican Church in Nineteenth-Century Britain: Hymns Ancient and Modern (1860–1875)* (Lewiston, NY: Mellen, 1989), 80.

76. Quoted in Bernarr Rainbow, *The Choral Revival in the Anglican Church, 1839–1872* (London: Barrie, 1970), 5n.

77. Dale Adelmann, *The Contribution of Cambridge Ecclesiologists to the Revival of Anglican Choral Worship, 1839–62* (Aldershot, UK: Ashgate, 1997), 8, 156–57.

78. Rainbow, *Choral Revival*, 69–70.

79. On choosing ancient hymns, see Adelmann, *Contribution of Cambridge Ecclesiologists*, 65; on identification, see Walter Hillsman, "The Victorian Revival of Plainsong in English: Its Usage under Tractarians and Ritualists," in *The Church and the Arts*, ed. Diana Wood, Studies in Church History 28 (Oxford: Blackwell, for the Ecclesiastical History Society, 1992), 410; on monodic form, see Franklin, *Nineteenth-Century Churches*, 476.

80. Ecclesiologist, n.s., 2, no. 11 (May 1846): 174.

81. Drain, *Anglican Church*, 146.

82. On the decline of plainsong, see Hillsman, "Victorian Revival," 412–13.

83. Adelmann, *Contribution of Cambridge Ecclesiologists*, 94.

84. Although I do not know how soon after its publication Christ Church obtained Dyce's edition, Hillsman notes that between 1843 and 1850, several leading Anglo-Catholic churches in London were incorporating plainsong in their services, including St. Andrew's, Wells Street ("Victorian Revival," 406–7). If Christ Church had no surpliced choir till 1849, and its plainsong was consequently not too polished, the fact that Rossetti has Maude, a character in her 1848 unpublished novella, describe St. Andrew's rather than Christ Church as having "the nearest English approach to vocal perfection" may not be surprising (Christina Rossetti, *Maude: Prose and Verse*, ed. R. W. Crump [Hamden, CT: Archon, 1976], 44, also 51–52).

85. W. M. Rossetti, "Memoir," lxxi, lx.

86. Ibid., lv.

87. Dinah Roe, *Christina Rossetti's Faithful Imagination: The Devotional Poetry and Prose* (New York: Palgrave, 2006), 112.

88. Contrast these vestments with the plain gown worn by preachers in most other Protestant churches at the time. The latter was "modeled after the black gown of the university professor" to evoke a "pastor-preacher-teacher" image rather than a "high church" or "priest" image (Joanne M. Pierce, "Vestments and Objects," in *The Oxford History of Christian Worship*, ed. Geoffrey Wainwright and Karen B. Westerfield Tucker [Oxford: Oxford University Press, 2006], 845). I suspect Congregationalist and Scotch Presbyterian ministers wore the black robe.

89. Allon quoted in Clyde Binfield, "A Chapel and Its Architect: James Cubitt and Union Chapel, Islington, 1874–1889," in *The Church and the Arts*, ed. Diana Wood, Studies in Church History 28 (Oxford: Blackwell, for the Ecclesiastical History Society, 1992), 430–31.

90. Walter Hillsman, "Women in Victorian Church Music: Their Social, Liturgical, and Performing Roles in Anglicanism," in *Women in the Church*, ed. W. J. Sheils and Diana Wood, Studies in Church History 27 (Oxford: Blackwell, for the Ecclesiastical History Society, 1990), 443–45.

91. *Ecclesiologist*, n.s.,2, no. 11 (May 1846): 174.

92. Burrows, *Half-Century of Christ Church*, 11.

93. John Shelton Reed, *Glorious Battle: The Cultural Politics of Victorian Anglo-Catholicism* (Nashville, TN: Vanderbilt University Press, 1996), 161, 189–95.

94. See Jan Marsh, *Christina Rossetti: A Writers' Life* (New York: Viking, 1995), 218–28, 433–35; Diane D'Amico, *Christina Rossetti: Faith, Gender and Time* (Baton Rouge: Louisiana State University Press, 1999), 94–117.

95. The letter to Webster reads in part, "Does it not appear as if the Bible was based upon an understood unalterable distinction between men and women, their position, duties, privileges? Not arrogating to myself but most earnestly desiring to attain to the character of a humble orthodox Xtian, so it does appear to me; not merely under the Old but also under the New Dispensation. The fact of the Priesthood being exclusively man's, leaves me in no doubt that the highest functions are not in this world open to both sexes: and if not all, then a selection must be made and a line drawn somewhere" (*LCR*, 2:158).

See Roe, *Christina Rossetti's Faithful Imagination*, chap. 4, for an excellent reading of the ambiguities in this letter, as well as Rossetti's thinking on women more broadly.

96. "But I endorse with my whole heart your remark on the paramount burden of responsibility: when one is strong one can by God's grace bear it; but when one is weak the pressure at times, or the *hauntingness*, may become fearful. And the books I write make me more and more glaringly inexcusable for my faults of all sorts, and shortcomings, and cowardice especially. Before very long I hope the S.P.C.K. will bring out another small prose volume of mine, but each volume heaps up my responsibility" (*LCR*, 3:100).

97. Yates, *Buildings, Faith and Worship*, 173–74.

98. Michael Fiedrowicz, "General Introduction," in *Expositions of the Psalms 1–32, Part 3*, vol. 15 of *The Works of Saint Augustine: A Translation for the 21st Century*, trans. Maria Boulding, ed. John E. Rotelle (New York: New City Press, 2000), 55.

Chapter 4: Manifestation, Aesthetics, and Community in Christina Rossetti's Verses

1. Lorraine Janzen Kooistra, *Christina Rossetti and Illustration: A Publishing History* (Athens: Ohio University Press, 2002), 146; David A. Kent, "Sequence and Meaning in Christina Rossetti's *Verses* (1893)," *Victorian Poetry* 17, no. 3 (1979): 260; Dinah Roe, *Christina Rossetti's Faithful Imagination: The Devotional Poetry and Prose* (New York: Palgrave, 2006), 4. See also Mary Arseneau, *Recovering Christina Rossetti: Female Community and Incarnational Poetics* (London: Palgrave, 2004).

2. Kent, "Sequence and Meaning"; David A. Kent, "W. M. Rossetti and the Editing of Christina Rossetti's Religious Poetry," *Pre-Raphaelite Review* 1, no. 2 (1978): 18–26; Diane D'Amico, *Christina Rossetti: Faith, Gender and Time* (Baton Rouge: Louisiana State University Press, 1999); Joel Westerholm, "In Defense of *Verses*: The Aesthetic Reputation of Christina Rossetti's Late Poetry," *Renascence* 51, no. 3 (1999): 191–203; Emma Mason, "'A Sort of Aesthetico-Catholic Revival': Christina Rossetti and the London Ritualist Scene," in *Outsiders Looking In: The Rossettis Then and Now*, ed. David Clifford and Laurence Roussillon (London: Anthem, 2004), 115–30; Constance W. Hassett, *Christina Rossetti: The Patience of Style* (Charlottesville: University of Virginia Press, 2005).

3. For a survey of criticism to 2006 on this subject, see Diane D'Amico and David A. Kent, "Rossetti and the Tractarians," *Victorian Poetry* 44, no. 1 (2006): 93–103. Roe's *Christina Rossetti's Faithful Imagination* includes a chapter on Rossetti's Tractarianism as well.

4. See John 7:24.

5. About these poems, we might observe also that Rossetti's Mary does not seek to understand her Son as the fulfillment of prophecy, as did Barrett Browning's. Rossetti's Mary, in fact, does not speak. Rather, another speaker attempts to describe her being.

6. Esther T. Hu, "Christina Rossetti, John Keble and the Divine Gaze," *Victorian Poetry* 46, no. 2 (2008): 175–89.

7. Alison Chapman, "Sonnet and Sonnet Sequence," in *A Companion to Victorian Poetry*, ed. Richard Cronin, Alison Chapman, and Antony H. Harrison (Oxford: Blackwell, 2002), 102.

8. The nine variations are *eecd, dece, eedc, edce, ecde, dcdc, cede, eced,* and *edec*.

9. These are *cdceed, ccddcd, cdcaac, cddced, cdcddc, cdcdcd,* and *cdccdc*.

10. Chapman, "Sonnet and Sonnet Sequence," 100.

11. John Keble, *Keble's Lectures on Poetry, 1832–1841*, 2 vols. (Oxford: Clarendon, 1912), 2:102.

12. Betty Flowers notes that the unpublished roundel has this note on the manuscript: "W.B.S. spurns the birthday (Sept. 12. 1887) tribute of CGR: *tableau* visible to the 'fine frenzied' mental eye." See Rossetti, *CP*, 1169.

13. David A. Kent, "'By thought, word, and deed': George Herbert and Christina Rossetti," in *The Achievement of Christina Rossetti*, ed. David A. Kent (Ithaca, NY: Cornell University Press, 1987), 259.

14. Ibid.; Gordon W. Lathrop, *Holy Things: A Liturgical Theology* (Minneapolis: Fortress, 1993), 19.

15. Roe also sees this function in the roundel. She remarks that "the 'formal scheme' of the roundel ["Judge nothing before the time," *CP*, 503] turns out to be very well-suited to Rossetti's theology" (*Christina Rossetti's Faithful Imagination*, 106).

16. Kent, "Sequence and Meaning," 262, 261.

17. Esther Hu has recently shown that for Rossetti, such discipleship included the trial of suffering. Hu situates Rossetti's poems on grief, pain, and suffering not within feminist arguments about masochism or self-renunciation (155) but within a Tractarian theology that affirmed that "God's character and purposes remain good even when his children endure pain" (156). See Esther T. Hu, "Christina Rossetti and the Poetics of Tractarian Suffering," in *Through a Glass Darkly: Suffering, the Sacred and the Sublime in Literature and Theory*, ed. Holly Faith Nelson, Lynn R. Szabo, Jens Zimmermann (Waterloo, ON: Wilfrid Laurier University Press, 2010), 155–67.

18. The biblical citation is from Hebrews 11:13.

19. David A. deSilva, *Sacramental Life: Spiritual Formation through the Book of Common Prayer* (Downers Grove, IL: IVP, 2008), 118–20.

20. Kooistra, *Christina Rossetti and Illustration*, 4, 67.

21. Jay A. Gertzman, *Fantasy, Fashion and Affection: Editions of Robert Herrick's Poetry for the Common Reader, 1810–1968* (Bowling Green: Bowling Green State University Popular Press, 1986), 49, 51, 217; Chapman, "Sonnet and Sonnet Sequence," 105.

22. Gertzman, *Fantasy, Fashion and Affection*, 49.

23. Kooistra, *Christina Rossetti and Illustration*, 28.

24. Kent, "'By thought,'" 257–72.

25. William Michael Rossetti, "Memoir," in *The Poetical Works of Christina Georgina Rossetti: With Memoir and Notes*, ed. William Michael Rossetti (New York: Georg Olms Verlag, 1970), lxix; Kent, "W. M. Rossetti," 22.

26. Roe, *Christina Rossetti's Faithful Imagination*, 9.

27. James 5:17.

28. 1 Kings 19; 2 Kings 2:11.

29. On the Tractarian preference for the earliest prayer book, see Peter B. Nockles, *The Oxford Movement in Context: Anglican High Churchmanship, 1760–1857* (Cambridge: Cambridge University Press, 1994), 218–22.

30. Jennifer Ann Wagner, *A Moment's Monument: Revisionary Poetics and the Nineteenth-Century English Sonnet* (Madison, NJ: Fairleigh Dickinson University Press, 1996), 39–40.

31. Boniface Lautz, *The Doctrine of the Communion of Saints in Anglican Theology, 1833–1963* (Ottawa: University of Ottawa Press, 1967), 37, 40.

32. Kent, "Sequence and Meaning," 262.

33. Hassett, *Christina Rossetti*, 233.

34. C. S. Lewis, *Mere Christianity* (Glasgow: Collins, 1952), 116.

35. John E. Tropman, *The Catholic Ethic and the Spirit of Community* (Washington, DC: Georgetown University Press, 2002), 68.

36. Roe, *Christina Rossetti's Faithful Imagination*, 194, 195, 174, 176.

37. See Arseneau, *Recovering Christina Rossetti*, 35–47.

38. Roe notes that Rossetti dedicated *The Face of the Deep* to the memory of her mother, and that her own 1895 copy of the book is inscribed "To my darling Mother, March, 1897" (*Christina Rossetti's Faithful Imagination*, 168). But religious communities also appear to have purchased the book: the first edition held by bookseller Leonard Roberts is signed and dated "Xmas 1892, Mary Burt" and bears the stamp of the Community of the Resurrection, an Anglican monastic order founded in Oxford in 1892. My thanks to the bookseller for this information.

39. D'Amico, *Christina Rossetti*, 170.

40. Kooistra, *Christina Rossetti and Illustration*, 147.

41. Alexis Weedon, *Victorian Publishing: The Economics of Book Production for a Mass Market, 1836–1916* (Aldershot, UK: Ashgate, 2003), 96–98.

42. Simon Eliot, *Some Patterns and Trends in British Publishing, 1800–1919* (London: Bibliographical Society, 1994), 72.

43. W. O. B. Allen and Edmund McClure, *Two Hundred Years: The History of the Society for Promoting Christian Knowledge, 1698–1898* (New York: Franklin, 1970), 455.

44. W. K. Lowther Clarke, *A History of the S.P.C.K.* (London: SPCK, 1959), 150.

45. Ibid., 151.

46. Mackenzie Bell, *Christina Rossetti: A Biographical and Critical Study* (New York: Haskell, 1971), 168.

47. Kooistra, *Christina Rossetti and Illustration*, 187, 175, 176.

48. Bell, *Biographical and Critical Study*, 180–81.

49. See, for example, *The Book of Praise Authorized by the General Assembly of the Presbyterian Church in Canada* (Oxford: Oxford University Press, 1918), *The Hymnary of the United Church of Canada, Authorized by the General Council* (Toronto: United Church, 1930), *The Baptist Church Hymnal* (London: Psalms and Hymns Trust, 1933), *The Methodist Hymnal: Official Hymnal of the Methodist Church* (Nashville, TN: Methodist, 1939), and Evan L. Bennett, ed., *The Hymnal: Army and Navy* (Washington, DC: GPO, 1942).

50. Allen and McClure, *Two Hundred Years*, 455, 456.

51. At least, I find it more probable that their widespread reception derives from a single, poetic source than from disparate prose sources; of the five poems that originally appeared in prose works, two were in *The Face of the Deep*, one in *Called to Be Saints*, and two in *Time Flies*. The five are "Love came down at Christmas," "None other Lamb, none other Name," "Sooner or later: yet at last," "We know not a voice of that River," and "O Christ, my God, who seest the unseen." The sixth non-*Verses* poem included in many hymnals is "In the bleak mid-winter."

Chapter 5: "The One Divine Influence at Work in the World"

1. Gill Gregory helpfully situates Procter's conversion within the larger context of Victorian anti-Catholic sentiments, describes Procter's enthusiasm for Father Faber's Oratorian preaching, and outlines how Procter's interests in the figure of Mary and in foreign places derive from the poet's Catholicism (*The Life and Work of Adelaide Procter: Poetry, Feminism and Fathers* [Aldershot, UK: Ashgate, 1998], 8–15). In her 1999 entry on Procter in *DLB*, Cheri Lin Larsen Hoeckley gives a brief but appreciative account of how Procter combines a "critique of traditional women's positions with Catholic theology," noting, "Female duty and political agitation for economic independence are two sides of the same coin for Procter, the coin of religious duty" ("Adelaide Anne Procter," in *Dictionary of Literary Biography: Victorian Women Poets*, ed. William B. Thesing [Farmington Hills, MI: Gale, 1999], 256, 258). Hoeckley elaborates on these points in "'Must Her Own Words Do All?': Domesticity, Catholicism, and Activism in Adelaide Anne Procter's Poems" (in *The Catholic Church and Unruly Women Writers: Critical Essays*, ed. Jeana Delrosso, Leigh Eicke, and Ana Kothe [New York: Palgrave Macmillan, 2007], 123–38); and in "Poetry, Activism and 'Our Lady of the Rosary': Adelaide Procter's Catholic Poetics in *A Chaplet of Verses*" (in *Sublimer Aspects: Interfaces between Literature, Aesthetics, and Theology*, ed. Natasha Duquette [Newcastle, UK: Cambridge Scholars Publishing, 2007], 145–59). Emma Mason treats these same subjects at greater length in a chapter on Procter in *Women Poets of the Nineteenth Century* (Tavistock, UK: Northcote House, 2006). I take up Mason's observation that the "disjunction between Procter's reserved nature and her passionate side was played out in her poetry ... and in some ways provides a commentary on the state of Catholicism in England" (91); however, I go further than Mason in asserting that the diverse Catholicism of the time actually helped *generate* Procter's reserved and passionate poetic styles.

2. Susan Drain, "Adelaide Anne Procter," in *Dictionary of Literary Biography*, vol. 32, *Victorian Poets before 1850*, ed. William E. Fredeman and Ira B. Nadel (Detroit: Gale, 1984), 234.

3. Procter's unpublished letters to Bessie Parkes are among the Personal Papers of Bessie Rayner Parkes, Girton College Archive, Cambridge, hereafter cited in the text as GCPP Parkes, followed by the catalogue number. See GCPP Parkes 8.37 for the reference to Procter's pew. Procter notes her conversion in GCPP Parkes 8.39. The letter bears no year but is dated August 22 at Brighton and refers to Procter's severe illness, most likely her last one. Because Procter died in February 1864, this letter was likely written in August 1863. In it, Procter notes that she has just celebrated the twelfth anniversary of her reception into the Roman Church. Procter's conversion has been variously stated as occurring in 1849, 1851, and 1853, but this letter and William J. Gordon-Gorman's *Converts to Rome: Since the Tractarian Movement to May 1899* (London, 1899; available through the Internet Archive, http://www.archive.org.) confirm 1851 as the correct year.

4. *Protestant Magazine*, n.s., 8, no. 2 (London 1846): 94; Thomas Earnshaw Bradley, ed., *The Lamp*, 4, no. 31 (August 14, 1852): 425.

5. Compare information in the 1839, 1851, and 1876 Catholic Directories, all available at http://books.google.com. Spanish Place details are on page 20, 36, and 110 of the directories, respectively. Benediction is a devotional ceremony in which the faithful are blessed

with the sacrament/host's being waved in the sign of the cross above them. Compline is an evening prayer service.

6. An oratory consists of a community of secular (i.e., not monastic) priests living under obedience to a rule, guided by a superior but not bound by vows. Its congregation consists only of the Fathers belonging to the rule, that is, it is not a parish church, though its services are open to the public.

7. Percy Fitzgerald, *Fifty Years of Catholic Life and Social Progress under Cardinals Wiseman, Manning, Vaughan, and Newman* (London: Unwin, 1901), 183. See also Mary Heimann, *Catholic Devotion in Victorian England* (Oxford: Clarendon, 1995), 26, 139.

8. Edward Norman, *The English Catholic Church in the Nineteenth Century* (Oxford: Clarendon, 1984), 88.

9. Richard Challoner, *The Garden of the Soul, or A Manual of Spiritual Exercises and Instructions* (Derby, 1843), 55, 73.

10. Frederick Faber, *Faber: Poet and Priest; Selected Letters, 1833–63*, ed. Raleigh Addington (Glamorgan, Wales: Brown, 1974), 247–48.

11. Heimann, *Catholic Devotion*, esp. 44, 10, and, for the quotation, 30.

12. "Golden Square Area: Warwick Street," in *Survey of London*, vols. 31 and 32, *St James Westminster, Part 2* (London: London City Council, 1963), 167–73. http://www.british-history.ac.uk/report.aspx?compid=41468.

13. See plate in *The London Oratory, 1849–1949* (London: Oratory of St. Philip Neri, 1949); see also "The London Oratory," in *Survey of London*, vol. 41, *Brompton* (London: Athlone Press for the Greater London Council, 1983), 50–57.

14. *London Oratory*, 7–8 and plates.

15. Bradley, *The Lamp*, 425.

16. The Mass is laid out in *The Roman Missal*, of which many editions are available. I used an edition/translation by the Very Rev. H. C. Husenbeth entitled *The Missal for the Use of the Laity* (London, 1853).

17. In the Asperges, the priest sprinkles the altar, the clergy, and the congregation with holy water while the choir sings a penitential Psalm verse. The sprinkling with water echoes the Mosaic act of sprinkling altar and people with the blood of sacrificed animals. Alluding to both baptism and sacrifice, it symbolizes the purification of the people. As such, it establishes unworthiness of self and the suffering sacrifice of Christ as important themes for the upcoming Mass.

18. The Right Rev. Doctor England, *The Roman Missal Translated into the English Language for the Use of the Laity* (Philadelphia, 1843), 9.

19. This was New Year's Day, a Saturday. Lowndes may also be accurate in her comment: Procter may have attended early morning Mass at St. Mary's, Moorfields, which offered Mass daily at 8:00, 9:00, and 10:00 a.m. (see *The Catholic Directory and Ecclesiastical Register* of 1851, p. 34). Procter does not mention this church in her correspondence, but according to Parkes, Procter's confessor was the Rev. Daniel Gilbert, who became affiliated with St. Mary's at some point in the 1850s. Bessie Parkes, *In a Walled Garden* (London: Ward and Downey, 1895), 175n. Available through the Victorian Women Writers Project, ed. Perry Willet, http://www.indiana.edu/~letrs/vwwp/belloc/walled.html.

20. Heimann, *Catholic Devotion*, 71.

21. Challoner, *Garden of the Soul*, 59.

22. T. E. Muir, *Roman Catholic Church Music in England, 1791–1914: A Handmaid of the Liturgy?* (Burlington, VT: Ashgate, 2008), 41–43.

23. Nicholas Schofield, *The Church of St. James, Spanish Place: A History and Guide* (London: St. James's Church, Spanish Place, 2005), 11–12.

24. Quoted in Thomas E. Woods, Jr., *Sacred Then and Sacred Now: The Return of the Old Latin Mass* (Fort Collins, CO: Roman Catholic Books, 2008), 8.

25. England, *Roman Missal Translated*, 24.

26. Ibid., 23–24.

27. Woods, *Sacred Then*, 7.

28. Lay reception is not necessary for Mass to be complete. Even in the early twentieth century, Communion was sometimes seen by many priests as "an unnecessary delay in saying Mass" (James F. White, *Roman Catholic Worship: Trent to Today*, 2nd ed. [Collegeville, MN: Liturgical Press, 2003], 88). The essential element is the consecration of the elements, followed by consumption by the priest (England, *Roman Missal Translated*, 9). One may speak of attending Mass—or, as Procter does, of "crawling" to Mass—without necessarily meaning one received Communion.

29. Several critics have related Procter's reserve to Tractarianism, a reasonable association given Procter's Anglican background. See, for example, Isobel Armstrong, *Victorian Poetry: Poetry, Poetics, Politics* (New York: Routledge, 1993), 337; Gill Gregory, "Adelaide Procter: A Poetics of Reserve and Passion," in *Women's Poetry, Late Romantic to Late Victorian: Gender and Genre, 1830–1900*, ed. Isobel Armstrong and Virginia Blain (New York: St. Martin's, 1999), 362–63; and Gill Gregory, *The Life and Work of Adelaide Procter* (Aldershot, UK: Ashgate, 1998), 68–118. However, there is no direct evidence of Procter engaging Tractarian preachers, writers, or writings before her conversion, and the usual linking of Procter to reserve through association with Faber loses some force when we discover that the postconversion Faber whom Procter admired gave up reserve, as this chapter later shows. I therefore associate Procter's reserve more with Tridentine than Tractarian experience.

30. Adelaide Procter, *The Poems of Adelaide A. Procter* (New York: Thomas Y. Crowell, [n.d.]; reprint, Whitefish, MT: Kessinger Publishing, [n.d.]), 386, lines 25–32. Hereafter cited in the text as *PAAP*.

31. Husenbeth, *Roman Missal*, 34 (my italics).

32. Quoted in Robert Gray, *Cardinal Manning: A Biography* (London: Weidenfeld, 1985), 177.

33. Ibid., 220–21.

34. Ibid., 149.

35. Other denominations also catechize laypeople into professed membership, but their liturgies do not usually embed a structural distinction between catechumens and professed.

36. On musical excellence and continental connections, see Muir, *Roman Catholic Church Music*, 75; on professionalism, see 80.

37. Ibid., 96–98.

38. Procter had originally written "Allegri and Marcello" in place of "The master Palestrina." See *Household Words* 12, no. 22 (1855): 515. Allegri and Marcello were early

baroque composers, Palestrina a Renaissance composer. In making the change, Procter extended the maiden's musical heritage further back in time and in the church.

39. In the poem, Procter writes "Scarlatti," not specifying whether she means the father (Alessandro) or the son (Domenico). However, Alessandro was an organist while Domenico composed for harpsichord—not a church instrument—so I am inclined to think she has the father in mind.

40. Mason, *Women Poets*, 110–11.

41. Because Mass began at 11:00 in both churches, Procter's underscoring of *sermon* here again highlights the change from the usual—for her, the Spanish Place—liturgical order.

42. Gray, *Cardinal Manning*, 87.

43. On Faber, see Ronald Chapman, *Father Faber* (London: Burns, 1961), 189; on Manning, see Gray, *Cardinal Manning*, 87.

44. Quoted in Edmund Sheridan Purcell, *Life of Cardinal Manning, Archbishop of Westminster*, 2 vols. (London, 1896), 2:725.

45. H. M. Gilbert, *The Story of the London Oratory Church* (London: Washbourne, 1934), 31.

46. Faber, *Faber: Poet and Priest*, 195.

47. John Bowden, *The Life and Letters of Frederick William Faber* (Baltimore, 1869), 462.

48. Wiseman quoted in ibid., 399–400.

49. Gray, *Cardinal Manning*, 209, 287.

50. Purcell, *Life of Cardinal Manning*, 2:718.

51. Frederick Faber, *The Blessed Sacrament* (London, 1855; reprint, Rockford, IL: Tan, 1978), 146.

52. See *The Prayer Book of the Oratory of St. Philip Neri, King William Street, Strand* (London, n.d.); and *Devotions to the Infant Jesus, as Practised in the Oratory, King William Street, Strand* (London, 1849).

53. White, *Roman Catholic Worship*, 85.

54. Chapman, *Father Faber*, 234.

55. The *American Ecclesiastical Review* notes that in 1879 the Sacred Congregation—the body that determines worship practices in the Roman Church—reasserted that it "does not countenance the practice of introducing hymns in the vernacular during the solemn Mass" although such hymns were permitted in extraliturgical services. See "Vernacular Hymns at Solemn Exposition of the Blessed Sacrament," *American Ecclesiastical Review* 7, no. 1 (1892): 457. See also Muir, *Roman Catholic Church Music*, 43.

56. Faber quoted in John Julian, ed., *A Dictionary of Hymnology Setting Forth the Origin and History of Christian Hymns of all Ages and Nations* (New York: Scribner's, 1892), 361.

57. On the animation of the evening services, see Bowden, *Life and Letters*, 383.

58. *London Oratory*, 8.

59. Fitzgerald, *Fifty Years of Catholic Life*, 183.

60. Pugin quoted in Denis Gwynn, *Lord Shrewsbury, Pugin and the Catholic Revival* (Westminster, MA: Newman, 1946), 125.

61. Guy Nicholls, "The Contribution of the Oratories to the Liturgical Life of England." In *The Birmingham Oratory*, October 1999, p. 8, http://www.birmingham-oratory.org.uk/Oratory/ALLOct99.pdf.

62. Frederick Faber, *Hymns* (London: Burns, 1861), 120, lines 1–4. Hereafter cited in the text as *Hymns*.

63. White, *Roman Catholic Worship*, 85; see also Carol Engelhardt Herringer, *Victorians and the Virgin Mary: Religion and Gender in England, 1830–85* (Manchester: Manchester University Press, 2008), 54.

64. R. S. Edgecombe, "From Wordsworth to Crashaw: The Poetical Career of Frederick William Faber," *English Studies* 5 (2000): 472, 477; see also Kirstie Blair, "Breaking Loose: Frederick Faber and the Failure of Reserve," *Victorian Poetry* 44, no. 1 (2006): 25, 39.

65. Frederick Faber, *Growth in Holiness* (London, 1854; reprint, Rockford, IL: Tan, 1978), 32.

66. Isobel Armstrong, "The Gush of the Feminine," in *Romantic Women Writers: Voices and Countervoices*, ed. Paula R. Feldman and Theresa M. Kelley (Hanover, NH: University Press of New England, 1995), 15, 16.

67. Isobel Armstrong, "Msrepresentation: Codes of Affect and Politics in Nineteenth-Century Women's Poetry," in *Women's Poetry, Late Romantic to Late Victorian: Gender and Genre, 1830–1900*, ed. Isobel Armstrong and Virginia Blain (New York: St. Martin's, 1999), 11.

68. Manning, for instance, recalled one priest who boasted that he had not brought any newcomers into the Church. See Gray, *Cardinal Manning*, 145.

69. John Bossy, *The English Catholic Community, 1570–1850* (New York: Oxford University Press, 1976), 386, 388.

70. Quoted in Gray, *Cardinal Manning*, 210.

71. See, for example, Jill Muller, *Gerard Manley Hopkins and Victorian Catholicism: A Heart in Hiding* (New York: Routledge, 2003), 41.

72. Ibid., 39, 40.

73. Heimann, *Catholic Devotion*, 163.

74. See, for example, *Faber: Poet and Priest*, 229, 231.

75. St. Francis de Sales, *Introduction to the Devout Life*, trans. Michael Day (London: Burns, 1956), 3, 1, 14.

76. Alphonsus Rodriguez, *On Christian Perfection for Persons Living in the World*, 2 vols. (London: Burns, n.d.), 1:54.

77. The list entails twenty works, in English and French, by authors such as Rodriguez, Veuillot, Newman, Ignatius, L'Abbé Chepay, Avrillon, de Sales, Lombez, and Lallemant (translated and with a preface by Faber). These are in addition to books Faber wrote himself, which Procter also owned.

78. De Sales, *Introduction to the Devout Life*, 117. Challoner's *The Garden of the Soul* includes ten meditations by de Sales, but this admonition is not among them, so Procter must have read de Sales directly as well.

79. Timothy R. Tangherlini, "'It Happened Not Too Far from Here…': A Survey of Legend Theory and Characterization," *Western Folklore* 49, no. 4 (1990): 385.

80. On Manning, see Purcell, *Life of Cardinal Manning*, 2:726; for Faber, see *Hymns*, xvii.

81. *Faber: Poet and Priest*, 242, 243.

82. Gray, *Cardinal Manning*, 206.

83. For a thorough study of Roman Catholic educational efforts in the nineteenth century, see Eric G. Tenbus, *English Catholics and the Education of the Poor, 1847–1902* (London: Pickering and Chatto, 2010). Tenbus demonstrates that English Catholics concurred on a philosophy of education that stressed the formation of character, doctrinal learning, and devotional practice (23–28). Faber, however, is notably absent among the Catholics Tenbus names who advocated strongly and politically for educational reform. The Catholic educational movement was strongest post-1870.

84. Heimann, *Catholic Devotion*, 156–61, 132–34.

85. Lauren M. Goodlad, *Victorian Literature and the Victorian State: Character and Governance in a Liberal Society* (Baltimore, MD: Johns Hopkins University Press, 2003), 38, 25, 20.

86. Heimann, *Catholic Devotion*, 157.

87. Josef L. Altholz, "Social Catholicism in England in the Age of the Devotional Revolution," in *Piety and Power in Ireland, 1760–1960*, ed. Stewart J. Brown and David W. Miller (Notre Dame, IN: University of Notre Dame Press, 2000), 211.

88. Quoted in Chapman, *Father Faber*, 232.

89. Altholz, "Social Catholicism," 215.

90. See Mary Poovey, *Making a Social Body: British Cultural Formation, 1830–1864* (Chicago: University of Chicago Press, 1995).

91. Muller, *Gerard Manley Hopkins*, 48.

92. Perhaps these beliefs led her, in her work among the Langham Place activists, to get more involved with women's employment than with women's education.

93. Jay P. Corrin, *Catholic Intellectuals and the Challenge of Democracy* (Notre Dame, IN: University of Notre Dame Press, 2002), 46.

94. See Roger Swift, "Crime and the Irish in Nineteenth-Century Britain," in *The Irish in Britain, 1815–1939*, ed. Roger Swift and Sheridan Gilley (Savage, MD: Barnes, 1989), 163–82.

95. Consider such representations in Elizabeth Gaskell's *North and South*, ed. Patricia Ingham (Harmondsworth, UK: Penguin, 1995), 144, 172.

96. Heimann, *Catholic Devotion*, 12.

97. Steven Fielding, *Class and Ethnicity: Irish Catholics in England, 1880–1939* (Philadelphia: Open University Press, 1993), 38.

98. Hoxie Neale Fairchild, *Religious Trends in English Poetry*, vol. 4, *1830–1880* (New York: Columbia University Press, 1957), 275.

Chapter 6: Religious-Poetic Strategies in Adelaide Procter's Lyrics, Legends, and Chaplets

1. I discount here the single poem published in 1843 in Heath's *Book of Beauty*, not because Procter's early choice of an illustrated literary annual is insignificant but because the ten-year gap between it and the next publications makes 1853 the better indicator of when Procter's poetic career really began. Procter died in 1864, at age thirty-eight, after a lengthy illness.

The Sisters of Mercy began as an Irish order that opened a convent in Bermondsey, London, in 1839. The order then expanded to open a convent in Cadogan Street, Chelsea, in 1845. Procter's sister Agnes became a Sister of Mercy in this convent, taking the name Sister Mary Francis (GCPP Parkes 11.51). When Daniel Gilbert, canon of the Roman Catholic Church of St. Mary Moorfields, founded the Providence Row Night Refuge, he asked the Sisters of Mercy to run it. It is possible that Agnes, as Sister Mary Francis, worked in the refuge, and that Procter's efforts on the refuge's behalf were a sign of support for her sister.

2. F. Elizabeth Gray observes that "while Procter's Catholicism is implicitly or explicitly treated in numerous verses, it is usually solely her narrative and feminist poems that have found a place in recent anthologies" (*Christian and Lyric Tradition in Victorian Women's Poetry* [New York: Routledge, 2010], 24). For this reason, I often quote Procter's religious poetry at length in this chapter.

3. Ibid., 220.

4. Compare Mark 10:17–22, where a rich young man asks Jesus what he must do to inherit eternal life. To Jesus's instruction to obey the commandments, the man replies that he has done so from his youth. At Jesus' instruction to sell all that he has and give to the poor, the man goes away sorrowful. Procter extends the conversation to make explicit what Jesus leaves implicit: her speaker has given to the poor and has even fasted and wept but—like the young man—has not yielded her heart to Christ.

5. For tabernacle and temple structures, see Exodus 26, especially verses 31–33, and 1 Kings 6, especially verses 16 and 31; for Uzzah's death after touching the ark, see 1 Chronicles 13:9–10.

6. Isobel Armstrong, *Victorian Poetry: Poetry, Poetics, Politics* (New York: Routledge, 1993), 337; Emma Mason, *Women Poets of the Nineteenth Century* (Tavistock, UK: Northcote House, 2006), 87.

7. The Right Rev. Doctor England, *The Roman Missal Translated into the English Language for the Use of the Laity* (Philadelphia, 1843), 24.

8. See "The Way Is Long and Dreary" at the Gilbert and Sullivan Archive, http://math.boisestate.edu/gas/other_sullivan/part_songs/long_dreary/long_dreary.html.

9. Esther T. Hu, "Christina Rossetti and the Poetics of Tractarian Suffering," in *Through a Glass Darkly: Suffering, the Sacred and the Sublime in Literature and Theory*, ed. Holly Faith Nelson, Lynn R. Szabo, and Jens Zimmermann (Waterloo, ON: Wilfrid Laurier University Press, 2010), 160.

10. Kirstie Blair, "John Keble and the Rhythm of Faith," *Essays in Criticism* 53 (2003): 133.

11. It appears, for example, in a 1933 Presbyterian hymnal (see *The Hymnal* [Philadelphia: Presbyterian Board of Christian Education]), a 1953 Baptist and Disciples of Christ hymnal (see *Christian Worship: A Hymnal* [St. Louis: Bethany]), a 1910 self-styled evangelical hymnal (see *Hymns of Worship and Service*, 22nd ed. [New York: Century]), and a 1939 nondenominational community-church hymnal (see Henry Hallam Tweedy, ed., *Christian Worship and Praise* [New York: Commission for Christian Worship and Praise]).

12. Newman wrote "The Pillar of the Cloud" in his Anglican years, but he reissued it without change in 1866, twenty-two years after his entry into the Roman Church. Presumably, then, a Roman Catholic reader such as Procter could find it worth emulating.

13. John Henry Newman, *Verses on Various Occasions*, Newman Reader (National Institute for Newman Studies, 2004), 156.

14. Marjorie Lang, "George Bell and Sons," in *Dictionary of Literary Biography*, vol. 106, *British Literary Publishing Houses, 1820–1880*, ed. Patricia J. Anderson and Jonathan Rose (Detroit: Gale, 1991), 25.

15. The *Chaplet* notice read: "*A Chaplet of Verses*. By Adelaide A. Procter. Author of *Legends and Lyrics*." See *Notes and Queries*, vol. 1, 3rd series, no. 20 (May 17, 1862): n.p. Compare this to the notice for the second series of *Legends and Lyrics* a year earlier: "Characterised by the same depth of poetic feeling as its predecessor, we can accord to this second volume of Miss Procter's *Poems* no higher praise—for it is high praise—than that it is in every way worthy of her." See *Notes and Queries*, vol. 11, 2nd series, no. 262 (January 5, 1861): 20.

16. Three of these palm-size cards remain at Girton College Archive, catalogued as Parkes 10.81.

17. Bessie Parkes, *In a Walled Garden* (London: Ward and Downey, 1895), 176. Available through the Victorian Women Writers Project, ed. Perry Willet, http://www.indiana.edu/~letrs/vwwp/belloc/walled.html.

18. For a discussion of the first gift-book edition of the combined *Legends and Lyrics*, see Lorraine Janzen Kooistra, *Poetry, Pictures, and Popular Publishing: The Illustrated Gift Book and Victorian Visual Culture, 1855–1875* (Athens: Ohio University Press, 2011), 153–66. Kooistra remarks that this edition "conferred cultural status and esteem" on its author and readers (153). Interestingly, she also describes the book as having a "missal-like quality" (155), a fitting term given Procter's Catholicism.

19. The 1868 edition of *A Chaplet of Verses* footnotes the table of contents with the remark, "Some of these poems were written twenty years ago: but only three of them have been previously published." The three previously published were "Ministering Angels" (in Heath's *Book of Beauty*, 1843), "Links with Heaven" (in *Victoria Regia*, 1861), and "The Old Year's Blessing" (in *English Woman's Journal*, 1861).

20. Parkes, *In a Walled Garden*, 175.

21. Carol Engelhardt Herringer, *Victorians and the Virgin Mary: Religion and Gender in England, 1830–85* (Manchester: Manchester University Press, 2008), 163, 164.

22. See Richard Challoner, *The Garden of the Soul, or A Manual of Spiritual Exercises and Instructions* (Derby, 1843), 291–92.

23. Cheri Lin Larsen Hoeckley, "'Must Her Own Words Do All?': Domesticity, Catholicism, and Activism in Adelaide Anne Procter's Poems," in *The Catholic Church and Unruly Women Writers: Critical Essays*, ed. Jeana Delrosso, Leigh Eicke, and Ana Kothe (New York: Palgrave Macmillan, 2007), 131.

24. Gray uses these terms in relation to another Procter poem, "One by One." See *Christian and Lyric Tradition*, 198.

25. Ibid., 92. Gray notes that the Victorian critic Edmund Clarence Stedman compares reading Procter's poetry generally to "telling one's beads" (201).

26. Kris Sommers, "Various Kinds of Rosaries and Chaplets," Marian Library/International Marian Research Institute, http://campus.udayton.edu/mary/resources/chaplet.html.

27. Christine A. Colón, "Lessons from the Medieval Convent: Adelaide Procter's 'A Legend of Provence,'" in *Beyond Arthurian Romances: The Reach of Victorian Medievalism*, ed. Lorretta M. Holloway and Jennifer A. Palmgren (New York: Palgrave Macmillan,

2005), 110, 108. Colón acknowledges that Procter's view of the medieval church is more romantic than realistic but suggests that for Procter "the image of what has been lost is more important than the reality of what was" (101). We will see this pattern again in the final section of this chapter.

28. Ibid., 102, 104, 113, 112. Hoeckley makes a similar point in "'Must Her Own Words'" when she notes "Procter's conviction that a Catholic spiritual economy rooted in justice overwhelms any domestic or political economy" (130).

29. While the poem does not identify its lady as a Catholic, its presentation of upper-class unfeelingness may derive from Procter's assumptions about—or perhaps knowledge of—aristocrats and gentry who attended Spanish Place. See also Cheri Lin Larsen Hoeckley, "Poetry, Activism and 'Our Lady of the Rosary': Adelaide Procter's Catholic Poetics in *A Chaplet of Verses*," in *Sublimer Aspects: Interfaces between Literature, Aesthetics, and Theology*, ed. Natasha Duquette (Newcastle, UK: Cambridge Scholars Publishing, 2007), 149.

Conclusion

1. James Stratten, "Increase of Faith," in *Freedom and Happiness in the Truth and Ways of Christ* (London, 1862), 77.

2. Proverbs 1:7; Deuteronomy 6:5; Luke 10:27.

3. Stanley Hauerwas and Ralph Wood, "How the Church Became Invisible: A Christian Reading of American Literary Tradition," *Religion and Literature* 38, no. 1 (2006): 61, 64, 87.

4. Procter's other Christmas poem, "A Christmas Carol," does the same in the lines "A new-born Infant, smiled" and "the Child we call our Jesus" (*PAAP*, 397.36, 51).

5. See Barry Spurr, *Anglo-Catholic in Religion: T. S. Eliot and Christianity* (Cambridge, UK: Lutterworth, 2010).

BIBLIOGRAPHY

Adelmann, Dale. *The Contribution of Cambridge Ecclesiologists to the Revival of Anglican Choral Worship, 1839–62*. Aldershot, UK: Ashgate, 1997.

Allen, W. O. B., and Edmund McClure. *Two Hundred Years: The History of the Society for Promoting Christian Knowledge, 1698–1898*. New York: Franklin, 1970.

Allon, Henry. "Scriptural Idea of a Christian Church." In *Services Connected with the Ordination of the Rev. Theophilus Lessey to the Pastoral Office over the Congregational Church at Barnsbury Chapel, Islington, on Tuesday, Dec. 7th, 1852*, 1–33. London, 1853.

Alone, Yet Not Alone; or, The Communion of Saints. London: SPCK, 1867.

Altholz, Josef L. "Social Catholicism in England in the Age of the Devotional Revolution." In *Piety and Power in Ireland, 1760–1960*, edited by Stewart J. Brown and David W. Miller, 209–19. Notre Dame, IN: University of Notre Dame Press, 2000.

Anderson, E. Byron. "Liturgical Catechesis: Congregational Practice as Formation." *Religious Education* 92, no. 3 (1997): 349–62.

Armstrong, Isobel. "The Gush of the Feminine." In *Romantic Women Writers: Voices and Countervoices*, edited by Paula R. Feldman and Theresa M. Kelley, 13–32. Hanover, NH: University Press of New England, 1995.

———. "Msrepresentation: Codes of Affect and Politics in Nineteenth-Century Women's Poetry." In *Women's Poetry, Late Romantic to Late Victorian: Gender and Genre, 1830–1900*, edited by Isobel Armstrong and Virginia Blain, 3–32. New York: St. Martin's, 1999.

———. *Victorian Poetry: Poetry, Poetics, Politics*. New York: Routledge, 1993.

Arnold, Matthew. *Culture and Anarchy and Other Writings*. Edited by Stefan Collini. Cambridge: Cambridge University Press, 1993.

Arnold, Richard. *The English Hymn: Studies in a Genre*. New York: Lang, 1995.

Arseneau, Mary. *Recovering Christina Rossetti: Female Community and Incarnational Poetics*. London: Palgrave, 2004.

Avery, Simon, and Rebecca Stott. *Elizabeth Barrett Browning*. London: Longman, 2003.

Banfield, Marie. "From Sentiment to Sentimentality: A Nineteenth-Century Lexigraphical Search." *19: Interdisciplinary Studies in the Long Nineteenth Century* 4 (2007): 1–11. www.19.bbk.ac.uk.

Bibliography

The Baptist Church Hymnal. Rev. ed. London: Psalms and Hymns Trust, 1933.

Barrett, Elizabeth Barrett. *Diary by E.B.B.: The Unpublished Diary of Elizabeth Barrett Barrett, 1831–1832*. Edited by Philip Kelley and Ronald Hudson. Athens: Ohio University Press, 1969.

Barrett Browning, Elizabeth. *See* Browning, Elizabeth Barrett.

Bauer, Carol, and Lawrence Ritt, eds. *Free and Ennobled: Source Readings in the Development of Victorian Feminism*. Oxford: Pergamon, 1979.

Bell, Mackenzie. *Christina Rossetti: A Biographical and Critical Study*. 1898. Reprint, New York: Haskell, 1971.

Bennett, Evan L., ed. *The Hymnal: Army and Navy*. Washington, DC: GPO, 1942.

Bentley, James. *Ritualism and Politics in Victorian Britain: The Attempt to Legislate for Belief*. Oxford: Oxford University Press, 1978.

Billone, Amy Christine. *Little Songs: Women, Silence, and the Nineteenth-Century Sonnet*. Columbus: Ohio State University Press, 2007.

Binfield, Clyde. "A Chapel and Its Architect: James Cubitt and Union Chapel, Islington, 1874–1889." In *The Church and the Arts*, edited by Diana Wood, 417–87. Studies in Church History 28. Oxford: Blackwell, for the Ecclesiastical History Society, 1992.

Bishop, Selma L., ed. *Isaac Watts: Hymns and Spiritual Songs, 1707–1748; A Study in Early Eighteenth Century Language Changes*. London: Faith, 1962.

Blackburn, John. *Congregational Year Book*. London: Congregational Union of England and Wales, 1847.

Blair, Kirstie. "Breaking Loose: Frederick Faber and the Failure of Reserve." *Victorian Poetry* 44, no. 1 (2006): 25–42.

———. "Church Architecture, Tractarian Poetry and the Forms of Faith." In *Shaping Belief: Culture, Politics and Religion in Nineteenth-Century Writing*, edited by Victoria Morgan and Clare Williams, 129–45. Liverpool: Liverpool University Press, 2008.

———. "John Keble and the Rhythm of Faith." *Essays in Criticism* 53 (2003): 129–51.

The Book of Common Prayer and Administration of the Sacraments and Other Rites and Ceremonies of the Church According to the Use of the Church of England. Cambridge: Cambridge University Press for the SPCK, [1880]. This edition and others also available at http://justus.anglican.org/resources/bcp/england.htm.

The Book of Praise Authorized by the General Assembly of the Presbyterian Church in Canada. Oxford: Oxford University Press, [1918].

Bossy, John. *The English Catholic Community, 1570–1850*. New York: Oxford University Press, 1976.

Bourdieu, Pierre. *The Logic of Practice*. Translated by Richard Nice. Stanford: Stanford University Press, 1990.

Bowden, John. *The Life and Letters of Frederick William Faber*. Baltimore, 1869.

Bradley, Thomas Earnshaw, ed. *The Lamp* 4, no. 31 (August 14, 1852).

Briggs, J. H. Y. "Image and Appearance: Some Sources for the History of Nineteenth Century Nonconformity (1)." *Baptist Quarterly* 23, no. 1 (1969): 15–31.

Brilioth, Yngve. *A Brief History of Preaching*. Translated by Karl E. Mattson. Philadelphia: Fortress, 1965.

Broadus, John A. *A Treatise on the Preparation and Delivery of Sermons*. New York, 1898.

Bibliography

Browning, Elizabeth Barrett. *Aurora Leigh*. Vol. 3 of *Works of Elizabeth Barrett Browning*. Edited by Sandra Donaldson. London: Pickering and Chatto, 2010.

———. *Elizabeth Barrett Browning's Letters to Mrs. David Ogilvy, 1849–1861*. Edited by Peter N. Heydon and Philip Kelley. London: John Murray, 1973.

———. *The Letters of Elizabeth Barrett Browning*. 2 vols. Edited by Frederic G. Kenyon. New York: Macmillan, 1898.

———. *The Letters of Elizabeth Barrett Browning to Her Sister Arabella*. 2 vols. Edited by Scott Lewis. Waco, TX: Wedgestone, 2002.

———. *Works of Elizabeth Barrett Browning*. 5 vols. Edited by Sandra Donaldson. London: Pickering and Chatto, 2010.

Browning, Elizabeth Barrett, and Robert Browning. *The Brownings' Correspondence*. 18 vols. to date. Edited by Phillip Kelley, Ronald Hudson, and Scott Lewis. Winfield, KS: Wedgestone, 1984– .

———. *Florentine Friends: The Letters of Elizabeth Barrett Browning and Robert Browning to Isa Blagden, 1850–1861*. Edited by Philip Kelley and Sandra Donaldson. Winfield, KS: Wedgestone; Waco, TX: Armstrong Browning Library, 2009.

———. *Letters of the Brownings to George Barrett*. Edited by Paul Landis with the assistance of Ronald E. Freeman. Urbana: University of Illinois Press, 1958.

Buchanan, James. *Analogy, Considered as a Guide to Truth, and Applied as an Aid to Faith*. Edinburgh, 1864.

Burrows, Henry W. *The Half-Century of Christ Church, St. Pancras, Albany Street*. London: Harrison and Sons, 1887.

Cameron, George G. *The Scots Kirk in London*. Oxford: Becket, 1979.

Camp, Nathan. "The Christian Poetics of *Aurora Leigh* (with Considerable Help from Emanuel Swedenborg)." *Studies in Browning and His Circle* 26 (2005): 62–72.

Carlyle, Thomas. "The Hero as Poet." Reprinted in *The Victorian Poet: Poetics and Persona*, edited by Joseph Bristow, 64–70. London: Croon, 1987.

———. *Past and Present*. Edited by Richard D. Altick. Boston: Houghton, 1965.

The Catholic Directory and Annual Register. London, 1839.

The Catholic Directory and Ecclesiastical Register. London, 1851.

The Catholic Directory, Ecclesiastical Register, and Almanac. London, 1876. The Internet Archive. http://www.archive.org/details/1876catholicdireoocathuoft.

Chadwick, Owen. *The Victorian Church*. Vol. 1, *1829–1859*. 3rd ed. London: Black, 1971.

Challoner, Richard. *The Garden of the Soul, or A Manual of Spiritual Exercises and Instructions*. Derby, 1843.

Chapman, Alison. "Sonnet and Sonnet Sequence." In *A Companion to Victorian Poetry*, edited by Richard Cronin, Alison Chapman, and Antony H. Harrison, 99–114. Oxford: Blackwell, 2002.

Chapman, Ronald. *Father Faber*. London: Burns, 1961.

Christ Church, Albany Street, renovation plans and inventory. London Metropolitan Archives P90 / CTC2.

Christian Worship: A Hymnal. St. Louis: Bethany, 1953.

Cianciola, Heather Shippen. "'Mine Earthly Heart Should Dare': Elizabeth Barrett's Devotional Poetry." *Christianity and Literature* 58, no. 3 (2009): 367–400.

Bibliography

Clark, Kenneth. *The Gothic Revival: An Essay in the History of Taste.* London: Murray, 1973.

Clarke, W. K. Lowther. *A History of the S.P.C.K.* London: SPCK, 1959.

Clarkson, Samuel. *Form or Freedom: Five Colloquies on Liturgies, Reported by a Manchester Congregationalist.* London, 1856.

Cohen, William A. *Embodied: Victorian Literature and the Senses.* Minneapolis: University of Minnesota Press, 2009.

Colón, Christine A. "Lessons from the Medieval Convent: Adelaide Procter's 'A Legend of Provence.'" In *Beyond Arthurian Romances: The Reach of Victorian Medievalism*, edited by Lorretta M. Holloway and Jennifer A. Palmgren, 95–115. New York: Palgrave Macmillan, 2005.

Conder, Geo. Wm. *Intelligent and True Worship: A Sermon Preached in the Congregational Church, Cheetham Hill, Aug. 22nd, 1869.* London, 1869.

Conder, Josiah, ed. *The Congregational Hymn Book.* London: Congregational Union of England and Wales, 1836.

The Congregational Service Book: A Form of Public Worship Designed for the Use of the Independent and Other Nonconformist Bodies in Great Britain. London, 1847.

Cooper, Helen. *Elizabeth Barrett Browning: Woman and Artist.* Chapel Hill: University of North Carolina Press, 1988.

Corrin, Jay P. *Catholic Intellectuals and the Challenge of Democracy.* Notre Dame, IN: University of Notre Dame Press, 2002.

Curl, James Stevens. *A Dictionary of Architecture.* Oxford University Press, 1999. Available at http://www.oxfordreference.com.

Dale, R. W. *Essays and Addresses.* 3rd ed. London: Hodder, 1891.

D'Amico, Diane. *Christina Rossetti: Faith, Gender and Time.* Baton Rouge: Louisiana State University Press, 1999.

———. "The House of Christina Rossetti: Domestic and Poetic Spaces." *Journal of Pre-Raphaelite Studies*, n.s., 19 (2010): 31–54.

D'Amico, Diane, and David A. Kent. "Rossetti and the Tractarians." *Victorian Poetry* 44, no. 1 (2006): 93–103.

David, Deirdre. *Intellectual Women and Victorian Patriarchy: Harriet Martineau, Elizabeth Barrett Browning, George Eliot.* London: Macmillan, 1987.

Davis, Philip. *The Oxford English Literary History.* Vol. 8, *1830–1880: The Victorians.* Oxford: Oxford University Press, 2002.

De Sales, St. Francis. *Introduction to the Devout Life.* Translated by Michael Day. London: Burns, 1956.

deSilva, David A. *Sacramental Life: Spiritual Formation through the Book of Common Prayer.* Downers Grove, IL: IVP, 2008.

Devotions to the Infant Jesus, as Practised in the Oratory, King William Street, Strand. London, 1849.

Dieleman, Karen. "Elizabeth Barrett Browning, Congregationalism, and Spirit Manifestation." *Victorians Institute Journal* 36 (2008): 103–22.

Drain, Susan. "Adelaide Anne Procter." In *Dictionary of Literary Biography*, vol. 32, *Victorian Poets before 1850*, edited by William E. Fredeman and Ira B. Nadel, 232–35. Detroit: Gale, 1984.

Bibliography

———. *The Anglican Church in Nineteenth-Century Britain: Hymns Ancient and Modern (1860–1875)*. Lewiston, NY: Mellen, 1989.

Drummond, Andrew L., and James Bulloch. *The Church in Victorian Scotland, 1843–1874*. Edinburgh: Saint Andrew, 1975.

The Ecclesiologist. Cambridge, 1841–68.

Edgecombe, R. S. "From Wordsworth to Crashaw: The Poetical Career of Frederick William Faber." *English Studies* 5 (2000): 472–83.

Edie, Fred P. "Liturgy, Emotion, and the Poetics of Being Human." *Religious Education* 96, no. 4 (2001): 474–88.

Edwards, O. C. *A History of Preaching*. Nashville, TN: Abingdon Press, 2004.

Elbow, Peter. *Everyone Can Write: Essays Toward a Hopeful Theory of Writing and Teaching Writing*. New York: Oxford University Press, 2000.

Eliot, Simon. *Some Patterns and Trends in British Publishing, 1800–1919*. London: Bibliographical Society, 1994.

Ellison, Robert H. *The Victorian Pulpit: Spoken and Written Sermons in Nineteenth-Century Britain*. Selinsgrove, PA: Susquehanna University Press, 1998.

England, the Right Rev. Doctor., trans. and ed. *The Roman Missal Translated into the English Language for the Use of the Laity*. Philadelphia, 1843.

Ewing, William, ed. *Annals of the Free Church of Scotland, 1843–1900*. 2 vols. Edinburgh: Clark, 1914.

Faber, Frederick. *The Blessed Sacrament*. London, 1855. Reprint, Rockford, IL: Tan, 1978.

———. *Faber: Poet and Priest; Selected Letters, 1833–63*. Edited by Raleigh Addington. Glamorgan, Wales: Brown, 1974.

———. *Growth in Holiness*. London, 1854. Reprint, Rockford, IL: Tan, 1978.

———. *Hymns*. London: Burns, 1861.

Faber, Heije. "The Meaning of Ritual in the Liturgy." In *Current Studies on Rituals: Perspectives for the Psychology of Religion*, edited by Hans-Günter Heimbrock and H. Barbara Boudewijnse, 43–56. Amsterdam: Rodopi, 1990.

Fairchild, Hoxie Neale. *Religious Trends in English Poetry*. Vol. 4, *1830–1880*. New York: Columbia University Press, 1957.

Fiedrowicz, Michael. "General Introduction." In *Expositions of the Psalms 1–32*, part 3, vol. 15 of *The Works of Saint Augustine: A Translation for the 21st Century*, translated by Maria Boulding, edited by John E. Rotelle, 13–66. New York: New City Press, 2000.

Fielding, Steven. *Class and Ethnicity: Irish Catholics in England, 1880–1939*. Philadelphia: Open University Press, 1993.

Fish, Henry Clay. *History and Repository of Pulpit Eloquence*. New York: Dodd, 1856.

Fitzgerald, Percy. *Fifty Years of Catholic Life and Social Progress under Cardinals Wiseman, Manning, Vaughan, and Newman*. London: Unwin, 1901.

Foley, Peter. "Anglican Communion: A Theological Consideration." In *Challenge and Hope: Epiphanies for Our Age*. Epiphany Study 2007. www.msgr.ca/msgr-3/Challenge_and_Hope 00.htm.

Forster, Margaret. *Elizabeth Barrett Browning: A Biography*. London: Chatto, 1988.

Franklin, R. W. *Nineteenth-Century Churches: The History of a New Catholicism in Württemberg, England, and France*. New York: Garland, 1987.

Bibliography

Gaskell, Elizabeth. *North and South*. Edited by Patricia Ingham. Harmondsworth, UK: Penguin, 1995.

Gertzman, Jay A. *Fantasy, Fashion and Affection: Editions of Robert Herrick's Poetry for the Common Reader, 1810–1968*. Bowling Green: Bowling Green State University Popular Press, 1986.

Gilbert, H. M. *The Story of the London Oratory Church*. London: Washbourne, 1934.

Girton College Personal Papers of Bessie Rayner Parkes. Girton College Archive, Cambridge.

"Golden Square Area: Warwick Street." In *Survey of London*, vols. 31 and 32, *St James Westminster, Part 2*, 167–73. London: London City Council, 1963. http://www.britishhistory.ac.uk/report.aspx?compid=41468.

Goodlad, Lauren M. *Victorian Literature and the Victorian State: Character and Governance in a Liberal Society*. Baltimore, MD: Johns Hopkins University Press, 2003.

Gordon-Gorman, William J. *Converts to Rome: Since the Tractarian Movement to May 1899*. 4th ed. London, 1899. Internet Archive. http://www.archive.org.

Gray, F. Elizabeth. *Christian and Lyric Tradition in Victorian Women's Poetry*. New York: Routledge, 2010.

Gray, Robert. *Cardinal Manning: A Biography*. London: Weidenfeld, 1985.

Green, Percy. *Paddington Chapel, 1813–1963*. London: Farmer, 1965.

Gregory, Gill. "Adelaide Procter: A Poetics of Reserve and Passion." In *Women's Poetry, Late Romantic to Late Victorian: Gender and Genre, 1830–1900*, edited by Isobel Armstrong and Virginia Blain, 355–72. New York: St. Martin's, 1999.

———. *The Life and Work of Adelaide Procter: Poetry, Feminism and Fathers*. Aldershot, UK: Ashgate, 1998.

Guthrie, Cliff. "Neurology, Ritual, and Religion: An Initial Exploration." *Proceedings of the North American Academy of Liturgy* (2000): 107–24.

Gwynn, Denis. *Lord Shrewsbury, Pugin and the Catholic Revival*. Westminster, MA: Newman, 1946.

Härdelin, Alf. *The Tractarian Understanding of the Eucharist*. Uppsala, Sweden: Almquist, 1965.

Harrington, E. C. *The Object, Importance, and Antiquity of the Rite of Consecration of Churches*. London: Rivington, 1844.

Harrison, Antony H. *Victorian Poets and the Politics of Culture: Discourse and Ideology*. Charlottesville: University Press of Virginia, 1998.

Hassett, Constance W. *Christina Rossetti: The Patience of Style*. Charlottesville: University of Virginia Press, 2005.

Hauerwas, Stanley, and Ralph Wood. "How the Church Became Invisible: A Christian Reading of American Literary Tradition." *Religion and Literature* 38, no. 1 (2006): 61–93.

Heimann, Mary. *Catholic Devotion in Victorian England*. Oxford: Clarendon, 1995.

Hendrikson, William. *New Testament Commentary: Exposition of the Gospel According to John*. Grand Rapids, MI: Baker, 1953.

Herringer, Carol Engelhardt. *Victorians and the Virgin Mary: Religion and Gender in England, 1830–85*. Manchester: Manchester University Press, 2008.

Hillsman, Walter. "The Victorian Revival of Plainsong in English: Its Usage under

Tractarians and Ritualists." In *The Church and the Arts*, edited by Diana Wood, 405–15. Studies in Church History 28. Oxford: Blackwell, for the Ecclesiastical History Society, 1992.

———. "Women in Victorian Church Music: Their Social, Liturgical, and Performing Roles in Anglicanism." In *Women in the Church*, edited by W. J. Sheils and Diana Wood, 443–52. Studies in Church History 27. Oxford: Blackwell, for the Ecclesiastical History Society, 1990.

Hoeckley, Cheri Lin Larsen. "Adelaide Anne Procter." In *Dictionary of Literary Biography: Victorian Women Poets*, edited by William B. Thesing, 252–58. Farmington Hills, MI: Gale, 1999.

———. "'Must Her Own Words Do All?': Domesticity, Catholicism, and Activism in Adelaide Anne Procter's Poems." In *The Catholic Church and Unruly Women Writers: Critical Essays*, edited by Jeana Delrosso, Leigh Eicke, and Ana Kothe, 123–38. New York: Palgrave Macmillan, 2007.

———. "Poetry, Activism and 'Our Lady of the Rosary': Adelaide Procter's Catholic Poetics in *A Chaplet of Verses*." In *Sublimer Aspects: Interfaces between Literature, Aesthetics, and Theology*, edited by Natasha Duquette, 145–59. Newcastle: Cambridge Scholars Publishing, 2007.

Hogue, David A. "Sensing the Other in Worship: Mirror Neurons and the Empathizing Brain." *Liturgy* 21, no. 3 (2006): 31–39.

Holloway, John. *The Victorian Sage: Studies in Argument*. Hamden, CT: Archon, 1962.

Holsinger, Bruce, ed. "Literary History and the Religious Turn: Announcing the New ELN." *ELN* 44, no. 1 (2006).

Hotz-Davies, Ingrid. *The Creation of Religious Identities by English Women Poets from the Seventeenth to the Early Twentieth Century*. Queenston, ON: Mellen, 2001.

Hu, Esther T. "Christina Rossetti and the Poetics of Tractarian Suffering." In *Through a Glass Darkly: Suffering, the Sacred and the Sublime in Literature and Theory*, edited by Holly Faith Nelson, Lynn R. Szabo, and Jens Zimmermann, 155–67. Waterloo, ON: Wilfrid Laurier University Press, 2010.

———. "Christina Rossetti, John Keble and the Divine Gaze." *Victorian Poetry* 46, no. 2 (2008): 175–89.

Husenbeth, the Very Rev. H. C., trans. and ed. *The Missal for the Use of the Laity*. London, 1853.

The Hymnal. Philadelphia: Presbyterian Board of Christian Education, 1933.

The Hymnary of the United Church of Canada, Authorized by the General Council. Toronto: United Church, 1930.

Hymns of Worship and Service. 22nd ed. New York: Century, 1910.

Inbody, Tyron. *The Faith of the Christian Church: An Introduction to Theology*. Grand Rapids, MI: Eerdmans, 2005.

Irwin, Kevin. *Liturgy, Prayer and Spirituality*. New York: Paulist Press, 1984.

Ives, David. *The Principles of Dissent from Church Establishments; with a Comparative View of the Modes of Worship of Churchmen and Orthodox Dissenters*. 3rd ed. London, 1833.

Johnson, Stephanie L. "*Aurora Leigh*'s Radical Youth: Derridean *Parergon* and the Narrative Frame in 'A Vision of Poets.'" *Victorian Poetry* 44, no. 4 (2006): 425–44.

Bibliography

Jones, R. Tudor. *Congregationalism in England, 1662–1962*. London: Independent, 1962.

Julian, John, ed. *A Dictionary of Hymnology Setting forth the Origin and History of Christian Hymns of All Ages and Nations*. New York: Scribner's, 1892.

Keaton, Maria. "Mystic, Madwoman or Metaphysic? The Analogical Theodicy of Christina Rossetti." In *Outsiders Looking In: The Rossettis, Then and Now*, edited by David Clifford and Laurence Roussillon, 145–54. London: Anthem, 2004.

Keble, John. *Keble's Lectures on Poetry, 1832–1841*. 2 vols. Oxford: Clarendon, 1912.

———. "On the Mysticism Attributed to the Fathers of the Church." Tract 89 of *Tracts for the Times*. Project Canterbury. http://anglicanhistory.org/tracts/tract89/.

Kelley, Philip, and Betty A. Coley. *The Browning Collections: A Reconstruction with Other Memorabilia*. Waci, TX: Armstrong Browning Library of Baylor University; Browning Institute; Mansell; Wedgestone, 1984.

Kent, David A. "'By thought, word, and deed': George Herbert and Christina Rossetti." In *The Achievement of Christina Rossetti*, edited by David A. Kent, 250–73. Ithaca, NY: Cornell University Press, 1987.

———. "Sequence and Meaning in Christina Rossetti's *Verses* (1893)." *Victorian Poetry* 17, no. 3 (1979): 259–64.

———. "W. M. Rossetti and the Editing of Christina Rossetti's Religious Poetry." *Pre-Raphaelite Review* 1, no. 2 (1978): 18–26.

The King James Version of the Bible. Grand Rapids, MI: Zondervan, n.d.

Kooistra, Lorraine Janzen. *Christina Rossetti and Illustration: A Publishing History*. Athens: Ohio University Press, 2002.

———. *Poetry, Pictures, and Popular Publishing: The Illustrated Gift Book and Victorian Visual Culture, 1855–1875*. Athens: Ohio University Press, 2011.

LaMonaca, Maria. *Masked Atheism: Catholicism and the Secular Victorian Home*. Columbus: Ohio State University Press, 2008.

Lang, Marjorie. "George Bell and Sons." In *Dictionary of Literary Biography*, vol. 106, *British Literary Publishing Houses, 1820–1880*, edited by Patricia J. Anderson and Jonathan Rose, 22–31. Detroit: Gale, 1991.

Lanham, Richard A. *Analyzing Prose*. 2nd ed. New York: Continuum, 2003.

Lathrop, Gordon W. *Holy Things: A Liturgical Theology*. Minneapolis: Fortress, 1993.

Latourette, Kenneth Scott. *A History of Christianity*, vol. 2. Rev. ed. New York: Harper, 1975.

Lautz, Boniface. *The Doctrine of the Communion of Saints in Anglican Theology, 1833–1963*. Ottawa: University of Ottawa Press, 1967.

Leighton, Angela. *Victorian Women Poets: Writing Against the Heart*. New York: Harvester, 1992.

Leuenberger, Samuel. *Archbishop Cranmer's Immortal Bequest: The Book of Common Prayer of the Church of England: An Evangelistic Liturgy*. Grand Rapids, MI: Eerdmans, 1990.

Lewis, C. S. *Mere Christianity*. Glasgow: Collins, 1952.

Lewis, Linda M. *Elizabeth Barrett Browning's Spiritual Progress*. Columbia: University of Missouri Press, 1998.

"The London Oratory." In *Survey of London*. Vol. 41, Brompton, 50–57. London: Athlone Press for the Greater London Council, 1983. http://www.british-history.ac.uk/report.aspx?compid=50008.

Bibliography

The London Oratory, 1849–1949. London: Oratory of St. Philip Neri, 1949.

Lundin, Roger. *Believing Again: Doubt and Faith in a Secular Age*. Grand Rapids, MI: Eerdmans, 2009.

MacHaffie, Barbara. *Her Story: Women in Christian Tradition*. Philadelphia: Fortress, 1986.

MacLeod, James Lachlan. "Race Theory and the Free Church of Scotland: A Nineteenth-Century Case Study." *Perspectives in Religious Studies* 25, no. 3 (1998): 227–47.

Marsh, Jan. *Christina Rossetti: A Writers' Life*. New York: Viking, 1995.

Mason, Emma. "'A Sort of Aesthetico-Catholic Revival': Christina Rossetti and the London Ritualist Scene." In *Outsiders Looking In: The Rossettis Then and Now*, edited by David Clifford and Laurence Roussillon, 115–30. London: Anthem, 2004.

———. *Women Poets of the Nineteenth Century*. Tavistock, UK: Northcote House, 2006.

McCarthy, William, and Elizabeth Draft, eds. *Anna Letitia Barbauld: Selected Poetry and Prose*. Peterborough, ON: Broadview, 2002.

Melnyk, Julie. "'Mighty Victims': Women Writers and the Feminization of Christ." *Victorian Literature and Culture* 31, no. 1 (2003): 131–57.

Mermin, Dorothy. *Elizabeth Barrett Browning: The Origins of a New Poetry*. Chicago: University of Chicago Press, 1989.

The Methodist Hymnal: Official Hymnal of the Methodist Church. Nashville, TN: Methodist, 1939.

Mitchell, Leonel L. *Praying Shapes Believing: A Theological Commentary on the Book of Common Prayer*. Harrisburg, PA: Morehouse, 1991.

Morgan, Thaïs E. "Victorian Sage Discourse and the Feminine: An Introduction." In *Victorian Sages and Cultural Discourses: Renegotiating Gender and Power*, edited by Thaïs E. Morgan, 1–18. New Brunswick, NJ: Rutgers University Press, 1990.

Muir, T. E. *Roman Catholic Church Music in England, 1791–1914: A Handmaid of the Liturgy?* Burlington, VT: Ashgate, 2008.

Muller, Jill. *Gerard Manley Hopkins and Victorian Catholicism: A Heart in Hiding*. New York: Routledge, 2003.

Murray, Mary Charles. "The Christian Zodiac on a Font at Hook Norton: Theology, Church, and Art." In *The Church and the Arts: Papers Read at the 1990 Summer Meeting and the 1991 Winter Meeting of the Ecclesiastical History Society*, edited by Diana Wood, 87–97. Oxford: Blackwell, 1992.

Nalbantian, Suzanne, and Jean-Pierre Changeux. "Neuroaesthetics: Neuroscientific Theory and Illustration from the Arts." *Interdisciplinary Science Reviews* 33, no. 4 (2008): 357–68.

Newman, John Henry. *Apologia Pro Vita Sua*. Edited by David J. DeLaura. New York: Norton, 1968.

———. "The Communion of Saints." In *Parochial and Plain Sermons*, vol. 4, 168–84. London: Longmans, 1909. Newman Reader. National Institute for Newman Studies, 2004. http://www.newmanreader.org/works/parochial/volume4/sermon1.html.

———. *Verses on Various Occasions*. Newman Reader. National Institute for Newman Studies, 2004. http://www.newmanreader.org/works/verses/verse90.html.

Nicholls, Guy. "The Contribution of the Oratories to the Liturgical Life of England." In *The Birmingham Oratory*. October 1999. http://www.birmingham-oratory.org.uk/Oratory/ALLOct99.pdf.

Bibliography

Nixon, Jude V. "Framing Victorian Religious Discourse: An Introduction." In *Victorian Religious Discourse: New Directions*, edited by Jude V. Nixon, 1–24. New York: Palgrave, 2004.

———. "'[S]he shall make all new': *Aurora Leigh* and Elizabeth Barrett Browning's Re-Gendering of the Apocalypse." *Studies in Browning and His Circle* 26 (2006): 72–93.

Nockles, Peter B. *The Oxford Movement in Context: Anglican High Churchmanship, 1760–1857*. Cambridge: Cambridge University Press, 1994.

Norman, Edward. *The English Catholic Church in the Nineteenth Century*. Oxford: Clarendon, 1984.

Notes and Queries. Vol. 11, 2nd series, no. 262 (January 5, 1861). Available through Internet Library of Early Journals, ILEJ Consortium 1997. http://www.bodley.ox.ac.uk/ilej/.

———. Vol. 1, 3rd series, no. 20 (May 17, 1862). Available through Internet Library of Early Journals, ILEJ Consortium 1997. http://www.bodley.ox.ac.uk/ilej/.

Nussbaum, Martha. *Upheavals of Thought: The Intelligence of Emotions*. New York: Cambridge University Press, 2001.

O'Day, Rosemary. "The Men from the Ministry." In *Religion in Victorian Britain*, vol. 2, *Controversies*, edited by Gerald Parsons, 258–79. Manchester: Manchester University Press, 1988.

Oxford English Dictionary. 3rd ed. Oxford University Press, 2006. http://dictionary.oed.com.

Paddington Chapel, Marylebone Road, London: Centenary, 1813–1913. London: Morton, [1913].

Paddington Chapel register of members. London Metropolitan Archives 4295 / B / 013.

Palmer, Samuel. *A New Directory for Nonconformist Churches: Containing Free Remarks on Their Mode of Public Worship, and a Plan for the Improvement of It*. London, 1812.

Parkes, Bessie. *In a Walled Garden*. London: Ward and Downey, 1895. Available through the Victorian Women Writers Project, edited by Perry Willet. http://www.indiana.edu/~letrs/vwwp/belloc/walled.html.

Parsons, Gerald. "From Dissenters to Free Churchmen: The Transitions of Victorian Nonconformity." In *Religion in Victorian Britain*, vol. 1, *Traditions*, edited by Gerald Parsons, 67–116. Manchester: Manchester University Press, 1988.

———. "Reform, Revival and Realignment: The Experience of Victorian Anglicanism." In *Religion in Victorian Britain*, vol. 1, *Traditions*, edited by Gerald Parsons, 14–66. Manchester: Manchester University Press, 1988.

Peel, Albert. *These Hundred Years: A History of the Congregational Union of England and Wales, 1831–1931*. London: Congregational Union of England and Wales, 1931.

Pierce, Joanne M. "Vestments and Objects." In *The Oxford History of Christian Worship*, edited by Geoffrey Wainwright and Karen B. Westerfield Tucker, 841–57. Oxford: Oxford University Press, 2006.

Poovey, Mary. *Making a Social Body: British Cultural Formation, 1830–1864*. Chicago: University of Chicago Press, 1995.

The Prayer-Book of the Oratory of St. Philip Neri, King William Street, Strand. London, n.d.

Procter, Adelaide. *The Poems of Adelaide A. Procter*. New York: Thomas Y. Crowell, n.d.; reprint, Whitefish, MT: Kessinger Publishing, n.d.

———. "A Tomb in Ghent." *Household Words* 12, no. 22 (1855): 515–18.

Bibliography

———. "The Way Is Long and Dreary." Gilbert and Sullivan Archive. http://math.boisestate.edu/gas/other_sullivan/part_songs/long_dreary/long_dreary.html.

Protestant Magazine. New series, 8, no. 2. London, 1846.

Purcell, Edmund Sheridan. *Life of Cardinal Manning, Archbishop of Westminster*. 2 vols. London, 1896.

Rainbow, Bernarr. *The Choral Revival in the Anglican Church, 1839–1872*. London: Barrie, 1970.

Reed, John Shelton. *Glorious Battle: The Cultural Politics of Victorian Anglo-Catholicism*. Nashville, TN: Vanderbilt University Press, 1996.

Reynolds, Margaret. "Critical Introduction." In *Aurora Leigh*, edited by Margaret Reynolds, 1–77. Athens: Ohio University Press, 1992.

Rodriguez, Alphonsus. *On Christian Perfection for Persons Living in the World*. 2 vols. London: Burns, n.d.

Roe, Dinah. *Christina Rossetti's Faithful Imagination: The Devotional Poetry and Prose*. New York: Palgrave, 2006.

Rossetti, Christina. *The Complete Poems*. Edited by R. W. Crump, with notes and introduction by Betty S. Flowers. Harmondsworth, UK: Penguin, 2001.

———. *The Face of the Deep: A Devotional Commentary on the Apocalypse*. London: SPCK, 1892.

———. *The Letters of Christina Rossetti*. 4 vols. Edited by Antony H. Harrison. Charlottesville: University Press of Virginia, 1997–2004.

———. *Maude: Prose and Verse*. Edited by R. W. Crump. Hamden, CT: Archon, 1976.

———. *Verses: Reprinted from* Called to Be Saints, Time Flies, *and* The Face of the Deep. London: SPCK, 1893.

Rossetti, William Michael. "Memoir." In *The Poetical Works of Christina Georgina Rossetti: With Memoir and Notes*, edited by William Michael Rossetti, xlv–lxxi. New York: Georg Olms Verlag, 1970.

Roston, Murray. *Prophet and Poet: The Bible and the Growth of Romanticism*. London: Faber, 1965.

Routley, Erik. *A Panorama of Christian Hymnody*. Collegeville, MN: Liturgical, 1979.

Rowell, Geoffrey. *The Vision Glorious: Themes and Personalities of the Catholic Revival in Anglicanism*. Oxford: Oxford University Press, 1983.

Roxborough, John. "The Legacy of Thomas Chalmers." *International Bulletin of Missionary Research* 23, no. 4 (1999): 173–76.

Ruskin, John. *The Works of John Ruskin*, vol. 18. Edited by E. T. Cook and Alexander Wedderburn. London: Allen, 1905.

Ryley, George Buchanan, and John M. McCandlish. *Scotland's Free Church*. Westminster, UK: Constable, 1893.

Sacred Rhetoric; or, The Art of Rhetoric as Applied to the Preaching of the Word of God. Dublin: Browne and Nolan, 1881.

Scheinberg, Cynthia. *Women's Poetry and Religion in Victorian England: Jewish Identity and Christian Culture*. Cambridge: Cambridge University Press, 2002.

Schofield, Nicholas. *The Church of St. James, Spanish Place: A History and Guide*. London: St. James's Church, Spanish Place, 2005.

Bibliography

Selbie, W. B. *Congregationalism*. London: Methuen, 1927.

Shuger, Debora K. *Sacred Rhetoric: The Christian Grand Style in the English Renaissance*. Princeton: Princeton University Press, 1988.

Slinn, E. Warwick. "Experimental Form in Victorian Poetry." In *The Cambridge Companion to Victorian Poetry*, edited by Joseph Bristow, 46–66. Cambridge: Cambridge University Press, 2000.

Smith, James K. A. *Desiring the Kingdom: Worship, Worldview and Cultural Formation*. Grand Rapids, MI: Baker, 2009.

———. *Introducing Radical Orthodoxy: Mapping a Post-secular Theology*. Grand Rapids, MI: Baker, 2004.

Sommers, Kris. "Various Kinds of Rosaries and Chaplets." Marian Library/International Marian Research Institute. http://campus.udayton.edu/mary/resources/chaplet.html.

Spinks, Bryan D. *Freedom or Order: The Eucharistic Liturgy in English Congregationalism 1645–1980*. Allison Park, PA: Pickwick, 1984.

Spurr, Barry. *Anglo-Catholic in Religion: T. S. Eliot and Christianity*. Cambridge, UK: Lutterworth, 2010.

Stephenson, Glennis. *Elizabeth Barrett Browning and the Poetry of Love*. Ann Arbor: UMI, 1989.

Stone, Marjorie. "Cursing as One of the Fine Arts: Elizabeth Barrett Browning's Political Poems." *Dalhousie Review* 66, no. 1–2 (1986): 155–73.

———. *Elizabeth Barrett Browning*. New York: St. Martin's, 1995.

———. "Genre Subversion and Gender Inversion: *The Princess* and *Aurora Leigh*." *Victorian Poetry* 25, no. 2 (1987). Reprinted in *Aurora Leigh: A Norton Critical Edition*, edited by Margaret Reynolds, 494–505. New York: Norton, 1996.

———. "A Heretic Believer: Victorian Religious Doubt and New Contexts for Elizabeth Barrett Browning's 'A Drama of Exile,' 'The Virgin Mary,' and 'The Runaway Slave at Pilgrim's Point.'" *Studies in Browning and His Circle* 26 (2005): 7–40.

Stratten, James. "Entrance to the Holiest by the Blood of Jesus." In *The Intermediate State and Other Discourses*, 88–120. London: James Nisbet, 1867.

———. "Increase of Faith." In *Freedom and Happiness in the Truth and Ways of Christ*, 77–100. London, 1862.

———. "Spiritual Declension." In *The Pastoral Echo: Nineteen Sermons by Eminent Dissenting Ministers and Others*, 185–97. London: W. Harding, 1837.

———. "The Titles and Offices of Christ." In *The Pastoral Echo: Nineteen Sermons by Eminent Dissenting Ministers and Others*, 97–112. London: W. Harding, 1837.

Swedenborg, Emmanuel. *True Christian Religion*. Translated by. John C. Ager. New York: American Swedenborg Printing and Publishing Society, 1906. Internet Sacred Text Archive. http://www.sacred-texts.com/swd/tcr/index.htm.

Swift, Roger. "Crime and the Irish in Nineteenth-Century Britain." In *The Irish in Britain, 1815–1939*, edited by Roger Swift and Sheridan Gilley, 163–82. Savage, MD: Barnes, 1989.

Tamke, Susan S. *Make a Joyful Noise Unto the Lord: Hymns as a Reflection of Victorian Social Attitudes*. Athens: Ohio University Press, 1978.

Tangherlini, Timothy R. "'It Happened Not Too Far from Here . . .': A Survey of Legend Theory and Characterization." *Western Folklore* 49, no. 4 (1990): 371–90.

Tate, Gregory. "Tennyson and the Embodied Mind." *Victorian Poetry* 47, no. 1 (2009): 61–80.

Taylor, Charles. *Modern Social Imaginaries*. Durham, NC: Duke University Press, 2004.

———. *A Secular Age*. Cambridge, MA: Belknap Press of Harvard University Press, 2007.

Taylor, Dennis. "The Need for a Religious Literary Criticism." In *Seeing into the Life of Things: Essays on Literature and Religious Experience*, edited by John L. Mahoney, 3–30. New York: Fordham University Press, 1998.

Tenbus, Eric G. *English Catholics and the Education of the Poor, 1847–1902*. London: Pickering and Chatto, 2010.

Tennyson, G. B. *Victorian Devotional Poetry: The Tractarian Mode*. Cambridge, MA: Harvard University Press, 1981.

Thompson, Paul. *William Butterfield*. London: Routledge, 1971.

Tracy, David. *The Analogical Imagination: Christian Theology and the Culture of Pluralism*. New York: Crossroad, 1991.

Tropman, John E. *The Catholic Ethic and the Spirit of Community*. Washington, DC: Georgetown University Press, 2002.

Tweedy, Henry Hallam, ed. *Christian Worship and Praise*. New York: Commission for Christian Worship and Praise, 1939.

Tyack, Geoffrey. *Sir James Pennethorne and the Making of Victorian London*. Cambridge: Cambridge University Press, 1992.

van der Lans, Jan M., and Henri Geerts. "The Impact of the Liturgical Setting: An Empirical Study from the Perspective of Environmental Psychology." In *Current Studies on Rituals: Perspectives for the Psychology of Religion*, edited by Hans-Günter Heimbrock and H. Barbara Boudewijnse, 87–102. Amsterdam: Rodopi, 1990.

"Vernacular Hymns at Solemn Exposition of the Blessed Sacrament." *American Ecclesiastical Review* 7, no. 1 (1892): 455–58.

Wagner, Jennifer Ann. *A Moment's Monument: Revisionary Poetics and the Nineteenth-Century English Sonnet*. Madison, NJ: Fairleigh Dickinson University Press, 1996.

Walker, Norman L. *Chapters from the History of the Free Church of Scotland*. Edinburgh: Oliphant, 1895.

Walker, Williston. *The Creeds and Platforms of Congregationalism*. Boston: Pilgrim, 1960.

Watson, J. R. *The English Hymn: A Critical and Historical Study*. Oxford: Clarendon, 1997.

Weedon, Alexis. *Victorian Publishing: The Economics of Book Production for a Mass Market, 1836–1916*. Aldershot, UK: Ashgate, 2003.

Westerholm, Joel. "In Defense of Verses: The Aesthetic Reputation of Christina Rossetti's Late Poetry." *Renascence* 51, no. 3 (1999): 191–203.

Wheeler, Michael. *The Old Enemies: Catholic and Protestant in Nineteenth-Century English Culture*. Cambridge: Cambridge University Press, 2006.

White, James F. *Roman Catholic Worship: Trent to Today*. 2nd ed. Collegeville, MN: Liturgical Press, 2003.

———. "The Spatial Setting." In *The Oxford History of Christian Worship*, edited by Geoffrey Wainwright and Karen B. Westerfield Tucker, 793–816. Oxford: Oxford University Press, 2006.

Bibliography

Williams, Isaac. "On Reserve in Communicating Religious Knowledge (continued)." Tract 87 of *Tracts for the Times*. Project Canterbury. http://anglicanhistory.org/tracts/tract87/.

Williams, Rowan. *Anglican Identities*. Cambridge, MA: Cowley, 2003.

Wilson, Elizabeth A. *Psychosomatic: Feminism and the Neurological Body*. Durham, NC: Duke University Press, 2004.

Woods, Thomas E., Jr. *Sacred Then and Sacred Now: The Return of the Old Latin Mass*. Fort Collins, CO: Roman Catholic Books, 2008.

Wörn, Alexandra M. B. "'Poetry is where God is': The Importance of Christian Faith and Theology in Elizabeth Barrett Browning's Life and Work." In *Victorian Religious Discourse: New Directions in Criticism*, edited by Jude V. Nixon, 235–52. Basingstoke, UK: Palgrave Macmillan, 2004.

Wylie, James A. *Disruption Worthies: A Memorial of 1843*. Edinburgh: Grange, 1881.

Yates, Nigel. *Anglican Ritualism in Victorian Britain, 1830–1910*. Oxford: Oxford University Press, 1999.

———. *Buildings, Faith, and Worship: The Liturgical Arrangement of Anglican Churches 1600–1900*. Oxford: Clarendon, 1991.

INDEX

Adelmann, Dale, 129
affect (affective), 8–9, 11–12, 15, 234, 255–56; in Barrett Browning's poetics, 28, 53–60, 64–74, 77–83, 86, 87–88, 99; in homiletic theory and practice, 53–55, 57–59, 180, 194–96, 199; in Procter's poetics, 178–79, 193–95, 199–202, 214, 228–34, 261; in revivalist exercises, 196–99. *See also* emotions (emotive)
altar: in Anglican Church, 104, 120–21, 122, 127, 132, 133, 277n50, 278n60; in Barrett Browning's poetry, 31, 51; Congregationalist rejection of, 30, 120; in Procter's poetry, 216, 236, 248; in Roman Catholic Church, 181, 182, 183, 184, 185, 186–87, 285n17; in Isaac Williams's poetry, 157
analogy (analogical language, analogical imagination), 112–17, 119–20, 140–43, 152–55, 162
Anderson, E. Byron, 9
Anglicanism: church consecration in, 103–4; Communion in, 18, 104–5, 114–15, 122, 127, 132, 275n6; and communion of saints, 109–10, 126–36, 163; ecclesiology in, 120–26, 132, 278n53; hierarchy in, 113, 131–34; historic orientations of, 103–5, 108, 109, 110–11, 113, 127, 170; hymns in, 104, 105, 129–30, 176; movements within, 112–13; postures of worship in, 101, 106, 107, 120; prayers in (collects), 104, 106–7, 109, 154; preaching in, 21, 114, 120–21, 135, 149; psalm singing in, 104, 109, 129, 130; ritualism in, 101–2, 112, 122, 126–34; sacramentalism in, 110–12, 113–14, 121–25 (*see also* reserve; Tractarianism). *See also* Christ Church, Albany Street
Anglo-Catholicism. *See* Anglicanism; Christ Church, Albany Street

architecture, 17–18, 30–31, 121–22, 181–82. *See also* church interiors; *names of individual churches*
Armstrong, Isobel, 199, 219
Arseneau, Mary, 126, 138, 274n2
Augustine, 12, 57, 135

baptism, 16, 32–33, 109, 122–23, 285n17
Barbauld, Anna, 41, 68
Barrett Browning, Elizabeth. *See* Browning, Elizabeth Barrett
Basil, 57, 79
Bell and Daldy (publishers), 228, 252
Bible (Scripture): Anglican approach to, 100, 104, 105–6, 108–9, 112–18; Barrett Browning on, 28, 39, 47, 49, 78, 269n43; Congregationalist approach to, 26, 30, 33, 38–39, 46–48, 108, 117; exegesis of, historical-grammatical method, 39, 45, 117; exegesis of, typological method, 115, 116, 259; Roman Catholic approach to, 183–84, 187, 257; Rossetti on, 133–34, 172
Blackburn, John, 30
Bonomi, Joseph, 181
Book of Common Prayer, The, 103–5, 108, 109, 112, 130, 134, 161, 275n6
Bourdieu, Pierre, 6, 7–8
Boyd, Hugh, 65, 72, 75
Bradley, Thomas Earnshaw (*The Lamp*), 181–82
Briggs, J., 29, 45
Brompton (London) Oratory, 178, 179, 181, 185, 207, 251; architecture and interior design of, 181–82; devotional books of, 235–36; music in, 191–92, 197–98; revivalist exercises of, 179–80, 193–94, 196–97, 248. *See also* Faber, Frederick; Procter, Adelaide: and church affiliation

Index

Browning, Elizabeth Barrett
    as biblical interpreter, 63–64, 69, 72, 75–80, 83–89, 95–96, 144–45
    and church affiliation, 25–28 (*see also* Congregationalism; Free Church of Scotland (Scotch Church); French Reformed Church; Paddington Chapel)
    and dialogue (dialogic), 50, 59–60, 62–63, 64–65, 75–77, 83, 85–87, 90, 91, 93–95
    and gender concerns, 50–51, 62–63, 64–65, 67, 74, 77–80, 83–85, 86–88, 92, 97–98
    and hymns, 28, 43–44, 62–63, 65–75, 82, 86 (*see also* hymns)
    and independence, 42, 62–63, 67, 97
    and languages, 39, 72, 89
    and poetic form, 62, 75–76, 82, 93, 107
    on poetry, 61 (*see also* poet-preacher)
    and preachers (preaching), 26, 27, 31, 52, 56, 57–58, 60, 71 (*see also* Greene, Henry; Gregory of Nazianzus; Hanna, Robert Maxwell; Stratten, James)
    religious imaginary of, 24–60
    and rhetoric, 25, 59–60, 63, 80–83, 95–96 (*see also* homiletics)
    and sacrament: Lord's Supper, 32–34
    and sacramentalism, 34–36
Browning, Elizabeth Barrett, works of
    Aurora Leigh, 34–36, 62–63, 91–98
    "The Book of the Poets," 34, 36
    "Christmas Gifts," 57, 256–57
    "A Curse for a Nation," 91, 98–99
    "The Dead Pan," 31, 89–90
    "A Drama of Exile," 34, 75, 83–84, 86–90, 117
    "The Dream: A Fragment," 63–64
    "Earth and Her Praisers," 36
    "An Essay on Mind," 31, 52
    "Hymn," 43, 66, 70
    "The Look," 145
    "The Meaning of the Look," 145
    "The Measure: Hymn IV," 43, 72–75
    "The Mediator: Hymn II," 43–44
    "Mountaineer and Poet," 91
    "Remonstrance," 65
    "The Seraphim," 75, 76–83, 117
    "Some Account of the Greek Christian Poets," 47, 56, 57
    "The Soul's Expression," 147
    "A Supplication for Love: Hymn I," 71
    "The Two Sayings," 145
    unpublished children's hymns, 67–70
    "The Virgin Mary to the Child Jesus," 75, 83–86, 224, 233
    "A Vision of Poets," 31, 51–52

    "The Weeping Saviour: Hymn III," 71
    "Who art thou of the veilëd countenance," 64–65
Browning, Pen, 28
Browning, Robert, 26, 27–28, 33–34, 58, 60, 189, 262
Buchanan, James, 115–16
Burrows, Henry W., 121–23, 127, 130
Butterfield, William, 122, 277n45
Calvin, John (Calvinism, Calvinist), 28, 29, 32, 33, 34, 40
Catholic Apostolic Church (Newman Street Church), 27
Chadwick, Owen, 46, 55
Challoner, Richard (*The Garden of the Soul*), 185–86, 197, 203–4, 226, 233
Changeux, Jean-Pierre, 10
chaplets, 196, 212, 234–36, 260
Chapman, Alison, 107, 147, 156
choirs, 127, 129–33, 183, 191, 222, 225, 285n17; in Rossetti's poetics, 165, 166
choral services, 129–31
Christ Church, Albany Street, 102, 121–25, 126, 127, 130–31, 133, 277n50, 278n53, 278n60
Christ Church, Woburn Square, 102, 176
Chrysostom, 47, 57, 79
church fathers, 47, 55–57. *See also* Augustine; Basil; Chrysostom; Gregory of Nazianzus
church furnishings. *See* altar; font; pulpit; table (for Lord's Supper)
church interiors: chancel, 104, 121, 122, 123, 132, 134, 157, 277n50, 278n53, 278n60; choir stall, 133, 277n45, 278n53, 278n60; gallery, 121, 126, 132, 278n53; nave, 105, 120, 122, 123, 157, 278n53; pews, 126, 130, 277n50, 278n53; sanctuary, 103, 122; stained glass windows, 31, 123, 124, 126, 157, 277n45
Cianciola, Heather Shippen, 83
class, 42; in relation to Congregationalism, 46; in Procter's poetics, 190–91, 206–8, 229, 244–49; in Rossetti's poetics, 134, 156, 167, 170–71, 173–75
Colón, Christine A., 241–42, 292n27
Communion, 18, 103, 104–05, 114–15, 122, 127, 132, 149–51, 275n6
communion of saints, 40–41, 109, 126–36; in Rossetti's poetics, 163–70, 175–76
Conder, Josiah, 38, 40–41
Conder, Mrs. J., 41
Congregational Hymn Book, The, 38, 40–41, 43, 70, 74

Index

Congregationalism: and the Bible, 26, 30–31, 33, 38–39, 46–48, 108, 117; chapels of, 30–31; and Free Church of Scotland, 26–27; hymns in, 28, 29, 37–38, 40–41, 65–66, 68, 129, 132 (see also *Congregational Hymn Book, The*); and independence 19, 26, 29, 39, 46–47; liturgical overview of, 19–20, 29–30; postures of worship in, 24, 37–38; prayer in, 19, 37; preachers in, 48–50 (see also Stratten, James); sacraments in, 29, 31–32 (see also baptism; Lord's Supper); sermons of, 45–46, 55 (see also homiletics); shifting theology of, 28–29

Congregational Service Book, The, 19

consecration: of bread and wine, 103–4, 110, 114, 120, 183, 184, 214; of church building, 103, 275n3

creeds, 15; Anglican adherence to, 104, 109; Congregationalist rejection of, 19, 39, 48; Roman Catholic adherence to, 182, 183, 185

Dale, R. W., 29
Damasio, Antonio, 10, 11
D'Amico, Diane, 104, 138, 173
Davis, Philip, 76, 112
"Declaration of the Faith" (Congregationalist), 39, 46–47, 48, 49, 97, 269n42
De Sales, St. Francis, 203–4
deSilva, David A., 106, 154
dialogue (dialogic): in Barrett Browning's poetics, 50, 59–60, 62–63, 64–65, 75–77, 83, 85–87, 90, 91, 93–95; in Christian liturgy generally, 15; in the Congregationalist imaginary, 30, 45–46, 49, 59
Dickens, Charles, 189, 211, 220, 229
didacticism, 4, 38, 41, 68, 70, 190–1, 199, 213, 243, 246–47
Dodsworth, William, 122, 127
Donne, John, 72, 79, 149
Drain, Susan, 43, 177, 235

Ecclesiological Society, 120–21, 122
Ecclesiologist, The, 121, 122, 123, 124
ecclesiology, 111–13, 120–26, 132, 157, 278n53
Edie, Fred P., 9, 10
education, 175, 195, 205–8, 289n83, 289n92
Edwards, O. C., 53–54
Elbow, Peter, 13–14
embodiment (embodied worship), 6, 8–15, 38, 68, 109, 146, 155, 199, 258–59
emotions (emotive), 12; as judgments of value, 66–67, 68, 74, 198–99, 234, 255; neuroscience on, 10–11; in Tractarian poetics, 149; in Victorian gender theory, 42. *See also* affect (affective)

Eucharist, 7, 16, 18

Faber, Frederick: and authority, 189; conversion of, 180, 198; devotional style of, 180, 181, 195, 196–98, 230–31; on education, 195, 205, 207; as hymnist and writer, 196–98, 208–9, 230; Marian devotion of, 196, 197–98, 230; as preacher, 194, 195, 196, 203
Procter's admiration of, 180, 204
feminism, 4, 10, 11, 12, 210, 255
Foley, Peter, 110–11
font, 122–23
Free Church of Scotland (Scotch Church), 26–28, 29, 30, 32, 33–34, 37, 48–49, 56, 262, 267n9–10, 271n62
French Reformed Church, 27, 33

Garden of the Soul, The, 185–86, 197, 203–4, 226, 233
gender (gender ideology), 2, 4, 9, 12, 262; in Barrett Browning's poetics, 47, 50–51, 62–63, 64–65, 67, 74, 77–80, 83–85, 86–88, 92, 97–98; in Rossetti's poetics, 132, 133–34, 139, 167, 169, 170–71; Victorian ideology of, 41–42, 53, 62–63, 133–34, 173. *See also* hierarchy, religious
genre, poetic. *See* hymns; legends; roundels; sonnets; *see also* poetic form *under names of individual poets*
Gilbert, Daniel, 229, 285n19, 290n1
Goodlad, Lauren, 206
Gray, Elizabeth F., 4–5, 234, 256, 290n2, 291n24
Greene, Henry, 60
Gregory, Gill, 189
Gregory of Nazianzus, 44, 47, 56–57, 59, 80–82, 257

habitus, 7–8
Hanna, Robert Maxwell, 27, 59
Hassett, Constance, 138, 168
Hauerwas, Stanley, and Ralph Wood, 255
Heimann, Mary, 181, 206
Herbert, George, 126, 139, 149, 158, 161
hierarchy, religious, 4; in Anglican Church, 131–34; Congregationalist opposition to, 39, 48–49; Free Church of Scotland opposition to, 26–27; in Roman Catholic Church, 188–89, 208, 213, 250–52
Hoeckley, Cheri Larsen, 234, 284n1, 292n28
Holloway, John, 50
homiletics, 53–60. *See also* preaching; sermon

Index

Hotz-Davies, Ingrid, 85
Hu, Esther, 143–44, 223–24, 282n17
hymnbooks, 38, 41, 125, 176, 197, 283n49, 290n11. See also *Congregational Hymn Book, The*; *Hymns Ancient and Modern*
hymns: in Anglicanism, 104, 105, 129–30, 176; for children, 68–70; as cognitive-emotive work, 66–67, 68, 78; in Congregationalism, 28, 29, 37–38, 40–41, 65–66, 68, 129, 132; conventions of, 42–43, 65–66, 74; as prayers, 38, 43–44, 68, 70, 74; in Roman Catholicism, 178, 180, 196–98, 208–9; as theological work, 40, 70; women's writing of, 41–42, 67. See also Browning, Elizabeth Barrett: and hymns; Watts, Isaac; Wesley (John and/or Charles; Wesleyans)
Hymns Ancient and Modern, 130, 176

imaginary. See religious imaginary; social imaginary
Inbody, Tyron, 18, 32
Ireland (the Irish), 113, 189, 205, 208–9; in Procter's poetics, 213, 249–50
Irving, Edward, 27, 52

Johnson, Stephanie, 51–52

Keble, John, 108, 117, 126, 127, 149, 157, 161–62, 189, 226, 262
Kent, David A., 137–38, 150, 152, 157–58, 167–68
Knox, John, 34
Kooistra, Lorraine Janzen, 137, 156, 173, 175–76

LaMonaca, Maria, 35–36
Lanham, Richard, 53
Latin liturgy: in Procter's poetics, 220–26, 236; in Roman Catholicism, 60, 178, 183–84, 185–87, 191, 197, 198–99
Lautz, Boniface, 127
lay devotion, 178, 203, 250–52
legends, 204–5, 238–244
Leuenberger, Samuel, 117
Lewis, C. S., 171
Lewis, Linda M., 78, 92
liturgy, 1, 6, 8–10, 12, 14, 150, 261–63; of Congregationalism, 24–25, 29–30, 37–38, 40–42, 48; of Holy Communion (Anglican), 102–12, 122, 124, 128–30, 132, 133, 137; of revivalist exercises (Roman Catholic), 178, 180, 193–94, 196–97; of Tridentine Mass (Roman Catholic), 178, 182–84; overview of Christian, 14–17. See also Latin liturgy

London Oratory. See Brompton (London) Oratory
Longinus, 54
Lord's Prayer, 104, 105, 109, 184
Lord's Supper, 18, 26, 32–34, 41, 103
Lowndes, Marie Belloc, 185
Lundin, Roger, 5, 35

manifestation (encounter): in Anglican imaginary, 100–101, 103, 111–12, 113–20; in Rossetti's poetics, 138, 140–46, 152, 168–69, 170
Manning, Henry Edward, 163, 180, 188–89, 194, 195, 202–3, 205–6
Marian devotion, 184, 196, 197–98, 201–2, 209, 225, 230–35, 236–38, 240–41, 245, 259–60
Mary, as poetic subject: in Barrett Browning's poetry, 84–86; in Faber's poetry, 197, 209, 230; in Procter's poetry, 201–2, 225, 230–35, 236–38, 240–41, 245, 259–60; in Rossetti's poetry, 141–42, 151, 258–59; for women writers, other than above, 41
Mary, Immaculate Conception of, 84, 197, 233
Mason, Emma, 138, 193, 219, 284n1
Mass (Tridentine), 178, 180, 182–87, 188, 190, 191
Mermin, Dorothy, 65
meter, poetic, 64, 74, 80–81, 198, 205, 226, 228, 234, 238, 240; blank verse, 64, 95; common measure, 43, 234
Morgan, Thaïs, 51
Muir, T. E., 186, 191

Nalbantian, Suzanne, 10–11
Neale, John Mason, 123–24
neuroscience, 10–11, 12, 17, 194
Newman, John Henry, 114, 127–28, 163, 178, 180, 195, 197, 203, 227–28, 290n12
Nixon, Jude V., 3–4, 92
Nussbaum, Martha, 66–67

Oratory. See Brompton (London) Oratory

Paddington Chapel, 25, 27, 28, 41, 52, 269n42, 270n62; architecture and interior design of, 30. See also Browning, Elizabeth Barrett: and church affiliation; Stratten, James
Palmer, Samuel, 1, 19–20, 37, 38
Parkes, Bessie Rayner, 179, 185, 204, 207, 229
Parsons, Gerald, 28–29, 40, 113
poet-preacher, 50, 52, 62–63, 90, 91–98
poet-priest, 52
poet-prophet, 50–51, 91–92, 96–98
pope, 28, 84, 186, 188–89, 213, 252, 256–57

Index

postures of worship, 13, 40; in Anglicanism and Rossetti's poetics, 101, 106, 107, 120, 124, 146, 152, 170; in Congregationalism and Barrett Browning's poetics 24, 37–38, 68–70, 74

practices, as formative, 1, 2, 6–10, 13–14, 19, 255–56, 262–63; for Barrett Browning's poetics, 24–25, 29–30, 38, 61–63; for Procter's poetics, 177–79, 210, 211–14; for Rossetti's poetics, 101–2, 136, 138–39

prayer, 15–16; collects, 104, 106–7, 109, 147, 154, 182, 183; form versus extemporaneous, 19, 37, 194, 269n37; poems as, 107–8, 144, 146, 155, 169, 170, 220–21, 222, 224–25, 226, 234, 236. *See also* chaplets; hymns: as prayers; Lord's Prayer; postures of worship

preachers: ordination of, 27, 48–49, 113, 132. *See also* Dale, R. W.; Faber, Frederick; Greene, Henry; Gregory of Nazianzus; Hanna, Robert Maxwell; homiletics; Manning, Henry Edward; preaching; Stratten, James; Wesley

preaching, 21, 31, 32, 49, 52, 54, 114, 120–21, 180, 194–96. *See also* homiletics; sermon

Presbyterianism, 27, 28, 32, 33, 176, 267n9–10, 271n62, 280n88

proclamation, 32, 100, 117, 145

Procter, Adelaide
and affect, 178–79, 193–95, 199–202, 214, 228–34, 261
and authority, 188–91, 246–47, 250–53
and church affiliation, 179–80, 193, 196, 199–200
and lay devotions, 186, 203–5, 212, 220–28, 229–30, 235, 250–52
and moral didacticism, 190–91, 213, 244–49
and poetic form, 190, 202, 204–5, 226–28, 230–36, 238–40, 251
publishing career of, 190, 211, 228–29, 252
and reserve, 187–88, 193, 210, 212, 214–19, 224, 233, 284n1, 286n29
and social conscience, 191, 208–9, 213, 229–30, 241–42, 244–49
See also religious imaginary: of Procter

Procter, Adelaide, works of
"The Annunciation," 236–38
"An Appeal: The Irish Church Mission," 249–50
"The Beggar," 248–49
"A Chant," 222–24
"A Chaplet of Flowers," 236
A Chaplet of Verses, 214–16, 224–38, 244–53; and affect, 201, 228, 230–33; in Catholic literary revival, 230, 238–44; as fundraiser, 211, 230; as lay devotional, 229–30, 235; liturgical parallels in, 220, 224–25; publishing of, 185, 190, 228–29; reception of, 229; and reserve, 214–16; social critique in, 244–49
"A Christmas Carol," 292n4
"Christmas Flowers," 259–61
"The Church in 1849," 251–52
"Comfort," 190
"Confido et Conquiesco," 225–26
"A Desire," 215–16
"Evening Chant," 201–2
"Give Me Thy Heart," 216–17
"Homeless," 247
"The Homeless Poor," 245–47
"The Inner Chamber," 217–18
"The Jubilee of 1850," 251–52
"Kyrie Eleison," 224–25
"A Legend of Bregenz," 238–40
"A Legend of Provence," 240–44
Legends and Lyrics, 186, 216–222, 228–29, 291n15, 291n18
"A Lost Chord," 192–93
"Milly's Expiation," 249
"The Names of Our Lady," 230–35
"Ora Pro Me," 225
"Our Daily Bread," 187–88
"Our Titles," 214–15, 252
"Per Pacem ad Lucem," 225–26, 226–28
"The Pilgrims," 220–21
"The Sacred Heart," 188, 235–36
"The Storm" 221–22, 225
"A Tomb in Ghent," 191–93
"Unexpressed," 218–19
"Unseen," 218

Procter, Edith, 179, 204

Providence Row Night Refuge, 211, 229–30, 241, 247, 290n1

Psalms (biblical book), 14, 19, 40, 43, 64, 72, 130, 134–35, 140, 183, 192, 285n17

psalm singing, 40, 104, 109, 130, 185

pulpit, 30–31, 120, 122, 277n45, 277n50

Reed, John Shelton, 133

religion: as formative of imaginary (*see* religious imaginary); as form of thinking, 3; in literary studies, 3–5, 255, 262–63

religious imaginary, 2, 5, 6, 7, 9, 12–22, 255–56, 262; of Barrett Browning, 24–60; of Procter, 177–210; of Rossetti, 102–36

reserve: in Procter's poetics, 193, 210, 212, 214–19, 224, 284n1, 286n29; in Roman Catholicism, 187–88, 233–34; in Rossetti's poetics, 101, 124, 126, 142–43, 167, 258, 259; Tractarian, 114–15, 122, 129, 149

Index

revivalism, Roman Catholic. *See* Brompton (London) Oratory
rhetoric: grand versus plain style, 53–54, 56, 95, 97. *See also* affect (affective); homiletics; sermocinatio
ritual(s), 6, 7, 14, 16, 31, 101, 149–50, 152, 178, 180, 239
ritualism, 101–2, 112, 122, 126–34, 163; in Rossetti's poetics, 125–26, 138, 139, 165, 167, 170
Rodriguez, Alphonsus, 203–4
Roe, Dinah, 131–32, 137, 138, 172, 282n15
Roman Catholicism: confraternities of, 206, 207 (*see also* Providence Row Night Refuge); hierarchy in, 188–89, 208, 250–52; hymns in, 178, 180, 196–98, 208–9; Latin liturgy in, 60, 178, 183–84, 185–87, 191, 197, 198–99; Mass (Tridentine) in, 178, 180, 182–87, 188, 190, 191; revivalism in, 179–80, 193–94, 196–97, 248. *See also* Brompton (London) Oratory; Faber, Frederick; Manning, Henry Edward; *Roman Missal, The*; St. James's Church
Roman Missal, The, 179, 184, 188, 291n18
Romanticism (Romantic), 24, 35–36, 54, 75–76, 128, 254
Rossetti, Christina
 and aesthetics, 124–26, 138–39, 143, 155–58, 174, 176
 and authority, 133–34
 and church affiliation, 102, 109, 123, 127, 176
 and gender concerns, 132, 133–34, 139, 167, 169, 170–71
 and poetic form, 107–8, 138–39, 146–52, 282n15
 and reserve, 101, 124, 126, 142–43, 167, 178, 258, 259 (*see also* Tractarianism)
 and ritualism in poetry, 125–26, 138, 139, 165, 167, 170
 and sacramentality in poetry, 140–43, 149–150
 See also religious imaginary: of Rossetti
Rossetti, Christina, works of
 "Advent Sunday," 118
 "After Communion," 215
 "Ah Lord, Lord, if my heart," 135–36, 167
 "All Saints," 159
 "All Saints: Martyrs," 165
 "Alone Lord God," 169
 "As the dove which found no rest," 119
 "As the sparks fly upwards," 159, 164
 "Awake, thou that sleepest," 174
 "Balm in Gilead," 142–43
 "Before the Throne," 166
 "Behold, it was very good," 166
 "Beloved, let us love," 118
 "A bundle of myrrh," 170
 Called to Be Saints, 160, 161, 173
 "Chastened not slain," 110
 "A chill blank world," 153
 "A Christmas Carol" ("In the bleak midwinter"), 257–59
 "Cried out with Tears," 168
 "The day is at hand," 154
 The Face of the Deep, 109–10, 138, 151, 158, 160, 161, 164, 172, 173, 174, 283n38
 "Feast of the Annunciation," 141–42
 "The General Assembly and Church of the Firstborn," 171
 "The goal in sight," 154
 "The gold of that land," 164
 "Good Friday Morning," 158
 "Her Seed," 154
 "Herself a rose who bore the Rose," 142, 233
 "The Iniquity of the Fathers upon the Children," 134
 "It is not death," 167
 "I will come and heal him," 159
 "Jerusalem of fire," 165
 "The joy of Saints," 159
 "Judge not according to the appearance," 141
 "Judge nothing before the time," 154
 "Let Patience have," 174
 "Life that was born today," 158
 "Lift up thine eyes" (in text as "Strain up thy hope"), 110
 "Like as the hart" (in text as "Kindle my burning"), 159
 "Looking back," 154
 "Lord, carry me," 146
 "Lord, grant me grace," 159
 "Lord, grant us eyes," 168–69
 "Lord, I am here," 146
 "Lord, I believe," 168
 "Lord, make me one," 165
 "Lord, make me pure," 107–8
 "Lord Jesus, who would think," 152
 "New creatures," 146, 159
 "O Christ our All in each," 149, 167
 "O foolish Soul," 159
 "O Jesu, better than Thy gifts," 153
 "O Lord, I am ashamed," 169
 "O Lord, on Whom we gaze" (in text as "Increase our faith"), 146
 "One of the Soldiers," 168

Index

"Our Church Palms are budding willow twigs," 125–26
"Our Mothers," 163–64
A Pageant and Other Poems, 148
"Palm Sunday," 16
"Passiontide," 168
"Peace I leave with you" (in text as "O my King"), 119
"A roundel seems to fit," 150
"Seven vials hold Thy wrath," 140–41
"Short is time," 153
"So brief a life," 153
"So great a cloud," 166
"St. Andrew's Church," 165
"St. John, Apostle," 159
"St. Peter once" (in text as "Open to Me"), 144
"Subject to like Passions," 160
"Then shall ye shout," 166
"This near-at-hand land," 153
"Thy fainting spouse," 118–19
"Thy lovely saints," 119
"Thy Name, O Christ, as incense," 152–53
Time Flies, 131–32, 142, 151, 158, 160, 173
"Time lengthening," 153
"Trinity Sunday," 118
"Tune me, O Lord," 167
"Unspotted lambs" (in text as "Unspotted doves"), 119
Verses, 137–76; and community or communion of saints, 134–36, 163–70; and encounter, 143–46; and liturgical calendar, 161–63; as outreach project, 173–76; poetic forms in, 147–52; publishing, pricing and reception of, 137–38; reserve and sacramentality in, 140–43; as revision, 158, 173; and spiritual journey, 152–54; structure of, 152–54, 158–61; titles in, 158–61; visual-verbal aesthetics of, 155–58
"Vigil of St. Peter," 143–44
"We are of those who tremble," 151
"What hath God wrought," 166
Rossetti, William Michael, 131, 158
roundels, 147–48, 150–52, 154, 282n15
Rowell, Geoffrey, 114, 121
Ruskin, John, 42

sacrament: of baptism, 16, 32, 89–90, 109, 122–23, 285n17; of Communion, 18, 103, 104–05, 114, 122, 127, 132, 149–51, 170, 275n6 (*see also* religious imaginary: of Rossetti); of Eucharist, 7, 16, 18; of Lord's Supper, 18, 26, 32–34, 41, 103; of Mass (Tridentine), 178, 180, 182–87, 188, 190, 191 (*see also* religious imaginary: of Procter); memorialist view of, 28, 32–33, 34, 120, 185; real presence in, 111, 114, 120
sacramentalism (sacramentality), 35–36, 111–12, 113–14, 121–25; in Rossetti's poetics, 140–43, 149–150
sage, 50–51, 92–93. *See also* poet-prophet
Scheinberg, Cynthia, 4, 5, 72, 84
Scoles, Joseph John, 181
Scotch Church. *See* Free Church of Scotland
Scripture. *See* Bible (Scripture)
sentiment. *See* affect (affective)
sermocinatio, 46, 56, 75, 85
sermon: in Anglicanism, 104, 105–6, 108, 114, 121, 122; in Congregationalism, 45–46, 54–56, 58–60, 77, 79–80, 254; in Roman Catholicism, 183, 187, 189, 193–96; as social, dialogic, 75–76. *See also* Gregory of Nazianzus; homiletics; preaching
Shuger, Debora, 53, 55
singing. *See* choirs; choral services; hymns; psalm singing
Sisters of Mercy, 211, 241, 289n1
Slinn, E. Warwick, 75–76, 93
Smith, James K. A., 6, 7, 8–9, 12, 14–17, 109
social imaginary, 6–7, 9
Society for Promoting Christian Knowledge (SPCK), 156, 173–76
sonnets, 107, 138–39, 147–50, 152, 156, 165, 168–69, 194, 202
Steele, Anne, 41
St. James's Church (Spanish Place), 178, 179, 185, 287n41, 292n29; architecture and interior design of, 181–82; music in, 191–92. *See also* Procter, Adelaide: and church affiliation
Stone, Marjorie, 84, 86, 92, 98
Stott, Rebecca, 59, 92, 94–95
Stratten, James, 58–59, 77, 79–80, 83, 254, 271n62
Swedenborg, Emmanuel (Swedenborgianism), 35, 36
Swinburne, Algernon Charles, 151

table (for Lord's Supper), 32, 33, 120
Tangherlini, Timothy R., 204
Taylor, Charles, 6, 7, 8
Taylor, Dennis, 3, 19
Tennyson, G. B., 13, 114–15

Index

theology: Anglican, 112–13, 127–28, 163–64; and Barrett Browning, 36, 43, 47, 56–57, 66, 68, 72; of church fathers, 56–57; Congregationalist, 26, 28–29, 34, 38–39, 46–47, 55; Faber and Manning's approach to, 195–96; and hymns, 38, 40–41, 42–43, 66, 68; and Procter, 194, 200; and Rossetti, 35, 173; and women's writing, 4–5, 51, 72. *See also* sacrament

Tractarianism, 56, 113–17, 127–28, 161–62, 163. *See also* Keble, John; reserve; sacramentalism (sacramentality); Williams, Isaac

Tracts for the Times, 116, 117

Tracy, David, 100–101, 115

Tropman, John, 171

Tyack, Geoffrey, 121, 122, 278n60

typology, 115, 116, 259

voice, 5, 6, 7, 13–14, 18, 19; in Barrett Browning's poetics, 67, 73–74, 75, 80, 93–96, 98–99; in Procter's poetics, 190–91, 213, 247, 248, 249–50; in Rossetti's poetics, 146, 165–66, 167–70

Wagner, Jennifer, 162
Watson, J. R., 70
Watts, Isaac, 28, 40, 43, 65–66, 68
Wesley (John and/or Charles; Wesleyans), 40, 58, 195
Wheeler, Michael, 55–56
Williams, Isaac, 116–17, 126, 157, 278n65
Wilson, Elizabeth A., 10, 11
Wordsworth, William, 162, 198

Zwingli, Ulrich, 32, 33